HELLENISTIC CULTURE AND SOCIETY

General Editors: Anthony W. Bulloch, Erich S. Gruen, A. A. Long,
and *Andrew F. Stewart*

Hellenistic Constructs

Hellenistic Constructs

Essays in Culture, History,
and Historiography

Paul Cartledge, Peter Garnsey, and Erich Gruen

UNIVERSITY OF CALIFORNIA PRESS
Berkeley   Los Angeles   London

University of California Press
Berkeley and Los Angeles, California

University of California Press, Ltd.
London, England

© 1997 by
The Regents of the University of California

Library of Congress Cataloging-in-Publication Data

Hellenistic constructs : essays in culture, history, and historiography / edited by
   Paul Cartledge, Peter Garnsey, and Erich Gruen.
      p.   cm. — (Hellenistic culture and society ; v. 26)
   Includes bibliographical references and index.
   ISBN 0-520-20676-2 (cloth : alk. paper)
      1. Hellenism.   2. Greece—Civilization.   3. Mediterranean Region—
   Civilization.   I. Cartledge, Paul.   II. Garnsey, Peter.   III. Gruen, Erich S.
   IV. Series : Hellenistic culture and society ; 26.
   DF77.H5463   1997
   938–DC21   97-7317
                                                                      CIP

Printed in the United States of America
9   8   7   6   5   4   3   2   1

CONTENTS

PREFACE AND ACKNOWLEDGEMENTS

The origins of this present collection lie in a seminar series held in Cambridge during the Lent Term 1993 under the direction of Paul Cartledge, Peter Garnsey, and Dorothy J. Thompson. Not all those who wished to offer a paper were in the event able to present it in Cambridge. We are happy to include several of those contributions here and regret that we were unable to accommodate all offers of papers. That so many did wish to contribute to the seminar was largely because it was dedicated to Frank Walbank, then approaching his eighty-fifth birthday and still astonishingly productive at the highest scholarly level (see Publications of F. W. Walbank, kindly prepared by Dorothy Thompson). We are delighted to repeat that dedication here.

Besides the contributors and other participants in the Cambridge seminar, the editors wish to thank warmly the officers of the University of California Press, especially Mary Lamprech, the Press's anonymous referees, and Judy Gaughan and Peter Wyetzner for their compilation of the volume's bibliography.

May 1997
Paul Cartledge, Peter Garnsey, Erich S. Gruen

Introduction

Paul Cartledge

I. HELLENISTIC STUDIES TODAY

Hellenistic studies are burgeoning today as perhaps never before. Publishers' series are dedicated specifically to their furtherance on both sides of the Atlantic, and since July 1995 the active reappraisal and radical revaluation of Hellenistic visual art have been complemented and enhanced by what the British Museum claims to be the first permanent Hellenistic gallery anywhere. Consequently, a full-scale review of the "state of the question" in Hellenistic studies today, or rather of the many diverse and highly complex questions at issue, would be not merely inappropriate in a volume such as the present collection of essays but beyond any ordinary mortal's capacity. Fortunately, the Hellenistic entity, period, age or world has not lacked for essays at overall characterization, with plentiful reference to the latest scholarship.[1] But what has principally eased my introductory task is a

---

For many suggestions and corrections I am most grateful above all to my co-editors, and also to Ricardo Martinez Lacy, Seth Schwartz, Dorothy Thompson, and Frank Walbank. The responsibility for the remaining errors of omission and commission is mine alone.

1. P. Green (ed.), *Hellenistic History and Culture* (Berkeley, 1993) 5–11 suggests reasons for "the contemporary renaissance in Hellenistic studies" (10), which now even have their own dedicated "small lexicon": H. H. Schmitt and E. Vogt (eds.), *Kleines Lexikon des Hellenismus*, 2nd ed. (Wiesbaden, 1993). Earlier surveys include J. B. Bury et al., *The Hellenistic Age* (Cambridge, 1923); P. Jouguet, *L'impérialisme macédonien et l'hellénisation de l'Orient* (Paris, 1937; repr. 1972 with add. bibl. 1937–1971); W. W. Tarn and G. T. Griffith, *Hellenistic Civilisation*, 3rd ed. (London, 1952); E. Badian, "The Hellenistic World," in H. Lloyd-Jones (ed.), *The Greeks* (Harmondsworth, 1965) ch. 10; C. Préaux, "Réflexions sur l'entité hellénistique," *ChrEg* 40 (1965) 129–39; A. H. M. Jones, "The Hellenistic Period," *PastPres* 27 (1964) 3–22; V. Ehrenberg, "The Hellenistic Age" (1964) repr. in *Man, State and*

characteristically wide-ranging, fair and incisive account of some "new trends and directions" in Hellenistic studies by Frank Walbank, a scholar (as well as a gentleman) who has towered over this field for more than half a century and has himself written probably the best concise survey of it.[2]

However precisely it is defined in time and space, the Hellenistic portion of Greek (or Graeco-Macedonian, Graeco-Roman, Graeco-Oriental) history has surely suffered from the outset from its unhappy title.[3] In ancient Greek *hellênizein* meant originally to speak Greek, and subsequently to behave like a Greek in other than linguistic ways too; but Greek-speakers were Hellenes, not Hellen*ists*, and in English at any rate the suffix "-istic" conjures up a notion of pale or failed imitation, Greek-ish, Greek-like, not the real pukka thing. It is no coincidence, perhaps, that two of the most interesting of modern English historical fictions about ancient Greece with Hellenistic settings are countercultural novels of political subversion—Naomi Mitchison's *The Corn King and the Spring Queen* (1933) and William Golding's posthumous (and unfinished) *The Double Tongue* (1995).

The inventor of the Hellenistic age or world—in the ancient Greek sense of its *prôtos heuretês*, the man later generations of scholars have come to see as its "onlie begetter"—is Johann-Gustav Droysen, who in 1836 labelled or rather baptised his creation as "Hellenismus," Greek-ism. (English "Hellenism," Greek-ness, would not be a correct translation of Droysen's German.) For him, this was a world-historical epoch of the first significance, not only and not so much in its own right but thanks chiefly to its missionary role of evangelical preparation for the predestined dawn of Christianity. Without the Graeco-Oriental cultural fusion ("Verschmelzung") of "Hellenismus," Droysen preached, the seed of the Christian gospel would have fallen on barren ground. In the happy event, it fell rather into a fertile seedbed of hellenizing Judaism watered by the universal fountain of Rome's global empire. Had Paul not been a hellenized Roman citizen, and had there not been suitably hellenized Jews both in Palestine and in the Jewish diaspora,

---

Deity: Essays in Ancient History (London, 1974) 64–106; R. Bichler, *"Hellenismus": Geschichte und Problematik eines Epochenbegriffs* (Darmstadt, 1983); S. Sherwin-White, "The Hellenistic World," *History Today* (December 1983) 45–48; L. Canfora, *Ellenismo* (Rome, 1987); H.-J. Gehrke, *Geschichte des Hellenismus* (Munich, 1990); P. Cabanes, *Le monde hellénistique de la mort d'Alexandre à la Paix d'Apamée* (Paris, 1995); C. Vial, *Les Grecs de la Paix d'Apamée à la bataille d'Actium* (Paris, 1995). See also n. 7.

2. F. W. Walbank, "The Hellenistic World: new trends and directions," *Scripta Classica Israelica* 11 (1991/92) 90–113; Walbank, *The Hellenistic World*, 2nd ed. (Glasgow, 1992); note also his "Recent work in Hellenistic history," *Dialogos* 3 (1996) 111–19.

3. Cf. S. Alcock, "Breaking up the Hellenistic World: survey and society," in I. Morris (ed.), *Classical Greece: Ancient Histories and Modern Archaeologies* (Cambridge, 1994) 171–90.

Christianity would have been doomed to remain, and probably soon wither and die, as a tiny, parochial Jewish sect. That the new religion spread and flourished as it did, "universally," was made possible, according to the Droysen version, only by the prior and surely divinely planned establishment of "Hellenismus," the Hellenistic world and its receptively fecund culture.[4]

Droysen's Hellenism, therefore, was without doubt an overwhelmingly good thing. However, in the eyes of most subsequent classical scholarship on the ancient Greeks, suffused as it soon became with an often uncritical adulation of Greek glory, it appeared almost entirely the reverse. The imaginary Greece that came to exercise its "tyranny" over Europe and America in the nineteenth and early twentieth century was not Droysen's "Hellenismus" but what had come to be called in basically art-historical terms "Classical Greece." This comprised the golden century and a half from the defeats of the invading Persians in Greece (490, 480–79 B.C.E.) to the defeat of the invaded Persian empire by Greeks under Alexander the Great (d. 323). This was the Greece of Pericles and Demosthenes, Herodotus and Thucydides, the great tragedians and Aristophanes, of Socrates, Plato and Aristotle, and of the Parthenon at Athens and Pheidias' chryselephantine statue of Zeus at Olympia. By comparison, so it was generally believed, the Hellenistic age could not but be construed and viewed as a decline, if not a catastrophe, of which the conquest of the Greek world by Rome was the perfectly apt symbol and expression.[5]

Despite and to a certain degree because of Droysen, this negative image has never quite been redressed, let alone expunged. It can, indeed, be questioned whether it is correct to speak of a self-contained Hellenistic age, epoch or period.[6] Even if the term is allowed, the Hellenistic entity still tends to be something of a stepchild, a Cinderella, in ancient Graeco-Roman historical studies. This is partly due to the dearth of ancient narrative sources that might give it a single, strong and coherent story line, partly thanks to the intrinsic difficulty of mastering the huge diversity of original written and non-written materials, and partly, as mentioned above, because of its

4. A. D. Momigliano, "Genesi storica e funzione attuale del concetto di Ellenismo" (1935) repr. in *Contributo alla storia degli studi classici* (Rome, 1955) 165–94; "J. G. Droysen between Greeks and Jews" (1970) repr. in G. Bowersock and T. J. Cornell (eds.), *Studies on Modern Scholarship* (Berkeley, 1994) 147–61; cf. Préaux, "Réflexions" 138; B. Bravo, *Philologie, histoire, philosophie de l'histoire* (Wroclaw, Warsaw and Cracow, 1968); H. Trevor-Roper, "Jacob Burckhardt," *ProcBritAc* 70 (1984) 359–78, at 376–77; J. R. Martinez Lacy, *Dos aproximaciones a la historiografía de la antigüedad clasica* (Mexico City, 1994) 65–80.

5. For powerful reflections on the modern historiography and ideology of "Classical Greece," see Morris, "Archaeologies of Greece," in Morris (ed.), *Classical Greece*, 8–47.

6. Bichler, "*Hellenismus*"; Canfora, *Ellenismo*.

seemingly unerasable cultural defects. This does not mean that it has failed to attract great, indeed some of the greatest, historical scholarship—far from it. In our century the names of Bickerman, Momigliano, Préaux, Robert, Rostovtzeff, Walbank and Édouard Will spring readily enough to mind. But whenever the attempt to do something more like justice to "Hellenism" begins to gather collective weight and seems to be tipping the balance from mere recuperation into positive approval, as it has in the eighties and nineties, it is noticeable how quickly it excites a powerful opposite reaction.

Thus, whereas Walbank in his recent review of scholarship could speak of "many Greek cities" developing "a flourishing social and intellectual life" in the Hellenistic era and finding "new avenues to self-definition," admittedly within the "limitations which the existence of monarchies imposed," Peter Green's massive survey was simultaneously painting an anti-Panglossian picture in which almost everything was for the worst in the worst of all possible worlds.[7] The present introduction, like the volume as a whole, will aim to hold the balance with a steady and impartial hand. What it will not aim to do is present an artificially tidied-up version of an in fact ever more messy scholarly arena, and what it cannot hope to do is in any sense "cover the field": students of Hellenistic philosophy and Hellenistic society (or rather societies), in particular, may well feel that they or their subject-areas are being somewhat unfairly shortchanged, whereas those unenthralled by matters economic may possibly feel the opposite.

The tide of academic culture-warring in its various guises and battle-grounds —especially the discourses or rhetorics of Orientalism and multi-culturalism, and the disputed validity of the (or a) Western literary canon—has washed fitfully over the shores of Greek and Hellenistic studies.[8] In response to the claim that the ancient Greeks were the original Oriental-ist sinners, uninterested in, contemptuous of or baffled by "alien wisdom," scholars including some Hellenistic specialists have countered that Ptolemaic Egypt and Seleucid Syria were precisely multicultural societies.[9] Both claim and counter-claim would seem to lack solid grounding, not least because

7. Walbank, "New trends" 95. P. Green, *From Alexander to Actium: The Historical Evolution of the Hellenistic Age* (Berkeley, 1990, corr. repr. 1993); rev. by D. Potter, *BMCR* 2.6 (1991) 357–63, with reply by Green, *BMCR* 6.4 (1995) 363–64. Green's generally downbeat position has been vigorously endorsed by V. D. Hanson, *The Other Greeks: The Family Farm and the Agrarian Roots of Western Civilization* (New York, 1995) e.g. 414.

8. E. Said, *Culture and Imperialism* (Harmondsworth, 1993); *Orientalism*, new ed. with "Afterword" (Harmondsworth, 1995); M. Bernal, *Black Athena: The Afro-Asiatic Roots of Classical Civilization*, 2 vols. (of 4) to date (London, 1987–1991). See also BAGNALL, below.

9. Momigliano, *Alien Wisdom: The Limits of Hellenization* (Cambridge, 1975); J. H. Johnson (ed.), *Life in a Multi-Cultural Society: Egypt from Cambyses to Constantine and Be-*

"Hellenism" and "hellenization" (by which may be meant the adoption or adaptation of Greek names, words and institutions, but also the reception of Greek political ideas, lifestyle and literary, artistic and architectural ideas and practices) are themselves contested terms. Hence, the "fusion" of Droysen, with its unscholarly implication of race, is now rightly seen to be quite inappropriate.[10] On the other hand, the notion of an ancient society treating members of very different cultures tolerantly on principle no less blatantly bears the hallmark of our contemporary times—or wishes.

The scholarly issue would now seem rather to turn on whether the essentially and enduringly separate Greek, Syrian, Egyptian and so forth cultural communities ever co-existed on a footing of anything remotely resembling equality.[11] Talk of a Greek "colonial" mentality and of "cultural and religious *apartheid*" in Egypt would suggest they did not.[12] In so far as cultural "hegemony" is a usable historiographical concept, that would appear to have remained firmly in Greek hands.[13] A more than ordinarily telling test case, both because it harks back to Droysen's original conception and because it involves religion at its core, is the encounter of Greeks and Jews.[14] Momigliano's contention that despite their having "so much in

---

yond (Chicago, 1992); K. Galinsky, *Classical and Modern Interactions: Postmodern Architecture, Multiculturalism, Decline, and Other Issues* (Austin, 1992); cf. E. J. Bickerman, *Institutions des Séleucides* (Paris, 1938); A. Kuhrt and S. Sherwin-White, *Hellenism in the East* (London, 1987); Sherwin-White and Kuhrt, *From Samarkhand to Sardis* (London and Berkeley, 1993); and now for the pre-Hellenistic background Kuhrt, *The Ancient Near East c.3000–330 BC*, 2 vols. (London and New York, 1995).

10. M. Hadas, *Hellenistic Culture, Fusion and Diffusion* (New York and London, 1959) unacceptably follows and extends Droysen's notion of "fusion"; *contra* P. Fraser, *CR* n.s. 11 (1961) 145–48. The racial dimension is still palpable in C. Schneider, *Kulturgeschichte des Hellenismus*, 2 vols. (Munich, 1967–1969): see *contra* O. Murray, *CR* n.s. 19 (1969) 69–72.

11. R. S. Bagnall, "Greeks and Egyptians: ethnicity, status and culture," in *Cleopatra's Egypt: Age of the Ptolemies* (Brooklyn Mus. Exhibition, 1988) 21–26; B. Virgilio (ed.), *Studi Ellenistici*, 3 vols. (Pisa, 1984, 1987, 1990) 1987: 107–89.

12. "Colonial mentality": Ed. Will, "Pour une 'anthropologie coloniale' du monde hellénistique," in J. W. Eadie and J. Ober (eds.), *The Craft of the Ancient Historian. Fest. C. G. Starr* (Lanham, 1985) 273–301. "Apartheid": Walbank, "New trends," 102; cf. N. Lewis, *Greeks in Ptolemaic Egypt: Case Studies in the Social History of the Hellenistic World* (New York, 1986) 135; A. E. Samuel, *From Athens to Alexandria: Hellenism and Social Goals in Ptolemaic Egypt* (Louvain, 1983), and *The Shifting Sands of History: Interpretations of Ptolemaic Egypt* (Lanham and London, 1989).

13. G. Shipley, "Distance, Development, Decline? World-systems analysis and the 'Hellenistic' world," in P. Bilde et al. (eds.), *Centre and Periphery in the Hellenistic World* (Aarhus, 1994) 271–84, at 282.

14. V. Tcherikover, *Hellenistic Civilisation and the Jews* (Philadelphia, 1959); M. Hengel, *Judaism and Hellenism* (London, 1974); *Jews, Greeks and Barbarians: Aspects of the Hellenization*

common, Greeks and Jews do not seem to have spoken to each other"[15] may need to be modified only a little. But that little is deeply significant. Even the Maccabees, the supreme symbol of Jewish repudiation of the Greek Other, fought their Graeco-Macedonian would-be overlords with Hellenistic rather than traditional Jewish military, diplomatic and institutional instruments.[16]

In another sense of culture—the "high" culture of the literary and visual arts, and of the multiplying fields of intellectual endeavour—the Hellenistic era has long been recognised as one of exceptional fertility, if not always of comparably desirable quality. In literary criticism and "hard" science, for example, Hellenistic scholars unquestionably set the agenda and the tone for future ages, including arguably our own.[17] But the question whether Hellenistic imaginative literature, historiography, and visual arts were as "good" as their Classical predecessors in all or most branches has often been answered negatively. Current perspectives and perceptions, however, would suggest that a far more positive appraisal is under way here, as in other areas.[18] The rehabilitation of Polybius by Walbank, for example, stands as a conspicuous monument and beacon of modern scholarship.[19] Another

---

of Judaism in the Pre-Christian Period (London, 1980); Momigliano, *Alien Wisdom*, 74–122; "Greek Culture and the Jews," in M. I. Finley (ed.), *The Greek Legacy: A New Appraisal* (Oxford, 1981) 325–46; *On Pagans, Jews and Christians* (Middletown, Conn., 1987); *Essays on Ancient and Modern Judaism* (Chicago, 1994); L. H. Feldman, *Jew and Gentile in the Ancient World: Attitudes and Interactions from Alexander to Justinian* (Princeton, 1993).

15. Momigliano, *Alien Wisdom*, 81.

16. Feldman, *Jew and Gentile*; cf. T. Rajak, "The Jews under Hasmonean rule," *CAH* IX, 2nd ed. (Cambridge, 1994), 274–309, at 280–87 ("The emergence of Judaea as a Hellenistic state"). See also Gruen, Millar, below.

17. P. M. Fraser, *Ptolemaic Alexandria*, 3 vols. (Oxford, 1972); A. W. Erskine, "Culture and power in Ptolemaic Egypt: The Museum and the Library of Alexandria," *G&R* 42 (1995) 38–48; J. Sirinelli, *Les enfants d'Alexandre: La littérature et la pensée grecques, 334 av. J.-C.—519 ap. J.-C.* (Paris, 1993).

18. See e.g. W. R. Connor, "Historical writing in the fourth century B.C. and in the Hellenistic period," in P. Easterling and B. M. W. Knox (eds.), *Cambridge History of Classical Literature* I. *Greek Literature* (Cambridge, 1985) 458–71; S. Goldhill, "The naive and knowing eye: ecphrasis and the culture of viewing in the Hellenistic world," in S. Goldhill and R. Osborne (eds.), *Art and Text in Ancient Greek Culture* (Cambridge, 1994) 197–223; D. Hahm, "Polybius' applied political theory," in A. Laks and M. Schofield (eds.), *Justice and Generosity: Studies in Hellenistic Social and Political Philosophy* (Cambridge, 1995) 7–47; N. Himmelmann, "Realistic art in Alexandria," *ProcBritAc* 67 (1981) 193–207; J. J. Pollitt, *Art in the Hellenistic Age* (Cambridge, 1986); C. M. Robertson, "What is 'Hellenistic' about Hellenistic art?" in Green (ed.) (n. 1) 67–103; R. R. R. Smith, *Hellenistic Sculpture* (London and New York, 1991).

19. Walbank, *A Historical Commentary on Polybius*, 3 vols. (Oxford, 1957, 1967, 1979); *Polybius* (Berkeley, 1972); "Polybius between Greece and Rome" (1974) repr. in *Selected*

instance of significant, if far more controversial, reappraisal is the positive role in practical politics that has been assigned to certain philosophers, contradicting the widespread notion of philosophical withdrawal in face of the new large, distant and impersonal Hellenistic political structures.[20] No less noteworthy in its own way is the extraordinary popular success of cheap translations of Epicurus' *Letter to Menoeceus* (one and a half million copies sold in a pocket Italian version within the first six months of its publication in 1993), which might seem to suggest that at any rate Epicureanism's upward mobility of esteem is not confined to the academic classes.[21]

How precisely the separate "national" communities of the Hellenistic world defined themselves as such has also been a matter for growing scholarly concern, again under the compulsion of our own fraught times.[22] Instead of race, it now tends to be ethnicity that occupies centre stage in the language of modern scholarship, although this relatively newfangled concept is in danger of seeming hardly less vacuous or ambiguous. A myth of common origin, and attachment to a defined territory, would appear to be two of the primary and constant criteria of ethnicity, with language coming a close third. But two Ptolemaic papyri well illustrate the problems of applying ethnic self-definition in practice: first, in the well known Zenon archive, a probably Arab camel driver complains that he has not been paid because he is a barbarian and "does not know how to *hellēnizein*," that is, behave like a Greek; in another text, a Greek complains no less bitterly that he is being treated unfairly because he is not a Macedonian. To complicate still further this Greek-Macedonian confusion, we might note that in the eyes of Ptolemaic officialdom a Jew could be accounted a "Hellene."[23] On the other side of the ledger, however, should be placed the homogenizing tendency of Ptolemaic (and Seleucid) military recruitment. What made and kept the Hellenistic kingdoms unitary monarchies were their armies, and in both Egypt and Syria these were significantly "polyethnic"

Papers: Studies in Greek and Roman History and Historiography (Cambridge, 1985) 280–97; cf. A. M. Eckstein, *Moral Vision in the Histories of Polybius* (Berkeley, 1994); and ECKSTEIN, below.

20. A. W. Erskine, *The Hellenistic Stoa: Political Thought and Action* (London, 1990). But see J. Annas, *The Morality of Happiness* (New York, 1993) esp. ch. 13 ("Justice").

21. Positive reappraisals of Hellenistic philosophies include M. Schofield, *The Stoic Idea of the City* (Cambridge, 1991); Annas, *Morality*; M. Nussbaum, *The Therapy of Desire: Theory and Practice in Hellenistic Ethics* (Princeton, 1994); and Laks and Schofield (eds.), *Justice and Generosity*.

22. A. W. Bulloch et al. (eds.), *Images and Ideologies: Self-Definition in the Hellenistic World* (Berkeley, 1993); Green (ed.), *Hellenistic History and Culture*.

23. Both texts are cited by Walbank, *Hellenistic World*, 115. Jews as "Hellenes": see THOMPSON, p. 247, below.

in composition.[24] A rather different source of ethnic confusion was that in the sight of both Greeks and Macedonians, and *a fortiori*, one presumes, of what W. W. Tarn called "culture-Greeks," the Romans were essentially "barbarians." Yet the latter not only became firmly established as the political lords and masters of the Greek world from the later third century B.C.E. onwards, but they did so in significant measure by means of proclaiming themselves to be adepts and devotees of Greek culture. It was only a matter of time, presumably, before "Romans" came to be constituted as a third term, between "Greeks" and "barbarians."[25]

Hellenistic politics, in the sense of the political events and processes that occurred within and between the new Hellenistic territorial and dynastic monarchies, are exceptionally confused and likely to remain confusing, despite the masterly syntheses of Will.[26] This is largely, though not entirely, a source problem. For many scholars, however, the key question has been not so much how and why such political relations were conducted, but whether or not the quintessentially Greek institution of the *polis* survived the establishment of the monarchies as a meaningful, lived reality in any shape or form. Hence *the* scholarly issue of Hellenistic politics has often been taken to be that of the crisis, decline and/or continuity of the *polis* as such, together with its associated civic identities.[27]

The standard answer given until quite recently was negative. Those who followed Aristotle in valuing uniquely highly the supposed autonomy and independence of the ideally free, sovereign and self-governing Greek citizen-state, and especially those who (unlike Aristotle) esteemed greatly its experiment in direct, participatory democracy, could not but deplore what they

24. M. M. Austin, "The Age of Kings from Alexander to the Roman conquest," in R. Browning (ed.), *The Greek World* (London and New York, 1985) 185–200, at 199; "Hellenistic kings, war and the economy," *CQ* n.s. 36 (1986) 450–66; cf. M. Launey, *Recherches sur les armées hellénistiques*, 2 vols. (Paris, 1949–1950, repr. with add. 1987); B. S. Strauss, "From Ethnicity to Status: Polyethnic armies and the making of the Hellenistic kingdoms" (forthcoming).

25. J.-L. Ferrary, *Philhellénisme et impérialisme: Aspects idéologiques de la conquête romaine du monde hellénistique* (Rome, 1988); R. Browning, "Greeks and Others: From Antiquity to the Renaissance," in his *History, Language and Literacy in the Byzantine World* (Northampton, 1989) ch. 2.

26. Ed. Will, *Histoire politique du monde hellénistique*, 2 vols., 2nd ed. (Nancy, 1979–1982); cf. Will, "Le monde hellénistique," in Will, Cl. Mossé and P. Goukowsky, *Le monde grec et l'Orient* II. *Le IVe siècle et l'époque hellénistique* (Paris, 1975). Problems of chronology: e.g. MATTINGLY, below.

27. See e.g. Cl. Mossé, "La crise de la 'polis' et la fin de la civilisation grecque," in Will et al., *Monde grec* II. 187–244; M. Wörrle and P. Zanker (eds.), *Stadtbild und Bürgerbild im Hellenismus* (Munich, 1995).

saw as the loss of political independence and vitality in the cities caused by direct monarchical intervention or by interference at the kings' behest, of which they took the suppression of democracy at Athens by Macedon to be the paradigmatic instance. The Romans on this view merely carried on where they had forced the Graeco-Macedonian kings to leave off, suppressing external independence and finally extinguishing such etiolated simulacra of democracy as still struggled feebly to persist.[28]

Against this once standard position—still cherished in some powerful quarters—there has been counterposed a far more optimistic interpretation.[29] Granted, the rise of Hellenistic monarchy and its *ex post facto* ideological justifications did undoubtedly affect the quality of political life in the old Greek cities.[30] But the outcome, on this alternative view, was by no means altogether negative. Citizens continued to act politically, even indeed democratically in some cases, well into the second century B.C.E. It was, moreover, a healthy sense of political self-identity that lay behind and helped to inspire political resistance to Rome. So far, in fact, was the Greek city from either dying on its feet or being murdered by external agencies that the *polis* of Hellenic type provided the model towards which indigenous towns within the Graeco-Macedonian hegemonial orbit tended to evolve spontaneously.[31]

The jury on that particular case is still out, partly because much of the evidence for the revised picture consists of official epigraphy that may not be

28. See e.g. G. E. M. de Ste. Croix, *The Class Struggle in the Ancient Greek World: From the Archaic Age to the Arab Conquests* (London and Ithaca, 1981, corr. impr. 1983); Green, *Alexander to Actium*; S. Alcock, *Graecia Capta: The Landscapes of Roman Greece* (Cambridge, 1993).

29. See esp. P. Gauthier, *Les cités grecques et leurs bienfaiteurs* (Paris, 1985); "Les cités hellénistiques," in M. H. Hansen (ed.), *The Ancient Greek City-State* (Copenhagen, 1993) 211–31; A. Giovannini, "Greek cities and Greek commonwealth," in Bulloch et al., *Images*, 265–86; E. S. Gruen, "The Polis in the Hellenistic World," in R. M. Rosen and J. Farrell (eds.), *NOMODEIKTES. Fest. M. Ostwald* (Ann Arbor, 1993) 339–54; F. Millar, "The Greek city in the Roman period," in Hansen (ed.), *City-State*, 232–60; P. Zanker, "Brüche im Bürgerbild? Zur bürgerlichen Selbstdarstellungen in den hellenistischen Städten," in Wörrle and Zanker, *Stadtbild*, 251–63; *Die Maske des Sokrates: Das Bild des Intellektuellen in der antiken Kunst* (Munich, 1995).

30. V. Ehrenberg, *The Greek State*, 2nd ed. (London, 1969) Part II; Chr. Habicht, *Gottmenschentum und griechische Städte*, 2nd ed. (Munich, 1970); Walbank, "Monarchies and Monarchic Ideas," in *CAH* VII.1, 2nd ed. (Cambridge, 1984) 62–100; "Könige als Götter: Überlegungen zum Herrscherkult von Alexander bis Augustus," *Chiron* 17 (1987) 365–82; K. Bringmann, "The King as Benefactor," in Bulloch et al., *Images*, 7–24; A. F. Stewart, *Faces of Power: Alexander's Image and Hellenistic Politics* (Berkeley, 1993); cf. S. Price, *Rituals and Power: The Roman Imperial Cult in Asia Minor* (Cambridge, 1984).

31. Ed. Will, "Poleis hellénistiques: Deux notes," *EchCl* n.s. 7 (1988) 329–52, at 349.

telling anything like the whole truth. It is, besides, considerably offset by both literary and archaeological testimony. There is, first, the persistent literary evidence of serious internal civil strife (*stasis*) between rich and poor citizens, not least in "old" Greece, with the poor demanding ever more insistently redistribution of land and cancellation of debts. These are the time-honoured slogans of oppressed peasantry, voiced by Greeks since the seventh century, but the economic oppression seems to have been compounded in Hellenistic times by a growing sense of political powerlessness.[32] Archaeologically, the evidence provided thus far by intensive field-survey consistently suggests a rather sudden and sharp decline of rural settlement and activity after about 250 B.C.E.; in particular, the available data for the fate of rural Greek sanctuary sites in the Hellenistic (and Roman) period would appear to point to "a major upheaval in the religious landscape, and thus to a radical restructuring of local allegiances and indeed emotions."[33] Even the fiercest advocates of continuing Hellenistic political vitality should concede at least that the nature of politics was being redefined in accordance with a new, more sociocultural than political, conception of citizenship. The general upwards revaluation of the status of women, or at any rate of free Greek citizen women in the cities, would tend to corroborate the inference of a corresponding devaluation of the civic-political status of their relatively disempowered menfolk.[34]

On the other hand, the creation or further development of the supra-*polis* entities that we call "leagues" is sufficient to disprove the notion that Greek political ingenuity was exhausted in the Hellenistic period. Whether or not these leagues were true federal states, those of Achaea and Aetolia above all certainly proved to be practical alternatives to the single *polis* as power units, during a period that saw the former great powers of the Classical period, Athens and Sparta, reduced internationally to near nullity.[35]

32. W. W. Tarn, "The social question in the third century," in Bury et al. (n. 1), 108–40; A. Fuks, "Patterns and types of social-economic revolution in Greece from the fourth to the second centuries B.C.," *Ancient Society* 5 (1974) 51–81, repr. as *Social Conflict in Ancient Greece* (Jerusalem and Leiden, 1984) ch. 2; Préaux, *Monde hellénistique*, 528; J. R. Martinez Lacy, *Rebeliones populares en la Grecia helenística* (Mexico City, 1995).

33. Alcock, "Minding the gap in Hellenistic and Roman Greece," in S. E. Alcock and R. G. Osborne (eds.), *Placing the Gods: Sanctuaries and Sacred Space in Ancient Greece* (Oxford, 1994) 247–61, at 261.

34. O. Murray, "Forms of sociality," in J.-P. Vernant (ed.), *The Greeks* (Chicago, 1995) 218–53, at 244–45; cf. S. Pomeroy, *Women in Hellenistic Egypt*, 2nd ed. (Detroit, 1990); P. Schmitt Pantel, *La cité au banquet: Histoire des repas publics dans les cités grecques* (Rome, 1992).

35. Walbank, "Were there Greek federal states?" *Scripta Classica Israelica* 3 (1976/77) 27–51, repr. in *Selected Papers*, 20–37; *Historical Commentary on Polybius* III (Oxford, 1979) 406–14.

For most individual Hellenistic *poleis*, therefore, the great game of international politics consisted essentially in diplomacy, all the more tricky in that it could not usually be backed by any credible threat of force. The concept of neutrality or non-alignment, dimly adumbrated in the Classical era, became understandably more popular, if no less hard to achieve.[36] The one Greek city to cut anything like a stylishly independent dash on the international scene for any length of time was Rhodes, but this revealingly was no traditional *polis*: the unified city was the product of a relatively very recent (408 B.C.E.) *sunoikismos*, and its democracy (or "democracy") was underpinned by a significantly polyethnic social and economic infrastructure.[37]

If we shift our gaze from politics to economics, we find the Russian émigré Mikhail I. Rostovtzeff still casting a long shadow. For sheer breadth and depth of empirical knowledge his work is unlikely to be equalled let alone surpassed. However, its theoretical, or more precisely ideological, structure is far more vulnerable to criticism, above all on grounds of anachronism but also for its Orientalism.[38] Rostovtzeff understood the Hellenistic world as a single, interdependent economic system characterized by sustained economic growth that was driven above all by long-distance interregional trade conducted by agents of a rising urban *bourgeoisie*. All four main elements of that picture—system, growth, trade, *bourgeoisie*—have come under intense and often successful attack.

A recent summarizing article offers a convenient handle on the principal issues.[39] Using Immanuel Wallerstein's "world-systems" model of the early-modern and modern economy as a means of "posing new questions about social, political and economic structures" in the Hellenistic world, Shipley plausibly doubts the existence of anything approaching a single economic system, let alone a world system, in the Hellenistic

---

Athens: Chr. Habicht, *Athen in Hellenistischer Zeit*, 2nd ed. (Munich, 1994); MATTINGLY, below. Sparta: P. Cartledge and A. Spawforth, *Hellenistic and Roman Sparta: A Tale of Two Cities* (London and New York, 1989).

36. R. A. Bauslaugh, *The Concept of Neutrality in Classical Greece* (Berkeley, 1991).

37. Besides Will (n. 26) see P. M. Fraser, *Rhodian Funerary Monuments* (Oxford, 1977).

38. M. I. Rostovtzeff, *Social and Economic History of the Hellenistic World*, 3 vols. (Oxford, 1941/1953); cf. C. B. Welles, "Michael I. Rostovtzeff," in *Fest. A. P. Usher* (Tübingen, 1956); J. Andreau, "Introduction" to *Histoire économique et sociale du monde hellénistique* (Paris, 1989); M. A. Wes, *Michael Rostovtzeff, Historian in Exile: Russian Roots in an American Context* (Stuttgart, 1990); J. R. Martinez Lacy, *Dos aproximaciones* (n. 4), 149–60; Momigliano, *Studies on Modern Scholarship*, 32–43.

39. Shipley, "Distance" (n. 13); cf. J. K. Davies, "Cultural, social and economic features of the Hellenistic world," *CAH* VII.1, 2nd ed. (Cambridge, 1984) 257–320.

epoch.[40]   As for growth, a tricky enough concept to pin down even in modern economics, its applicability to any preindustrial economic order is yet more doubtful. So far as any supposed central management of growth is concerned, Shipley properly distinguishes between the kings' undoubted concern to maximize revenues *via* taxation (royal monopolies, crops, etc.) and the rationality of managed economic maximization *per se* with which they have sometimes been credited. The latter he considers to have been non-existent: "The king was above all a military and religious leader, not an economic bureaucrat."[41]

In any case, even if there really was growth, development or progress—whom did it benefit? Although Rostovtzeff identified the Hellenistic period as one characterized largely by economic prosperity, involving progress in production, active commerce and accumulation of capital, he was perfectly well aware that such overall prosperity could go hand in hand with an unsatisfactory lot for the working classes (about whom, admittedly, he found relatively little to say). Economic growth or prosperity, in other words, must not be viewed only from the perspective of the politically dominant partners in any relationship. Robert Sallares, for example, has postulated a probable socio-economic crisis of overpopulation during the third century, explicable in biological-demographic terms, that would have differentially affected the poor and marginal farmers.[42] In the peripheral Peloponnese, the material evidence of intensive archaeological field-survey seems to confirm objectively the literary evidence strongly suggesting that ownership of land had become polarized.[43] In the Aegean, too, the gap between the rich and the non-rich demonstrably widened, leading here as elsewhere to the increased prevalence of economically motivated *stasis* and revolution noticed above. Outside the old Greek city areas, unfreedom in the shape of serfdom increased, or at any rate persisted to an extent probably underestimated even by de Ste. Croix.[44]

---

40. See now G. Reger, *Regionalism and Change in the Economy of Independent Delos, 314–167 B.C.* (Berkeley, 1994).

41. Samuel, *From Athens to Alexandria* (n. 12) has likewise emphasised the persistence of traditional economic outlooks and practices.

42. R. Sallares, *The Ecology of the Ancient Greek World* (London, 1991).

43. Alcock, *Graecia Capta*; M. H. Jameson, C. N. Runnels and Tj. van Andel, *A Greek Countryside: The Southern Argolid from Prehistory to the Present Day* (Stanford, 1994) 394.

44. Ste. Croix, *Class Struggle*, 155–57; cf. H. Kreissig, *Wirtschaft und Gesellschaft im Seleukidenreich* (Berlin/Ost, 1978); *Geschichte des Hellenismus* (Berlin/Ost, 1984); "Weiteres zum Hellenismus," *Klio* 67 (1985) 603–607; D. Rathbone, "The ancient economy in Graeco-Roman Egypt," in L. Criscuolo and G. Geraci (eds.), *Egitto e storia antica dall' ellenismo all' età araba* (Bologna, 1989) 159–76.

Thirdly, trade. Rostovtzeff stood somewhere between the "primitivist" Karl Bücher and the "modernist" Eduard Meyer on the issues of the nature of "the ancient economy" and the role of markets therein, though appreciably nearer to the latter.[45] Following Immanuel Wallerstein, Shipley fruitfully steers the argument away from the rather sterile modernist/primitivist debate to the issue of "distance-related effects": how far were surpluses diverted from peripheral to core areas? to what degree did centralised power affect the growth or decline of subject territories? was regional economic specialisation promoted, enforced or inhibited from the political centres? His balanced conclusion is that although royal politico-military power could still determine economic success, the monarchies at most accelerated existing changes, for example regional economic interdependence, whereas other significant changes, such as the rise in the status and cosmopolitanism of traders, occurred independently of royal initiative or intervention.[46]

Fourthly, new urban amenities certainly were developed. Indeed, Hellenistic Alexandria (the subject or setting of some of C. P. Cavafy's finest poems) and Antioch were among the first truly urban centres of the ancient Greek world, and their amenities might profit indigenous populations as well as Greeks and Macedonians. But, despite Rostovtzeff, there was probably no new urban "bourgeoisie"—this seems to be just an urban myth. It may be more helpful to speak of a growing urban "middle class," but Rostovtzeff's assumption that they were the people chiefly responsible for the hellenization (and later romanization) of the Hellenistic world—what became the eastern, predominantly hellenophone half of the Roman Empire—was the fruit more of wishful ideology than empirical analysis.

The "dawn" of Rome's empire and "the coming of Rome" to the Greek East have, not unnaturally, excited a huge scholarly literature, whether the process of conquest has been seen primarily in political or in cultural terms, or as a mixture of the two elements.[47] Some of the most interesting contributions to this research have focussed on non-Greek, politico-cultural resistance to Hellenism, and on Greek politico-cultural resistance to Rome.[48]

45. M. I. Finley (ed.), *The Bücher-Meyer Controversy* (New York, 1979); S. Meikle, "Modernism, economics, and the ancient economy," *PCPS* n.s. 41 (1995) 174–91.

46. See also Fraser, *Rhodian Funerary Monuments*.

47. Badian, *Foreign Clientelae (264–70 B.C.)* (Oxford, 1958); R. M. Errington, *The Dawn of Empire: Rome's Rise to World Power* (London, 1971); E. S. Gruen, *The Hellenistic World and the Coming of Rome*, 2 vols. (Berkeley, 1984, repr. in 1 vol. 1986); Ferrary, *Philhellénisme* (n. 25); Cartledge and Spawforth, *Hellenistic and Roman Sparta*, chs. 5–6; Cl. Nicolet, *Rome et la conquête du monde méditerranéen* II. *Genèse d'un empire*, 2nd ed. (Paris, 1991).

48. S. K. Eddy, *The King is Dead: Studies in Near Eastern Resistance to Hellenism* (Lincoln, 1961); J. Deininger, *Der politische Widerstand gegen Rom in Griechenland* (Berlin, 1971).

The problem posed to the conquered Greeks, Macedonians and "culture-Greeks" by the "barbarian" status of their Roman conquerors has already been glanced at; here, it may be worth dwelling briefly on the question of Roman motives and techniques of conquest.[49] At one level, clearly, war and imperialism had a positive feedback effect on other sub-systems of Roman society, politics and culture. But whether the Romans' extra-Italian empire was sought and gained for primarily economic reasons, as opposed to being subsequently exploited for massive economic advantage but sought—if sought at all—for primarily political reasons, is still moot.[50] No less controversial is the good or bad faith of certain elite Romans in their professions of "philhellenism," the most famous—or notorious—case being T. Quinctius Flamininus' open declaration of Greek freedom and independence in 196 B.C.E.[51]

A new reading of the Philodemos Papyrus (col. 72) from Herculaneum seems to show the late-second-century Stoic Panaitios, or a pupil of his, being described or rather hailed as Rhodes' "new" or "second founder," because through his friendship with Rome he "allowed [his] native city to recover freedom."[52] This rather remarkable testimony to the apparently effectual participation of Hellenistic philosophers in international diplomacy, if that is what it is, must be set, however, against the very clear thrust of Roman policy towards internal Greek city politics. When their Greek subjects interpreted freedom too literally or liberally as meaning the freedom of the poor masses to have the sort of democratic constitution they wished, then the Roman panjandrums consistently felt constrained to curtail it in the name of good domestic order and international stability, not to mention the interests of their allies in the Greek upper classes.[53] The Romans, like other peoples and polities of the Hellenistic world, were adept at inventing pedigrees and traditions so as to legitimate their present self-perceptions

49. Romans' imperialism: W. V. Harris, *War and Imperialism in Republican Rome* (Oxford, 1979, repr. with new preface 1984); Harris (ed.), *The Imperialism of Mid-Republican Rome* (Rome, 1984); Gruen, *Hellenistic World*.

50. Harris, *War*, argues for conscious seeking, Gruen, *Hellenistic World*, equally firmly against.

51. Badian, *Titus Quinctius Flamininus: Philhellenism and Realpolitik* (Cincinnati, 1970).

52. FERRARY, below, p. 119 n. 57.

53. Walbank, "The causes of Greek decline," *JHS* 64 (1944) 10–20, at 14; J. Touloumakos, *Der Einfluss Roms auf die Staatsform der griechischen Stadtstaaten des Festlandes und der Inseln im ersten und zweiten Jhdt. v. Chr.* (Göttingen, 1967); J. Briscoe, "Rome and the class struggle in the Greek states, 200–146 B.C." (1967) repr. in M. I. Finley (ed.), *Studies in Ancient Society* (London, 1974) 53–73; R. Bernhardt, *Polis und römische Herrschaft in der späten Republik (149–31 v. Chr.)* (Berlin and New York, 1985).

and self-constructions; indeed, they were even prepared to flirt with a certain Greek ancestry.[54] But when it came to mundane dealings with their Greek subjects, pragmatism not sentiment was the order of the day: "If you want to understand Greece under the Romans," as Momigliano once epigrammatically put it, "read Polybius and whatever you may believe to be Posidonius; if you want to understand Rome ruling Greece, read Plautus, Cato—and Mommsen."[55]

II. INTRODUCTION TO THIS VOLUME

The present volume opens with a sequence of four essays concerned in one way or another with the connected themes of Hellenistic self-definition through the manipulation of legend and fable, the invention of tradition and creative mythopoeia. ALCOCK's archaeologically based essay returns to the Greek fountainhead and explores the Hellenistic concern for linking the present to the past as expressed religiously in the worship of Homeric heroes.[56] Such relatively small-scale cults, scattered across the Old Greek portions of the Hellenistic world from Samothrace to Ithaca, might have served one or more functions, including those of elite legitimation, symbolic protection or the fostering of a sense of communal identity. The dynamic explanation she offers for the cults' prevalence in the Hellenistic era is the Greeks' self-conscious yearning for a suitably epic and panhellenic pedigree, either real or fictive, a yearning born of the threat to the independent life of their small cities.

To Peter GREEN, well known as a conspicuously unsentimental critic and lively translator (in more than once sense) of ancient Greek and Roman cultural productions for modern general audiences, is owed one of the latest attempts at an overall interpretation of the Hellenistic age. This is not exactly the most upbeat of interpretations, since for him the Hellenistic age by and large means the pessimistic story of three centuries of hastening decline.[57] But in the present volume Green approaches the Hellenistic world on its own terms, through its myth-making, and by way of one of the most self-conscious of its literary fictions, the *Argonautica* of Apollonius of Rhodes

---

54. E.J. Bickerman, "Origines Gentium" *CP* 47 (1952) 65–81; E. Rawson, *The Spartan Tradition in European Thought* (Oxford, 1969, repr. 1991); cf. E.J. Hobsbawm and T. Ranger (eds.), *The Invention of Tradition* (Cambridge, 1983).

55. Momigliano, *Alien Wisdom*, 49; cf. Gruen, *Studies in Greek Culture and Roman Policy* (Leiden, 1990). On Posidonius, see also BRINGMANN and GARNSEY, below.

56. See more generally Alcock, "Minding the gap" (n. 33) 258.

57. See above, n. 7.

(who produced most of his work at the cultural epicentre of Alexandria). What strikes Green about Apollonius, and his perhaps close contemporary Dionysios Skytobrachion of Mytilene, is the continuity of Greek mythopoeic tradition that their work embodies, rather than any significant changes that he would have expected them to introduce in this otherwise (as he sees it) comprehensively and distinctively altered Hellenistic era.

The next two essays explore Jewish-Hellenic interactions, again within a mythopoeic framework. The coming of Hellenism must have seemed a threat to a society as self-consciously separate and as acutely aware of its peculiar role and mission as ancient Israelite society apparently was. One way of dealing with this threat was to turn the tables on one's adversaries, as GRUEN shows in an essay that explains how certain Jewish intellectuals had absorbed enough of Hellenic culture to be able to assimilate it to Judaism rather than themselves becoming hellenized by their contact with the Greek genre of literary fable. This Jewish cultural reception of Hellenism is to be compared, and contrasted, with that practised by the contemporary Romans.[58] MILLAR, for his part, pursues the theme of Jewish-Greek interaction in a different direction, by way of one of Elias Bickerman's "four strange books of the Bible," namely Daniel.[59] The early part of his essay explores the Jewish response to a succession of foreign empires through a broad range of sources, including Daniel (conventionally dated to the 160s B.C.E.). The conclusion stresses, against other scholarly opinion, that the various sections of Daniel are in fact structurally integrated, and emphasises the Maccabean crisis as a motive for recounting the sequence of empires. More research along the lines Millar adumbrates would clearly be welcome.

The two following essays in different ways concern the coming of Rome to the Greek world and the Greeks' responses to it, pragmatic, ideological or both. In his earlier major book FERRARY had argued that "philhellenism" was both a genuine Roman stance towards aspects of Greek high culture and a weapon of ideological warfare wielded by the Roman governing class as a means of enabling the subaltern Greeks to come to terms with their subordination to the Roman barbarian. Here, he advances on a rather narrower front, considering the effect of personal patronage by influential Romans on the affairs of Greek states in the Hellenistic period. He rightly dissents from the thesis of Ernst Badian that the Roman institution of *clientela* constituted an alien intrusion into a world that operated internationally

58. Gruen, *Studies*; *Culture and National Identity in Republican Rome* (Ithaca and London, 1992).

59. Bickerman, *Four Strange Books of the Bible: Jonah, Daniel, Koheleth, Esther* (New York, 1984).

on quite other lines, and he stresses instead the practical interrelationship between *clientela* and the Greek socio-political institution of *proxenia*.[60] It is worth adding that the relationship had also, and perhaps no less important, symbolic ramifications. Ferrary's essay closes neatly with Polybius, about whom much more anon.

MATTINGLY patiently collects the testimonia on Athenian relations with Hellenistic monarchies and with Rome, mainly in the second century B.C.E.[61] The vast bulk of the evidence consists of honorific decrees, either for Athenians who advocated their city's cause in foreign capitals or for monarchs and their immediate entourage. Behind their calm and immobile surface there no doubt lies a sometimes quite frantic diplomacy aimed presumably at conciliating as many relevantly powerful foreigners as possible at the same time. But very few of the decrees, unfortunately, indicate the precise character of the services for which the individuals were honoured.

Rather than epigraphy, the primary source material and objective of study in the next three historiographical essays are the two leading figures of Hellenistic history writing, Polybius and Posidonius. Reversing their chronological order, we print next BRINGMANN's acute analysis of two questions concerning Posidonius, in themselves relatively minor and quite independent but connected by him in such a way as to illuminate the larger and more interesting issues of the Syrian Greek author's ideas of historical causality and historiographical propriety. The thesis proposed is that the Stoic Posidonius, in order to flesh out his portrayal of Athenion as a paradigm of the false philosopher turned arch-tyrant, constructively contaminated his colourful account of Athenion's brief tyranny at Athens in 88 B.C.E., the terminal date of his history, with material belonging originally to the later tyranny of Aristion (87 B.C.E.). GARNSEY takes a different and unusual approach to Posidonius the philosophic historian, by reexamining an alleged "fragment" of his work about a particular group of unfree Hellenistic people (the Mariandynoi of Greek Heracleia on the Black Sea) in the light of the Middle Stoa's scantily attested—and, in Garnsey's view, little developed—attitude to slavery in general. Conclusions are mostly negative, but, in so far as Garnsey can firmly detach Posidonius thereby from any possible implication with Aristotelian natural slavery doctrine, none the less valuable for that.[62]

60. Badian, *Foreign Clientelae*.

61. See also Chr. Habicht, *Athen in Hellenistischer Zeit*, 140–230, s.v. "Politik"; S. V. Tracy, *Attic Letter Cutters of 229–86 B.C.* (Princeton, 1990).

62. See also P. Garnsey, *Ideas of Slavery from Aristotle to Augustine* (Cambridge, 1996) 146–50.

With ECKSTEIN's essay we come head-on to Polybius, who serves also as prime source for the essay immediately following. Polybius characterized his history as "pragmatic" or transactional. By this linguistic device and in numerous other ways he plainly sought to represent his historiography as marking a return in essentials to the sort of history practised in the fifth and fourth centuries B.C.E. by Thucydides and the Oxyrhynchus Historian, and thus a decisive break with the dominant trends of Hellenistic historical writing encapsulated (so he claimed) in Timaeus and "tragic" history.[63] Polybius' rhetoric, when combined with the modern political-scientific approach to foreign relations known variously as realism or neo-realism, has encouraged the view that Polybius strove, successfully, to eliminate from his history any strong moral standpoint. Eckstein's project, both in his recent book and rather differently here, is to restore Polybius' moral judgmentalism to what he considers its proper, that is a central, place.[64] Condemnations of self-indulgence, greed and cowardice are not on this estimation mere grace notes but essential vehicles of Polybius' historical understanding and explanation. Furthermore, by pointing out that Polybius liberally imputed vices to the Romans as well as to the Greeks and Macedonians, Eckstein effectively counters the widespread notion that Polybius regarded the Romans as by nature a fundamentally superior people.

HERMAN's essay also draws heavily on Polybius, but to different effect: like the immediately succeeding essay, it is above all a venture in comparative history and historiography. For Herman's aim is to develop a theory of the workings of Hellenistic court society by applying retrospectively a version of that formulated by Norbert Elias in relation to the court of Louis XIV. Thus, although Polybius' strong republican bias against Hellenistic courts and courtiers has doubtless obscured more than somewhat their standard structures and routine functions and activities, Herman nevertheless sees plotting, intrigue and bickering among courtiers, and relentless rivalry between them and the king, as very much the Hellenistic courtly norm.[65] Herman provides also a new account of the networks of associations between elite members of Greek communities and the men at court that help to explain both the

---

63. Walbank, *Polybius*, *passim*; cf. Connor, "Historical writing" (n. 18).

64. Eckstein, *Moral Vision*.

65. Compare the following generalisation prompted by analysis of a more recent "court": "The rule of a court conceals a political anarchy in which jealous feudatories, with their private armies and reservations of public resources, are secretly bargaining, and may openly fight, for the reversion or preservation of power"—H. Trevor-Roper, *The Last Days of Hitler*, 7th ed. (London, 1995) 209.

international outreach of these court societies and the modes of recruitment into their circles.[66]

BAGNALL's comparativism is of a different kind, consisting in an attempt to expose the limitations of a "colonial" model for the understanding of Ptolemaic Egypt. Under this broad rubric Bagnall provocatively treats the work not only of Edward Said but also of Édouard Will as presenting interpretative paradigms that are to be avoided. Bagnall's essay, though primarily an exercise in negative criticism, does also allude to the improved understanding to be derived from consulting imaginative literature produced by the victims of what he considers a hierarchical—not necessarily "colonial"—system of domination.

Finally, we return to political economy with THOMPSON's essay on Ptolemaic fiscality as represented in a variety of papyrus materials including not yet published tax registers; this draws both on her own previous influential work and on collaborative work in progress on the nuts and bolts of Ptolemaic administration.[67] The central questions addressed concern the bureaucracy's character and efficiency, but rarely if ever, as Thompson duly underlines, does the evidence available or likely to become available provide clear-cut and decisive answers. What, for example, accounts for the progressive lowering of the tax rate and extension of exemptions? Loopholes in tax collection there undoubtedly were, as in all systems, but how far and by whom, typically, were they exploited in Ptolemaic Egypt? Any future work in this area will have to start from the basis and database established by Thompson and her collaborators. But it seems only fitting to end this introduction on an interrogative note.

66. See also Herman, "The 'friends' of the early Hellenistic rulers: servants or officials?" *Talanta* 12/13 (1980/81) 103–49; *Ritualised Friendship and the Greek City* (Cambridge, 1987).

67. D. J. Thompson, *Memphis under the Ptolemies* (Princeton, 1988).

ONE

The Heroic Past in a Hellenistic Present

Susan E. Alcock

In the early 1970s, an enigma was discovered at the Sanctuary of the
Great Gods (the Megaloi Theoi) on Samothrace. Built within a retaining
wall, near structures identified as ritual dining rooms, was what appeared
to be the stomion, or entrance, of a Bronze Age tholos tomb, complete
with rough polygonal "Cyclopean" masonry, a huge fieldstone lintel and a
relieving triangle formed by two porous sandstone blocks (Figure 1). Yet this
Samothracian tholos is doubly false: first because no tomb lies within (the
passageway ends after some two meters) and again because it is not of Bronze
Age date. The "tholos" belongs instead to the Hellenistic era, constructed
when the retaining wall was built around the end of the third or beginning
of the second century B.C.[1] "Enigma" was the designation given to this
monument by the Samothracian investigators, and it has indeed remained
more or less a hapax among ancient architectural oddities; certainly no
other Hellenistic constructions appear directly to emulate Mycenaean tholoi.
Concentrating only on its formal characteristics, however, may not be the
most fruitful way to consider this pseudo-tholos. Instead, the monument can
be challenged for what it appears to represent, becoming a springboard for

This essay is dedicated to Frank W. Walbank, a Hellenistic hero if ever there was one.
It first appeared in *Echos du monde classique / Classical Views* 38, n.s. 13 (1994) 221–34. I thank
the editors of that journal for kindly allowing me to reprint the piece (with some minor
revisions) here, as well as the editors of this volume for inviting me to do so.
    1. J. R. McCredie, "Recent investigations in Samothrace, 1965–74," in U. Jantzen,
ed., *Neue Forschungen in Griechischen Heiligtümern* (Tübingen, 1976) 91–102, esp. 98–99; J. R.
McCredie, "A Samothracian enigma," *Hesperia* 43 (1974) 454–59; S. G. Cole, *Megaloi
Theoi: The Cult of the Great Gods at Samothrace* (Leiden, 1984) 8; H. Ehrhardt, *Samothrake:
Heiligtümer in ihrer Landschaft und Geschichte als Zeugen antiken Geisteslebens* (Stuttgart, 1985)
183–87, figs. 48–49.

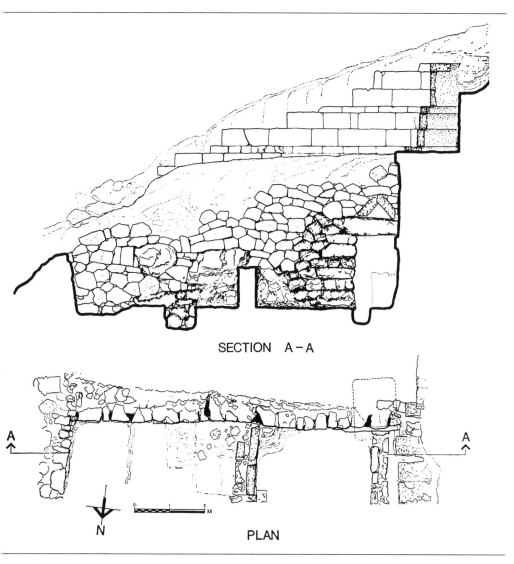

SECTION A – A

PLAN

N

Figure 1. Sanctuary of the Great Gods, Samothrace. Retaining wall (elevation and plan)
with pseudo-tholos in right corner (Courtesy of the American School of Classical Studies
at Athens)

questioning Hellenistic concern with the age of heroes or, to put it another way, for exploring the heroic past in a Hellenistic present.

A Hellenistic concern for linking the present to the past has already been observed in other spheres of behavior, notably in the form of cult at Bronze Age tholos tombs. This phenomenon has been identified, with varying degrees of certainty, in several parts of the Greek mainland and on Crete.[2] The precise identity of the recipients of such cult has been much debated, particularly in relation to similar practices in earlier, Geometric and Archaic times. While likely, it is impossible to be certain that this post-classical attention was dedicated to figures who would have been explicitly recognized and venerated as "heroes," and the term "hero" in itself poses a complex problem of definition. Most fundamentally, however, such rituals manifest a desire to invoke powerful elements drawn from the past at a time in the history of the Greek city which, if not the period of crisis and disintegration that was once envisioned, was surely still a time of stress and transformation.[3]

Taking a cue from post-classical tomb cult, a tentative pattern could be proposed: the representation in material culture of Hellenistic veneration for an antique and yet still compelling past. This paper will attempt to unfold that perceived pattern still further by examining the Hellenistic fate of cults attested to a specific group of heroes—named epic heroes, Homeric heroes—and to other figures linked to the Heroic Age. What will be monitored in the individual cases considered are what developments and what transformations, if any, took place in cults of this sort during Hellenistic times.[4] This type of period-oriented investigation runs counter to many traditional approaches to Greek religious practice which tend, based on a

2. Cult at Bronze Age tombs, after an initial florescence in the Geometric period, reappears in the fourth century B.C. and after; see S. E. Alcock, "Tomb cult and the post-classical polis," *AJA* 95 (1991) 447–67.

3. For recent discussion of the Geometric cult and the definition of the term "hero," see for example: I. Morris, "Tomb cult and the 'Greek Renaissance': the past in the present in the 8th century B.C.," *Antiquity* 62 (1988) 750–61; J. Whitley, "Tomb cult and hero cult: the uses of the past in Archaic Greece," in N. Spencer, ed., *Time, Tradition and Society in Greek Archaeology: Bridging the "Great Divide"* (London, 1995) 43–63; C. Antonaccio, "The archaeology of ancestors," in C. Dougherty and L. Kurke, eds., *Cultural Poetics in Archaic Greece* (Cambridge, 1993) 46–70, and *An Archaeology of Ancestors: Tomb Cult and Hero Cult in Early Greece* (Lanham, Maryland, 1995); E. Kearns, *The Heroes of Attica* (London, 1989) 1–9.

4. It should be noted that, with the exception of Achilles at Troy, this analysis focuses on mainland Greece and the islands (the territory of "Old Greece") and does not consider the issue of heroic cult in the Hellenistic kingdoms beyond.

somewhat haphazard mixture of literary references, to stress its synchronic nature. Such static reconstructions are now being challenged with the help of archaeological data, and in this context these data will be employed where possible. The available archaeological evidence is, admittedly, often less than impeccable; many of the investigations involved were of early date and problematic design. Yet in by far the majority of instances, it is only with archaeological help that variations in either the practice, or the intensity, of cult can be measured over time. While the following review does not deal comprehensively with all epic or heroic age cults in Hellenistic Greece, it does for the most part cover the ones for which we have some degree of archaeological evidence.

We can begin the review with Agamemnon, "lord of men." Agamemnon was worshipped at the Agamemnoneion, excavated by the British School at Athens in their Mycenae campaigns of the earlier part of the twentieth century. The cult of Agamemnon was apparently not linked with the supposed site of his tomb; Pausanias (2.16.6) reports his grave within the citadel, while the shrine in question lies about one kilometer outside the settlement's walls. The location of the Agamemnoneion was nonetheless tied to that community by its proximity to a Mycenaean causeway, a recognizably Cyclopean structure on the road to Prosymna. Cult activity began at this site in the eighth century B.C. (the period of Geometric tomb cult); in the Archaic period an enclosure was built and cult continued "well into Hellenistic times."[5] Finds indicate drinking and feasting in honor of the dedicatee, together with what Cook called "embarrassingly appropriate" louteria. As for the Hellenistic period proper, excavations revealed a renewal of the sanctuary; published details are few, but it is clear that the temenos was remodelled with features such as a green schist pavement and a new roof for the enclosure. At this time inscriptions on ceramic offerings also clearly identify the recipient of worship as Agamemnon, an attribution that cannot be definitively made for the previous centuries of worship and indeed is frequently doubted.[6]

---

5. J. M. Cook, "The cult of Agamemnon at Mycenae," in *Geras Antoniou Keramopoullou* (Athens, 1953) 112–14; J. M. Cook, "Mycenae 1939–52: the Agamemnoneion," *BSA* 48 (1953) 30–68, esp. 32–33, 62–65 and fig. 6; R. Hägg, "Gifts to the heroes in Geometric and Archaic Greece," in T. Linders and G. C. Nordquist, eds., *Gifts to the Gods* (Uppsala, 1987) 93–99, esp. 96–98.

6. Several scholars have queried the early date of the epic hero's worship at this locale, arguing for an originally female dedicatee: F. de Polignac, *La naissance de la cité grecque* (Paris, 1984) 130–31; Antonaccio (n. 3) 67 n. 36; C. Morgan and T. Whitelaw, "Pots and politics: ceramic evidence for the rise of the Argive state," *AJA* 95 (1991) 88–90.

Mycenae had been destroyed by Argos in the fifth century B.C.; this rebuilding of the Agamemnoneion is generally assumed to have been contemporaneous with its reoccupation as an Argive *kôme* in the third/second century B.C. The reestablishment of the site was short-lived, enduring only a century or so.[7] Despite the short life of the *kôme*, however, further observations can be made about the possible interaction of the new Argive inhabitants with Mycenae's ancient monuments. At three of the nine Bronze Age tholoi at Mycenae (Epano Phournos, Tomb of Aegisthus, Tomb of Clytemnestra), finds of associated later pottery at least raise the possibility of some form of post-classical cult, although the evidence is admittedly poor.[8] It is also worth noting that the Hellenistic theater constructed in the *kôme* was built across the dromos of the Tomb of Clytemnestra. That juxtaposition was long thought to be a meaningless association, on the assumption that later builders were unaware of the tomb's presence. Subsequent observation has shown, however, that seats of the theater actually rest directly upon the wall blocks of the dromos.[9] Our interpretations of such spatial annexation of monuments may require revising, to credit Greeks of the historical period with greater sensitivity to past human landscapes, and with a greater interest in forging physical linkages between old and new elements.[10]

Bonds between Heroic and Hellenistic Mycenae can be taken a step further. Michael Jameson recently raised some provocative points about the relationship of Argos and Mycenae, or rather of Argos and Mycenae's legendary repute. He noted, for example, the appropriation by Argos of Mycenae's other "local hero," Perseus. Perseus appears on Argive coins; in the Roman period his honors were voted to Argive benefactors. From epigraphic evidence, Jameson also observed that, although under Argive

7. On the Hellenistic settlement: C. A. Boethius, "Excavations at Mycenae XI. Hellenistic Mycenae," *BSA* 25 (1921–1923) 409–28; J. A. Dengate, "Coins from the Mycenae excavations, 1939–62," *BSA* 69 (1974) 95–102.

8. A. J. B. Wace, "Excavations at Mycenae IX: the tholos tombs," *BSA* 25 (1921–1923) 292–316, 357–76; A. J. B. Wace, M. S. F. Hood and J. M. Cook, "Mycenae, 1939–52: the Epano Phournos tholos tomb," *BSA* 48 (1953) 69–83, esp. 81, 83; Alcock (n. 2) 464 for references.

9. C. Antonaccio, "The Archaeology of Early Greek 'Hero Cult,'" (Ph.D. Diss. Princeton, 1987) 62–65; H. Thompson, "The tomb of Clytemnestra revisited," in K. DeVries, ed., *From Athens to Gordion: The Papers of a Memorial Symposium for Rodney S. Young* (Philadelphia, 1980) 3–9, esp. 7–9; Boethius (n. 7) 418.

10. C. Antonaccio, "Placing the past: the Bronze Age in the cultic topography of Early Greece" (pp. 79–104) and the other papers in S. E. Alcock and R. Osborne, eds., *Placing the Gods: Sanctuaries and Sacred Space in Ancient Greece* (Oxford, 1994).

control, Mycenae appeared to possess special rights, notably in retaining an independent ephebeia, an unusual privilege for a *kôme*:

> ... can it be that Argos encouraged those of its citizens who lived off the land of the former Mycenaean territory to revive old cults and traditions for the sake of their prestige and aura of antiquity, even as they undertook the rebuilding of the Agamemnoneion?[11]

Turning from the Hellenistic treatment of Agamemnon, of Perseus and of strong-walled Mycenae itself, the second case to consider is that of wily Odysseus and the Polis Cave on Ithaka. Finds from the cave span the period from the Bronze Age to the Roman era, but exactly who received cult at any particular time remains a confused matter: Athena and Hera are attested in the seventh century B.C., masks of Artemis are present, and a third-century B.C. votive to the Nymphs was also found. The first dedication to Odysseus proper belongs no earlier than the Hellenistic period, when his name can be reconstructed on a female mask of a style dating to the second/first century B.C. It is not impossible that Odysseus was worshiped in the cave before then, unrecorded but sharing the sacred space with other deities. On the other hand, to judge from present evidence at least, the possibility cannot be ruled out that Odysseus began to receive worship at the Polis Cave only at some point during the Hellenistic period.[12] What can be said with confidence is that excavation recovered noteworthy amounts of Hellenistic pottery (moldmade bowls, West Slope ware) and female masks, a common votive at this time and, at least in that one case, a type associated with the hero. Even more significant is the sanctuary's reorganization with the erection of a temenos wall, dated not earlier than 300 B.C. Games of the Odysseia are known to have been celebrated on Ithaka, possibly in connection with this cult place. These contests, again, are first certainly attested in the Hellenistic age; the festival appears to have been of some consequence, with cities as far afield as Magnesia being invited in 206 B.C.[13]

11. M. H. Jameson, "Perseus, the hero of Mykenai," in R. Hägg and G. C. Nordquist, eds., *Celebrations of Death and Divinity in the Bronze Age Argolid* (Stockholm, 1990) 213–22, at p. 222. Honors, e.g. *IG* 4.606; ephebeia, *IG* 4.497 (ca. 195 B.C.); cf. Pausanias 2.21.6–7.

12. See n. 6 on the possible late arrival of Agamemnon as a cult figure at the Agamemnoneion. Similar arguments have been made about Menelaus and the Lakonian Menelaion, where the first dedications are to Helen only: H. W. Catling, "Excavations at the Menelaion, Sparta, 1973–76," *Archaeological Reports* (1976–1977) 24–42; H. W. Catling and H. Cavanagh, "Two inscribed bronzes from the Menelaion, Sparta," *Kadmos* 15 (1976) 145–57.

13. T. Hadzisteliou Price, "Hero cult in the 'Age of Homer' and earlier," in G. W. Bowersock, W. Burkert and M. C. J. Putnam, eds., *Arktouros: Hellenic Studies Presented to*

Whenever epic hero cults are discussed, three instances immediately spring to mind: the Agamemnoneion, the Polis Cave and the Menelaion, the shrine of Menelaus and Helen in Lakonia. Yet the Menelaion does not appear to follow all the developments observed in the first two cases. Cult activity at the site of Therapne began in the eighth century B.C., continuing at least well into the Hellenistic period and possibly running even later. The latest major renewal of the shrine building itself, however, dated to the fifth century B.C., although inscribed tiles do suggest some third- and first-century B.C. work on associated site structures (possibly a storeroom or house for shrine personnel). Following the site's most recent excavator, Hector Catling, it can be stated that the post-classical history of the shrine remains poorly understood and—at this point at any rate—the Menelaion can contribute little secure information to the present investigation.[14]

Another more ambiguous case is that of the tomb of Achilles in the Troad—archaeologically ambiguous, it should be said, for there is no doubt but that the site believed to be his grave was recognized and honored in Hellenistic times. Alexander, as Plutarch tells us, went to Ilium where:

> ... he sacrificed to Athena and poured libations to the heroes. Furthermore the gravestone of Achilles he anointed with oil, ran a race by it with his companions, naked, as is the custom, and then crowned it with garlands, pronouncing the hero happy in having, while he lived, a faithful friend, and after death, a great herald of his fame... (*Alexander* 15.4–5)

Alexander's fascination with the works of Homer is celebrated, of course, as was his claim to genealogical descent from the most famous of epic heroes. But Alexander was hardly unique in his obsession about "where Homer

---

Bernard M. W. Knox on the Occasion of his 65th Birthday (Berlin, 1979) 221–22; S. Benton, "A votive offering to Odysseus," *Antiquity* 10 (1936) 350; S. Benton, "Excavations in Ithaca, III. The cave at Pólis, I," *BSA* 35 (1934–1935) 45–73, esp. 54–55; S. Benton, "Excavations in Ithaca, III. The cave at Pólis, II," *BSA* 39 (1938–1939) 1–51, esp. 31–38, 43–45. It has been suggested that, after the sanctuary's refurbishment, some of its dedicatory tripods had been arranged "to give it an image consistent with that of the cave of Odysseus in *Odyssey* 13.13–14 and 363–71"; see François de Polignac, "Mediation, competition and sovereignty: the evolution of rural sanctuaries in Geometric Greece," in S. E. Alcock and R. Osborne, eds., *Placing the Gods: Sanctuaries and Sacred Space in Ancient Greece* (Oxford, 1994) 11 n. 23.

14. H. W. Catling, *Archaeological Reports* (1975–1976) 14–15; Catling (n. 12) 41–42; P. Cartledge, *Sparta and Lakonia. A Regional History 1300–362 B.C.* (London, 1979) 121; Catling and Cavanagh (n. 12); A. J. B. Wace, M. S. Thompson and J. P. Droop, "Laconia I. Excavations at Sparta, 1909: The Menelaion," *BSA* 15 (1908–1909) 108–57, esp. 113; P. Cartledge and A. Spawforth, *Hellenistic and Roman Sparta: A Tale of Two Cities* (London, 1989) 195.

happened." Hellenistic scholars agonized, much as their successors would, over recalcitrant Homeric geography: as Cook noted, "The ancients too had their 'False Troy' heresy, their problem of the 'Springs of Scamander,' their 'No Space for the Battlefield' quandary …"[15] Today the site of Besik Tepe is often, if far from universally, thought to be the tomb of Achilles hallowed in ancient times. From Schliemann and Dörpfeld's work at this mound came a small quantity of fourth/third-century B.C. pottery. The paucity of this material allowed it to be readily dismissed as extraneous to the site itself (which is, of course, a prehistoric tell), clearly an easier explanation than having to envisage later additions to the mound or imagining that "such a tumulus would have been thrown up in Hellenistic times."[16] In light of developments at other epic cult places, however, perhaps such a scenario is not as implausible as would once have been thought; there may have been some incentive for the site's reorganization in the Hellenistic period. The nature of the archaeological evidence allows nothing more definite to be said but, through textual evidence at any rate, signs of Hellenistic veneration at the tombs of heroes appear in the plain of windy Troy itself.

In Boeotian Thebes, Hector provides another instance of Hellenistic hero cult based more on texts than archaeology. An oracle urged the Thebans to worship Hector if they wished the city to prosper, and we are told that the bones of Hector were transferred from Ophryneion in the Troad to Thebes. All the extant literary evidence for the cult dates to the Hellenistic era, probably the early third century B.C. or at the very earliest the end of the fourth century. Farnell noted, and others have agreed, that the tradition does indeed appear to belong to this "late" period, with Schachter suggesting that the transfer might be connected with the rebuilding of Thebes by Kassandros and with the possible consolation offered by one sacked city

---

15. J. M. Cook, *The Troad* (Oxford, 1973) 186–88, quote at 188; J. M. Cook, "The topography of the plain of Troy," in L. Foxhall and J. K. Davies, eds., *The Trojan War: Its Historicity and Context* (Bristol, 1984) 163–72; cf. W. Leaf, *Troy: A Study in Homeric Geography* (London, 1912). For Hellenistic and Roman visitors to Troy, see C. C. Vermeule III, "Neon Ilion and Ilium Novum: Kings, soldiers, citizens and tourists at Classical Troy," in J. B. Carter and S. P. Morris, eds., *The Ages of Homer* (Austin, 1995) 467–82.

16. Cook (n. 15) 173–74, quote at 174. Another possible case of restoration at this tumulus, however, is suggested by Cook who notes that the present cone at Besik Tepe could have been added by Caracalla to match the tumulus of Festus, the emperor's favorite: Cook ("The topography," n. 15) 171 n. 2. For other perspectives on cults of Achilles: J. Hooker, "The cults of Achilles," *RhM* 131 (1988) 1–7; G. Hedreen, "The cult of Achilles in the Euxine," *Hesperia* 60 (1991) 313–30.

to another.[17]   Pausanias (9.18.5) reports that Hector's tomb was "near the spring of Oidipous," but no archaeological evidence can yet be brought to bear on this Theban cult. Literary testimony for its inception, nonetheless, appears well anchored in the Hellenistic age.[18]

Hector, representing the losing side in the Trojan struggle, is the last of the specifically Homeric heroes to be discussed here. Yet other figures drawn from the heroic age, or associated with that particular past, can also usefully be considered. In Boeotian Orchomenos, for example, stands the Treasury of Minyas, a Bronze Age tholos tomb. The structure has apparently been visible throughout the ages, Pausanias declaring it "a wonder second to none" (9.38.2). The tomb was first explored archaeologically by Schliemann, who discovered a deep stratum of ash and burned material, possibly consonant with ritual sacrifices. In the center of the circular tholos space were found the remains of a substantial marble statue base, together with marble statue fragments. Schliemann dated these internal improvements to the "Macedonian" era, arguing the tomb had been turned at that time into some form of sanctuary complex. The identity and range of cult recipients remain unclear. From the Hellenistic period appears an inscription to Hera Teleia; in Roman times the tomb seems to have become a focus for the imperial cult.[19] Perhaps there was no heroic presence at all here, although, as the Polis Cave and many other sanctuaries suggest, heroes and deities could closely co-exist.[20] As for which hero might have been honored here in Hellenistic times, the benefit of the doubt (with cautious use of Pausanias' second-century A.D. identification) must go to Minyas, the legendary founder of Orchomenos and, incidentally, an important figure in various heroic genealogies.[21]

17. L. R. Farnell, *Greek Hero Cults and Ideas of Immortality* (Oxford, 1921) 328–29; A. Schachter, *Cults of Boeotia* 1. *Acheloos to Hera* (London, 1981) 233–34, which collects the ancient testimonia.

18. S. Symeonoglou, *The Topography of Thebes from the Bronze Age to Modern Times* (Princeton, 1985) 193–94; "Thebai (Boiotien)," in *Paulys Real-Encyclopädie* 5A.1514–15 (Stuttgart, 1934).

19. H. Schliemann, "Exploration of the Boeotian Orchomenos," *JHS* 2 (1881) 122–63, esp. 137–39; A. K. Orlandos, "Ergasiai en tôi tholôtôi taphôi Orchomenou," *AD* 1 (1915) 51–53; J. G. Frazer, *Pausanias' Description of Greece*, vol. 5 (London, 1898) 189.

20. E. Kearns, "Between god and man: status and function of heroes and their sanctuaries," in A. Schachter and J. Bingen, eds., *Le sanctuaire grec* (Geneva, 1992) 65–99, esp. 77–93.

21. "Minyas" in *Paulys Real-Encyclopädie* 15.2014–18 (Stuttgart, 1932); cf. Homer, *Iliad* 2.511. Paul Wallace has suggested that the tomb became the repository of Hesiod's bones, but his arguments have not been generally accepted: P. W. Wallace, "The tomb of Hesiod and the Treasury of Minyas at Orkhomenos," in J. M. Fossey and H. Giroux,

In light of the foregoing review, we can now return to the "Samothracian enigma" with which we began. The Hellenistic period, as is well known, proved a growth time for the cult of the Great Gods. At the Samothracian sanctuary, a number of Hellenistic structures use rough polygonal masonry in a kind of "Cyclopean"-looking style, a phenomenon which is in itself of some interest.[22] But the pseudo-tholos goes well beyond such low-level suggestive quotations in its emulation of a Bronze Age, and potentially heroic, tomb. This "Mycenaeanizing" entrance has been most specifically associated with Eëtion, son of Elektra and Zeus and founder of the island's mysteries; his brother Dardanos left Samothrace to become the ancestor of Trojan kings. It has been suggested by McCredie that the monument served as the cenotaph of Eëtion, who was vaporized by a thunderbolt from Zeus and thus did not require a proper tomb.[23] If such an association, which is certainly plausible, is also correct, then we find here an overt Hellenistic correlation of hero cult with Mycenaean burial forms.

At this point one might with some justice protest that there need be no correlation between epic tomb types and those tholoi venerated in post-classical tomb cult and in some of the contexts reviewed here (e.g. Orchomenos, Samothrace). Homeric heroes, of course, are cremated and buried in tumuli (*Iliad* 10.415; 11.166, 371; 23. 256; 24.349, 799). And it is striking that cases of unambiguous epic hero cult (the Agamemnoneion, the Polis cave, the Menelaion) are not focused upon tholos tombs, or indeed upon any obvious kind of monumental grave at all. Does that rule out, however, the possibility that heroic significance was attached to certain tombs (now known to date to the Bronze Age) by individuals in later historical periods? I believe that would call for too narrow an interpretation, failing to allow for later mental associations, connections drawn between certain places named in epic (a Mycenae, an Orchomenos) and still-visible structures of perceived antiquity and power, characterized not least by the seemingly superhuman workmanship of Cyclopean masonry.

---

eds., *Proceedings of the Third International Conference on Boeotian Antiquities* (Amsterdam, 1985) 165–71; cf. Frazer (n. 19) 189.

22. McCredie ("Samothracian," n. 1) 457; A. Conze et al., *Untersuchungen auf Samothrake* (Vienna, 1875) pl. VII; H. Seyrig, "Sur l'antiquité des remparts de Samothrace," *BCH* 51 (1927) 353–68, esp. 366–67.

23. McCredie ("Samothracian," n. 1) 458–59; ("Recent," n. 1) 98–99; Cole (n. 1) 3–4; W. Burkert, "Concordia Discors: the literary and the archaeological evidence on the sanctuary of Samothrace," in N. Marinatos and R. Hägg, eds., *Greek Sanctuaries: New Approaches* (London, 1993) 178–91, esp. 185–86. By Hellenistic times, the Theban story of Harmonia and Kadmos had been woven into this tale, with Harmonia being Elektra's third child; she wed Kadmos on Samothrace.

The antiquarian interests and historicizing tendencies of the Hellenistic age, to be further discussed below, would have contributed strongly to such associations. The epic tradition was a potent force, but one not incapable of modification. We could, for example, note another variation: Homer has Achilles and Patroclus buried in a single tomb, yet in antiquity two distinct graves were often identified and venerated separately.[24] Divergence from epic "truth" may remain a problem, but it is not sufficient to disengage the link between Bronze Age tombs and Hellenistic heroic affections.

It seems fair to summarize this review by saying that, in the Hellenistic age, cults of heroes (and other heroic characters) witness a resurgence of interest, expressed in certain cases through some form of monumentalization (attested at the Agamemnoneion, Polis Cave, Treasury of Minyas, and Samothrace). Literary evidence, too, offers instances of Hellenistic heroic veneration (Hector, Achilles). These cults are not necessarily new, in fact few appear to originate in Hellenistic times; but some *intensification* of cult practice in this epoch seems to have taken place. When combined with the practice of post-classical tomb cult, the tentative theme with which this paper began—the power of the heroic past in a Hellenistic present—is much reinforced, and now requires explication.

In accounting for post-classical tomb cult, while acknowledging the polyvalence of ritual in general and the ambiguity and flexibility of the concept of the hero in particular,[25] I suggested that one of the more powerful forces behind renewed activity at Bronze Age tombs was the need for élite legitimization within the life of the Greek city. Aristocratic families, it has often been remarked, took on greater responsibility within Hellenistic civic affairs, especially in their role as benefactors (*euergetai*). While current revisionist views argue for the continued vitality of cities at this time, it would nonetheless be going too far to deny completely the existence of new structural tensions. One stress point, certainly, must have been the role of these wealthy benefactors in relation to civic ideology. Many changes can be identified in what might be called the symbolic atmosphere of the Hellenistic city: the resumption, and acceptance, of monumental burial; commemorative communal celebrations designed to mourn the prominent and benevolent dead; the very application of the term "hero" to those recently deceased

---

24. Arrian 1.12.1; Plutarch, *Alexander* 15.4–5; Strabo 13.1.32; cf. Cook (*Troad*, n. 15) 160.

25. On the polyvalence of ritual: C. Bell, *Ritual Theory, Ritual Practice* (New York, 1992). Geometric tomb cult, for example, has accumulated a wide range of explanatory baggage, yet much recent scholarship on the subject accepts this diversity; Morris (n. 3); J. Whitley, "Early states and hero cults: a reappraisal," *JHS* 108 (1988) 173–82.

or even still living. Tomb cult can be linked to a general appropriation of "civic memory" by civic élites as yet another way to achieve prominence, and to perpetuate a new social order.[26]

The new attentions paid in Hellenistic times to the cults reviewed here would fit well within this general explanatory framework. The family trees of aristocratic clans were, after all, carefully cultivated to take firm root in heroic soil. Fictive genealogies were not new in the Hellenistic period, but in this age such claims could be more openly expressed, more publicly asserted. An additional consideration is the fact that the very degree of investment needed to improve and formalize these cult spaces suggests the involvement of more prosperous interests. Élite priorities, the determination to control collective memory and to annex the power thus provided, seem a convincing way to account—in part—for the patterns observed. On the other hand, the extent to which more community-oriented goals might be served by such cults can be considered, in this returning to the more traditional notion of the hero as a force for group solidarity and cohesion. The use of Mycenae's various heroes and monuments by Argos could be held up as an example of a community consciously employing antiquities and antique traditions for the sake of civic prestige.[27] Thebes annexing the bones of Hector, perhaps at a particularly traumatic time in its history, may represent another more communally-based impetus to cult. Given the complexity of ritual practice, neither of these possibilities—élite manipulation or communal concern—is mutually exclusive.

The objection might be raised that all the foregoing arguments take for granted, and merely presuppose, the power of the heroic past. In some senses, that might be secure enough ground to defend: Homer and his heroes were always challenging and commanding presences. Yet if the aim in this paper is to achieve some kind of historical and dynamic perspective, then it must be asked *why*, for the Hellenistic age specifically, the heroic age proved such a magnetic force. A start could be made by examining the once-popular notion of the influence of epic, the spread of which, after all, was once the predominant explanation for Geometric cult at Bronze Age

26. L. Robert, *Études anatoliennes. Recherches sur les inscriptions grecques de l'Asie Mineure* (Amsterdam, 1970) 45–49; Alcock (n. 2) 456–58. I am greatly indebted to Pauline Schmitt Pantel's work on this subject; e.g. "Le festin dans la fête de la cité grecque hellénistique," in *La fête, pratique et discours* (Paris, 1981) 85–95.

27. Inscribed tiles indicate that the Hellenistic enclosure at the Agamemnoneion was public in character: Cook ("Mycenae 1939–52," n. 5) 33 and n. 2, 66. The Argive annexation of the panhellenic Nemean Games is another aspect of the city's symbolic expansion: S. G. Miller, *Nemea: A Guide to the Site and the Museum* (Berkeley, 1990) 20, 23–24, 57.

tombs.[28] More recent interpretations of Geometric activity, however, prefer accounts more rooted in social conditions of the time, as I have likewise proposed for similar cults in the post-classical era. Yet just how disconnected is the reading of epic from social and political development? Ian Morris has argued that the use and abuse of Homer was an implicit factor in the turmoil surrounding the rise of the *polis*.[29] What about the potential disorder of its later transformations?

Readings of Homer do not, of course, remain static over the centuries, as each age engages with its own questions and priorities.[30] In the Hellenistic period, Homer became the subject of much philosophical, scientific and antiquarian debate, as seen in the controversies over Homeric topography. Most interpretative work so far on the "Hellenistic Homer" has operated at this erudite level—for example, research on Aristarchus and the Alexandrian Mouseion. While it might seem difficult to move from that level of discourse to what are, after all, small-scale shrines on the Greek mainland, the influence of Homer, and his evocation of the heroic age, nevertheless emerge as a pervasive element in Hellenistic society.[31] So what additional pressures, what particular expectations, might have been placed upon readings of the poet at this time? Two suggestions can be put forward: first, a reliance upon Homer's universal appeal and his unquestionable authority, and second, a dependence upon his presentation of the heroic past and its lineages.

The cults discussed in this paper were indeed relatively small-scale, yet it would be a mistake, for that reason, to remove them completely from wider trends within the Hellenistic world, not least the changing scale of Hellenistic society. Many scholars have noted various political responses growing out of the increasing interaction of great and small powers at this time (e.g. the growing permeability of *polis* boundaries, acts of *sympoliteia*, or development of federal leagues). In the religious sphere, the popularity of "universal" deities, gods perceived to transcend former political and even

---

28. Farnell (n. 17) 340–42; J. N. Coldstream, "Hero cults in the age of Homer," *JHS* 96 (1976) 8–17. This explanation was employed by Cook for the development of the Agamemnoneion ("Cult," n. 5) 33 and by Benton at the Polis cave ("Pólis, I," n. 13) 56.

29. I. Morris, "The use and abuse of Homer," *ClAnt* 5 (1986) 81–138.

30. R. Lamberton, "Introduction" and the other essays in R. Lamberton and J. J. Keaney, eds., *Homer's Ancient Readers* (Princeton, 1992), vii–xxiv; I. Morris and B. Powell, eds., *A New Companion to Homer* (Leiden, New York, and Köln, 1997).

31. K. McNamee, "Aristarchus and 'Everyman's' Homer," *GRBS* 22 (1981) 247–55. For a recent innovative study of the place of Homer and the heroic past in fourth century Macedonian culture, see A. Cohen, "Alexander and Achilles—Macedonians and 'Mycenaeans,' " in J. B. Carter and S. P. Morris, eds., *The Ages of Homer* (Austin, 1995) 483–505.

cosmological boundaries, has also been long observed (e.g. Isis, Asklepios, or the Great Gods on Samothrace). What has this to do with Homeric heroes? Given Hellenistic political conditions, locally generated claims to territory and prestige were now not purely internal affairs; externally powerful states were often involved. Low-key cults, of geographically restricted interest, held little appeal and exerted little influence over the distant authorities who could now dictate the political landscape. But a shrine to Odysseus, a cult of Agamemnon: these were names with which to conjure, with Homer (*the* poet) a solid bulwark in the background. Even the Romans knew their Homer, and that would become no small matter. Epic heroes, it has often been said, are panhellenic heroes, and that became a special distinction in the expanded world view of the Hellenistic age. This is by no means to suggest that local hero cults went defunct at this time, any more than that the traditional civic gods were suddenly neglected. But in the competitive atmosphere of the Hellenistic world, a claim to heroic associations became one ritual means by which to articulate local histories and local strengths to outside authorities.

My second suggestion revolves around the ability of Homer and of the heroic age to offer a sense of origin and identity. Underlying this need, indeed behind all this rather tangled web of motivations, is the issue of Hellenistic historicism. Louis Robert, among others, has spoken of the yearning on the part of Hellenistic communities for a history, either real or "invented." These were times that saw collective history become a matter for study, collation, and recording. Stress was laid upon recovering and celebrating origin myths and legends, on establishing pedigrees running back into the mists of time.[32] In part, this self-consciousness appears a product of the threat to the independent life of small cities, a threat rooted in Hellenistic times which grew apace under the Roman empire. The right to privilege, the very right to existence, increasingly had to be demanded upon historic grounds. Yet this search transcended matters of mercenary self-protection. As Paul Veyne put it, etiology "spoke from a need for political identity." Ancestries and origins, invoked through myth and ritual, could be used to claim kinship with other cities, to establish status, and to secure identity. Heroes were especially instrumental in this process, for they above all possessed a comprehensible genealogy, capable of yielding plausible chronologies and webs of inter-relationships. Hellenistic scholars charted the generations, measuring with what Veyne termed "the thread of time" the distance between heroes and

---

32. See, for example, L. Robert, "Une épigramme satirique d'Automédon et Athènes au début de l'empire," *REG* 94 (1981) 338–61. On civic genealogies, G. Rogers, *The Sacred Identity of Ephesos: Foundation Myths of a Roman City* (London, 1991).

the present day.[33] Genealogy provided that longed-for sense of local history and identity, and the heroic age anchored that thread of time.

Élite legitimation, civic prestige, symbolic protection, a sense of communal identity: all of these may go some way to explaining the appeal of a Hellenistic heroic past. In the end, it is worth raising the more general question: "which past?" It has long been recognized, for example, that Pausanias and other voices of the Second Sophistic to some extent evade the recent past, the history of Greece under Roman domination. In countless other contexts, there are numerous equally revealing episodes of histories accepted and histories rejected.[34] If it is accepted that the Greeks of the Hellenistic age felt some special kinship, had some special need of the heroic age, then the Samothracian pseudo-tholos becomes somewhat less enigmatic—and so, more importantly, does the Hellenistic period.

33. P. Veyne, *Did the Greeks Believe in Their Myths? An Essay on the Constitutive Imagination.* Translated by Paula Wissing (Chicago, 1988) 76–78.

34. E. Hobsbawm and T. Ranger, eds., *The Invention of Tradition* (Cambridge, 1983). On Roman Greece: E. L. Bowie, "Greeks and their past in the Second Sophistic," in M. I. Finley, ed., *Studies in Ancient Society* (London, 1974) 166–209; C. Habicht, *Pausanias' Guide to Ancient Greece* (Berkeley, 1985) 104 n. 34; S. E. Alcock, *Graecia Capta: The Landscapes of Roman Greece* (Cambridge, 1993) 28–29. See also Cartledge and Spawforth (n. 14) 190–211.

TWO

"These fragments have I shored against my ruins": Apollonios Rhodios and the Social Revalidation of Myth for a New Age

Peter Green

These myths or current stories, the spontaneous and earliest growth of the Grecian mind, constituted at the same time the entire intellectual stock of the age to which they belonged. They are the common root of all those different ramifications into which the mental activity of the Greeks subsequently diverged; containing, as it were, the preface and germ of the positive history and philosophy, the dogmatic theology and the professed romance, which we shall hereafter trace each in its separate development. They furnished aliment to the curiosity, and solution to the vague doubts and aspirations, of the age; they explained the origin of those customs and standing peculiarities with which men were familiar; they impressed moral lessons, awakened patriotic sympathies, and exhibited in detail the shadowy, but anxious, presentiments of the vulgar as to the agency of the gods; moreover they satisfied that craving for adventure and appetite for the marvellous, which has in modern times become the province of fiction proper.

G. GROTE, *A HISTORY OF GREECE* (1888 ED.), VOL. I, 309

Some years ago, when composing a chapter on Apollonios for my general survey of the Hellenistic era, I posed the following question (Green 1990 214): "How, asked the Psalmist, shall we sing the Lord's song in a strange land? And how, in their luxurious enclave or ghetto, were these Egyptian (or Cyrenaic) Greeks to maintain the matrix of sustaining myth that grew up amid warring Mycenaean baronies in central Greece and the Peloponnese?" If

I would like to acknowledge here the very great help I have had from the editors of this volume, in particular Erich Gruen and Paul Cartledge, whose ingenious suggestions for restructuring an originally unwieldy and ill-proportioned essay were matched only by the patience with which they waited for my revisions. It goes without saying that I remain responsible for the many defects which (I am uneasily aware) still remain, perhaps inevitably, in my treatment of a topic by its very nature as elusive as Proteus himself.

I am rash enough to attempt a solution now, it is in large measure thanks to Frank Walbank's work: he, above any other historian, has shown me over the years how scrupulous scholarship and imaginative insight can combine to irradiate even the most recalcitrant problems. In particular, while pursuing my own researches for the present paper, I have always had in mind Frank's lapidary essay on "History and Tragedy."[1] His perception of the early and fundamental link between the two is only one of the many insights it has given me: if there is any merit in what follows here, let that stand as a tribute to his inspiring example.

Almost the only undebated aspect of Greek myth is its extraordinarily long-enduring significance. When the Homeric epics were first conceived, Jason's ship *Argo* was already πᾶσι μέλουσα,[2] a familiar public topic,[3] and Nilsson's correlation of the major cycles of myth with known Mycenaean sites (a theory that has withstood much criticism[4]) took the kernel at least of this material back into the Aegean Bronze Age. But it was not only of great antiquity: it seemed indestructible. Hellenistic Alexandria made an industry out of it. *Graecia capta* found Rome equally receptive: Tiberius' obsessive passion for the arcana of mythology was notorious.[5] Revealing, too: the questions with which he tried to floor the grammarians ("Who was Hecuba's mother? What name did Achilles go under when disguised as a girl? What songs did the Sirens sing?") all tacitly assume the possibility of eliciting a truthful answer, i.e. concede the fundamental *historicity* of myth.

My prime interest is, broadly speaking, historical. What did the Greeks themselves value about myth? How much, and in what way, did those values change between Mycenaean and Greco-Roman times? What factors—

---

1. Originally published in *Historia* 9 (1960) 216–34, and reprinted as ch. xv (224–41) of *Selected Papers: Studies in Greek and Roman History and Historiography* (Cambridge, 1985).

2. Hom. *Od.* 12.70. The debate as to whether the epithet should be treated as one word or two goes back to Aristarchus' day: see Dräger 14 and n. 7 for a conspectus of scholarship.

3. Schol. ad loc. [Dind. II 535.6f.]: ἐπίθετον τῆς Ἀργοῦς ἀπὸ τοῦ πᾶσιν ἐν ἐπιμελείᾳ εἶναι διὰ τοῦ κλέος.

4. See Vermeule's remarks in M. P. Nilsson, *The Mycenaean Origin of Greek Mythology*, (Berkeley, 1932, repr. with intro. and bib. by E. Vermeule, 1972) vii–xiii, and Nilsson's own arguments, with especial relevance for the present discussion, in ch. ii, § 7, 127–58.

5. Suet. *Tib.* 70.3: Maxime tamen curauit notitiam historiae fabularis usque ad ineptias atque derisum; nam et grammaticos . . . eius modi fere quaestionibus experiebatur: "Quae mater Hecubae, quod Achilli nomen inter uirgines fuisset, quid Sirenes cantare sint solitae."

social, psychological, geographical, intellectual, literary, scientific—were ultimately responsible? Because of the variety and complexity of the Greek mythic tradition, not to mention perennial, and endemic, scholarly disagreements over its interpretation, I have chosen to use as a test case one particular myth, that of the Argonauts, and restrict my study of its evolution to the period between Homer and Apollonios Rhodios. This has several advantages. The Argonaut myth is one, primarily, of heroic *action*: despite its accretion of magic and *Märchen* (cf. Buxton 75–76), it falls essentially into the historicising category—with a background eloquent of early trade, the foundation of colonies, Mediterranean exploration, genealogical links with the heroic past, the commemoration of that past for its κλέος, and its use as an empowering model of conduct, a validation, a guide to Greek individual and public identity. Further, it possesses three key narratives, one archaic (Pindar's Fourth *Pythian*), and two Hellenistic (Apollonios' *Argonautika*, and the *Argonautai* of Dionysios Skytobrachion, summarized at length by Diodoros) to use as indices of change. Lastly, by cutting my study short in the mid-third century I can for the most part avoid the mythically complicating intrusion of the Roman factor.[6]

The social mutation of myth, in its wider context, forms one facet of what is perhaps the most influential factor in all Greek history: the rapid expansion of rational knowledge generated by the so-called "Greek miracle," the sixth-century B.C. intellectual breakthrough in Ionia, and the on-going conflict this created between new perceptions and old beliefs, setting heart against head, tribe against polis, what Gilbert Murray called the Inherited Conglomerate[7] against innovative thought (often labelled "secular," but in fact, as we shall see, rather "anti-Olympian": not the same thing at all). The degree to which, at all levels, the strands of past belief and future reason remained in acute conflict, not merely between intellectuals and the masses, but *within individuals*, supplying (for example) the terrible tension that dominates such plays as Sophokles' *Ajax* or *Antigone*, is central to any understanding of Greek society.

The deep and instinctive conservatism of all but the most progressive Greek intellectual thinking—τιμιώτατον γὰρ τὸ πρεσβύτατον, said Aristotle (*Met.* A3, 983b32)—has often elicited comment,[8] but its impact on mythic

---

6. Cf. A. D. Momigliano, *On Pagans, Jews and Christians* (Middletown, CT., 1987), 264–88.

7. G. Murray, *Greek Studies* (Oxford, 1947) 66–67, cited by Dodds 179.

8. Most strikingly by Van Groningen, 1–12, who surveys our sources from Homer to Aristotle. For the status quo as the economic ideal cf. A. E. Samuel, *From Athens to*

historiography has not, I think, been fully appreciated. This obsession with the past, above all the heroic past, was ubiquitous and intense. To an overwhelming extent the past and everything it stood for had been *better*, and it was not only Homer's heroes[9] who thought so. Plato, Isocrates, Aristotle all shared the same outlook: when they attacked witnesses to that lost world it was for misrepresenting it.[10] Thus challenges to the validity of the myths in which its essence was enshrined could not but arouse intense antagonism, confusion, and distress.

Efforts at reconciliation, with all the redefining and reinterpretation of evidence that these entail, were made, and made in good faith. Criticism certainly existed, but on almost every occasion aimed to remove false accretions, not to deny the ultimate truth or kernel of the myth as such. In particular, the *historical existence* of the Heroic Age, however the truth of that claim be defined (cf. Veyne 1, chs. i, vii), remained an article of faith, not merely in Apollonios' day—when we find an exact contemporary (264/3) working out the chronology of such events as Deukalion's Flood (1528), the Amazon campaign against Athens (1256) and the beginning of the Trojan War (1218)[11]—but as late as the third century A.D., when the rationalizing Eusebius, similarly, provides specific dates for such events as Laius' rape of Chrysippus (1303)[!] and (with at least antiquarian interest for the present discussion) the voyage of the Argonauts (1264).[12] From the very beginning the mythic past was firmly situated in historical time, its basic events accepted as fact, its heroic protagonists linked both to the prior "age of origins" and to the purely human era that succeeded it (Brillante 101–102).

Alexandria: Hellenism and Social Goals in Ptolemaic Egypt (Louvain, 1983) 123, and Green 1990 363–67, 374–75.

9. E.g. *Il.* 1.260–61, 5.302, 447; *Od.* 8.223.

10. Plat. *Phileb.* 16C: Socrates speaks of οἱ μὲν παλαιοί, κρείττονες ἡμῶν καὶ ἐγγυτέρω θεῶν οἰκοῦντες. Isocrates, as Van Groningen comments (7), "places everything which he thinks desirable in the past; the Athens of former days was exemplary; only imitations of the forefathers can bring real prosperity . . . with him 'the excellency of the fathers' becomes a synonym of the fathers themselves." For ἡ τῶν προγόνων ἀρετή see Isokr. 12.5, 15.76. For the spirit of emulating the past cf. 5.113–14, 6.12–13, 6.98, 7.84, 8.93, 12.137, 15.114, and in general, *Orat.* 4 and 7. Aristotle believed that "antiquity appears to be a near approach to what is by nature," *Rhet.* 2.9.9, 1387a16 (trans. Van Groningen).

11. The Marmor Parium (*FGrH* 239 §§ 4, 21, 23: cf. Dowden 51–52).

12. See *Eusebi Chronicorum Canonum Quae Supersunt*, ed. A. Schoene, H. Petermann, and E. Roediger (Berlin, 1866, repr. Dublin/Zürich, 1967), vol. ii, 44–47. Eusebius dated to the "years after Abraham." It has been calculated that 1 Abr. = 2016 B.C.: see E. J. Bickerman, *Chronology of the Ancient World*, 2nd ed. (London, 1980) 87–88. Cf. Veyne 111.

The "age of heroes" was seen as remote (and hence difficult of access), but no less real than contemporary history, and similarly located in time and place. The main impression conveyed by the "age of origins," on the other hand, as reflected in Hesiod and his successors, is neither moral nor foundational, but a huge, and characteristic, sense of relief at having moved from the nothingness of monsters and chaos to a world of reasoned order, identifiable existence. Further, those ancient genealogical links that constituted one of the chief reasons for the importance attached to the mythical past also, as Rosalind Thomas points out, largely ignored the centuries intervening between heroic ancestor and present-day (alleged) descendant.[13] While oral memory extended back only about three generations, mythic memory jumped the gap to what Kipling in his *Just-So Stories*, with exquisite accuracy, termed the "high and far-off times." Compared with the Egyptians, of course (cf. Hdt. 2.143[14]), the Greeks were mere Balkan parvenus; and indeed there is something oddly makeshift about their "time of origins."

Makeshift or not, the Greek mythic tradition certainly filled a need, satisfying the aspirations and emotions of endless generations. In what way, we well may ask, did it achieve this end? Buxton has recently outlined four general categories which (with one striking exception) do appear to cover the most important functions that myth performed for its Greek adherents.[15] (1) The preservation of great deeds from the heroic past, what Homer described (*Il.* 9.189) as κλέα ἀνδρῶν and Hesiod (*Th.* 100) as κλεῖα προτέρων ἀνθρώπων. This constitutes the primary purpose of early epic, and remains a prominent ideal for Herodotos, Pindar, and the orators. (2) The didactic and educational function, the furnishing of mythical παραδείγματα, "moral exemplars, cautionary tales and formulation in gnomic utterance of moral, and indeed of technical, wisdom" (Heath 47).The source of such guidance was universally assumed to lie in the heroic past. But that past was also attacked by progressive moralists. Archaic primitivism and bluntness

---

13. Thomas 177–78: her whole section "Genealogy and the Genealogists" (173–95) is of great interest in this context.

14. Herodotos' anecdote on the snubbing of Hekataios by Egyptian priests may, in detail, be *ben trovato* rather than strictly true, but the significance lies in its being told by a Greek. For a good analysis see Alan B. Lloyd's *Herodotus Book Two: Commentary* 99–182 (Leiden and New York, 1988) 107–108. The ambivalent Greek attitude to Egyptian antiquity and the sheer *size* of Egyptian temples, strange beasts, etc., is betrayed by their vocabulary: such words as κροκόδειλος, πυραμίς, ὀβελίσκος, στροῦθος, used to signify "crocodile," "pyramid," "obelisk," or "ostrich," originally meant, respectively, "house-lizard," "honey-cake" (pyramidally shaped), "spit" and "sparrow."

15. In ch. ix, "The Actors' Perceptions," 169–81.

were becoming an embarrassment. (3) The element of *entertainment*, achieved in particular by playing on the emotions (θέλγω, τέρπω) with the retelling of famous *gestes*. This attitude, of course, also attracted the censure of serious moralists, Stoics in particular.[16]   (4) "The role of myths in explaining the present in terms of its origins" (Buxton 177). Such appeals to the past for authorization or empowerment could, and did, operate to powerful effect not only in foundation-cum-charter myths and genealogical stemmata, backing up territorial or family claims, but also—an overlap, I think, with category (2)—in moral decisions or personal conduct.

We have here no mention, as a fifth category, of what might be thought the most important of all, i.e. religion.[17]   Buxton does recognise (145) the brute and crucial fact that archaic Greek divinities, as portrayed in myth, "are neither good nor evil, but powerful," an *aperçu* that applies even to Zeus;[18] that their motives are petty and personal, their relations with one another "based on a combination of violence, deception, negotiation and reciprocity" (146).   But (like so many) he shies away from the unpalatable implications of all this by treating an essentially religious phenomenon as not really religious at all, though it is precisely here that we find the archetypal layer of stubborn and irrational belief which formed the living core of Greek myth, and fought so protracted a battle against the inroads of knowledge and reason.

The evidence suggests a world where Chaos, the Unknown, still looms dauntingly near;[19] where μίασμα is as real, and lethal, as bubonic plague; where gods wholly devoid of moral sense, immortal and narcissistic, subject the world to their unpredictable and arbitrary whims; where human

---

16. Strabo, summing up much earlier Hellenistic thinking about myth at the opening of his *Geography*—see in particular 1.1.10, C.7, 1.2.3, C.15–16, 1.2.8–10, C.19–21—scathingly dismisses Eratosthenes' argument that a poet should aim to provide pleasure rather than instruction (ψυχαγωγίας, οὐ διδασκαλίας): 1.2.3, C.15, ad init., repeated at 1.1.10, C.7, ad fin.

17. I do not propose here to enter into yet another argument, at this point, of "what I think religion is," which would be wholly irrelevant to my present purpose: my concern is with what, on the evidence, *the Greeks* took to be, and did about, *their* religion.

18. Cf. M. P. Nilsson, "Die Griechengötter und die Gerechtigkeit," *Opuscula Selecta* (Lund, 1951–1960), vol. iii, 303–21, esp. 315, tellingly cited by Buxton, 145 n. 1.

19. C. Geertz, "Religion as a Culture System," *Anthropological Approaches to the Study of Religion*, ed. M. Banton (London, 1966) 14, cites Suzanne Langer as arguing that Man "can adapt himself somehow to anything his imagination can cope with; but he cannot deal with Chaos," and goes on to isolate three points at which Chaos seriously threatens man's integrity: "at the limits of his analytic capacities, at the limits of his powers of endurance, and at the limits of his moral insight." I owe this reference to Gould (p. 5).

virtue and good intentions count for nothing in the divine scheme of things. Knowledge of natural functions (e.g. rain, thunder, lightning) is limited, and the gods' powers (since the unknown is automatically seen as an instrumental perquisite of divinity) correspondingly enhanced, thus intensifying human ἀμηχανία, which not only survives, well-documented, in the lyric poetry of the period,[20] but also, of course, appears—not, I would argue, by accident—as a prominent leitmotif in Apollonios' portrayal of Jason. This grim archetypal scenario forms the imprinted legacy of centuries: elements of it persist, uncomfortable ghosts, throughout Greco-Roman history.

The atavistic phenomena and attitudes outlined above came under sustained attack on several fronts, all directly connected with the expansion of knowledge, the development of λόγος at the expense of μῦθος. To begin with, for centuries Greek geographical knowledge had been virtually limited to the eastern half of the Mediterranean, and even there not all that far into the hinterland: Greeks, as Socrates remarks in the *Phaedo* (109B), stuck to the coast like frogs round a pond. The Black Sea—something to which the myth of the Clashing Rocks bears eloquent witness—was largely ἄπειρον, as far as Aegean Greeks were concerned, till the eighth century B.C. at the very earliest,[21] while Kolchis, so prominent in the Argonaut myth, and referred to in the earliest literature, shows no real physical traces of Greek presence till ca. 550 (Braund 92–93). The chronological time-lag between literary and archaeological evidence indicates a period when myth could still flourish unchecked.

It was, of course, the great outburst of colonisation and trade from the late eighth century onward which radically expanded Greek physical knowledge of the whole Mediterranean basin. Very soon the journeys traditionally taken by Odysseus and *Argo* became regular shipping routes, which posed an interesting problem of how to accommodate various mythic θαύματα. As the boundaries of knowledge spread, travellers' tales were steadily forced further and further towards the still unexplored periphery.[22] The geographical map began to slough off its original symbolic form, and

20. Snell 72–75, cf. 102: "Die Hilflosigkeit ist ein wesentliches Motiv der frühgriechischen persönlichen Lyrik, das der Dichter dazu führt, von ihrem Innern, ihrer Seele, von der Tiefe ihres Empfindens zu sprechen."

21. Boardman (1980) 240. E. H. Minns, *Scythians and Greeks* (Cambridge, 1913) 9 refers to the trepidation with which Greeks for long contemplated a Black Sea voyage.

22. Cf. Nestle 132: "Und auch die Welt war eine andere geworden: je mehr sich durch kolonisatorische Unternehmungen in 8. und 7. Jahrhundert und durch Entdeckungsfahrten, wie die des Skylax von Karyanda von der Indusmündung bis ins Rote Meer, der geographische Horizont erweitert hatte, desto mehr mußten die Märchenländer

bend mythic belief to physical fact. Nothing, perhaps, had so profound an impact on the *Weltanschauung* of the archaic era as Herodotos' flat rejection, thrice repeated,[23] of the stream of Ocean.

One significant by-product of this geographical expansion was a more sceptical attitude, at least among a minority, to the kind of primaeval θαύματα involving disregard for the normal laws of nature: three-headed dogs, fire-breathing brazen bulls, winged horses or heroes, the Chimaira, and so on. Yet they all turn up again in Pliny's *Natural History* (7.9–32), to survive, recycled, in mediaeval bestiaries and the *Travels of Sir John Mandeville*. This is significant. We sometimes assume that λόγος, when it comes, will always be welcome, that μῦθος is awaiting enlightenment. It was not so then; it is not so now. Heart and head remain in stubborn opposition. μῦθος persists against all odds.[24]

But the growth of knowledge altered more than external and visible facts: in several fundamental ways it transformed Greek social, moral, and even religious attitudes. What had been almost totally lacking still in the archaic age was any developed sense of *individual moral responsibility*, in heaven as on earth. Tribal authoritarianism had ruled through power, as Hesiod's ancient fable of the Hawk and the Nightingale, with its Near Eastern associations, starkly demonstrates;[25] it was the drive towards civilised urbanism, combined

---

und ihre Fabulistik, wie sie etwa noch das Arimaspenepos des Aristeas von Prokonnesos beherrschte, zurückweichen und fragwürdig werden."

23. Hdt. 2.23, 4.8, 4.36. The last of these passages is the most interesting, since it also contains a brisk dismissal of the (largely symbolic) Anaximandran map. The persistence of geographical myth, however, can be judged from the fact that though Herodotos correctly identified the Caspian as an inland sea rather than an inlet of Ocean (1.203), thus replacing water by land as an eastern boundary, it was not long before the old view was reinstated, largely as the result of propaganda on behalf of Alexander (Romm 34, 42–43).

24. Paul Veyne himself provides a remarkable instance of this (p. 87): "For my part, I hold ghosts to be simple fictions but perceive their truth nevertheless. I am almost neurotically afraid of them, and the months I spent sorting through the papers of a dead friend were an extended nightmare. At the very moment I type these pages I feel the hairs stand up on the back of my neck." An interesting "bridge from myth in history to myth versus history" is provided by Herodotos' account (9.26–28) of the dispute between Athens and Tegea, at the battle of Plataia in 479, over which should have precedence of position in the front line. Mythic antecedents are justified by the historian's anachronistic rhetorical topoi. See Cartledge 1993 28.

25. Hes. *WD* 202–12. For this fable's Sumerian, Babylonian, and other Near Eastern antecedents see P. Walcot, *Hesiod and the Near East* (Cardiff, 1966) 90, and M. L. West, *Hesiod: Works and Days* (Oxford, 1978) 204–205. It is interesting how modern scholars, these two included, so often understate (to put it mildly) the bleak amorality here, which

with written law-codes and a growing taste for ἰσονομία, that made men look askance at arbitrary conduct of any sort. The virtues of cooperation militated against heroic egotism. Town life softened outspokenness, produced in time the middle-class virtues of euphemism—"dirty talk" (αἰσχρολογία) is a term not found before the fourth century[26]—and domestic respectability.[27] Divine behavior, being rooted in archaic religious and mythic tradition, was getting further and further out of step with human conduct.

The central function of myth in validating genealogies and territorial claims also meant, inevitably, that political propaganda, including on occasion the forgery of documents and interpolation of traditional texts, would not seldom influence the evolution of a mythic tradition. An ingenious but decidedly *parti pris* reworking of myth by the epic poet Eumelos attempted, as we shall see, to transfer Medea's ancestry to Corinth. What becomes clear from such incidents is the overriding centrality of myth to the *self-definition and self-esteem* of any family or polis.[28]

Lastly, the spread of literacy, and the beginning of efforts (first visible in Hesiod) to systematise and categorise the vast heterogeneous body of Hellenic myth, meant that any would-be mythographer was going to be confronted by a bewildering range of independent local variants. We hear a good deal nowadays about Greek mythology's "tolerance of plurality . . . the compatibility of alternatives is basic to Greek mythology" (Buxton 177, 179). But what seems to me far more likely than a state of affairs that found conflicting plurality natural (can this ever in fact have happened?) is a growing confusion caused by improved communications, which progressively broke down the barriers between hitherto isolated enclaves, and thus released

anticipates by centuries the attitude of the Athenians in the Melian Dialogue (Thuc. 5.89, cf. 105.2), ἐπισταμένους πρὸς εἰδότας ὅτι δίκαια μὲν ἐν τ᾽ ἀνθρωπείῳ λόγῳ ἀπὸ τῆς ἴσης ἀνάγκης κρίνεται, δυνατὰ δὲ οἱ προύχοντες πράσσουσι καὶ οἱ ἀσθενεῖς ξυγχωροῦσιν.

26. Xen. *Lac.* 5.6; Arist. *Eth. Nic.* 1128a23.

27. This trait was so marked in Athens as to become a topic for derisive outsider jokes: see Plut. *Sol.* 15.2–3.: Ἃ δ᾽ οὖν οἱ νεώτεροι τοὺς Ἀθηναίους λέγουσι τὰς τῶν πραγμάτων δυσχερείας ὀνόμασι χρηστοῖς καὶ φιλανθρώποις ἐπικαλύπτοντας ἀστείως ὑποκορίζεσθαι, τὰς μὲν πόρνας ἑταίρας, τοὺς δὲ φόρους συντάξεις, φυλακὰς δὲ τὰς φρουρὰς τῶν πόλεων, οἴκημα δὲ τὸ δεσμωτήριον καλοῦντας . . .

28. Wickersham, to his credit, sees this very clearly, when he talks (23–24) of "the centrality of myth to a polis' self-concept, and how all its myths are interwoven. The historical loss of Salamis changed Megara's and everyone's view of what it meant to be Megara. Megara became not only a city that did not now have Salamis, but one that perhaps never really did. A way had to be found to reconnect, or else the loss would be compounded; all the rest of the myths predicated upon Megarian kinship with Ajax and possession of Salamis were shaken."

a variety of irreconcilable variant myths into common circulation. Since all traditions commanded respect, contradictory voices had somehow to be accommodated.

Historians and mythographers, faced with such attacks, set themselves to "save the appearances" (σώζειν τὰ φαινόμενα) by either explaining away or reinterpreting those elements of each μῦθος which seemed incompatible with the rational demands of λόγος. To this end they developed two interpretative methods, rationalization and allegory, each justifying apparently impossible, undesirable, or irreconcilable characters and events by explaining that they were not in fact what they appeared to be. In this sense there is comparatively little difference between historical misinterpretation or symbol: Zeus can just as easily be anaxagorized in the form of Νοῦς as euhemerized into a dead king deified for his achievements on earth. The distinction lies in the attitude to the past which each approach implies: the one embraces inner, the other outer, reality. While rationalisation trawls for historical reality distorted by misunderstanding, poetic vision, or propaganda, allegory seeks an abstract inner truth independent of any specific or physical actuality, the hidden verity beneath the surface of things.

Allegory, despite its inherent inanities, was there to stay.[29] The idea spread like wildfire: its main usefulness for the modern historian is to demonstrate just how firm a grip the myths still had on society, that they were felt worth thus rescuing at all costs. Rationalising critics sought different targets. Where allegory chiefly concerned itself with sanitizing the *repugnant or undesirable*—divine adulteries, mutual violence, or similar improprieties liable to shock or reduce veneration in the human observer—rationalisation, finding such activities only too credible (if not necessarily desirable), preferred to concentrate on the *physically or historically impossible*.[30] "By discarding the over-mythical," Dikaiarchos pronounced, "one reduces it, through reason, to natural reality."[31] Prodikos and Euhemeros at one stroke solved the awkward

29. Buxton 73 sketches its *Nachleben* from Boccaccio (the Danaïds' endless and futile pouring out of liquid = a warning against male sexual indulgence!) through Vico (the Theban Spartoi = "protagonists in an early class struggle") to Max Müller's "theory that Greek myths are disguised accounts of celestial phenomena" and, in our own day, the Jungian pattern of psychic archetypes.

30. Feeney 36 points out, interestingly (though he does not suggest, and I am not sure, what the significance might be), that for Homer the "rationalizing angle" is very rare in the *Iliad* scholia, being largely confined to those of the *Odyssey* and to Eustathius.

31. Quoted by Porph. *De Abstin.* 4.1.2 (ed. M. Patillon, A. P. Segonds, and L. Brisson [Paris, 1995] = Müller *FHG* 2.225 = fr. 49 Wehrli): τὸ δὲ λίαν μυθικὸν ἀφέντας εἰς τὸ διὰ τοῦ λόγου φυσικὸν ἀνάγειν. The Budé editors translate this as "laissant ce qui est trop légendaire, restituer la réalité en se fondant sur la raison."

divine-human nexus by explaining away the Olympians, and demi-gods like Herakles, as great kings and leaders in the "high and far-off times" who had been deified by their grateful subjects,[32] thus firmly anchoring them in historical time and at a human level.

Far from dislodging the mythic world, in fact, rationalisation made a remarkably thorough job of historicising it. Modern historiographical concerns remained virtually non-existent through antiquity. Even Herodotos and Thucydides, in their opening chapters (Dowden 46), see early myth as "distorted remnants of history." The Greco-Roman period might usher in a deeper scepticism,[33] with Lucretius complaining that centaurs could never have existed *duplici natura et corpore bino / ex alienigenis membris compacta,*[34] but rationalisation of such species, plainly *contra naturam,* had been going on for centuries. This industry was associated with the name of Palaiphatos, possibly a student of Aristotle.[35] Most of the "Palaiphatan" rationalizing glosses that have come down to us follow a regular pattern: e.g., the Chimaira (Pal. xxviii) was really a volcanic mountain in Anatolia, the flanks of which were haunted by a lion and a serpent. Far-fetched though his efforts to save the mythic phenomena were, Palaiphatos remains perhaps antiquity's most eloquent witness to the truth that even die-hard sceptics wanted no more than to purge myth of its factually or morally unacceptable accretions; basic faith in its fundamental historicity remained unshaken until far on in the Christian era.

In many ways the Argonaut myth is an ideal example to test against these findings. It is extremely ancient; the many features from *Märchen* it contains give it an archetypal validity; it preserves great deeds from the

---

32. The subject is vast, and I can no more than touch on it here. For Prodikos as anticipating Euhemeros see Henrichs 1975, 1976, and 1984 340–41. For the fragments of Euhemeros (updating *FGrH* 63) see now Winiarczyk (bibliogr.). There is no satisfactory monograph: useful comments in the introduction and commentary of the Italian ed. of G. Vallauri, *Euemero di Messene* (Turin, 1956). See also P. M. Fraser, *Ptolemaic Alexandria* (Oxford, 1972) 1.289–95; Feeney 31–32; Henrichs 1984 346–49; Buffière 1956 245–48; Dowden 50.

33. See the apt examples (Philostr. *Heroic.* 7.9, p. 136; Cic. *ND* 3.16.40, *De Div.* 2.57.117; Paus. 1.30.3) cited by Veyne 71–72, and add the stern remarks of Dion. Hal. *Ant. Rom.* 2.20.1–2.

34. 5.879–80. William Empson wittily reworked this as the beginning of his poem "Invitation to Juno," *Collected Poems* (London, 1955) 5: "Lucretius could not credit centaurs; / such bicycle he deemed asynchronous."

35. Festa xxxiii–xlvi: his argument that the four Suda entries s.v. Παλαίφατος (= *FGrH* 44T1–4) all in fact refer to the same person is highly convincing.

heroic past; despite the carping of some modern critics, it is compulsively entertaining; it lays down an empowering pattern for explorative colonizing ventures, and embodies key instances of divine intrusion in human affairs at moments of crisis. All five categories of myth are thus covered in it. The basic structure of the narrative was established early, and remained constant enough to give identifiable significance to such exceptions as are found.[36] Since its geographical venue is an Unknown that becomes, in course of time, thoroughly explored, and indeed absorbed into the οἰκουμένη, we can measure the value placed on the Unknown *per se* by observing what steps are taken, between the Archaic and the Hellenistic periods, to preserve it. The myth also has its quota of paranormal θαύματα: how far are these modified to meet the standards of a more critical age? It offers ample opportunity for political propaganda: do such considerations change the substance of the myth in any fundamental sense? To what extent, by Apollonios' day, have allegory or rationalization modified it? Last, and perhaps most important, how far, and in what way, do changing moral, social, and religious assumptions affect the myth's interpretation? In particular, what can we learn from comparing, say, Pindar's *Fourth Pythian* of 462 B.C. with the third-century epic by Apollonios—or, perhaps as important, Apollonios' version with the more or less contemporary[37] account by Dionysios Skytobrachion?

Beye (42) skilfully isolates the universal folk-tale motifs incorporated in the Medeia-Aiëtes-Jason narrative, which he describes as "a commonplace around the world":[38] "A young prince comes to the home of a hostile being who puts him to severe trials in which he is helped by the daughter of his

36. Cf. Hunter 1989 12–14.

37. Till recently it was taken for granted, on the basis of Suet. *De Gramm.* 7, that Dionysios Skytobrachion was very slightly older than M. Antonius Gnipho, and thus active in the early decades of the first century B.C. Rusten, however (85–92), argues very persuasively, beginning with the evidence of P. Hibeh 2.186, for a date in the mid *third* century, "the period between 270 (the approximate day the θεοὶ ἀδελφοί were introduced) and 220 B.C." If he is right (and I am convinced he is), then Skytobrachion and Apollonios were contemporaries, a fact with significant implications for their respective versions of the Argonauts' quest.

38. See Andrew Lang, *Custom and Myth* (London 1885) 87–102. Buxton (75–76) points out further details: Jason (like Herakles, Bellerophon and Perseus) is sent out on his seemingly impossible quest because his presence threatens a ruler's authority. After winning through, to maturity as well as success, he returns (like Orestes or Odysseus) to "a household disrupted through usurpation." It is also true that Medeia shows a quite remarkable talent throughout for *disrupting households* (in Kolchis, Iolkos, Corinth, and Athens): on this cf. J. O. de G. Hanson, "The Secret of Medea's Success," *G&R* 12 (1965) 54–61. Remove Medeia, and we have another familiar variant (Meuli 3–4 and n. 1): the

host. After succeeding at the imposed task, he elopes with the girl and is pursued. They elude their pursuer by throwing things in his wake which must be collected." (This of course is the precise category into which the story of Theseus, Minos and Ariadne also falls: no accident that Apollonios mischievously makes Jason use it [3.998–1004, 1074–76] to allay Medeia's fears.) The references in Homer and Hesiod are casual enough to assume widespread familiarity. In the *Iliad*, Iolkos is ruled by Pelias' grandson Eumelos (2.711–15), and Lemnos by a son of Jason and Hypsipyle (7.467–69). The *Odyssey* knows Tyro as mother of Pelias (by Poseidon) and Aison (by Kretheus) (11.253–9); Aiëtes and his sister Circe are referred to (10.135–39; for the genealogy cf. Hes. *Theog.* 956–62) and Circe is located on the island of Aiaia (10.135, 12.3–4: still in the lands of the dawn). Circe herself (12.59–72)—not only Aiëtes' sister but, thus, Medeia's aunt—describes *Argo* to Odysseus as πᾶσι μέλουσα (70), and explains how, because of Hera's love for Jason (72), this vessel alone escaped the Wandering Rocks (Πλαγκταί) during the Argonauts' voyage home from Aiëtes' realm.

The Hesiodic fragments contain various references, e.g. to Jason's education by Cheiron, to Phrixos, Helle, and the Ram, and to Phineus' delivery from the Harpies by the Boreads,[39] which indicate general familiarity with the standard narrative. One important fragment (241 Merkelbach-West) gives a clearly early return route for *Argo*, familiar to Hekataios (*FGrH* 1F18a) and utilised still by Pindar (*Pyth.* 4.251–52), from the Black Sea by way of the Phasis River (first mentioned at *Theog.* 340), from which they debouch into Ocean, returning eventually to Libya and the Mediterranean; but after Herodotos' rejection of Ocean as a geographical entity (above, p. 42), the general pressure to rewrite this part of the journey became, eventually, irresistible.[40] The *Theogony* (992–1002) gives the whole myth in capsule form: Jason's accomplishment of the challenge set by Pelias ὑβριστής, his return to Iolkos with Aiëtes' daughter Medeia, their marriage, the birth of a son Medeios—μεγάλου δὲ Διὸς νόος ἐξετελεῖτο.

---

hero whose efforts to win a prize are aided by companions with an assortment of magical talents. Functionally, Medeia replaces these; yet the companions remain—significantly diminished, but still stronger, more individualized figures (Beye 43) than "the mostly faceless, forlorn, weak, and cowardly men who tag along after Odysseus." When we compare *Odyssey* and *Argonautika*, this is a point worth remembering.

39. Frs. 38–42, 68–9, 150–51, 156 Merkelbach-West. Other reff. collected by Braswell 8–10.

40. Vian 1981 16–20. Antimachos however, ca. 400, still stuck to the Ocean route, thus demonstrating that for some the power of tradition could eclipse even demonstrable physical proof: frs. 64–65 Wyss (p. 35) = schol. Ap. Rhod. 4.259 and 1153, with Wyss' note on fr. 65.

One point that emerges very clearly, from this and other evidence,[41] is that Medeia *was originally an immortal goddess*; a fact not only important for the interpretation of our later literary sources, but also for explaining one otherwise odd aspect of the iconographic tradition. A number of Attic vases, as well as two Etruscan mirrors, dating from ca. 500 to the late fourth century, unmistakably portray Medeia rejuvenating, not, as we might expect, the aged Aison, but Jason himself.[42] The reason is not far to seek. Medeia ἀθάνατος is anxious not to fall into the same trap as did Eos with Priam's brother Tithonos, for whom she won from Zeus immortality but not youth, leaving him a withered yet indestructible husk, a kind of semi-human cicada.[43] The irony, when we reflect on Medeia's later attitude to Jason, is palpable.

As has often been pointed out,[44] there is no direct correlation between the literary and the visual interpretations of myth. Literary motifs tend to be ignored by artists—who, on the other hand, will often pick up visually promising episodes omitted from the surviving literary record, a salutary reminder of the patchy nature of our evidence. It follows that any social or mythical conclusions drawn from iconography are highly uncertain, except within very broad limits, and this should be borne in mind when considering what follows. Many identifications, too, are speculative in the extreme. For example, what *may* be the earliest illustration of the Argonaut legend, on a Late Geometric Theban vase dated ca. 735–710, shows a male and female figure holding hands at the stern of what looks like a schematised pentekonter (thirty-nine rowers actually visible). Jason and Medeia about to board *Argo*? It would be encouraging to believe so. But the scene has also been interpreted as the rape of Helen by Paris (Hampe), or as the *departure* of *Argo*, so that the

---

41. See schol. Eur. *Med.* 9, citing Mousaios; cf. M. L. West, *Hesiod: Theogony* (Oxford, 1966) 429: "Medea's place in this catalogue means that she is immortal." Note her attachment to Achilles in Elysion (Ibyk. fr. 10, Simon. fr. 53). See also *LIMC* s.v. "Medeia" 386, and Jessen 1896 743–44.

42. *LIMC* s.v. "Iason" nos. 58–64. It might be argued that the inscription on the hydria of ca. 470 (no. 62), IAΣΩN, was simply a careless reversal for AIΣΩN; but this would explain neither the prevalence of the motif elsewhere, nor the clear reference to it by both Pherecydes and Simonides (Page *PMG* fr. 548, citing the *argumentum* to Euripides' *Medea*, repeated in schol. Aristoph. *Kn.* 1321).

43. See *HHAphr* 218–38, with Hom. *Il.* 20–237, *Od.* 5.1–2; for the tradition of Tithonos being eventually turned into a cicada see Hellanikos *FGrH* 4F140, and in general Gantz 36–37.

44. See, e.g., Boardman 1974 215–16, 1975 223–24, 1989 222. For what follows, in addition to the relevant articles in *LIMC*, see also Vojatzi 28–94; Braswell 19–23; and Schefold 1989 15–39, 1993 261–69.

woman then becomes Hypsipyle or Hera (Morrison and Williams); or even as "an everyday event ... the captain just stepping on board after saying good-bye to his wife" (Wilamowitz).[45] If *Argo* was really πᾶσι μέλουσα in this period—if, indeed, as we have every reason to suppose, all the main mythic cycles were flourishing—then we can only suppose that, for whatever reason,[46] the urge to represent them visually had not yet developed to any significant extent, though between 700 and ca. 580 one or two subjects did get treated, e.g. the flight of the Harpies, and Medeia's magical rejuvenation of Aison and others by boiling them in a cauldron.[47]

When we move into the sixth and early fifth centuries, we find two items of archaic visual evidence concerning the Argonaut myth that are both significant and surprising, since they point to a far earlier genesis for the "Hellenistic" elements in Apollonios' epic—specifically, the erotic motif and the concept of Jason as ἀμήχανος—than has hitherto been supposed. The first is the representation of Jason and Medeia on the famous Chest of Kypselos, a Corinthian votive offering at Olympia no longer extant, but seen and described by Pausanias, and datable to ca. 580/70 B.C.: "Jason is

45. J. S. Morrison and R. T. Williams, *Greek Oared Ships 900–322 B.C.* (Cambridge, 1968) 29, with pl. 4e; B. I. Nadel, "The Euxine Pontos as seen by the Greeks" *Epigraphica* 53 (1991) 272 with n. 19; G. S. Kirk, "Ships on Geometric vases," *ABSA* 44 (1949) 149–50 (citing Hampe and Wilamowitz) with pl. 40. It is hard to argue with Kirk's flat assertion that not one Geometric representation is definitely identifiable with any episode from heroic saga or epic.

46. I am not persuaded by Schefold's argument (1989 9), "daß die Sagen von den Argonauten und von Theben erst gegen 600 eine epische Fassung erhielten, die vorbildlich geworden ist" as an explanation for the comparative absence of illustrative material prior to this date. That Eumelos of Corinth initiated such epic treatment for the Argonaut legend is pure speculation, and that artists were incapable of portraying episodes from myth without a *vorbildlich* epic to show them the way is nonsense.

47. The seventh century offers a meagre crop of possibilities: items asterisked (*) indicate dubious or speculative identifications; a double asterisk (**) doubles the improbability (when *LIMC* says "Deutung unsicher," this is normally an understatement). All references are to *LIMC*; all dates are approximate within a range of two decades; figures are of item nos., not pp. 700: *Medeia or Hera with Jason (s.v. "Hera" 450: Perachora relief). 660: *Hypsipyle episode (s.v. "Argonautai" 30: Boeotian pithos relief). 650: ? Medeia dealing with three-headed [!] serpent (s.v. "Medeia" 2: Etruscan amphora). 640: **Boreads (s.v. "Boreadai" 28, 34: Aeginetan pyxis, Spartan seal-ring). 630: Medeia (named) rejuvenating a man (unnamed) in a cauldron (s.v. "Medeia" 1: Etruscan olpe). 620: Harpies (named) in flight, pursued (? by Boreads) (s.v. "Harpyiai" 1: Attic BF). 610: *Jason being disgorged from serpent's mouth [see above] (s.v. "Iason" 30, 31: Corinthian aryballoi). 600: ** Boreads (s.v. "Boreadai" 29: Tanagra alabastron). 600: *Jason with head in serpent's jaws (s.v. "Iason" 77: Attic BF lekythos). I am particularly doubtful about the Boreads: any kind of winged demon is liable to be thus labelled by someone.

standing to the right of Medeia, who is seated on a throne, with Aphrodite on her left. An inscription above them reads: 'Jason marries Medeia, as Aphrodite commands.' "[48] The erotic motif, far from being a Hellenistic, or even a Euripidean, addition, is there from the beginning.

As for the ἀμηχανία, we have already (above, p. 41) seen that as a characteristic feature of archaic literature; but in Jason's case it acquires powerful support from the visual record. A famous red-figure cup by Douris, ca. 480–470 B.C., often reproduced,[49] shows Jason being disgorged, passive and flaccid, by the guardian serpent while Athena looks on, very much in charge, and the Fleece hangs in the background. It is a commonplace that we have here "a version of the myth unknown in the literary tradition" (Braswell 21); on the other hand in both Corinthian (late seventh century) and Etruscan (early to mid-fifth century) art we find this incident portrayed: it was clearly both traditional and widespread.[50] Could there be a more eloquent expression of ἀμηχανία? Hardly. Do we have here an early, "monstrous" strand of the legend? Almost certainly. Is this what explains the literary silence? If so, what audience, in the years after Marathon, would enjoy the *visual* evidence of discomfiture, but baulk at its *verbal* representation? We also have to consider, in the same context, a column-krater of ca. 470/460, showing "a remarkably puny Jason" (Braswell 21) reaching up for the Fleece, watched by Athena and an unidentified, but tall and heroic, male figure.[51] The tradition of inadequacy, so clear in Apollonios, seems now, like his central erotic motif, to have well-established earlier, indeed archaic, precedent.

There is little more of value, in the present context, that can be drawn from the iconographic tradition. Most positive preferences can be explained in terms of illustrative suitability; arguments *ex silentio* (e.g. why does no artist exploit the drama of Jason's first one-sandalled encounter with Pelias before the Pompeian wall-painters?[52]) lack force when the surviving evidence is so

---

48. Paus. 5.18.3: Μηδείας δὲ ἐπὶ θρόνου καθημένης Ἰάσων ἐν δεξιᾷ, τῇ δὲ Ἀφροδίτη παρέστηκε· γέγραπται δὲ καὶ ἐπίγραμμα ἐπ' αὐτοῖς· Μήδειαν Ἰάσων γαμέει, κελεύεται δ' Ἀφροδίτα.

49. E.g. Boardman 1975 no. 288; Schefold 1989 31, no. 14; Green 1990 211, fig. 78.

50. *LIMC* s.v. "Iason," 632 (nos. 30–35).

51. *LIMC* s.v. "Iason," 632–33 (no. 36 = "Argonautai" no. 12, and thus cited by Braswell 21). Radermacher's suggestion (169) that this New York vase-painting can be dismissed as "eine Parodie des Abenteuers im Drama, vielleicht Satyrspiel" I find less than convincing.

52. Schefold 1989 21 uses Pompeii 111–436 (from IX 5, 18) to illustrate this scene. The dangers are beautifully illustrated by *LIMC* "Iason" B.2. The relevant scene on this mid-fourth-century calyx-krater was, till recently, identified (by Webster and Meyer among others) as a scene from Euripides' *Stheneboea*. New arguments (Bulle, Simon) claim it shows Jason's arrival in Iolkos while Pelias is sacrificing to Poseidon. What (to quote

fragmentary.[53] *Argo* and her crew are portrayed as early as 570, and fairly frequently thereafter. Popular scenes include Phrixos either being carried by, or sacrificing, the ram; the Harpies assailing Phineus and being pursued by the Boreads (though this motif, like the portrayal of monsters in general, ends earlier than most[54]); Jason (with or without Medeia and her box of *pharmaka*) snatching the Fleece from the serpent, or, rather less often, taming the fiery bulls; Amykos boxing, or being punished for his brutality (but not, as most literary sources have it, killed in combat).[55] Variants abound. On one early column-krater (*LIMC* s.v. "Iason" 7: ca. 570) Jason (appropriately, given the etymology of his name) appears to be healing Phineus' blindness: no literary source mentions this. In two late-fifth-century kraters Talos is shown being subdued by the Dioscuri (again, unconnected with this episode in any known literary source), though Medeia also seems to be "hexing" him,

---

LIMC's accurate description) do we in fact *see*? "A half-draped youth wearing a pilos leans on a staff before an old man who is in the act of pouring from a phiale; at l. a woman peers from an open doorway." Are we seriously asked to make a confident identification from evidence such as this?

53. There is, for example, a single surviving bronze group that *may* portray Euphemos and Triton (the copy of a work *probably* executed in the mid-third century B.C.: Curtius ap. *LIMC* s.v. "Argonautai" 37). Even if its attribution should be correct, its relationship (if any) to Pind. *Pyth.* 4.28–49 and Ap. Rhod. 4.1547–85, 1731–64 (cf. Hdt. 4.179) remains quite uncertain, despite the confidence of Schefold (1989 36–37, with pl. 18), Braswell 90, and Vojatzi 157, n. 398. Reasonable doubts expressed by Herter, *JAW* [Bursian] 285 ([1944/5] 1956) 398.

54. Even so, though the bulk of the Gorgons, Chimaeras, and hero-versus-monster duels are gone by soon after 530 (Boardman 1975 223), the Harpies-Phineus-Boreads theme survives till the closing years of the fifth century: see *LIMC* s.v. "Phineus I" 11.

55. I am not including here representations either of the Calydonian boar-hunt or of the funeral games for Pelias, both of which fall outside the limits of this survey. The same is true of the iconography of Circe (all referring to the *Odyssey*), and that of Peleus and Thetis: though their relationship is referred to by Ap. (4.805–809, 816–17, 865–84), it is in no way integral to the Argonaut myth. *Argo* and the Argonauts: *LIMC* s.v. "Argonautai" 1, 2 (cf. Schefold 1993 263–64, pl. 283 for this relief from the Sikyonian treasury at Delphi, ca. 570), 3–11, 17 [570–230 B.C.]. Phrixos and the ram: *LIMC* 1–16, 20–27, 45–48, 51, app. a–b, d–g [560–250 B.C.]. The Harpies and Phineus: *LIMC* s.v. "Harpyiai" 1–3, 8–26, 28; s.v. "Phineus I," 1–16, 18–22 [570–400 B.C.]. Jason and the Serpent/Fleece: *LIMC* s.v. "Iason" 22–24, 36–42, cf. 57 [470–310 B.C.]. Jason and the bulls: ibid. 15–17 [440–320 B.C.]. Amykos: *LIMC* s.v. "Amykos" 1–15, 17 [430–250 B.C.]. The authors vouching for his death include Ap. Rhod. 2.90–97, Apollod. 1.9.20, Hygin. *Fab.* 17. Theocr. 22.120–34 has Polydeukes stop short (but not far) of killing him, merely exacting a promise from him "never again deliberately to be a vexation to strangers" (134). The leitmotif of Amykos being tied up to a tree is sometimes supposed to derive (on no real evidence) from Sophocles' lost play *Amykos*: Beckel, *LIMC* s.v. "Amykos" p. 741.

as in the version by Apollonios (4.1638–75).[56] The most exploited scene of all, at first sight surprisingly, has to do with the golden apples of the Hesperides; but the reason for this may be no more than the involvement in it of that ever-popular figure Herakles.[57]

Our literary sources suggest that the main lines of the Argonaut myth were established early, but that this did nothing to prevent considerable variation of detail, whether through local preference or social evolution. The iconographic tradition, as we see, precisely confirms such a finding. It also suggests that one of the sharpest divergences was that between written and visual interpretation. Yet both, we should never forget, were supported by an oral tradition: the *anecdotal* nature of early Greek illustrative art makes this very clear. In other words, the visual record preserves something of a sub-literary, vernacular, and archaic handing-down of myth which writers—by and large well-educated, morally progressive, and attuned to the new polis morality (above, p. 43)—found an increasing embarrassment, and thus preferred to ignore. Jason ignominiously swallowed and then disgorged by the serpent offers a classic instance of this.[58]

The earliest stratum of the Argonauts' journey, as we have seen, took them into the Unknown. "In general," Strabo says (1.2.10, C.21), "the men of that time [Homer's contemporaries] regarded the Pontic Sea as though it were another Ocean, and thought that those who sailed thither were going off the map (ἐκτοπίζειν) as surely as those who ventured far beyond the Pillars [of Herakles]." The business of accommodating the

---

56. *LIMC* s.v. "Talos I," nos. 4–5, well illustrated in Schefold 1989, pls. 17b and 18, pp. 35–36. See also M. Robertson, "The death of Talos," *JHS* 97 (1977) 158–60, for the depiction of Medeia's use of the evil eye, and M. Dickie, "Talos bewitched: magic, atomic theory and paradoxography in Apollonios' *Argonautika* 4.1638–1688," in *Papers of the Leeds international Latin Seminar*, sixth volume, 1990: *Roman poetry and drama, Greek epic, comedy, rhetoric*, ed. F. Cairns and M. Heath [*ARCA* no. 29] (Leeds, 1990) 267–96. Ap.schol. 1646–48 suggests that Ap.'s version of Talos' death derived from Sophocles' lost play *Daidalos*. Apollod. 1.9.26 mentions several other versions: that Medeia drove him mad with her *pharmaka* (note the presence of her *pyxis* in the Ruvo krater), and then removed the nail or plug that held in his life-giving ichor; or, alternatively, that Talos was shot in the ankle by Poias.

57. *LIMC* s.v. "Hesperides" 1–5a (solo), 6–8 (with Herakles: alarmed), 24–46 (with Herakles: calm), 54–62 (with other heroes or deities), 64–66 (misc. dub.) [570–250 B.C.].

58. The motif recurs elsewhere (e.g. in Indian, Irish, and Icelandic folk-tradition) as well as, most obviously, in the Biblical story of Jonah, and seems to belong to the basic stock of giant-and-dragon *Märchen*: see J. G. Frazer, *Folklore in the Old Testament* (London, 1918) vol. iii, 82.

myth to geographical exploration began early. Other aspects of the "high and far-off times" could, as we shall see, be accepted, even if not reconcilable with current realities: the heroes might indeed have walked with gods, conquered monsters now extinct, possessed—innately or by magic (the latter still, of course, flourishing)—superhuman powers. But their world, the stage on which their *gestes* took place, was fixed and immutable. All that changed was the degree of human knowledge concerning it, the proportion of Unknown to Known. The huge colonizing expansion between the eighth and the sixth centuries, from the western Mediterranean to the furthest shores of the Black Sea,[59] filled gaps in the Hellenes' *mappa mundi* with irrefutable geographical realities very different from the quasi-symbolic and largely imaginary constructs of early saga. This proved the mythic tradition's most vulnerable feature, and in the Argonaut legend it played a large and crucial part.

About Aiaia and Kolchis there was nothing to be done. As early as Mimnermos' day (frs. 11, 11a West) they had become, as the eastern kingdom of Aiëtes son of Helios, a fixture: it was from Aiaia, Aiëtes' city, in Mimnermos' text uncompromisingly located by the stream of Ocean, that Jason brought back "the great Fleece" (μέγα κῶας: our first surviving reference to it).[60] The Argonauts' outward route was now immutable. In consequence, two things happened: both Kolchis and the Clashing Rocks lost their original significance as part of a *rite de passage* into the kind of fairyland Odysseus describes for the Phaeacians,[61] and in course of time Aiaia's earlier association with Ocean was quietly abandoned. (Pindar is the last writer—a few years before Herodotos—to use Ocean as part of the Argonauts' route, or to regard the Pillars as a liminal barrier.[62]) The filling up of the Mediterranean map brought about some interesting relocations. Plausible but unfamiliar geography became much sought after. South Italy, Sicily, and the West in general were obvious targets. Though for Homer Circe is located in the East

59. Boardman 1980 chs. v–vi, 161–266, provides an excellent general survey.

60. Both quotations are preserved by Strabo (1.2.40, C. 46–47), and his Augustan comments are revealing in themselves. Homer, he argues, mixes history and myth. For Strabo the characters and events of the Argonaut legend are unquestioningly assumed to be historical: it is only Ocean that belongs to myth. After all, he says, the voyage was made in "familiar and populous regions" (ἐν γνωρίμοις τόποις καὶ εὐανδροῦσι), which of course by Strabo's day Kolchis had become: hence the appropriate epithet for *Argo* of πᾶσι μέλουσα, most inappropriate in the case of Ocean!

61. Beye 43–44; J. Lindsay, *The Clashing Rocks* (London, 1965) 7–37.

62. See *Ol.* 3. 43–45, where, discussing the Ἡρακλέος σταλᾶν he writes, with extraordinary passion and emphasis: τὸ πόρσω δ᾽ ἔστι σοφοῖς ἄβατον κἀσόφοις. οὔ νιν διώξω· κεινὸς εἴην.

(*Od.* 12.3–4) by Hesiod's day (*Theog.* 1011–15) she is already the mother, by Odysseus, of two sons, Agrios and Latinos, who rule over the Tyrrhenians; Aiaia is very soon located off the Italian coast, midway between Rome and Naples. An ingenious—and scandalous—anecdote explained Circe's move: she had poisoned the king her husband, and needed to take a *very* long trip in a hurry.[63]

Thus Pindar's *Fourth Pythian*, composed (like the *Fifth*) in 462 B.C. to honor the chariot victory by Arkesilas IV, king of Cyrene, at Delphi, stands at a critical point in the transmission of the Argonaut myth, on the very edge of the final opening up of the whole Mediterranean world. There are, in fact, several highly interesting features in it from the viewpoint of my present discussion.[64] To begin with, it has been politically adapted to the needs of Pindar's patron. When Eumelos of Corinth did the same thing earlier for his city, manufacturing a local ancestry for Aiëtes and Medeia,[65] the changes were not incorporated into the general tradition, and impressed only an assortment of German scholars.[66] But with Euphemos (already commemorated on the Chest of Kypselos as a charioteer, Paus. 5.17.4) and the clod of earth symbolising the colonization of Cyrene from Thera, the Argonauts are firmly and permanently linked to North Africa: Battos I, seventeenth in descent from Euphemos, was the founder, and Arkesilas IV, Pindar's patron, his eighth successor.[67] The loss of the clod described by Medeia during the course of her Pindaric prophecy (38–49) provides an explanation for the delay in colonization.

Thus at one level, the affirmation of genealogy, Pindar's use of the Argonaut myth performs a central and traditional function. We may note, however, that in his eagerness to pay Arkesilas the proper degree of respect he at one point alters the basic narrative in a manner as embarrassing as it is ludicrous: he places the landfall on Lemnos, and the subsequent mass impregnation of the Λαμνιᾶν ἀνδροφόνων, not during the Argonauts'

---

63. Vian 1980 122; Hunter 1989 133.

64. Segal (8) nicely summarizes its main ingredients: "Pindar brings together in a tour de force epic adventure, foundation legends, love, magic, family conflict, and cosmogonic myths."

65. For a brilliant analysis of Eumelos' appropriative scheme see Huxley ch. v, "Eumelos, the early Argonautika and related epics," 60–84, and cf. Beye 46.

66. E.g. Friedländer 313–17, Radermacher 227–29, Lesky 43–50. Dräger 2–11, cf. 24–30, comes as a welcome contrast.

67. See F. Chamoux, *Cyrène sous la Monarchie des Battiades* (Paris, 1953) 115–210. Hdt. 4.159–65 has an account of the first six Battiad kings. Cf. Braswell 89–90 and 153.

outward voyage,[68] but on their return from Kolchis, with Medeia very much in evidence. The idea of Jason's bride fuming in jealousy while her husband dealt with Hypsipyle (even though a fair anticipation of coming events in Corinth) bothered critics in antiquity and has spawned some unlikely theories among modern scholars.[69] With exemplary common sense, Braswell (348) explains what Pindar is about. His patron's heroic pedigree must be the climax of the narrative; equally important, "the claim of the Euphemids to Libyan sovereignty would be psychologically (if not logically) stronger if Euphemus' natural son had been sired after his father's receipt of the symbol [the clod of earth] rather than before." Royal flattery, in short, easily outclassed dramatic realism, and sharp literary critics were probably not thick on the ground in fifth-century Cyrene.

Medeia's centrality to the myth was undeniable, and seems to have caused Pindar some problems. As Segal says (6), "she at once brings into the story the atmosphere of a fabulous world close to the gods," and indeed Pindar obliquely recognizes her immortal status by referring—perhaps metaphorically, perhaps not—to her ἀθανάτου στόματος (11). However, his prime concern is with masculine heroic or athletic *kleos*, and here Medeia's role in the Argonaut legend constitutes a distinct embarrassment.[70] Its hero not only succumbs to her womanly charms, which is bad enough, but, far worse, can vanquish fire-breathing bulls and serpent, and thus win the Fleece, only through her indispensable aid. There are two kinds of magic involved here, and neither is really compatible with Pindar's ideal.[71] What he celebrates is the age of the great *kouroi*, and as Beye remarks (48), his Jason, with that fine manly figure and flowing locks, courtly yet decisive, compared by wondering bystanders to Apollo or Ares, is very much in the *kouros* tradition. Hera engenders in him and his companions (184–87) an "all-persuasive sweet desire"

---

68. As all other accounts seem to have done: see Apollod. 1.9.17 with Frazer's note ad loc., 98–99.

69. See schol. Pind. *Pyth.* 4.252, and cf. Braswell 347. As Beye remarks (47), "scholars who worry about Medea's virtue when she travels alone with the crew in Apollonios' fourth book narrative must find this assault on her sensibilities impossibly trying." But he himself is not much better, arguing that "what Pindar says makes little difference: he has achieved the absolute separation of form from content," a *reductio ad absurdum* of the apolitical literary attitude.

70. Segal 165: "To Pindar, as to other Greek poets from Homer to Euripides, female sexuality appears as a mode of treacherous craft (μῆτις), deceptive ornamentation, beguiling persuasion, and quasi-magical drugs, unguents, or enchantments."

71. On the other hand Pindar is also already infected with fifth-century moral delicacy: he carefully ignores Medea's murder of Apsyrtos in the same spirit with which he shrinks from calling any god a cannibal for snacking off the shoulder of Pelops: see *Ol.* 1.51–52.

(παμπειθῆ γλυχὺν πόθον) for the voyage, not to skulk at home in safety, but to pursue "the finest elixir (φάρμαχον) of his excellence" with his coevals.

That word φάρμαχον,[72] boldly transferred from Medeia to Jason himself, reveals a quite breathtakingly ingenious solution. If magic there must be, let the *kouros* have it first. But that is not all. In addition to cultivating his own heroic φάρμαχον, as above, Jason also receives lessons in erotic magic, complete with ἴυγξ and incantations, from Aphrodite—the first of mankind to be so honored. The reversal of roles is complete: far from Medeia bewitching Jason, it is Jason himself who employs the devices of love-magic to dominate Medeia's heart, destroy her filial reverence, and fill her with a longing for Greece (213–19). His need for *her* φάρμαχα (tactfully reduced here to mere "advice," ἐφετμαῖς, though she herself is παμφαρμάχου) has been anticipated and eclipsed by his own superior powers. Blending politeness and diplomacy with heroic magnificence (Segal 7), this Jason emerges as a born leader. Pindar's Medeia is left with the restricted and formal role, acceptable in a woman (Cassandra at once springs to mind, not to mention the Pythia), of prophetess.

For the two centuries between Pindar and Apollonios evidence is sketchy and puzzles abound. The biggest single influence on the *Argonautika* is commonly said to be Euripides' *Medea* of 431; yet no one could guess this from the iconographic evidence, which largely ignores Medeia as *Kindermörderin* till the Roman period, when the motif suddenly acquires great popularity.[73] It would be useful if we had more of the *Lyde* of Antimachos (ca. 400), which *inter alia* told the story of the expedition from the building of *Argo* to the episode in Libya (frs. 56–65 Wyss)—especially since from fr. 64 (= schol. Ap. Rhod. 4.1153) we learn that Antimachos made Jason and Medeia ἐν Κόλχοις πλησίον τοῦ ποταμοῦ μιγῆναι. Hellanikos of Lesbos (late fifth century), the first Greek author to attempt to date myths (Dowden 44–45), was also in the business of "providing Athenian nobles with heroic pedigrees" (Forsdyke 143–46), and had a good deal of recondite knowledge about the Argonaut tradition (*FGrH* 4F122–33);[74] his attitude was probably not far removed from that of Isocrates, who used examples

72. In an otherwise excellent note (271–72) Braswell misses the significance of φάρμαχον in this context.

73. *LIMC* s.v. "Medeia," 391–92 lists only three fourth-century South Italian vases (nos. 29–31) directly connected to the murders, plus five (35–37, 39–40) of Medeia in her *Schlangenwagen*, which are in all likelihood also inspired by Euripides' treatment.

74. See e.g. 4F 127 = schol. Ap. Rhod. 2.1144, where he informs us that Helle met her end off Paktye.

culled from before the Trojan War to demonstrate the character and power of Athens.[75]

Hints and guesses, as Eliot said: hints followed by guesses. As we move into the fourth century allegory and rationalizing meet us on every hand.[76] But here an odd fact strikes us. None of the allegorizing that has survived, except insofar as Herakles (allegorized *ad nauseam*) is involved, concerns the Argonaut myth. None of our ancient testimonia, including late collections such as that of Antoninus Liberalis, nor the most exhaustive modern survey, that by Félix Buffière, can produce a single instance of genuine Argonautic allegory. In a myth where the allegorizing imagination could surely have had ample scope (e.g. over the Fleece, or the Clashing Rocks, or the tests imposed by Aiëtes), history remains silent. Perhaps it was felt that this archaic tale of theft, seduction, and murder (including fratricide) was past rescuing in moral terms; more probably the answer lies in Homer's preëminence as a universal icon and educational tool,[77] which meant that would-be moral whitewashers concentrated on his *Iliad* and *Odyssey* to the exclusion of all else (Buffière, *passim*). The Argonaut legend, on the other hand, tended to be tinkered with by rationalizing romantics anxious to preserve—at varying levels—their suspension of disbelief. That cheerful realist Diogenes of Sinope "used to say that Medeia was clever, but no magician."[78] Herodoros' most interesting reference to the Argonauts is the claim (shared by Sophocles and Euripides) that they simplified their return voyage—thus incidentally also saving the geographical appearances—by coming back the way they had gone.[79]

---

75. Isocr. 4 (*Panegyr.*) §§ 54–56. Invoking the case of the protection given to Herakles' sons fleeing from Eurystheus, Isocrates justifies his choice parenthetically: ἐκεῖθεν γὰρ δίκαιον τὰς πίστεις λαμβάνειν τοὺς ὑπὲρ τῶν πατρίων ἀμφισβητοῦντας. What he believed about the myths is open to doubt: when praising Athens in connection with Demeter and the Mysteries (ibid. § 28), he argues καὶ γὰρ εἰ μυθώδης ὁ λόγος γέγονεν, ὅμως αὐτῷ καὶ νῦν ῥηθῆναι προσήκει, a calculated ambiguity, which could be taken to indicate either pious belief or a knowing accommodation with tradition.

76. Both are prominent in Herodoros (?430–?360 B.C.), who wrote not only an *Argonautika*, but also a 17-book work on Herakles: *FGrH* 31 F 5–10, 38–55 (*Argonautika*), 13–37 (*Heraklesgeschichte*). Cf. Nestle 146–48.

77. As Long (1992 44) justly remarks, "All Greek literature and art, and just about all Greek philosophy, resonate against the background of Homer": a truth that the translator of Apollonios, to look no further, is never allowed to forget for long.

78. Cited by Stobaeus, 3.29.92: ὁ Διογένης ἔλεγε τὴν Μήδειαν σοφήν, ἀλλ' οὐ φαρμακίδα γενέσθαι.

79. Soph. fr. 547 Radt; Eur. *Med.* 432, 1263–64; Herodoros *FGrH* 31 F 10 = schol. Ap. Rhod. 4.259.

What even Plato and Aristotle both assume, and pursue, is that never-queried underlying kernel of historical truth in myth. For Plato, τὸ ψεῦδος is a φάρμακον: "Since we don't know the truth about the ancients, may it not be useful to approximate falsity to truth as closely as possible?" (*Rep.* 382C–D). He will impugn an aristocrat's moral character, but never question his pedigree (*Theaet.* 174E–175B). This lends extra edge to his attacks, following Xenophanes, on Homer, Hesiod and other poets for immorally misrepresenting ancient mythic truths (*Rep.* 377D). Censorship was thus justified on didactic grounds (*Rep.* 378D), a view which left the field wide open for appearance-saving reinterpretations.[80] Aristotle, who sought to defend poetry against Plato's strictures,[81] had a low opinion of history, regarding it as a mess of particulars lacking universalism (*Poetics* 1451b 5–11). Despite this, he had no time for allegory (*Met.* 1000a 19), which for him was a mere decoration or sweetener that made truth more palatable (*Met.* 1074b 1). Unable to credit nectar and ambrosia (*Met.* 1000a 12), he still, like everyone else, accepted Theseus as a historical character, and seemingly the Minotaur too (ap. Plut. *Thes.* 16.2). His attempt to bridge the gap between the heroic and the historical period involved a curiously class-conscious compromise: "Only the leaders of the ancients were heroes—the people were merely men" (*Probl.* 922b).

Aristotle's distaste for allegory, however, was more than compensated for by the enthusiasm in this area which Stoics such as Apollonios' near-contemporary Chrysippus displayed. As Long says (1992 64), "What passes under the name of Stoic allegorizing is the Stoic interpretation of myth." Veyne (65) puts it less politely, but with equal accuracy: "Since the Stoics are certain beforehand that myth and poetry speak the truth, they have only to put them to torture [i.e. on the Procrustean bed of allegory] to reconcile them with this truth." Chrysippus was at least capable of making the process enjoyable, and at the same time of deeply shocking all those who, with more than Victorian fervor, opposed anything even faintly redolent of αἰσχρολογία: a certain notorious painting in Argos, of Hera fellating Zeus, he interpreted to mean "that Matter receives and holds within itself the spermatic λόγοι of the deity destined for the ordering of the Whole."[82] Mythic conservatism and moral prudery were between them in real danger,

---

80. Cf. Thomas 174–75; Buffière 33–34, 230–1; Dowden 47–49; Buxton 20, 160; Heath 41–42; Feeney 25–26.

81. Cf. Feeney 25–31; Heath 42–44 with further bibliography.

82. Cf. H. von Arnim, *Stoicorum Veterum Fragmenta* [*SVF*] (Leipzig, 1903), vol. ii, 314, nos. 1071–75. The citation quoted in the text is from Origen (fr. 1074): ὅτι τοὺς σπερματικοὺς λόγους τοῦ θεοῦ ἡ ὕλη παραδεξαμένη ἔχει ἐν ἑαυτῇ εἰς κατακόσμησιν τῶν ὅλων. Diog. Laert. (7.187 = no. 1071) coyly refrains from explaining what is going on, and insists that the interpretation (which he does not describe, merely referring to

by the mid-third century, of creating a literary *reductio ad absurdum* for both rationalization and allegory.

In such a world, what kind of approach to the Argonautic myth should we expect? It so happens that for the mid-third century, the apogee of the Alexandrian age, we possess, in addition to Apollonios' *Argonautika*, an extensive and fairly close summary (Diod. Sic. 4.40–56) of the prose *Argonautai* by Dionysios Skytobrachion ("Leather-Arm": perhaps an allusion to the quantity of his published work), a scholar from Mytilene.[83] To judge the current attitude to myth (though it lacks a date for the expedition, such as Eusebius provides) we also have the chronological list of the Parian Marble (264/3), which, as we have seen (above, p. 38), makes no distinction between mythical and historical events, attributing firm dates to both with equal confidence. When we compare these three very different texts, what instantly strikes us, significantly enough, is the one central feature they all have in common: that unquestioning belief in the *historicity* of mythic tradition which this essay began by examining. Where they differ is in the means chosen—rationalization, chronological specificity, aetiologizing traditionalism—to save the appearances in a new, cosmopolitan, and more sceptical age.

Skytobrachion's *Argonautai* is heavily rationalistic throughout, attempting, as Rusten says (93–94), "to explain the fabulous stories connected with the heroes as misunderstandings of perfectly ordinary events, by putting forward a version which preserved τὸ εἰκός, i.e. something which could actually have happened but was later 'mythologised' into an improbable fantasy." The Symplegades are simply ignored: Jason and his companions "set sail from Thrace and enter Pontos" (44.7).[84] To explain Aietes' fire-breathing bulls (ταῦροι), and the unsleeping serpent (δράκων) that guarded

---

it as something ἃ μηδεὶς ἠτυχηκὼς μολύνειν τὸ στόμα εἴποι ἄν—I don't think this was meant to be funny) has to be Chrysippos' own invention. Other writers (Clement, Theophilos, Origen as above) are not so delicate: πρὸς τ' τοῦ Διὸς αἰδοίῳ φύρων τῆς Ἥρας τὸ πρόσωπον (Clement, fr. 1072).

83. In what follows I am heavily indebted to Rusten's exemplary analysis, in particular 1–21 and 93–101. In particular, I am convinced by his careful arguments leading to the conclusion that Skytobrachion's work can "be dated roughly to the period between 270 (the approximate date the θεοὶ ἀδελφοί were introduced) and 220 B.C. (P. Hibeh 2.186)," with a mid-century median, and by his comparison of Diodoros' summary with the citations of Dionysios in the scholia to Apollonios to demonstrate the generally close and faithful nature of that summary: see 13, 28, 93.

84. All references to Skytobrachion's *Argonautai* are to the relevant chapter and section in Book IV of Diodoros. Since Rusten's monograph is not widely available I have not used the numbers he assigns to this and other texts in his collection of the fragments.

the Fleece, Skytobrachion falls back on that ever-popular device, the onomastic homonym: the ταῦροι were in fact fierce Taurian guards, while the
sacred grove was watched over (simple error!) by a man named Drakon.
Similarly with the magical flying ram (χριός): one of the two rationalizations
here reported identifies this Krios as Phrixos' *paidagogos*, who was sacrificed
(no reason given) on arrival in Kolchis, and his skin flayed off and hung up.
Since an oracle stated that Aiëtes would die should it be removed, the king
had it gilded to convince the sentinels it was worth guarding [!] (47.2–3, 5).[85]
The alternative explanation makes this χριός a ship with a ram as figure-
head, from which Helle fell overboard in the throes of *mal de mer* (47.4).[86] It is
surprising that Skytobrachion does not, like Strabo (1.2.39, C.45) and others,
rationalize the expedition as a colonisers' quest for gold.

There are several significant variations to the traditional narrative. To
begin with, Jason himself is credited with the building of *Argo* (41.1–2). This is
a change that first appears in Herodotos (4.179.1), but may well have been
introduced here to offset the fact that in the Skytobrachion version it is Herakles who leads the expedition and remains with it throughout (41.3, 49.6: see
below). The entire episode on Lemnos is omitted, perhaps as improper: one
of Skytobrachion's more remarkable achievements is to eliminate throughout what had been the *Ur*-myth's strongest motivating factor, i.e. sex. The
itinerary is also altered: not only, as we might expect, to get rid of *Argo*'s
more exotic return peregrinations (Italy, North Africa, the Danube, Po, and
Rhône), but also to include two unforeseen landfalls, at Sigeion in the Troad
and the Tauric Chersonese (42.1–7, 44.7, 47.2)—the latter probably for no
better reason than to justify the existence of those "Taurian" guards (and to
emphasize the barbarous habit of ξενοκτονία, well documented in the Chersonese). Skytobrachion, like Herodoros, Callimachus, and the dramatists,[87]

85. 47.2–3, 5. One of the more pleasant paradoxes about Dionysios Skytobrachion is
that his rationalisations are not seldom at least as incredible as the mythical θαύματα
they are designed to replace: why Pelias should have gone to the trouble of sending
an expedition to fetch back a servant's flayed skin, gilded or not, is a question left
unaddressed. At the same time we should note that the names (Drakon, Krios) actually
existed, and that the Ταῦροι were a real tribe (Rusten 94).

86. Though Skytobrachion's rational mind cannot accept a flying ram, he seemingly
has no trouble with a sea-monster that picks off coastal victims (42.3). Similarly he has
no hesitation in accepting oracles, the Samothracian mysteries, the miraculous calming
of storms, or equally miraculous twin stars descending above the Dioscuri (Rusten 95
with nn. 9–10). Social pressures may well have applied here: even the most determined
ancient rationalist is unlikely to have exposed himself to the public charge of atheism.

87. Soph. *Scyth*. fr. 547 Pearson, Eur. *Med*. 432, 1263, Herodoros *FGrH* 31 F 10, Callim.
fr. 9 Pfeiffer.

sends the Argonauts home by their outward route, with stops at Byzantion and Samothrace then rather than earlier.

The most striking element in Skytobrachion's account, however, is something familiar to us from the political myth of panhellenism, and recently the subject of several excellent studies:[88] the systematic effort at Hellenic self-definition by contrast with the Barbarian Other. From the very beginning of this narrative it is emphasized that the inhabitants of the Black Sea region in those days were fierce, savage and murderous, ξενοκτονούντων τῶν ἐγχωρίων τοὺς καταπλέοντας (40.4). Against them stands Herakles, Hellene *par excellence*, famous civilizer in distant lands, who deals appropriately with savagery wherever it may be found. At Sigeion he rescues Laomedon's daughter Hesione from a sea-monster.[89] The Phineus episode, far from having the Boreads rescue a blinded Phineus from the Harpies, and Phineus reward them with a prophecy of their coming vicissitudes, ends with Herakles and the Boreads killing Phineus for his treatment of his children.[90] The early *kleos* that Herakles wins on the expedition, in fact, chiefly consists "in leading the Argonauts against a variety of cruel barbarian kings" (Rusten 97). The voyage once over, he founds the Olympic Games, proceeding thence to further glory with a band of young followers—not alone: rationalism forbids (53.4–7). It is hard not to see this treatment as in some sense propaganda for Ptolemy II's vigorous program of colonial expansion.[91]

Of course, the acme of barbarian cruelty is encountered in Kolchis; and here we note another predictable revision of traditional legend. Medeia—

88. See in particular E. Hall, *Inventing the Barbarian: Greek Self-Definition through Tragedy* (Oxford, 1989), P. Georges, *Barbarian Asia and the Greek Experience: From the Archaic Period to the Age of Xenophon* (Baltimore and London, 1994), and Cartledge 1993, ch. iii, "Alien Wisdom: Greek v. Barbarian," 36–62. Cf. also my "The Metamorphosis of the Barbarian: Athenian Panhellenism in a Changing World," in R. W. Wallace and E. M. Harris, eds., *Transitions to Empire: Essays in Greco-Roman History, 360–146 B.C., in Honor of E. Badian* (Norman and London, 1996), 5–36.

89. Though the story of Laomedon's cheating Apollo and Poseidon (when they were doomed by Zeus to labor at building the walls of Troy for him) is as old as Homer (*Il.* 21.441–57), Skytobrachion seems to have been the first to record the matter of Hesione's rescue by Herakles, with its tell-tale resemblance to the episode of Perseus' very similar rescue of Andromeda. See Apollod. 2.5.9, and Frazer *ad loc.*, pp. 206–208, n. 2. All other surviving references are late.

90. See 43.3–44.7 *passim*, fleshed out by schol. Ap. Rhod. 2.206–208b = *FGrH* 31 F 19.

91. For lavish celebration of this policy cf. Theocr. 17.85–94, and for the background Green 1990 146. In Skytobrachion the familiar ploy of a Hellenic mission (whether of conquest, enlightenment, or one followed by the other) among the savage *barbaroi*, a theme exploited by orators and politicians ever since the Persian Wars, comes across very clearly.

uncanny virgin, enchantress, full of old divinity—is rationalized into a liberal humanist's dream. Skytobrachion, like Diogenes before him (above, p. 57) finds her σοφήν, but no φαρμακίδα—at least, not in any magical sense. Rather than a witch, she is a skilled medical herbalist, who rapidly heals any Argonauts' battle-wounds (48.5). At high risk to herself she fights her father's policy of ξενοκτονία, springing victims from prison and facilitating their escape. Arrested for these activities, she escapes at the time of the Argonauts' arrival and seeks refuge with them. Her relationship with Jason is based on mutual self-interest (46.4: τὸ κοινὸν συμφέρον) rather than passion: no arrows of Eros here. Nor do we hear a word about the murder of Apsyrtos: only the monstrous behavior of Pelias (50.1–2, cf. 6) can bring this Medeia to kill after years of selfless work for mankind's benefit.[92] Her one bravura act is her entry into Iolkos (51.1–5), disguised as an old woman (the better to impress with her ability to rejuvenate by secretly removing her make-up); and even then, after persuading Pelias' daughters to cut their father up and boil him, she delicately avoids staying on to witness the butchery (52.1–4). It is not even a case of all passion spent: in this Shavian world reason is promoted as a desirable substitute for all the passions, sex as well as ξενοκτονία.

Where Skytobrachion reveals most of the intellectual trends of his age, Apollonios' *Argonautika* is, by contrast, quite astonishingly independent (to coin a paradox) in its traditionalism. The one basic quality both versions share is a sense of a Hellenic venture to the world's end, a confrontation between Greek civilization and barbarian savagery, deepened in Apollonios' case by the increasingly alien tribes encountered along the southern shore of the Black Sea during *Argo*'s outward voyage. There may be a political element at work here—Ptolemy II not only nursed expansionist dreams, but liked to think of himself, *qua* Alexander's successor, as a protector of Greeks and Greek interests—but the underlying belief rested on that fundamental Hellenocentrism, or Panhellenism, which had been a constant factor in Greek affairs at least since the Persian Wars.[93] The geographical boundaries might have expanded—Alexander, of course, had opened up the οἰκουμένη in a wholly unprecedented fashion—but this had merely sharpened the Hellenic appetite for empire. The new world that emerged had also— and here we come back to the question posed at the beginning of this essay—produced a deep sense of deracination among emigrant Greeks, in

92. In the same way, years later in Corinth, it takes Jason's betrayal to evoke her innate barbarian ὠμότης (54.7).

93. Fusillo 162–67; Hunter 1993 159–60, who also cites E. E. Rice, *The Grand Procession of Ptolemy Philadelphus* (Oxford, 1983) 106–107. Cf. Green, above, n. 88.

particular the intellectuals of Alexandria. *Mutatis mutandis*, they faced the same agonizing dilemma as their ancestors in fifth-century Athens. Reason dictated a rejection of the heroic past; but emotion cried out for a return to one's ancient roots. The cry of μέγα βιβλίον μέγα κακόν was matched by an ever-increasing addiction to aetiologizing. *Credo quia impossibile est*: what Apollonios attempted in the *Argonautika* was a reconciliation of opposites, an epic *geste* as experienced by heroic yet vulnerable human beings.

His decision to frame his narrative as an epic poem in itself represents a decision of great significance. The Callimachean rejection of this genre was due at least as much to social and historical realities as to literary theory. Hunter (1993 154) sees the central issue very clearly:

> The decision to write *epic* in such a society, even (or particularly) an epic which constantly sets out to explore the cracks in what are set up as Homeric certainties, carried special weight.... [T]he status of epic as embodiment and transmitter of traditional values is in constant tension with the novelty and literariness of Apollonius' project.... Apollonius must emphasise fracture and discontinuity both within the "heroic" age itself and between the past and the present, *as well as* the unbroken chain which bound his readers to the pre-Homeric heroes of his story.

Skytobrachion, by rejecting both epic form (in favor of prose narrative: the E. V. Rieu of antiquity, I've always thought) and most aspects of the mythical that clashed with his circumscribed rationalism, refashioned the Argonaut legend as an unremarkable adventure novel, which not only lacked "the grandeur of epic or tragedy" (Rusten 101) but virtually wrote the heroic age out of existence. This was to ignore the problem rather than grapple with it.

Apollonios, far bolder, sought no such easy and dishonest palliatives. The first, and one of the most remarkable, things that emerges from his narrative is that it never falls back on rationalism, and is also virtually free of allegory,[94] as though that particular intellectual tradition, of cosmetic patching for unwilling sceptics, had never existed. θαύματα of every sort—the Clashing Rocks, Aiëtes' fire-breathing bulls, the Spartoi, Talos, the Nereïds, Medeia's magic—are accepted without demur, as integral features of the heroic Unknown. There is no attempt, for instance, to *explain away* the Clashing Rocks, in the style of some modern scholars, e.g.

---

94. Hunter 1993 80–83, 154, makes an attempt to find "near-allegories" in, e.g., the Harpies or Iris; but neither these examples, nor his suggestion that the Argonauts' adventures in Libya (Book IV) are "a kind of allegory of the Alexandrian Greeks lost in the cultural desert of North Africa," do I find really convincing.

as memories of encounters with icebergs in the Arctic;[95] nor to eliminate their awkward physicality by allegorizing them as some kind of moral hazard. Apollonios was, however, forced to accept one addition to the legend made necessary by exploration: the fusing of the rocks once they had been successfully navigated (2.604–606). Pindar (*Pyth.* 4.210–11) was right to describe this necessary end of an archaic belief as a τελευτάν, a kind of death (Braswell 293).

In sharp and deliberate contrast, the exploring Hellenes who penetrate this barbarous Bronze Age world of wonders and magic are drawn very much as Apollonios' contemporaries: enterprising yet vulnerable, wholly Hellenistic in their reactions, and human to a fault.[96] The confrontation of old and new, operating at social, mythical, and literary levels simultaneously, is what gives Apollonios' narrative its penetration and originality. The one great exception to this company of Hellenistic Candides, of course, is Herakles: a giant of gargantuan appetites, overwhelming strength and unruly bisexual passions, who himself embodies the outsize virtues and vices of the heroic age. His mere presence threatens to destroy all proportion and harmony among Apollonios' latter-day Argonauts, whose understated virtues tend more towards the cooperative. Muscle-bound, ruled by his obsolete code, an embarrassing anachronism from a culture in which, "when the typical hero found his path to fame and glory blocked, his instinct was to batter his own or someone else's head against the obstacle until something broke,"[97] he serves briefly as object-lesson, and then is left behind—his absence unnoticed, for all his bulk, by the departing company.[98] It is doubly ironic that the uncontrolled violence which breaks

95. See J. G. Frazer's edition of Apollodoros (London, 1921), vol. ii, app. v, 355–58: he is probably right that the Clashing Rocks are an archetypal fairy-tale, with parallel versions recounted by (among others) Rumanians, Russians, and Eskimos.

96. We may note that the one supernatural item that actually accompanies them is *Argo*'s "speaking beam," part of the tradition at least as early as Aeschylus' day (fr. 36 Mette), "carpentered into the forekeel" by Athena herself (1.524–27), and silent throughout the voyage until, with dramatic force all the greater for its rarity of utterance, it conveys Zeus' wrath at the murder of Apsyrtos (4.585–88).

97. W. B. Stanford, *The Ulysses Theme* (Oxford, 1954) 73.

98. See Ap. Rhod. 1.862–74, 992–1011, and especially 1153–1272. Apollonios is not above sly mischief at Herakles' expense: this hero did not get a rowing-bench amidships simply as a mark of honor, but also (bearing in mind his enormous size) in order to preserve *Argo*'s equilibrium: 1.399–400, 531–33. (There existed a tradition that *Argo* herself rejected Herakles because of his weight: schol. 1.1289–91; Antimachos fr. 58 Wyss; Pherecydes *FGrH* 3 F 111a = Apollod. 1.9.19.) There is also high comedy in his determination, in a kind of strong-man frenzy, to continue rowing when the winds are blowing again and everyone else has stopped (1.1161–71). The crew's failure to notice his absence [!] on

his oar should lead, step by step, to his loss of Hylas and his severance from the expedition.

Apollonios' treatment of Herakles nicely symbolizes the ambiguous tensions in any attempt by men of the Hellenistic age to come to terms with their ancient heroic heritage. Recognition and acceptance of the past are essential, he is saying, but its reinstatement would be sheer disaster; a Herakles in Ptolemaic Alexandria would upset the boat in a more than literal sense. The Argonauts on several occasions (2.145–53, 2.774–95, 3.1232–44, 4.1436–82) lament his irreplaceable absence; but they have in fact managed quite well without him (e.g. in the matter of boxing, one of his specialties, successfully putting up Polydeuces against Amykos, 2.20–97), and, faced among the Hesperides with evidence of his destructive passage, make it clear, despite their protestations (4.1458–60), that they are in fact much happier regretting Herakles' absence than dealing with his monstrous and unmanageable presence. On the other hand he had to be handled delicately: he was claimed as an "ancestor" by the Ptolemies, and thus much written about by Alexandrian court poets.[99] Dealing with his violent, emotional, and intermittently comic character thus presented a problem in the ethics of patronage in addition to everything else.[100]

Herakles is indeed (Hunter 1993 26) "anomalous among the Argonauts"; the longing for his superhuman aid, as Burkert sees (1985 210), bears all the marks of a wish-fulfilment fantasy (perhaps not entirely surprising in those who habitually hired mercenaries to do their fighting for them). To interpret the traditional myth in terms of human psychology, even while accepting its magical elements, meant, first and foremost, dropping Herakles from the narrative, "bestial and godlike" (Feeney 98), letting him slouch off towards ultimate deification. Like the madman in drama, he would have made nonsense of moral issues, and indeed of personal relationships, continually acting as a lumbering *semideus ex machina*: what would have become of the dramatic tension, let alone Jason's complex relationship with Medeia, had Herakles been there at every turn to obliterate the opposition?[101]

---

leaving Mysia (1.1273–83) should thus be seen as witty paradox rather than a regrettable lapse from realism.

99. See J. Rostropowicz, "Das Heraklesbild in den Argonautika des Apollonios Rhodios," *Act. Class. Univ. Scient. Debreceniensis* 26 (1990) 31–34.

100. This, however, seems not to have proved too much of a deterrent: see, e.g., Callim. *H.* 3.145–61 and Theocr. 17.26–33. More difficult was Hera's famous distaste for Herakles, since Hera figures throughout as the Argonauts' patron.

101. In fact we get a fairly clear picture of the results from Skytobrachion's version of events: see Diod. Sic. 4.48–49.

This is clearly why most versions of the myth remove him from the narrative at an early stage.[102] Apollonios, however, keeps him long enough to get some fun out of making this polyphiloprogenitive stud upbraid his comrades (1.865–74) for dallying too long in the beds of the Lemnian women.[103] The paradoxes of Herakles' nature have led scholars both ancient and modern to extrapolate a moral, civilizing aspect of him to offset the guzzler, rapist, and murderer: Cynics and Stoics, indeed, turned him into a kind of muscular saint.[104] But this is surely no more than the attempt (with which we are now familiar) to clear up some of the hero's more embarrassing archaic features by means of allegory,[105] a pitfall which Apollonios carefully—and characteristically—avoids.

For some time now the *communis opinio* about the *Argonautika* has stressed its acute literary self-consciousness, and in particular the way in which it echoes, varies, or subverts Homer (we hardly need telling that as a scholar Apollonios wrote on Homeric epic).[106] Though I am not primarily concerned here with literary problems, this erudite awareness is important for evaluating the *perspective* (for want of a better term) that Apollonios gives to his quest into past time, his evocation of the heroic age, even his aetiologizing search for roots. In *creative* time Apollonios wrote some four centuries after Homer, who becomes his legacy: as Eliot once remarked of past writers, "We know more than they did; and they are that which we know." But in *mythic* time, of course, the Argonauts' expedition to Kolchis belongs to the generation *before* the Trojan War: Cheiron's wife cradles the baby Achilles as she waves

102. Testimonia conveniently tabulated by Clauss, 176 and n. 1: Herodoros even claims (*FGrH* 31 F 41) that Herakles never sailed with the expedition at all, being at the time enslaved to Omphale, thus reminding us of his internal antitheses: as Burkert 1985 says (210) "the glorious hero is also a slave, a woman, and a madman."

103. Hunter 1993 33–34 is sensible on this point: whatever this speech may be, it is not, as has sometimes been suggested (Fränkel 1968 and Vian *ad loc.*), an old-fashioned declaration of misogyny by a high-minded heroic paederast.

104. Feeney 95–98 offers a good example of this.

105. As in the famous moral lesson, attributed to Prodikos by Xenophon (*Mem.* 2.1.21–33), of "Herakles at the crossroads."

106. See R. Pfeiffer, *A History of Classical Scholarship from the Beginnings to the end of the Hellenistic Age* (Oxford, 1968) 140–45. It is perhaps worth pointing out in this context that, for a scholar, Apollonios evinces a striking practical knowledge and love of the sea and seafaring: cf. J. Rostropowicz, "The Argonautica by Apollonius of Rhodes as a nautical epos: remarks on the realities of navigation," *Eos* 88 (1990) 107–17. The passage of the Symplegades (2.549–97) is a physically compelling hands-on description; and there is a similar precision and authenticity about the details of *Argo*'s launching (1.363–93), probably picked up in the Rhodian shipyards. See F. Chamoux, "Le lancement du navire Argo," *Bull. de la Soc. Nat. des Antiq. de France* (1983 [1985]) 45–49, and cf. 4.887–91.

them on their way (1.556–58). Thus by a kind of mythic intertextuality knowledge can jump forwards as well as backwards, offering to Apollonios an irresistible opening for deadpan narratological jokes, and to the modern historian enlightenment regarding ancient chronological awareness.

Both combine to solve one of the oddest problems in the *Argonautika* (4.784–90). Hera has requested Thetis to convoy the Argonauts past the dangers (well-known to Homer's Odysseus) of Scylla and Charybdis and the Wandering Rocks (Πλαγκταί), all located in the Straits of Messina. But then she says: "You know how ... I saved [Jason and his crew] as they threaded the Wandering / Rocks, with their fearfully roaring fiery tempests." Thetis is being asked to do what Hera asserts she has once already done; but in fact this will be *Argo*'s first passage through the strait. Was Hera really talking about the Clashing Rocks (Συμπληγάδες)? Hardly: Apollonios never confuses the two, and on that earlier occasion it was Athena, not Hera, who got *Argo* through.[107] Textual emendation has proved equally inadequate.[108] As always with Apollonios, Homer helps. Describing the Πλαγκταί to Odysseus, Circe warns him (*Od.* 12.69–72, trans. Lattimore): "That way the only seagoing ship to get through was Argo, / who is in all men's minds [πᾶσι μέλουσα], on her way home from Aiëtes; / and even she would have been driven on the great rocks that time, / but *Hera saw her through*, out of her great love for Jason" [emphasis mine]. These were famous lines, like *Argo* herself "in all men's minds," certainly those of Apollonios' audience. What Hera in effect says to Thetis is: "Well, I hardly need to repeat how I saved the Argonauts from the Wandering Rocks: you know your Homer as well as I do, and it's all in there."[109] The Homeric tag, suddenly shifted from its frame and thus relocated, is as arresting—and was meant to be—as another Hellenistic innovation, those looming high-relief fighters on the steps up to the Great Altar at Pergamon, which "set foot, hand and knee on the actual treads on which the worshipper mounted to the altar."[110]

Yet the most crucial element in the Argonauts' Unknown, as for the entire mythical era—above all by way of validation, belief, and instrument

---

107. Vian 1981 41–43, demolishing earlier theories by E. Livrea, *Apollonii Rhodii Argonautikon Liber IV* (Firenze, 1973) 234–36, and M. Campbell, "Further notes on Apollonius Rhodius," *CQ* 21 (1976) 416, and pointing out, *inter alia*, that the "fearfully roaring fiery tempests" (πυρὸς δειναὶ βρομέουσι θύελλαι) could refer *only* to the volcanic Πλαγκταί.

108. See, e.g., Fränkel 1968 534–36; G. Giangrande, *Zu Sprachgebrauch, Technik, und Text des Apollonios Rhodios* (Amsterdam, 1973) 37.

109. Hunter 1993 97 asks, casually, "Has Thetis read *Odyssey* 12 with its reference to Ἀργὼ πασιμέλουσα ... or has she read the *Argonautica*?" but does not follow up the implications of his own question.

110. Martin Robertson, *A History of Greek Art* (Cambridge, 1975) vol. i, 538.

of cultural definition—had to be τὸ θεῖον, the divine, primarily as godhead, i.e. major and minor deities, but also including θαύματα, magic, and the numinous in all its various manifestations. Like Athenians of the Periclean age, torn between the Inherited Conglomerate and the sophistries of the New Rationalism,[111] Alexandrians in the mid-third century B.C. found their yearning for old roots and past certainties under constant assault by forces such as Euhemerism; no one, it is safe to say, had forgotten the hymn with which, in 291, Athenians greeted Demetrios Poliorcetes:[112] "The other gods are far away, / or cannot hear, / or are nonexistent, or care nothing for us; but *you* are here, and visible to us, / not carved in wood or stone, but real, / so to you we pray." The other side of the coin is well exemplified, five or six years later, again in Athens, by the passionate outburst of a comic poet, Philippides, precisely *against* those blasphemous usurpations of godhead by Demetrios which, he asserts, have been directly responsible for Athens' misfortunes.[113] The split was not between two groups, but personal and internal. The resultant stresses are easily imagined.

It would be surprising had Apollonios *not* been affected by three centuries of rationalising criticism in the area of religion: the remarkable thing is how little impact it had on his work. Xenophanes' lethal dismissal of divine anthropomorphism (Kirk-Raven-Schofield frs. 167–69) has produced a certain awkwardness (perhaps calculated, sometimes witty) over the physical aspects of deity. Athena is weighty (cf. *Il.* 5.838–39) but can still travel by cloud (*Arg.* 2.538–40), and at the Clashing Rocks thrusts *Argo* through with one hand while bracing herself against a rock with the other (2.598–99). Are the Argonauts thought of as seeing her? Probably not (Feeney 74), any more than they see the Nereïds performing a similar function in the Straits of Messina (4.930–64). What is their relative size? We aren't told. Hera, Athena and Aphrodite, during their famous meeting at the beginning of Book 3, bear more resemblance, *pace* Feeney (78), to the gossiping Alexandrian ladies of Theocritus (*Id.* 15) than to Homeric deities. In the delineation of Triton, as Feeney says (79), "the norms of anthropomorphism are adhered to in order to be destabilized." But such instances apart, what is striking is the all-pervasive degree of Apollonios' *anti*-rationalism,

---

111. Penetratingly analyzed by E. R. Dodds in *The Greeks and the Irrational* (Berkeley, 1951), ch. vi, "Rationalism and Reaction in the Classical Age," 179–206.

112. Duris of Samos cited by Athen. 6. 253e; cf. Green 1990 55.

113. Philippides fr. 25 Kock. The blasphemies he catalogues—improper interference with the sacred calendar, using Athena's shrine on the Acropolis to house courtesans—as well as the signs of ill omen (frostbitten vines, a tear in the sail of the sacred ship during the Panathenaic procession) that were thought to have come about as a result, are also listed in Plut. *Demetr.* 10,12,23,26 and 27.

confronted with which (Feeney 67) "Xenophanes and Plato would have re-coiled in disdain." Indeed, in many ways the *Argonautika* can be read as a subtle indictment of the whole Protagorean πάντων χρημάτων μέτρον ἄνθρωπος formulation, the arrogance and inadequacy of which, after the events of the past two centuries, and despite Euhemerism, it was becoming increasingly hard to deny.

This, surely, is the common factor linking a whole range of symptoms apparent throughout the poem: above all that pervasive sense of human uncertainty, inadequacy, and ignorance in the face of an Unknown that extends from the motives of the gods to the unpredictability of the future, from magic and other counter-natural powers to the cracks in the fabric of the heroic ethos. Judged in these terms, Jason's much-debated ἀμηχανία, far from being a flaw, could be interpreted as a realistic recognition of man's limitations. Zeus is never seen, and recognition of his divine will (at least before the murder of Apsyrtos) remains fragmentary,[114] though at the same time his divine struggle for power may be quietly illuminating the all-too-similar deadly strife among Alexander's successors.[115] Hera's revenge against Pelias is worked out by using Medeia as an unconscious agent; the emphasis in the *Argonautika* on human decision-making is balanced against the lack of knowledge on which such decisions are based, the arbitrary and unsuspected machinations of the gods: "for the most part, Apollonius' characters struggle in a cloud of ignorance and doubt" (Hunter 1993 79). Phineus demonstrates the inadequacy of human prophecy, the ineluctable force of divine vengeance (2.250–51, 314–16). Deity no longer, as in Homer, consorts with mortals. These archaic gods are remote, unknowable, and in epiphany, as Apollo over Thynias, terrifying.[116]

We see then, in the end, that the fragments Apollonios has shored against his ruins are in essence not merely literary, or nostalgic, or indeed really fragments at all. What we rather find in the *Argonautika* is a remarkably consistent and thorough reversion to that archaic world-view consciously

114. Feeney 58–62, 65–67, Hunter 1993 79–80.

115. Feeney 68–69 perceives Apollonios' emphasis on struggle and usurpation in references to Zeus, but does not draw what seems to me the inevitable conclusion from it.

116. See 2.669–79. Many scholars have pointed out that Apollo's visitation here would inevitably evoke comparison with his murderous attack on the Greek camp in the *Iliad* (1.43–52): see, e.g., Feeney 50–51, 75. But the demonstration of power over Thynias, sometimes seen as a contrast to Homer's dark assault, is in fact at least as awe-inspiring. To rationalise this epiphany as no more than "a poetic version of sunrise" (Hunter 1987 52–53, repeated 1993 80) is to lapse into the kind of flaccid symbolism favored by Palaiphatos and Skytobrachion, not to mention the egregious Max Müller, who characterized Herakles' pyre on Oita as one more beautiful sunset.

discarded by the intellectual pioneers of the Periclean age—on the dead-end of which allegorists and rationalists were still hopefully battening. Like Euripides at the close of his life, when he wrote the *Bacchai*, Apollonios has seen, with deadly clarity, that reason alone is not enough, that the dimension of the Unknown formulated by myth has shrunk little if at all. There is no discussion here of the already old chestnut (Hunter 1993 80) of whether Homer's gods "were 'real' or were 'metaphors' to be allegorized away": their power, tangible existence and inscrutable control of mortal affairs permeate the entire narrative.

Perhaps most remarkably, the Fleece itself, the *raison d'être* of the entire epic *geste*, remains a complete (and highly numinous) mystery. The full reason for its Grail-like desirability, that can send a shipload of heroes to Kolchis and back, is never explained. We are not even told what generates its unearthly magical glow (4.172–73, 177–78, 185). Apollonios, speaking of its "ruddy blush like a flame" (173), clearly is visualizing a deep metallic red-gold such as that of the royal *larnax* from Tomb II at Vergina: what substance are we looking at here? We can ignore (as does Apollonios) the numerous bathetic rationalizations (Braund 23–25). The Fleece was a magical symbol: of supernatural power, of entitlement, above all of kingship. The bravest thing Jason ever does in this poem is to consummate his marriage on it (4.1141–43), an act as potentially dangerous as laying impious hands on the Ark of the Covenant.

Apollonios was not, as we have seen, wholly immune to the pressures of his age; but these were restricted, in the first instance, to the necessary changes imposed by the expansion of geographical knowledge—i.e. by a genuine, *physical* diminution of the Unknown. He will not, for example, indulge arbitrarily in what came to be called ἐξωκεανισμός, that wandering off the known map which got so bad a mauling in his day (Romm 194–96). His journey home for the Argonauts, even though it works its way into Switzerland by way of the Po, returning to the Mediterranean (via a non-existent confluence) down the Rhône (4.552–651), never strays off into that Ocean so remorselessly deconstructed by Herodotos—indeed, at one point Hera in person turns *Argo* back (4.637–44)—and carefully follows the track of Odysseus' Western wanderings as identified by earlier writers.[117]

117. It is a nice point (setting mythical chronology—Argonauts before Odysseus—against writers' time—Apollonios after Homer) as to whether this "Western route" is to be thought of as having been laid out by Odysseus or the Argonauts. The tendency in antiquity (when both were treated as historical) was to give preference to the Argonauts; the balance today (when both are regarded as "mythical" in the modern sense) is to opt for Odysseus: see e.g. Beye ch. iv. Further bibliography in Romm, 194 n. 51.

Apollonios' many literary concessions to Callimachean fashion do not for one moment affect his basic approach to the past. At heart he embraces the ancient epic tradition with a courage that in the mid-third century can only astonish us (and is more than sufficient to explain the tradition, whether true or false, of his quarrel with Callimachus): scorning to euhemerize the gods; not questioning the αἴτια, but accepting and going beyond them; not rationalizing or allegorizing clashing rocks or fiery bulls, but taking them in his stride as an integral part of those "high and far-off times" that exist no longer, yet must be preserved for ever in men's memories, a guard against intellectual *hubris*, a reminder and validation of everything it meant to be a Greek.[118] That is why the intellectually fashionable Skytobrachion survives only in epitome, whereas Pindar and Apollonios have lived through the centuries to delight and inspire us still today.

118. Cf. Green 1990 206–15.

THREE

Fact and Fiction: Jewish Legends in a Hellenistic Context

Erich S. Gruen

— I —

The terms *Ioudaismos* and *Hellenismos* first appear in the text of II Maccabees. That work provides the *locus classicus* for confrontation between the two cultures, a buttress for the idea that a clash or competition characterized the encounter. The coming of Hellenism to the land of the Jews, so it has been inferred, brought a threat to tradition and faith. Increasing Hellenization entailed erosion of ancestral Jewish practice or belief. And the Jews faced a choice of either assimilation or resistance to Hellenism.[1]

This paper adheres closely to the lecture delivered in January 1993 at the Cambridge Ancient History Seminar honoring Frank Walbank—mentor, guide, and inspiration to all who have labored in the fields of Hellenistic studies for the past two generations. Footnotes have been added to supply essential citations, selective references to modern work, and some evaluation of the scholarship. The paper's principal purpose is to lay out ideas and research plans for a larger study to come.

    1. The influential work of M. Hengel, *Judaism and Hellenism* (London, 1974) makes a strong case for the Hellenization of Judaea which, however, in his view, encountered vigorous Jewish resistance after the early 2nd century B.C.E. See the summary of his interpretation at I, 247–54. The recent and broad-ranging study of L. H. Feldman, *Jew and Gentile in the Ancient World* (Princeton, 1993), takes sharp issue with Hengel's findings on the spread of Hellenism among the Jews and attributes Jewish success to an internal strength and vitality that overcame the challenge of Greek culture; see, especially, 42–44, 416–22. Both scholars, however, operate from the premise that Jews who did not resist the blandishments of paganism ran the risk of succumbing to assimilation. A similar struggle is outlined by V. Tcherikover, *Hellenistic Civilization and the Jews* (Philadelphia, 1959) 152–74, 193–203; cf. C. Habicht, *JhrbHeidAkad* (1974) 97–110; A. Momigliano, *RivStorItal* 88 (1976) 425–43 = *Essays on Ancient and Modern Judaism* (Chicago, 1994) 10–28. For S. J. D. Cohen, the Maccabaean crisis stimulated the Jews to develop a sense of identity that would

72

Various statements in II Maccabees ostensibly lend weight to the conclusion. New institutions introduced by the High Priest Jason in the 170s B.C.E., namely the gymnasium and the ephebate, were, according to that text, the "height of Hellenism."[2] He had the Jews conform to the "Greek style of life."[3] And in three separate passages, the author of II Maccabees refers to those who fought for Judas Maccabaeus and resisted the persecutor Antiochus Epiphanes as adherents of *Ioudaismos*.[4] Hence it is not surprising that Hellenism and Judaism have regularly been reckoned as competing systems.

Yet a peculiar paradox lies here. The very work that employs those terms, its author a staunch advocate of the Maccabaean cause and fiercely hostile to the Seleucid invader, was composed in Greek and addressed to a readership conversant with the language. Outside that text, one would be hard pressed to find testimony to any conflict between Hellenism and Judaism in contemporary or near contemporary texts. No evidence for cultural strife appears in I Maccabees. It is absent also from the work of Ben Sira, written in the early second century. Ben Sira denounces those who fall away from righteousness, tyrannize the poor, and abandon fear of the Lord or the teachings of the law. But he nowhere contrasts Jews and Greeks or suggests a struggle for the conscience of his fellow-Jews being waged by Hellenizers and traditionalists.[5] Nor can one discern such a struggle in the Book of Daniel, composed at the very time of the Maccabaean revolt. The apocalyptic visions allude to contests among the Hellenistic powers and forecast delivery of the Jews from the foreign oppressor—but no cultural contest for the soul of Judaism.[6] In fact, not even II Maccabees juxtaposes the terms *Ioudaismos* and *Hellenismos* or expresses them as competing opposites. It is a mistake to imagine a zero-sum game, in which every gain for Hellenism was a loss for Judaism or vice-versa. That sort of analysis, as an increasing number of scholars now acknowledge, is simplistic and misleading.[7] Adaptation to Hellenic culture did not require

---

highlight their own distinctiveness and allow them to resist the forces of assimilation, in P. Bilde et al., *Religion and Religious Practice in the Seleucid Kingdom* (Aarhus, 1990) 204–23.

2. II Macc. 4.13: ἀκμή τις Ἑλληνισμοῦ.

3. II Macc. 4.10: πρὸς τὸν Ἑλληνικὸν χαρακτῆρα; cf. 6.9, 11.24.

4. II Macc. 2.21, 8.1, 14.38.

5. See the cogent remarks of J. Goldstein in E.P. Sanders, *Jewish and Christian Self-Definition* (Philadelphia, 1981) 70–81. *Contra*: Hengel, *Judaism and Hellenism*, I, 131–53; A. Momigliano, *Alien Wisdom* (Cambridge, 1975) 95.

6. Dan. 11.2–12.3. See Momigliano, *Alien Wisdom* 109–12.

7. Cf. E. Will and Cl. Orrieux, *Ioudaismos-Hellenismos* (Nancy, 1986) 120–36; G. Delling, *ANRW* II.20.1 (1987) 3–39; L. Grabbe, *Judaism from Cyrus to Hadrian* (Minneapolis, 1992) I, 169–70.

compromise of Jewish precepts or conscience. When a Greek gymnasium was introduced into Jerusalem, it was installed by a Jewish High Priest. And other priests soon engaged in wrestling matches in the palaestra.[8] They plainly did not reckon such activities as undermining their priestly duties. The idea of an irremediable cultural conflict needs to be abandoned.

A different and more interesting line of inquiry warrants attention. How did Jewish intellectuals accommodate themselves to the larger cultural world of the Mediterranean—while at the same time reaffirming the character of their own traditions within it? The subject, of course, is massive and daunting. Only a select portion of it can be touched on here. This is not the place to pronounce on a number of matters that have been much discussed and defy treatment within a limited compass—such as how far Greek culture had penetrated Palestine in the Hellenistic period and how profound or superficial that penetration was, or to what degree Palestinian Judaism represented an entity distinct from "Hellenistic" Judaism of the Diaspora. Nor can one outline in brief the influence of Greek language, literature, philosophy, historiography, political theory, and art upon Judaism. Analyses along these lines, however learned and insightful, too often tend to presuppose passive receptivity on the part of Jewish thinkers to Hellenic culture, a one-way street. What this paper seeks to stress is a more dynamic relationship, an active engagement by Jews with the traditions of Hellas which they recast and refashioned for their own purposes. One form of such activity comes under investigation here, an especially intriguing one: the elaboration of legends, fictions, and inventions, by which the Jews both connected themselves with a Hellenic cultural legacy and simultaneously defined a distinctive cultural identity of their own.

— II —

The first and most revealing category of such stories involves putative kinship associations. The tracing of relationships between cities, states, or peoples through supposed genealogical links and imagined common ancestors regularly appears in Greek literary speculation—a familiar feature in Hellenic folklore and legend. It makes a more striking impression, however, to find tales of this sort attesting connections between Greeks and Jews.

A notable fiction stands in the forefront. Tradition had it that Jews and Spartans both descended from the line of Abraham. The web of tales requires only brief summary here. The subject has been treated more

8. II Macc. 4.12, 4.14.

extensively elsewhere.[9] A diplomatic correspondence, consisting of three letters, recorded in I Maccabees and reproduced in a variant form by Josephus, constitutes the central testimony. The exchange began with a missive from King Areus to the Judaean High Priest Onias, ostensibly in the early third century B.C.E. Areus declared a blood tie between the two people, deriving from their common ancestor Abraham. He drew that information, so he claimed, from a written document in Sparta.[10] More than a century later, the Maccabaean leader Jonathan, successor of Judas, resumed relations with an embassy to Sparta, addressing the Lacedaemonians as ἀδελφοί and renewing the relations of friendship and alliance between the peoples.[11] The Spartans responded in kind. Some time later, when Simon had taken the reins from the fallen Jonathan, envoys from their state reached Jerusalem, greeted the Jews as brothers, proclaimed their intent to renew friendship and alliance, and announced that the association would be preserved in written form in the Spartan archives.[12]

The authenticity of that correspondence has long engendered debate and controversy—with an increasing inclination toward belief. Some have proposed that King Areus' scribes managed to learn Aramaic and composed a letter in that language, or that the Spartans had read the Scriptures even before appearance of the Septuagint, or indeed that they had learned of the patriarch Abraham from reading Hecataeus of Abdera—of course, in some portion of his work that we no longer possess.[13] These exercises in imagination can be set aside. Areus, the enterprising and aggressive Spartan ruler of the early third century, had no need for the moral or substantive support of a remote dependency of the Ptolemaic empire. Nor would the Jews of the second century find any special political or diplomatic advantage in claiming connection with Sparta.

Two points only call for emphasis here. The kinship affiliation carried cultural, not political, implications. And it was an invention by the Jews. Abraham as ultimate progenitor makes the matter clear. Further, Areus is

9. See E. S. Gruen, "The Purported Jewish-Spartan Affiliation," in R. W. Wallace and E. M. Harris, eds., *Transitions to Empire: Essays in Greco-Roman History, 360–146 B.C., in Honor of E. Badian* (Norman, Oklahoma, 1996) 254–69.

10. I Macc. 12.20–23; Jos. *Ant.* 12.225–27.

11. I Macc. 6.12–18; Jos. *Ant.* 12.225–27, 13.164–70.

12. I Macc. 14.16–23; cf. Jos. *Ant.* 13.170.

13. For bibliography, see B. Cardauns, *Hermes* 95 (1967) 317–18, n. 1; R. Katzoff, *AJP* 106 (1985) 485, n. 1; Cl. Orrieux in R. Lonis, *L'étranger dans le monde grec: Actes du colloque organisé par l'Institut d'Études Anciennes* (Nancy, 1987) 187, n. 7; more recently, P. Cartledge and A. Spawforth, *Hellenistic and Roman Sparta* (London, 1989) 36–37, 239, n. 22. See, further, Gruen in Wallace and Harris, *Transitions to Empire*, 254–69.

made to express himself in terms that sound suspiciously Biblical: "your cattle and goods are ours, and ours are yours."[14] And, equally revealing, the tone of Jonathan's letter to the Spartans conveys a distinctively Jewish orientation toward the relationship. Jonathan sets on record Jewish successes accomplished through divine grace and without aid of Spartans or others.

He reassures his Lacedaemonian allies that they can count on Jewish intercession through sacrifices and prayers, as is only proper for kinsmen.[15] The Jews, in other words, secured for Sparta the favor of the true god. The tone has a distinctly patronizing ring. Jonathan represents his people as indulgent benefactors.

Wherein lay the stimulus for this invention? Jewish intellectuals did not rush to attach themselves to a Hellenic heritage. The fictive forefather was Abraham, not Heracles. The Jews, to be sure, were claiming links with a Greek community. But this fable represents a Jewish endeavor to fit Greeks into their own traditions rather than to seek assimilation to Hellenism.

The pattern repeats itself. An equally remarkable tradition derives from an obscure and untraceable writer named Cleodemus Malchus, cited by Alexander Polyhistor and preserved by Josephus and Eusebius.[16] Cleodemus, conventionally dated to the second century B.C.E., claims Moses as his authority, an ostensible reference to the book of Genesis. In his version, Abraham's children by Katoura included three sons named Assouri, Apher, and Aphran. Assouri became namesake of Assyria, the others of the city of Apher and the land of Africa respectively. The latter two made their way to Africa, there to participate in Heracles' successful crusade against the Libyan giant Antaeus. Heracles then proceeded to marry the daughter of Aphran, from whom the whole continent of Africa took its name.

The author Cleodemus Malchus escapes identification. A variety of modern conjectures have labeled him as either Jew, Samaritan, Syrian, Phoenician, Carthaginian, or some combination thereof.[17] No definitive solution is forthcoming, nor is one necessary. The scholarly debate operates on the assumption that if we could determine Cleodemus' nationality, we could

14. I Macc. 12.23.

15. I Macc. 12.9–15.

16. Jos. *Ant.* 1.239–41; Eus. *PE* 9.20.2–4.

17. Important treatments by J. Freudenthal, *Alexander Polyhistor und die von ihm erhaltenen Reste jüdischer und samaritanischer Geschichtswerke* (Breslau, 1875) 130–36, and N. Walter, *Jüdische Schriften aus hellenistisch-römischer Zeit*, I.2 (Gütersloh, 1973) 115–18. See the valuable text, commentary, notes and bibliography of C. R. Holladay, *Fragments from Hellenistic Jewish Authors*, vol. I: *Historians* (Chico, Calif., 1983) 245–59.

discern the motives for the invention. But nothing shows that Cleodemus invented it anyway; we know only that Polyhistor found it in that source. The story itself could have originated earlier, elsewhere, and under any number of possible circumstances. What matters is not the origin of the legend but its meaning and implications. As with the Spartan-Jewish connection, the link between Abraham and Heracles represents an *interpretatio Judaica*, not *Graeca*. The line begins with the Hebrew patriarch, his grandson has the honor of a continent named after him, and Heracles' victory becomes by inference the outcome of Jewish intervention. The Greek hero gains stature by marrying into the house of Abraham. The fashioner of the narrative employed Hellenic tradition in the service of Jewish enhancement. What had been a Greek legend of Heracles bringing Hellenic civilization to barbarous Libya became transformed into one that implicitly gave that distinction to the line of Abraham.

The process can be further illustrated. An interesting item surfaces in a decree of Pergamum, at least as conveyed by Josephus.[18] The historian dates it to the late second century and records it in a section of his work devoted to listing Roman edicts and pronouncements that had been issued in favor of the Jews over the centuries, thereby to indicate the high esteem in which his people were held.[19] The Pergamene decree was prompted by the Romans who sought to show backing for Jewish interests around the eastern Mediterranean. This supposed document, however, in addition to expressing the usual sentiments about friendship and benefactions, also makes reference to an ancient association between Pergamenes and Jews that dates back to the time of Abraham, "father of all Hebrews." One might observe further that the relationship is claimed on the basis of documents found in the public records of Pergamum.[20] That claim closely parallels the notice in the purported letter of Areus that he came upon knowledge of the Jewish-Spartan kinship through a Spartan document, a γραφή.[21] Neither text, of course, gives any reason to believe in the authenticity of the relationship or, for that matter, the documents. That Pergamenes would express themselves in this fashion in a public decree is most implausible. But the texts indicate a pattern whereby Jewish writers conjured up Greek records to substantiate connections between the two peoples. The Pergamene decree does not allude to συγγένεια, only to φιλία. As in the other instances, however, it

18. Jos. *Ant.* 14.247–55.

19. On the authenticity of these documents, a much disputed matter, see, most recently, M. Pucci Ben Zeev, *SCI* 13 (1994) 46–59, with bibliography.

20. Jos. *Ant.* 14.255: ἐν τοῖς δημοσίοις εὑρίσκομεν γράμμασιν.

21. I Macc. 12.21: εὑρέθη ἐν γραφῇ.

gives primacy to the Jews. The inception of the relationship is dated by allusion to Abraham.

Diverse and diverting tales evidently circulated that certified kinship links and invented reasons for believing them. One sets the origins of the Jews in Crete, offering as testimony the resemblance of the name *Iudaei* to that of *Idaei*, the Cretan people who dwelled under Mt. Ida. Another pointed to the ostensible similarity between the names Hierosolyma (Jerusalem) and the Solymoi whom Homer lists among Lycian peoples, thus making the Jews derive from Asia Minor. Testimony on these postulated Jewish beginnings is preserved by Tacitus, his sources irrecoverable.[22] They may well stem from Greek speculation, the standard and familiar practice of ascribing Greek origins to alien peoples. But one can easily surmise that tales of this kind were picked up and developed by Hellenizing Jews who took pleasure in finding their ancestors linked with the epic traditions of Greece. They provided a convenient means whereby the Jews could reinvent themselves in a Hellenistic context.

— III —

We turn now to a second category of comforting fictions: the romantic tales that place Jews in confrontation or collaboration with rulers of the Hellenistic world. Most of those that survive, in one form or another, involve the Ptolemies, and were doubtless conceived or adapted by Alexandrian Jews. But the most celebrated narrative in this category stands outside the Ptolemaic context: the purported visit of Alexander the Great to Jerusalem.

The story, as preserved in Josephus, contains two or three separate strands awkwardly woven into one.[23] The central thread, however, has Alexander, at the head of his mighty host, march with hostile intent against the capital of the Jews. The High Priest Jaddus had declined to send him aid and had maintained his allegiance to Persia. Alexander would now wreak vengeance. Jaddus and his people were terrified, offered sacrifice to Jehovah, and prayed for deliverance from the Macedonian juggernaut. And Jehovah spoke to Jaddus in his dream, bidding him decorate the city with wreaths, have all the citizens dressed in white and himself decked out in priestly robes, and meet the Macedonian forces in person. This, of course, they did. When Alexander saw the white-clad Jewish populace, the High Priest

---

22. Tac. *Hist.* 5.2.

23. Jos. *Ant.* 11.317–39. Among modern treatments, see Momigliano, *Athenaeum* 57 (1979) 442–48; S. J. D. Cohen, *AJS Review* 78 (1982–1983) 41–68; D. Golan, *Berliner Theologische Zeitschrift* 8 (1991) 19–30.

in resplendent blue and gold, a mitre on his head with a gold plate on which was inscribed the name of Jehovah, the Macedonian monarch halted his invasion forthwith. Alexander the Great fell on his knees, performed *proskynesis* before the priest, and proclaimed that his god was the great god who had appeared to him also in a dream, clad in similar garb, and had promised him conquest of the Persian empire. The king then conducted his own sacrifices to Jehovah in the Temple and under the direction of the High Priest. A copy of the Book of Daniel was produced to authorize the prophecy that a Greek would dismantle the empire of the Persians. And Alexander proceeded to grant a variety of privileges not only to the Jews of Palestine but to those in Babylon and Media as well, a happy and satisfying conclusion.

The tale is outright fabrication. Alexander never approached Jerusalem. All the historical narratives of his march make it clear that he went straight to Egypt after the siege of Gaza and that, on his return trip, he went directly from Egypt to Tyre and from there to North Syria and Mesopotamia.[24] One need not pursue the implausible details in the rest of the story— like the presentation of the Book of Daniel a century and a half before it was composed! The fabrication itself is of central importance. It does not, as one might have expected, present Alexander as villain, have him humiliated by Jehovah and his priests, and bring the Jews to triumph. Alexander's reputation, in fact, remains unscarred. The episode reaffirms his stature as great conqueror, indeed now furnishes a satisfactory Jewish explanation for his successes. It is the Jewish god who guarantees him his conquest of Persia. The Macedonian turns from potential foe to actual friend.

The story, in short, implies a partnership between Jews and Greeks. Alexander will fulfill his promised destiny because Jehovah decrees it. The king correspondingly honors that deity and his chosen people with special prerogatives, the right to live under their own laws and exemption from taxes every seventh year. The Jewish state thereby becomes an integral part of the Macedonian empire, while holding a distinctive and privileged position at the behest of its ruler. And the centerpiece of the narrative is a solemn vindication of the Jewish faith. Those elements and implications make this fable an illuminating exemplar of Jewish recreation of historical narrative to suit the larger world of power politics while dramatizing their own centrality within it.

---

24. Arrian 3.1.1, 3.6.1, 3.6.4, 3.7.1–3; Diod. 17.49.1, 17.52.6; Curt. Ruf. 4.7.1–2, 4.8.9– 16; Plut. *Alex.* 29.1, 31.1. Golan's effort to defend the substance of the tradition, *Berliner Theologische Zeitschrift* 8 (1991) 19–30, does not explain the silence of these narratives.

The text of III Maccabees furnishes another tale of this variety, though with somewhat different import.[25] Ptolemy IV Philopator of Egypt appears as villain of the piece. After the battle of Raphia in 217, Philopator decided to visit Jerusalem and, impressed by its Temple, sought to enter the inner sanctuary. To the Jews, of course, that would constitute sacrilege. They refused the request, but Ptolemy insisted upon access and endeavored to force his way in. The Jews turned in prayer to Jehovah who paid heed to his people and struck Ptolemy down. The king then abandoned his plan but returned to Alexandria determined to have his revenge. This time he directed that all Jews in his realm be registered, branded with the ivy leaf of Dionysus, and reduced to the status of servitude. When the Jews resisted, Philopator had them rounded up and herded into the hippodrome in Alexandria where they were to be trampled by five hundred crazed elephants, drugged with huge quantities of frankincense and unmixed wine. The mass murder was twice postponed when the Lord intervened to afflict Ptolemy with sleep or a temporary bout of amnesia. And when all was at last in readiness and the intoxicated pachyderms were loosed upon the multitude, Jehovah once again heeded the call of his people. Two angels of the Lord arrived in the nick of time, interposing themselves between the Jews and the inebriated beasts who then turned tail and crushed the soldiers of the king. Ptolemy now saw the light, released the Jews, created a new festival in their honor, and instructed all his governors to assure their protection. The Jews thus emerged with greater authority and higher esteem.

Much of the discussion on this romantic narrative has concentrated on its date and on the historicity of its contents. Josephus supplies a suspiciously similar story about Ptolemy VIII Physcon who set intoxicated elephants upon the Jewish backers of his political rivals—only to have the beasts turn against his own supporters. Scholars divide on whether the true persecution belongs in Ptolemy VIII's reign, wrongly shifted by III Maccabees to Ptolemy IV, or vice-versa. Others find a historical basis in a much later time, either in the Augustan era or in the reign of Caligula, thus dating III Maccabees to the time of the Roman Empire.[26] No need to enter into that particular controversy here. It may well be fruitless to seek an appropriate occasion

25. A useful discussion, with translation, notes, and bibliography by H. Anderson in J. H. Charlesworth, *The Old Testament Pseudepigrapha*, vol. 2 (New York, 1985) 509–29.

26. Among the more important discussions, see J. Moreau, *ChrEg* 31 (1941) 111–22; M. Hadas, *The Third and Fourth Books of Maccabees* (New York, 1953); J. J. Collins, *Between Athens and Jerusalem: Jewish Identity in the Hellenistic Diaspora* (New York, 1983) 104–11; E. Schürer, *The History of the Jewish People in the Age of Jesus Christ (175 B.C.–A.D. 135)*, rev. ed. by G. Vermes, F. Millar, and M. Goodman (Edinburgh, 1986) III.1, 537–42; A. Paul, *ANRW* II.20.1 (1987) 298–336; F. Parente, *Henoch* 10 (1988) 143–82.

or period to which the narrative refers. A folk-tale of this sort could well serve more than one purpose. The historicity of the events, in any case, has less importance than the perception of the Jewish place in the larger world as reflected in the text. The story offers a valuable perspective on the manner in which Jews conceived their situation within a Hellenistic kingdom.

The narrative plainly has a sharper tone and delivers a more pointed blast at the excesses of Hellenistic rule than does the fictitious tale of Alexander and the Jews. That does not mean, however, as some commentators have suggested, that it is a piece of subversive literature or a document of Jewish resistance to Hellenic overlordship. In fact, the author more than once insists upon Jewish good will and loyalty to the crown, an allegiance to the monarchy that is unwavering—unless, of course, it conflicts with the demands of ancestral law.[27] And when Ptolemy relented, acknowledged the power of the Jewish god, and ordered his officials to secure Jewish rights, the cordial relationship between monarch and subjects resumed.[28] The king, however, remained in control.[29] So the message of III Maccabees is quite compatible with that of the Alexander narrative. Jewish faith is once again vindicated, the Macedonian king mends his ways, recognizes the magnitude of the Jewish divinity, and becomes protector of the Jews themselves. Both of these stories concede by implication a subordinate status for the Jews in the political and military circumstances of the Hellenistic world. But in the fantasy of the fable, the rulers also pay special respect to that particular segment of their subjects.

In this connection, some comments on the famous "Letter of Aristeas" seem requisite.[30] The text, as is well known, concerns the supposed decision of Ptolemy II Philadelphus, on the advice of his librarian Demetrius of Phaleron, to have the Pentateuch translated into Greek and added to the Alexandrian library. The king, portrayed as a lover of learning and culture, and impressed by what he had heard about the Hebrew books of the law, sent to the High Priest in Jerusalem, respectfully requesting that he provide scholars of exemplary morality, knowledge of the law, and learned in Greek to translate the books of Moses. The High Priest duly selected six men who fit that description from each of the twelve tribes to bring their skills to Alexandria. Ptolemy then interrogated them in a long, drawn-out banquet

27. III Macc. 3.2–4, 7.7.

28. III Macc. 6.36–41, 7.10–13.

29. Cf. III Macc. 7.20.

30. A serviceable bibliography in Schürer, *History of the Jewish People*, rev. ed. by Vermes et al., III.1, 685–87.

that lasted seven days, putting a host of philosophical questions to them, mostly taken from Greek political theory on the nature of kingship, and seeking advice on the proper means of royal governance. The Jewish sages responded to each with answers derived from their own traditions, though expressed in Hellenic form and argument, stressing trust in god as the fundamental principle. The king and his assembled philosophers were mightily impressed by Jewish wisdom, filled with admiration for the intellectuals sent by the High Priest. Those seventy-two scholars proceeded to produce their translation in precisely seventy-two days. And when the new text was read, Ptolemy marveled at the genius of the Jewish lawgiver who had composed the Pentateuch. The king then sent back the translators with lavish gifts and his compliments to the High Priest in Jerusalem.

Yet another discussion of this much discussed text would be inappropriate. Debate continues on its date, purpose, and historical value. Some reckon it as a treatise designed to counteract the largely negative portrait of Ptolemaic kingship contained in III Maccabees by presenting a more favorable image and suggesting a harmonious relationship between Jews and Greeks—or, conversely, that the Letter of Aristeas came first, genuinely reflecting a happy period of collaboration in the early Ptolemaic era that later turned sour, thereby generating III Maccabees. Others propose that it defended the Septuagint as against a newer translation perhaps deriving from the Jewish community in Leontopolis, or, on a different theory, that it promoted the Septuagint as a new translation against postulated earlier versions. In certain interpretations, it was directed generally to the Hellenic world, a broadcast of Jewish wisdom and religious superiority. Others view it, however, as a manifesto by Alexandrian Jews, with their openness toward Hellenism, in response to the more isolationist Jews of Palestine. And yet another analysis regards its audience as Alexandrian Jews themselves, thus to reconcile their ancestral faith with Greek culture. Comparable differences exist on the date. Efforts to elicit a suitable time have depended on postulating an occasion. On one view, composition came ca. 170 B.C.E., when Antiochus Epiphanes threatened the Jewish community in Jerusalem, thus inspiring the Jews of Alexandria to stress the ties that linked Jews and Greeks. On another, the letter of Aristeas belongs in the late second century B.C.E., reflecting the Hellenizing tendencies that characterized not only Alexandrian Jews but also the Hasmonean dynasty in Judaea.[31] All of this represents a mere sampling

---

31. Diverse and conflicting opinions on these and other matters may be found, e.g., in S. Tracy, *YCS* 1 (1928) 241–52; Hadas, *HTR* 42 (1949) 175–84; Tcherikover, *HTR* 51 (1958) 59–85; Jellicoe, *NTS* 12 (1966) 144–50; O. Murray, *JTS* 18 (1967) 337–71; E. van't Dack, *Studia Hellenistica* 16 (1968) 263–78; G. E. Howard, *JTS* 22 (1971) 337–48; Schürer,

of the innumerable proposals and conjectures that have issued forth on the character and objectives of this text. For our purposes only a few central points need emphasis.

The letter of Aristeas expresses a deep unity between Palestinian and Diaspora Judaism. It has the Bible of Egyptian Judaism, the Septuagint, derive from the authority of the High Priest and scholars of Jerusalem. At the same time it gives voice to a genuine harmony between the Hellenistic ruler and the adherents of Judaism. As in the other texts treated here, the Greek monarch commands the political scene. The translation project is his decision, he summons the translators to Alexandria, he interrogates them, and he rewards them upon completion of their task.[32] The creation of the Septuagint, therefore, emerges as consequence of Ptolemy Philadelphus' cultural sensitivities and broad learning, a new addition to the holdings of the Ptolemaic monarchy. But, of course, the Letter of Aristeas also highlights the profound respect allegedly shown to Judaism by the pagan king. The author of the Letter has Ptolemy evince high regard for Jewish law and religious observances, makes him the grateful recipient of Jewish wisdom whose insistence on divine underpinnings for kingly behavior eclipses the tenets of Greek philosophy—and even has him serve a kosher meal to his Jewish guests.[33] It is quite inadequate to characterize this and similar fictions as Jewish apologetic or Jewish propaganda. The saga constitutes more than rationalization for the Septuagint, justification for Diaspora Judaism, or a reactive pamphlet to III Maccabees. The positive and inventive features of the Letter of Aristeas merit greater stress. It has the *pagan* monarch initiate a project to bring *Jewish* sagacity into the service of a Hellenistic kingdom. In this way it both underscores the genuine power relationship—the Greek king calls the shots—and it also privileges Jewish tradition over Greek learning.

Space does not permit examination of further instances in this category of Jewish fictions. But mention might be made, in passing, of the tales of the Tobiads, recorded or embellished by Josephus.[34] The Tobiads constituted a family of financial officials in the employ of the Ptolemaic monarchy,

History of the Jewish People, rev. ed. by Vermes et al., III.1, 677–87; L. Troiani in B. Virgilio, *Studi Ellenistici* 2 (1987) 31–61. And see now the acute comments by G. Boccaccini, *Middle Judaism: Jewish Thought, 300 B.C.E to 200 C.E.* (Minneapolis, 1991) 163–85.

32. *LetAris*, 9–12, 38–40, 124, 173–75, 187–294 (the banquet), 317–21.

33. *LetAris*, 124–25, 174–81, 293–94, 317.

34. Jos. *Ant.* 12.154–236. See especially the discussions of Tcherikover, *Hellenistic Civilization and the Jews*, 126–42; Hengel, *Judaism and Hellenism*, I, 267–77; Goldstein in J. Neusner, *Christianity, Judaism, and Other Greco-Roman Cults: Studies for Morton Smith at Sixty*, Part III (Leiden, 1975) 85–123; and D. Gera in A. Kasher, U. Rappaport, and G. Fuks, *Greece and Rome in Eretz Israel* (Jerusalem, 1990) 21–38.

having obtained royal favor through use of their wits and mental agility. The tales correspond very loosely to the Joseph story in the Book of Genesis, but tailored and elaborated to suit the Hellenistic context. They too are normally treated as propaganda vehicles either for heirs of the Tobiads or for their rivals the Oniads. But the motif itself has greater significance. Once again Jewish figures serve the Ptolemaic crown, in this case Jewish tax collectors and financiers. But these Jewish figures are the shrewd, clever, and successful manipulators who win the high regard of the Ptolemies.

One last example in this category. The Jew as trusted counselor of the pagan king appears in another purported letter. This one comes at the outset of II Maccabees, a communiqué from the people of Jerusalem to the Jews in Egypt. Its addressee is a certain Aristobulus, identified as of high priestly family and also as *didaskalos*, tutor, of Ptolemy.[35] Once again the Jew is servant of the king—but his intellectual and spiritual superior.

— IV —

A third and final category of Jewish imaginative fabrication deserves attention: the tales that trace Hellenic culture itself to Jewish influence.

One may take as a revealing instance the romance composed by the Egyptian-Jewish writer Artapanus in the third or second century B.C.E. The lengthiest and most substantial fragment from that work concerns Moses.[36] Artapanus' retelling of the Moses saga draws only in part on the Biblical version in the Book of Exodus and depends largely on creative inspiration. Moses does not take on the conventional role as the great lawgiver to the Israelites. Rather, he appears as author of most of the intellectual, religious, and cultural institutions among the Egyptians. They include technological innovations, political structures, priestly organization, philosophical learning, and even animal worship. And, for good measure, Moses, after defeating the Ethiopians, taught them the practice of circumcision. But Moses did not

35. II Macc. 1.10.
36. The fragments, conveyed by Alexander Polyhistor, are preserved by Eusebius and Clement of Alexandria. For Artapanus' version of the Moses story, see Euseb. *PE* 9.27.1–37; Clement *Strom.* 1.154.2–3. A convenient text, with translation, commentary, notes, and bibliography, in Holladay, *Fragments*, I, 189–243. Important treatments by Freudenthal, *Alexander Polyhistor*, 143–74, 215–18; D. L. Tiede, *The Charismatic Figure as Miracle Worker* (Missoula, 1972) 146–77; Holladay, *THEIOS ANER in Hellenistic Judaism* (Missoula, 1977) 199–232; and G. E. Sterling, *Historiography and Self-Definition: Josephos, Luke-Acts, and Apologetic Historiography* (Leiden, 1992) 167–86. See also the useful discussions by Collins in Charlesworth, *Old Testament Pseudepigrapha*, 2, 889–903 and Schürer, *History of the Jewish People*, rev. ed. by Vermes et al., III.1, 521–25, with additional bibliography.

neglect the Greeks. According to Artapanus, he was much revered by that people, identified by them with the mythical Greek poet Mousaios, an identification inspired by the similarity of names—a typical Hellenic inference. In that guise he was reckoned as the teacher of Orpheus. And, in a particularly syncretistic analysis, Artapanus has the Egyptians make Moses equivalent to Hermes because of his skill in interpreting sacred texts. This is the Hermes whom Egyptians identified with their god Thot and who, in Greek mythology, appears as patron god of literature and the arts.[37] Moses thus takes his place as culture hero *par excellence*, a source of inspiration to Hebrews, Egyptians, and Greeks alike.

How does one interpret the objective of Artapanus? The usual answer regards his work as a piece of apologetic propaganda, responding to antisemitic critics of the Jews, an example of what has been called "competitive historiography." So, for instance, whereas tracts hostile to the Jews had accused Moses of endeavoring to stamp out animal worship, Artapanus has him invent the institution himself.[38] If this is a response to critics, it is at least quite an imaginative one. But Artapanus goes well beyond mere polemics. He was plainly very familiar with Egyptian institutions and religious traditions. His narrative appears aimed at demonstrating that the Jews, far from being aliens or outsiders in that culture, were its originators. They belong in Egypt as its most important denizens. Artapanus, of course, only ostensibly deals with Egypt of the Pharaohs. In fact, his eye is trained upon contemporary Hellenistic Egypt. Hence, Moses in the form of Mousaios or Hermes emerges also as cultural progenitor of Hellas itself.

Jewish contribution to Greek culture has a more central place in the work of the Alexandrian Jew Aristobulus. Only a few fragments of his writings survive, preserved primarily by Eusebius.[39] Aristobulus dedicated his book, we are told, to Ptolemy the king, a king whom Eusebius and Clement of Alexandria took to be Ptolemy VI Philometor.[40] If so, that would

37. Euseb. *PE* 9.27.6. See G. Mussies in M. Heerma van Voss et al., *Studies in Egyptian Religion* (Leiden, 1982) 89–120.

38. So, e.g., P. M. Fraser, *Ptolemaic Alexandria* (Oxford, 1972) 705–706, 714; Collins, *Between Athens and Jerusalem*, 33–35; Schürer, *History of the Jewish People*, rev. ed. by Vermes et al., III.1, 522–23; Sterling, *Historiography and Self-Definition*, 182–84. A modified version in Holladay, *THEIOS ANER*, 212–18. But see Tiede, *Charismatic Figure*, 175–76.

39. Euseb. *HE* 7.32.16–18; *PE* 8.9.38–8.10.17, 13.12.1–16. The major modern treatment by N. Walter, *Der Thoraausleger Aristobulus* (Berlin, 1964), with extensive bibliography. Additional titles and discussion in Schürer, *History of the Jewish People*, rev. ed. by Vermes et al., III.1, 579–87. And see now C. R. Holladay, *Fragments from Hellenistic Jewish Authors*, vol. 3: *Aristobulus* (Atlanta, 1995).

40. Euseb. *PE* 8.9.38; Clement, *Strom.* 1.150.1, 5.97.

make our author the same Aristobulus whom II Maccabees describes as tutor to Ptolemy Philometor. Of course, a nice—and rare—coincidence of testimony along such lines immediately makes it suspect to some scholars. So, it has been argued, Eusebius and Clement simply inferred from the forged letter in II Maccabees that their Aristobulus was tutor of Philometor. Or the reverse can be postulated: the forger of the letter knew of Aristobulus' dedication of his book to a Ptolemy and conjectured that he was Philometor's tutor.[41] We do not need to decide the question. Nor is it vital to determine whether Aristobulus' allusion to the story of the Septuagint translation means that he knew the Letter of Aristeas, or vice-versa, or that both drew on a common source.[42] What matters is the content of the work, fascinating and revealing.

Aristobulus had read widely in the works of Greek authors—including some that they probably never wrote. And he regularly ascribes the wisdom and insights found therein to the Jewish lore with which he assumes their familiarity. So, Plato found the source for his *Laws* in the Pentateuch, Pythagorean philosophy was an adaptation of Hebraic doctrine, and all Greek philosophical ideas with a monotheistic tinge derived from the Bible.[43] Aristobulus names in this connection not only Pythagoras, Socrates, and Plato, but even the Hellenistic writer Aratus, author of an astronomical poem, the *Phaenomena*, which he traces to Jewish influence.[44] Nor is that all. The Jewish reverence for the Sabbath, according to Aristobulus, found its way into the verses of Homer and Hesiod—of which he supplies a few examples, some of them spurious and possibly his own inventions.[45] And he reaches back to a mythological past: Orpheus imitated Moses in his verses on the Hieros Logos.[46] Of course, in the time of Homer and Hesiod, or even Socrates and Plato, the Septuagint had not yet been composed; the Hebrew Bible was still unavailable to Greek readers. Aristobulus recognized the problem—and then got around it. He simply postulated some earlier and superseded translation of the Pentateuch into Greek so as to make its doctrines accessible to early Hellenic poets and philosophers.[47]

41. See the arguments of Walter, *Thoraausleger*, 13–26; Hengel, *Judaism and Hellenism*, II, 106–107; Schürer, *History of the Jewish People*, rev. ed. by Vermes et al., III.1, 579–80; and Y. A. Collins in Charlesworth, *Old Testament Pseudepigrapha*, 832–33.

42. Euseb. *PE* 13.12.1–2. Cf. Walter, *Thoraausleger*, 88–103; Fraser, *Ptolemaic Alexandria*, II, 964; Schürer, *History of the Jewish People*, rev. ed. by Vermes et al., III.1, 580–81.

43. Euseb. *PE* 13.12.1, 13.12.4, 13.12.6.

44. Euseb. *PE* 13.12.6–7.

45. Euseb. *PE* 13.12.9–15.

46. Euseb. *PE* 13.12.4.

47. Euseb. *PE* 13.12.1–2.

Modern scholars commonly describe Aristobulus as a serious philosopher, well trained in Hellenic teachings. Perhaps so. But Aristobulus needs to be given his due in another realm: the most striking features of the fragments are the inventiveness and the imaginative reconstructions that amalgamate Jewish pronouncements with Greek philosophy and poetry. In this regard his mission parallels that of the other texts discussed above. And, equally important, the assimilation once more is not that of Judaism to Hellenism but the other way around.

The attribution of monotheistic sentiments to Greek poets became an increasingly stimulating activity for ingenious Jewish forgers. Their passion for ascribing to celebrated Hellenic literary artists attitudes toward the spirituality, unity, and transcendence of God that corresponded to Jewish belief has added considerably to our stock of spurious verses. Fictitious fragments or, at best, highly selective lines of this sort were assigned to Hesiod, Pythagoras, Aeschylus, Sophocles, Euripides, and comic writers like Epicharmus, Diphilus, Philemon, and Menander.[48] And that is not even to mention fictitious fragments of the fictitious poets Orpheus and Linus.[49] Jewish ingenuity here outdid itself. One noteworthy illustration might be offered. Among the verses attributed to the legendary Orpheus, recorded in the pages of Aristobulus, were noble sentiments about the transcendent glory of God that is invisible to mortals. Orpheus himself can make out only his traces and sees him as if engulfed in a cloud. But that is better than most mortals—with one exception. One man alone has seen God, says Orpheus: the man of the Chaldees, i.e., Abraham.[50] So, even the most noble of poets, the quintessential singer Orpheus who understands the nature of monotheism, has to give precedence to the Hebrew patriarch.

— V —

The reinterpretation of authentic sentiments and the inventions of bogus utterances give insight into the motives of Jews learned in Hellenic literature and lore. These works go beyond what is conventionally termed apologetic writing. They do not represent mere defensive, rear-guard action by a be-leaguered minority in an alien world. What stands out is the aggressive inventiveness of the stories. The Jews, of course, were in no position to challenge the political supremacy of Hellenistic powers, whether in Palestine or in the Diaspora. And they did not do so. They accepted, even

---

48. Cf. Clement *Strom.* 5.112–14, 5.118–22, 5.127–31.
49. Euseb. *PE* 13.12.4–5, 13.12.16; Clement *Strom.* 5.116.2, 5.123–26, 5.128.3.
50. Euseb. *PE* 13.12.4–5; Clement *Strom.* 5.123

acknowledged their subordinate political status. But by selectively appro-
priating Hellenic culture, they could redefine it in their own terms, adopting
categories and genres that would be familiar to a pagan readership but
making more vivid the spiritual and intellectual precedence that the Jewish
audience associated with their own traditions. Through creative fictions like
kinship connections, tales of homage paid by Hellenic rulers to Jewish values,
and the supposed Jewish roots of Greek culture, the Jews not only affirmed
their place in the larger Hellenistic community. They also articulated their
special identity in a form that bolstered self-esteem by accepting honestly
their political subordination but asserting—perhaps not so honestly—their
cultural ascendancy.

FOUR

Hellenistic History in a Near Eastern Perspective: The Book of Daniel

Fergus Millar

I. THE BACKGROUND

As with so many aspects of Hellenistic history, it is best to begin with the words of Polybius:

> I shall bring the whole narrative of events to a conclusion, narrating finally the expedition of Antiochus Epiphanes against Egypt, the war with Perseus and the abolition of the Macedonian monarchy.

Polybius is here developing his "second introduction," in the first few chapters of Book 3, in which he goes on to explain that, after all, he has changed his mind about the terminal date. It was not now to be, in modern terms, 168 B.C., but 146. For his secondary purpose would be to examine how the Romans had used the power that they had gained, and the new terminal point would be the destruction of Carthage and the disaster which happened in Greece in the same year: "the withdrawal of the Macedonians from their alliance with Rome and that of the Lacedaemonians from the Achaean League, and hereupon the beginning and end of the general calamity that overtook Greece."[1]

Artistically, it might be argued that it would have been better to keep to the original plan, to cover the period (221/0–168 B.C.) in which "in not quite fifty-three years all parts of the *oikoumené* fell under the single rule (ἀρχή)

I am very grateful to Martin Goodman, Tessa Rajak and Geza Vermes for various forms of help, guidance and correction in the preparation of this paper.

1. The "second introduction" occupies Bk. 3.1–5. The passages quoted, from the Loeb translation, are 3.7–8 and 5.6.

of the Romans."[2]   The period had been one of rapid evolution, and the theme had coherence and dramatic force. As Peter Derow showed some years ago, what Polybius meant by ἀρχή was not the formation of Roman provinces, but the developing capacity to defeat some peoples or rulers and give instructions to others.[3]   Both aspects of Roman domination are perfectly exemplified in the book (29) which would have formed the original conclusion: the defeat of Perseus at the battle of Pydna, and the famous scene outside Alexandria when the Roman *legatus*, Popilius Laenas, ordered the Seleucid king Antiochus IV Epiphanes to abandon the siege of the city and go home.[4] Polybius could not of course know that, in historiographical terms, this moment had already acquired a significance even greater than it manifestly had as a historical event. For the author of Daniel had already made it the latest event to be recorded in the Hebrew Bible (11.30): "For the ships of Chittim will come against him; therefore he will be disheartened and return."

The connections and contrasts between Polybius and Daniel are far more profound, however, than this accidental conjunction. In Polybius' conception of history, the Romans were seen as taking their place in a succession of world rulers: first the Persians, then the Spartans, then the Macedonians and now the Romans (1.2). Moreover, it was in his originally planned final book, 29, that Polybius included an extended quotation of the reflections of Demetrius of Phalerum, meditating on the destruction of the Persian Empire by Alexander:[5]

> For if you consider not countless years or many generations, but merely the last fifty years, you will read in them the cruelty of Fortune. I ask you, do you think that fifty years ago either the Persians and the Persian king or the Macedonians and the king of Macedon, if some god had foretold the future to them, would ever have believed that at the time when we live, the very name of the Persians would have perished utterly—the Persians who were masters of almost the whole world—and that the Macedonians, whose name was formerly almost unknown, would now be the lords of it all?

The idea that the history of mere "events" was something superficial or insignificant would have amazed Demetrius and his contemporaries in the Greek world, just as it would have surprised later observers in the Near East who reflected on the devastating impact of Alexander's conquests. One such

2. Polybius 1.1.
3. P. Derow, "Polybius, Rome and the East," *JRS* 69 (1979) 1–15.
4. Polybius 29.27.
5. Polybius 29.21.3–4, Loeb translation.

was the author of 1 Maccabees, writing (almost certainly) some time towards the end of the second century B.C. His work opens as follows:[6]

> And it came to pass after the victory of Alexander the son of Philip the Macedonian, who came from the land of Chittim (ἐκ τῆς γῆς Χεττιμ), that he smote Darius, king of the Persians and Medes, and ruled in his stead, beginning in Greece. He waged many wars and captured strongholds and slew (the) kings of the land. He pressed forward to the ends of the earth and took spoils from a multitude of peoples, and the earth was silent before him, and he was exalted and his heart filled with pride.

We can assume that in Judaea itself Alexander's passage, from Tyre down the coast to Egypt, will have made a corresponding impact. The only detailed narrative reflection of it from a Jewish perspective which we have, however, is a legend, or perhaps better a religious historical novella, which Josephus incorporated in Book 11 of his *Antiquities*.[7]

We shall return briefly later to the significance of Josephus' use here of Daniel, which in fact had not yet been written. It is more important to stress at this point that the still developing corpus of Biblical works did incorporate a reasonably complete historical narrative, or series of narratives, relating the impact on the Jewish community of a succession of Near Eastern empires, going back through the Persian empire of the Achaemenids to the Babylonian and Assyrian empires. To go no further back, the book of Kings contained a historical narrative from the end of King David's reign to the Babylonian Captivity. The two books of Chronicles retold the story from the time of Saul onwards, continuing to a rather brief account of the Captivity, and ending triumphantly with the victory of Cyrus over the Babylonian dynasty (539 B.C.) and the return from the Captivity:[8]

> In the first year of Cyrus king of Persia (KWRŠ MLK PRS)—to fulfil the word of Yahweh through Jeremiah—Yahweh roused the spirit of Cyrus king

---

6. 1 *Macc.* 1.1. The sequence of tenses in this section is not clear, and the translation is hypothetical. For a basic discussion of 1 Macc., generally thought to be a Greek version of a Hebrew or Aramaic original, see E. Schürer, *History of the Jewish People*, ed. G. Vermes, F. Millar and M. Goodman, vol. 3.1 (Edinburgh, 1986) 180–85. A relatively early date of writing, of around 130 B.C., is argued by S. Schwartz, "Israel and the Nations Roundabout: 1 Maccabees and the Hasmonean Expansion," *JournJewStud* 42 (1991) 1–38.

7. Josephus, *Ant.* 11.8.1–9 (304–47); Loeb translation of 8.5 (336). See e.g. A. D. Momigliano, "Flavius Josephus and Alexander's Visit to Jerusalem," *Athenaeum* 57 (1979) 442–48 = *Settimo contributo alla storia degli studi classici e del mondo antico* (Rome, 1984) 319–29.

8. 2 Chron. 36.22–23, trans. *New Jerusalem Bible*.

of Persia to issue a proclamation and to have it publicly displayed throughout his kingdom: "Cyrus king of Persia says this: 'Yahweh, the God of Heaven, has given me all the kingdoms of the earth and has appointed me to build him a Temple in Jerusalem, which is in Judah. Whoever there is among you of all his people, may his God be with him! Let him go up.'"

As is evident, Chronicles could not have been written as it stands before the Achaemenid period, and it is sometimes argued that it was written, or edited, as late as the early Hellenistic period. The same must apply to the book of Ezra (which begins with a slightly extended version of the same proclamation by Cyrus) and of Nehemiah, which between them relate, within a structure which is chronologically confused and not mutually related as between the two books, the restoration of the Temple and the re-establishment of Jewish worship and observances under the Achaemenids, thus taking the story to some (now indeterminable) point in the fifth century.[9]

An alternative version of the same story (but equally confused in its conception of the sequence of Persian kings) was constructed at some time in the Hellenistic period, using material found also in 2 Chronicles, Ezra, and Nehemiah, and provides a continuous narrative going from Josiah to Ezra. This is the important and highly puzzling text called 1 Esdras, which may have been composed originally in Hebrew or Aramaic, but certainly existed in Greek by the time of Josephus, who used it for his *Antiquities*.[10]

Its significance in this context is simply as another sign of awareness within Jewish culture of the national tradition as a historical narrative, and as one whose course had been dependent on the attitudes and actions of a succession of external rulers. Such an awareness was quite compatible with a lack of complete clarity as to which ruler had succeeded which, or even as to which empire had been which. It was this sometimes confused impression of a sequence of empires and rulers which provided the framework for a group of three religiously-inspired historical novels, one of which, Esther, was to be incorporated in the Hebrew Bible, while Tobit and Judith appeared in the Christian Bible in Greek, which we refer to for convenience as the Septuagint.[11] (In consequence, all three appear in Catholic Bibles, but only Esther in Protestant ones.) Tobit is set in the Assyrian empire of the eighth to

9. See O. Eissfeldt, *The Old Testament* (Oxford, 1965) 529f. (Chronicles); 541f. (Ezra and Nehemiah); H. G. M. Williamson, *The New Century Bible Commentary: 1 and 2 Chronicles* (Grand Rapids, Michigan, 1982); idem, *World Biblical Commentary* 16: *Ezra, Nehemiah* (Waco, Texas, 1985).

10. For a detailed survey of the problems see E. Schürer, *op. cit.* (n. 6), vol. 3.2 (1987) 708–18.

11. See the fundamental article by M. Hengel, to which I am extremely indebted, "Die Septuaginta als 'christliche Schriftensammlung': Ihre Vorgeschichte und das Problem

seventh century. The hero is introduced as one who "in the days of Shalmaneser king of the Assyrian empire was carried away captive out of Thisbe which is on the right hand of Kedesh Naphtali in Upper Galilee." Thenceforward he lived in Nineveh, in the reigns of Shalmaneser (V), Sennacherib and Esarhaddon (the sequence is historical, if incomplete, the respective dates being 726–722, 704–681 and 680–669 B.C.). The full text of Tobit survives only in Greek, but it is of crucial importance that fragments in Aramaic, with one in Hebrew, have been found in Qumran.[12] The work is thus almost certainly a Semitic-language composition of the early Hellenistic period.

Judith, by contrast, confuses the Assyrian and Babylonian Empires: "It was in the twelfth year of Nebuchadnezzar who reigned over the Assyrians in the great city of Nineveh." The historical Nebuchadnezzar was of course a Babylonian king (see p. 99 below). There is no trace of the (probable) Semitic original of the Greek text of Judith; and only general arguments from the religious and nationalistic tone of the story of Judith and Holofernes might perhaps suggest that it *could* belong in the Maccabean period.[13]

As for Esther, if we ignore an inept introductory paragraph added to the Greek version, which confuses the Persian and Babylonian empires (as does indeed a reference to Esther's father in 2.5–6), it is firmly set in the Persian empire, in the reign of a king 'HŠWRWŠ (Ahasuerus-Artaxerxes), who ruled from Susa over an empire which stretched from India to Kush, and who had an army of Persians and Medes (ḤYL PRS WMDY). The whole story of Esther is re-told in detail by Josephus in the *Antiquities*, where it is set in the fifth century.[14] As a literary work, it was certainly in existence by the second century B.C. at the latest. A note at the end of the Greek version claims that one Dositheos had "brought" the letter concerning Purim (described in 9.20–22) in the fourth year of Ptolemy and Cleopatra, after it had been translated by Lysimachus, a Jerusalemite. If this reference is authentic, and not merely a piece of pseudo-historical colouring, the date referred to is 88/7 B.C. There are no known fragments from Qumran, making this the only book of the Hebrew Bible not represented there.[15]

ihres Kanons," in M. Hengel and A. M. Schwemer, eds., *Die Septuaginta zwischen Judentum und Christentum* (Tübingen, 1994) 182–284.

12. For Tobit see R. H. Charles, *Apocrypha and Pseudepigrapha of the Old Testament*, vol. 1 (Oxford, 1913) 174f.; P. Deselaers, *Das Buch Tobit* (Tübingen, 1982); Schürer, *op. cit.* (n. 6), vol. 3.1 (1986) 222f. (pp. 224–45 for Qumran fragments 4Q 196–200, to be edited by J. A. Fitzmyer in *Documents from the Judaean Desert* 19, *Parabiblical Texts*, Part 2).

13. See Charles, *op. cit.*, 174f.; Eissfeldt, *op. cit.*, 585f.; Schürer, *op. cit.*, 216f.

14. Josephus, *Ant.* 11.6.1–13 (184–296).

15. For Esther see Eissfeldt, *op. cit.*, 505f., and 591–92 (the additions). For the additions see also Schürer, vol. 3.2, 718f.

The establishment of the feast of Purim thus was, or was made into, the central point of this vivid court-narrative, and this feature is reflected clearly in 2 Maccabees, surely written in the second half of the second century B.C. This book ends with the defeat of the Seleucid general Nicanor in 161 B.C., and the decision to celebrate the "day of Nicanor" on the thirteenth of Adar, on the day before "the day of Mordechai": τὴν τρισκαιδεκάτην τοῦ δωδεκάτου μηνός—Ἀδαρ λέγεται τῇ Συριακῇ φωνῇ—πρὸ μιᾶς ἡμέρας τῆς Μαρδοχαϊκῆς ἡμέρας: "the thirteenth day of the twelfth month—it is called Adar in the Syrian language—one day before the day of Mordechai."[16] Purim was thus already established as a festival, and was already associated with the story of Esther, Haman and Mordechai. Esther is thus (perhaps) roughly contemporary with Daniel, or might be as much as a couple of centuries earlier. It shares with Daniel the use of history, and the deployment of an alien court as a stage for the demonstration of Jewish piety.

II. THE BOOK OF DANIEL

These varied works, for all the problems of date, authorship, intention and original language which they present, are enough to set the framework for Daniel, and to suggest how the successive Near Eastern empires, and the relationship of the Jewish community to them, could be used in Jewish historical and semi-historical works of the late Achaemenid and earlier Hellenistic period, in ways which ranged from sequential narratives of events to colourful and improving historical novels.

As will be obvious, this paper will make no attempt even to indicate all the problems which surround Daniel: the question, for instance, of whether there had been earlier versions before the (indisputable) redaction of the canonical Hebrew and Aramaic text in the 160s B.C.; the meanings intended by the anonymous author to be attached to the symbols incorporated in the dreams and visions which it recounts; whether even after the 160s variant "Daniel" texts were in circulation; the dates and origins of the two established Greek versions; and the interpretation of the text in the New Testament, in Josephus, by Christian commentators, such as Hippolytus and Jerome, or by Daniel's brilliant pagan commentator, Porphyry. All that is intended here is to set out the most elementary facts and then to present an analysis of the structure of the text that will show just how detailed a use it makes of Near Eastern history from the sixth century up to the 160s B.C.

As for the date and context of the canonical Daniel as we have it, no serious commentator would now question Porphyry's demonstration that

---

16. 2 Macc. 15.36.

the work belongs in the 160s under Antiochus IV Epiphanes, and that up to and including that point the prophecies in it are pseudo-prophecies, relating and giving meaning to events which had already occurred. At the time when the author was completing the work, the imposition of the "abomination of desolation" in 167 had occurred, and the restoration of the Temple cult in 164 had not.[17] The "reception" of Daniel is a topic which could take many volumes and is integral to early Christianity, in particular to the notion of Jesus as a "Son of Man" (see briefly p. 103 below). But it may be noted that stories which form part of "our" Daniel are alluded to in 1 Maccabees, which (as above) dates to the later second century B.C., or (less probably) to the early first. In the "testament of Mattathias" in 1 Maccabees 2, recounting historical examples of pious Jews, there appear (2.59) Ananias, Azarias and Misael saved from the furnace (cf. Daniel 3); and (2.60) Daniel saved from the lion (cf. Daniel 6). Similar allusions appear in 3 Maccabees (perhaps of the first century B.C.) and 4 Maccabees (probably of the first century A.D.).[18]

Much more important still is the fact that actual fragments of the canonical Daniel (as well as other Daniel-like prophetic fragments) are known from Qumran and would thus count among the textual attestations from the ancient world which are closest in time to the original composition.[19] The earliest of the Daniel fragments from Qumran Cave IV covers sections of chapters 10–11, and is thought to date from the late second century B.C., thus only some half a century after the composition of these chapters. The

17. For the essential treatments and bibliography see R. H. Charles, *A Critical and Exegetical Commentary on the Book of Daniel* (Oxford, 1929); F. L. Hartman and A. A. De Lella, *The Book of Daniel, Anchor Bible* 23 (New York, 1978); Schürer, *op. cit.*, vol. 3.1 (1986) 245f.; and now the massive commentary by J. J. Collins, *Daniel: A Commentary on the Book of Daniel* (Minneapolis, 1993). Note also E. Bickerman, *Four Strange Books of the Bible: Jonah, Daniel, Koheleth, Esther* (New York, 1987), and A. S. van der Woude, ed., *The Book of Daniel in the Light of New Findings* (Leuven, 1993). In this latter collection note esp. M. Delcor, "L'histoire selon le livre de Daniel, notamment au chapitre 11," 365–86, and C. C. Caragounis, "History and Supra-history: Daniel and the Four Empires," 387–97.

18. 3 Macc. 6 (the prayer of Eleazar): section 6 (three companions in Babylonia saved from furnace); and 7 (Daniel saved from lion). See J. H. Charlesworth, *Old Testament Pseudepigrapha*, vol. 2 (London, 1985) 509. Cf. 4 Macc. 13.9, 16.3, 16.21, 18.3. See E. Bickerman, "The Date of Fourth Maccabees," *Studies in Jewish and Christian History*, vol. 1 (Leiden, 1976) 276ff., Charlesworth, *op. cit.*, 531f.

19. See E. Ulrich, "Daniel Manuscripts from Qumran I," *BASOR* 268 (1987) 17–37; "II," *BASOR* 274 (1989) 3–26. Note in particular the Aramaic "son of God" fragment, discussed by G. Vermes in "Qumran Forum Miscellanea I," *JournJewStud* 43 (1992) 299–305, on pp. 301–303; translated in G. Vermes, *The Dead Sea Scrolls in English*[4] (London, 1995) 331–32.

fragments also confirm that the shift from Hebrew to Aramaic and back characteristic of the canonical Daniel (2.4b-7.28 is in Aramaic, the rest in Hebrew) was already present in the texts circulating in the late Hellenistic period. At some point which remains open to debate two different Greek translations were made, one of which came to be that which formed part of Christian *codices* of the Bible and is therefore labelled as the Septuagint-text— quite unhistorically, since the legendary account of the translation carried out by seventy-two elders under Ptolemy Philadelphus related only to the five books of Moses, and at that time (the third century B.C.) the canonical Daniel had not been written. The other is that ascribed to Theodotion, alleged to have worked in the second century A.D. But a text which was at any rate close to his is quoted by writers of the first century A.D. In particular, a "pre-Theodotion" version seems to lie behind some passages in the New Testament.[20] But it is futile to try to see the earliest history of the translation of Daniel into Greek in terms of specific and distinct "versions" represented in later manuscripts. For by far the most important known user of the Greek Daniel is Josephus, in Book 10 of the *Antiquities*, written in Rome in the 80s A.D.[21] His paraphrase of Daniel incorporates readings which are shared with either the "Septuagint" text or the "Theodotion" one, or with neither.[22]

It is in fact not unlikely that Daniel had been translated into Greek, perhaps more than once, as early as the later Hellenistic period, as we know was the case with Esther (p. 93 above) and with the *Wisdom* of Ben Sira (Ecclesiasticus).[23] But all we can be certain of is that it was in circulation in Hebrew and Aramaic by the end of the second century B.C., and in Greek also by the first century A.D..

20. For these questions, which I do not attempt to go into further, see M. Harl, G. Dorival and O. Munnich, *La Bible grecque des Septante* (Paris, 1988), and the important article by M. Hengel, *op. cit.*, n. 11 above. I am very grateful to Tessa Rajak for allowing me to see the text of her unpublished paper "The Jewish Reception of the LXX in the First and Second Centuries A.D.: Some Thoughts on Josephus and LXX Daniel."

21. *Ant.* 10.10.1–6 (186–218); 11.2–7 (229–81). See most recently G. Vermes, "Josephus' Treatment of the Book of Daniel," *JournJewStud* 47 (1991) 149–66, and S. Mason, "Josephus, Daniel and the Flavian House," in F. Parente and J. Sievers, eds., *Josephus and the History of the Greco-Roman Period* (Leiden, 1994) 161–91.

22. See J. Ziegler, ed., *Susanna, Daniel: Bel et Draco* (Göttingen Septuagint, vol. 16.2, 1954) 22. As does Rahlfs in his standard edition, Ziegler prints both texts.

23. See the *Wisdom* of Ben Sira, *prol.* 27–30: ἐν γὰρ τ᾽ ὀγδόῳ καὶ τριακόστ᾽ ἔτει ἐπὶ τοῦ Εὐεργέτου βασιλέως παραγενηθεὶς εἰς Αἴγυπτον ... ἀναγκαιότατον ἐθέμην καὶ αὐτός τινα προσενέγκασθαι σπουδὴν καὶ φιλοπονίαν τοῦ μεθερμηνεῦσαι τήνδε τὴν βίβλον. The year is 132 B.C.

Josephus, as we saw earlier in relation to Alexander's legendary visit to Jerusalem (p. 91 above), accepted "Daniel" as a historical personage of the sixth century B.C. living under the Babylonian Captivity, and hence treated his dreams and visions as genuinely prophetic. He thus equally took the references in Daniel to Antiochus Epiphanes as prophetic, and also understood the prophetic element as including the Roman Empire. Whether Josephus interpreted Daniel as specifically foretelling the destruction of the Temple in A.D. 70 is, unfortunately, unclear, owing to a problem in the text. According to a possible reconstruction of his text, Josephus wrote as follows:[24]

> And there would arise from their number a certain king who would make war on the Jewish nation and their laws, deprive them of the form of government based on these laws, spoil the temple and prevent the sacrifices from being offered for three years. And these misfortunes our nation did in fact come to experience under Antiochus Epiphanes, just as Daniel many years before saw and wrote that they would happen. In the same manner Daniel also wrote about the empire of the Romans and that Jerusalem would be taken by them and the temple laid waste.

Josephus' recognition that Daniel did indeed speak about Antiochus Epiphanes is however quite unambiguous, and he reverts to this point (which is not in his main source, 1 Maccabees) when he comes to relate Antiochus' desecration of the Temple in 167 B.C.:[25]

> Now the desecration of the temple came about in accordance with the prophecy of Daniel, which had been made four hundred and eight years before; for he had revealed that the Macedonians would destroy it.

He thus supplied nearly all the evidence for Porphyry's correct deduction that this prophecy was a pseudo-prophecy, but of course without drawing this conclusion himself.[26]

---

24. Josephus, *Ant.* 10.10.7 (275–76), Loeb trans. In the last sentence the equivalent of τὸν αὐτὸν δὲ τρόπον ὁ Δανίηλος γὰρ περὶ τῆς Ῥωμαίων ἡγεμονίας ἀνέγραψε, καὶ ὅτι ὑπ' αὐτῶν [αἱρεθήσεται τὰ Ἱεροσόλυμα καὶ ὁ ναὸς] ἠρεμωθήσεται is omitted in the Latin version. The words bracketed are supplied only from John Chrysostom, *Adv. Iudaeos* 5.8 (Migne, *PG* XLVIII, col. 897). See R. Wilken, *John Chrysostom and the Jews* (Berkeley, 1983), esp. 134f.

25. *Ant.* 12.7.6 (322), Loeb trans.

26. Porphyry's argument is preserved in Jerome's *Commentary on Daniel, Corpus Christ. Lat.* LXXVA, p. 771; the relevant passage is reproduced and translated in M. Stern, *Greek and Latin Authors on Jews and Judaism*, vol. 2 (Jerusalem, 1980) no. 464A.

III. DANIEL: NARRATIVE STRUCTURE

It was a pseudo-prophecy, however, and Daniel does preserve for us a unique representation, written in the mid-Hellenistic period, of how Jewish piety and religious knowledge had been deployed under a series of foreign empires, Babylonian, Persian and Macedonian, over a period of four hundred years. The following tabulation makes no attempt to go into interpretative details, but is concerned to do two things: to make clear the literary structure of the work, which means primarily the relationship between "authorial voice" (first person and third person), narrative and interpretation; and to set out summarily the real identities and dates of the rulers to whom the work refers.[27]

It will be seen that in form and character the work divides into four distinct sections. In (1), covering chapters 1–6, a series of narratives, in the third person, with no identified narrator, and designed to demonstrate the operation of Jewish piety, are interspersed with dreams and portents external to Daniel, which are then provided with interpretations by him. In (2), covering chapters 7–10—or perhaps better chapters 7–8, with chapters 9–10 forming a sort of transition to (3)—Daniel himself has very detailed prophetic dreams, occasionally described in the third person (7.1; 10.1), but related by him in the first person, whose interpretation, in even greater detail, is supplied first by an anonymous figure to whom he turns (7.16), and then by Gabriel (8.17). Chapters 9–10 move on to prayers by Daniel and to exchanges between Gabriel and Daniel, both related by Daniel in the first person. Section (3) covers chapter 11.1–34, and contains a continuous series of historical prophecies addressed to Daniel by an angelic being who is not specifically named (11.1: W'TH 'MT 'GYD LK / καὶ νῦν ἀλήθειαν ἀναγγελῶ σοι ["Theodotion"]—"and now I will declare to you the truth"). The literary structure of this section is quite different, in that there is no division between the material and its interpretation. The narrative, interspersed with interpretation and comment by the same speaker, covers nearly four centuries, from the beginning of the Achaemenid period to the middle of the reign of Antiochus Epiphanes.

Finally, there is section (4), covering chapter 11.35 to the end of chapter 12, the only truly prophetic part of the whole work, which looks forward, in very significant style, to events which really had not yet occurred (and never did).

---

27. For these identifications, and the historical framework in general, see now Amélie Kuhrt, *The Ancient Near East c. 3000–330 B.C.*, vols. 1 and 2 (London, 1995). Volume 2 covers, among other things, the Neo-Assyrian Empire (ch. 9), Babylonia ca. 900–539 (ch. 11), and the Achaemenid Empire (ch. 13).

In literary structure, however, this section is continuous with (3) and is also placed in the mouth of the same angelic being.

Section (1)

Narrative; dreams and visions	Interpretations
Ch. 1 Capture of Jerusalem by Nebuchadnezzar (II) of Babylon [604–562 B.C.]. Daniel, Hananiah, Mishael and Azariah selected for court service. They refuse royal rations. This continues to "first year of Cyrus" [539 B.C.].	
Ch. 2 Year "2" of Nebuchadnezzar. His dream.	
	Daniel interprets dream: image of gold, silver, brass, iron; indicates four successive kingdoms, to be followed by eternal kingdom.
Ch. 3 Nebuchadnezzar sets up golden image. Hananiah (Shedrach), Mishael (Meshach) and Azariah (Abednego) refuse to worship. Placed in furnace, saved. Nebuchadnezzar orders all to respect their God.	
Ch. 4 Nebuchadnezzar's dream of tree (related in first person).	
	Daniel interprets: dream portends Nebuchadnezzar's expulsion from kingdom, to live in fields.
Nebuchadnezzar is expelled and then restored, and worships God (related in third, then first, person).	
Ch. 5 Feast of Belshazzar, "son" of Nebuchadnezzar [= Bel-shar-uṣur, ruling in Babylon as "royal prince" in the absence of his father, Nabonidus (555–539 B.C.)]. Vessels from Temple used. Writing on the wall.	

Section (1) *(continued)*

Narrative; dreams and visions	*Interpretations*
	Daniel interprets writing: kingdom to be given to Medes and Persians (MDY WPRS).
Belshazzar killed. Kingdom taken by "Darius the Mede" [in fact by Cyrus, 539 B.C.].	
Ch. 6 Darius forbids prayer to man or god, except himself. Daniel prays all the same. Thrown to lions, saved. Darius orders observance of Daniel's God. Daniel prospers in reign of Darius (I?) [522–486 B.C.] and Cyrus [539/30 B.C.].	

Section (2)

Narrative; dreams and visions	*Interpretations*
Ch. 7 Daniel's dream of four beasts; 4th beast with 10 horns, and 11th which destroys 3 of others. Day of judgement. Beast (4th?) slain. Reign of one "like a son of man" (KBR 'NŠ, 7.13).	
	Interpretation given *to* Daniel by unnamed person (7.16). Four kings/kingdoms. 10 kings of 4th kingdom. Persecution by 11th. Dominion to be given to "the people of the saints of the most high" ('M QDYŠY 'LYWNYN, 7.27).
Ch. 8 Daniel's dream (in "year 3 of Belshazzar"). Ram, defeated by goat from west. His horn broken, and replaced by four horns. From one of them comes little horn, who magnifies himself, and destroys daily sacrifice (TMYD, 8.11) and sanctuary.	

Section (2) *(continued)*

Narrative; dreams and visions	*Interpretations*
	Interpretation given *to* Daniel by Gabriel (named in 8.17): ram is king of Media and Persia (MDY WPRS); goat is king of Greece (MLK YWN) [Alexander, 336–323 B.C.]. Four kingdoms. Then persecuting king [Antiochus Epiphanes, 175–164 B.C.].
Ch. 9 Daniel's vision (in year 1 of Darius "son of Ahasuerus" (DRYWŠ BN 'ḤŠWRWŠ) [522 B.C.? Or Darius II, 423–405 B.C.?]; he understands Jeremiah's prediction of 70-year desolation of Jerusalem. Daniel's prayer. Gabriel appears to Daniel, predicts cessation of sacrifice and offering, and imposition of "abomination of desolation" (ŠQWṢYM MŠMM / βδέλυγμα τῶν ἐρημώσεων, 9.27).	
Ch. 10 Year 3 of Cyrus king of Persia (KWRŠ MLK PRS) [537 B.C.?]. Daniel's vision of angel (not named), and then of (different?) person "like a son of man" (KDMWT BNY 'DM, 10.16, cf. 7.13). Latter announces prophecy, "what is written in the book of truth" (BKTB 'MT, 10.21).	

Section (3)

Ch. 11	1–2	The same person (angel?) prophesies course of events from Darius "the Mede" (or Cyrus, as in LXX and "Theodotion"). Three more kings in Persia (LPRS). Fourth [Xerxes, 486–465 B.C.?] will attack "all the kingdom of Greece" (HKL 'T MLKWT YWN).
	3	Mighty king will arise [Alexander].
	4	Kingdom divided into four [early Hellenistic monarchies].
	5	Strength of "king of south" (MLK HNGB) [Ptolemy I, 306–285 B.C.].

6   Marriage of daughter of king of south to king of north (MLK
         HṢPWN). Marriage breaks down. [Berenice, daughter of Ptolemy II
         Philadelphus, marries Antiochus II Theos, ca. 252 B.C.]

7–8   Invasion by "king of south." Spoils carried to Egypt (MṢRYM).
         [Ptolemy III Euergetes, 247–222 B.C., and Third Syrian War, 246–
         241 B.C.; for spoils, cf. Adoulis inscription, 238 B.C., *OGIS* 54; Canopus
         decree, *OGIS* 56.]

11–12   Victory of "king of south" over "king of north." [Ptolemy IV defeats
         Antiochus III at Raphia, 217 B.C.]

13–17   Conquests by "king of north." [Conquest of Coele Syria and Pales-
         tine by Antiochus III, 202/1–200 B.C.]

17   Marriage-alliance between kings. [Cleopatra, daughter of Anti-
         ochus III, marries Ptolemy V Epiphanes, 194/3 B.C.]

18   (King of north) turns to isles. Frustrated. [(?) Antiochus III, in Asia
         Minor, Greece, conflict with Rome, defeat at Magnesia, treaty of
         Apamea, 192–188 B.C.]

19   Return; death. [Death of Antiochus III in Elymais, 187 B.C.]

20   His successor, death of. [Seleucus IV Philopator, 187–175 B.C.]

21–34   "King of north" invades kingdom of south, returns, action against
         holy covenant. Second invasion, stopped by "ships of Kittim"
         (ṢYYM KTYM, 11.30). Action against sanctuary, suppression of
         daily sacrifice (TMYD), imposition of "the abomination of deso-
         lation" (ŠQWṢ MŠMM / βδέλυγμα ἐρημώσεως). Resistance be-
         gins. [Antiochus IV Epiphanes 175–164 B.C. Invasion of Egypt,
         170/169 B.C. Second invasion, 168 B.C., stopped by Roman emissary,
         Popilius Laenas. Suppression of Temple cult, 167 B.C. Maccabean
         revolt begins.]

Section (4)

35–45   Prophecies of prospective last part of Antiochus' reign. Angel
         Michael, delivery of Israel. Resurrection and Day of Judgement.

5–13   Daniel reports final vision and message.

11   From cessation of daily sacrifice (TMYD) and imposition of "abom-
         ination of desolation" (ŠQWṢ ŠMM / τὸ βδέλυγμα [τῆς] ἐρη-
         μώσεως) 1290 days.

IV. CONCLUSION: DANIEL AND HISTORY

Many aspects of the text of Daniel, heavily loaded with often enigmatic
symbols and with religious meaning, have an important place in the history
of Judaism and Christianity. It is only necessary to note, first, the earliest
unambiguous appearance in Jewish literature of the notions of a day of

judgement and of the resurrection of the virtuous (12.2: "Of those who lie sleeping in the dust of the earth many will awake, some to everlasting life, some to shame and everlasting disgrace").[28] Second, there is the (highly enigmatic) symbolism of the one "like a son of man" (KBR 'NŠ) seen "coming on the clouds of heaven" (7.13–14), whose relevance to New Testament imagery is obvious.[29]

My concern here is however only to stress, firstly, how closely integrated the various sections of Daniel are one with another, and to suggest how profoundly they are related to the Maccabean crisis. Cyrus is mentioned already in 1.21, and the Medes and Persians appear first in 5.28, while the Hellenistic monarchies and Antiochus Epiphanes are mentioned already in chapters 7–8. In chapter 9 we have the first of three appearances (9.27, 11.31, 12.11) of the suppression of the daily sacrifice in the Temple (TMYD) and the imposition of the "abomination of desolation." Equally important, even the earlier part of the work is dominated by concerns over the personal observation of Judaism, concerns which it is tempting to interpret as reflecting the strains imposed by the persecution under Antiochus from 167 B.C. onwards, which was noteworthy for being directed not only at the Temple cult, but at the private observance of Judaism.[30] Hence there are references to the avoidance of unclean food (ch. 1); the worship of pagan gods (ch. 3); and the offering of prayers to deities, or supposed deities (ch. 6). In spite of the drastic successive shifts in "authorial voice," literary form and narrative structure which characterise this quite brief work, it may be suggested that in its conceptions and concerns it can be seen as a unity, and one which reflects the great crisis of the 160s.

For historians of the Classical world, however, what is most distinctive and significant about Daniel is the representation, through the medium of narratives, dreams and prophecies, of a succession of Near Eastern empires, in steadily increasing detail and accuracy, from the Neo-Babylonian empire through Achaemenid Persia to Alexander, and then to the Seleucids and Ptolemies. Viewed literally, there are in these representations various mistakes, misidentifications and transpositions. But, taken as a series, the

28. See G. W. E. Nickelsburg, *Resurrection, Immortality and Eternal Life in Intertestamental Judaism* (Cambridge, Mass., 1972); E. P. Sanders, *Judaism: Practice and Belief 63 BCE–66 CE* (London and Philadelphia, 1992) 298f.

29. See e.g. M. Black, *An Aramaic Approach to Gospels and Acts*[3] (Oxford, 1967), App. E (G. Vermes); G. Vermes, *Jesus the Jew* (London, 1973) 160f.; Schürer, vol. 2 (1979) 488f.; C. Rowland, *The Open Heaven: A Study of Apocalyptic in Judaism and Early Christianity* (London, 1982); J. Ashton, *Understanding the Fourth Gospel* (Oxford, 1991) 337f.

30. For my view of this see "The Background to the Maccabean Revolution: Reflections on Martin Hengel's *Judaism and Hellenism*," *JournJewStud* 29 (1978) 1–21.

picture presented by Daniel is indeed that which Momigliano argued should
be seen as a borrowing from the Greek world, namely the notion of history
as a succession of world empires.[31] In terms of the subsequent history of
the world the issues which were stirred up by Antiochus' persecution and
the Maccabean counter-revolution, and which gave rise to the composition
of the book of Daniel as we have it, had a significance far greater than
any other aspect of the Hellenistic period. For it was in the persecution of
the 160s and the resistance to it that Jewish monotheism, its sacrificial cult
and the personal observances required of its adherents faced and survived
their greatest test. But even as regards ancient political history, and the
representation in literature of the successive regimes which had claimed
domination over the peoples of the Near East, Daniel can add a dimension
and the sense of a longer perspective which even Polybius was not in a position
to attach to those drastic swings of fortune which took place in 168 B.C., the
year at which his great work had originally been intended to end. But, as
history, Daniel's brief and allusive representations of selected episodes, taken
largely out of context and seen from a very precise and limited viewpoint,
cannot of course compare with Polybius' profound conception of how events
in different parts of the *oikoumené* had come to be interlinked and to form a
single causative sequence. For an understanding of Hellenistic history we
will still depend on Polybius, and on his greatest modern interpreter.

31. See A. D. Momigliano, "The Origins of Universal History," *AnnScNormSupPisa*,
ser. 3, 12.2 (1982) 533–60 = *On Pagans, Jews and Christians* (Middletown, Conn., 1987)
31–57.

FIVE

The Hellenistic World
and Roman Political Patronage

Jean-Louis Ferrary

This text is a revised version of a lecture which I had the honour to deliver in the Cambridge Ancient History seminar, when a programme on Hellenistic society and culture was organized in honour of Frank Walbank during the Lent term of 1993. I had just written my (still unpublished) report for the International Congress of Greek and Latin Epigraphy entitled "From Hellenistic to Roman euergetism," in which I also considered the problem of Roman political patronage in the Hellenistic world.[1] The first part of my argument will concern Greek cities and their Roman patrons, beginning with the epigraphic evidence; in the second part, I shall discuss the problem of patronage as a key to the interpretation of Roman policy in the Hellenistic World. My plan is in a way the opposite of Ernst Badian's in his *Foreign Clientelae*, but my conclusions will lead me to a point more or less halfway between the maximalist and minimalist interpretations of Ernst Badian and Erich Gruen on the importance of patronage in the Roman conquest of the Greek World and the history of the cities in the Republican period.[2]

I. GREEK CITIES AND THEIR ROMAN PATRONS

The Hellenistic World had a large vocabulary for benefactors or protectors of cities (*euergetes, soter, kedemon, ktistes, proxenos*). The introduction of the

1. I had already approached the subject in *Philhellénisme et impérialisme* (Rome, 1988), especially 117–32, and I thought a synthesis of my reflections and conclusions on this topic could be of interest for a seminar in the presence of Frank Walbank. I should like to thank Michael Crawford for improving my English text.

2. E. Badian, *Foreign Clientelae (264–70 B.C.)* (Oxford, 1958); E. S. Gruen, *The Hellenistic World and the Coming of Rome* (Berkeley, 1984), especially 158–200.

transliteration *patron* and of the derivatives *patroneia* and *patroneuein* cannot but mean that Greeks became aware of a character specific to Roman patronage. Louis Harmand's thesis on *Le patronat sur les collectivités publiques des origines au Bas-Empire* is of little use, and particularly inadequate with regard to Greek inscriptions.[3] Several papers of John Nicols[4] are to be followed by a book, *The patronage of communities in the Roman Empire*, mainly concerned with the Principate, and Claude Eilers' Oxford thesis on Roman patrons of Greek cities remains unpublished. At present, we have J. Touloumakos' article "Zum römischen Gemeindepatronat im griechischen Osten,"[5] but I cannot agree with many of his conclusions: e.g., that *patroneia*, in the eyes of the Greeks, primarily evokes the relationship between patron and freedman and implies a close dependence of the city on its patron; that a text such as *IGR* 4.968 proves that Roman patronage was imposed on the Hellenistic world by the Senate with the double aim of reminding Greek cities of their duties and of making Roman aristocrats give up traditional Hellenic honours; that such a policy, inspired by none other than Cato the Censor, eventually failed; that patronage was never able to supplant traditional Hellenic honours; that the scarcity of inscriptions with the precision πάτρων διὰ προγόνων implies that Roman patronage was unable to preserve its hereditary character in the Hellenic world; and that the Greeks never viewed Roman power as a form of *patroneia*.

In fact, *patron* and *patroneia* do not seem to appear in Greek inscriptions before the last third of the second century B.C., when the introduction of direct rule in Macedonia and part of Achaia (146), and later in Asia (129), greatly increased, even for free cities, the need to plead their cause before the Senate. From a famous decree of Abdera,[6] we know that the Ionian free city of Teos had patrons who agreed to intercede on behalf of Abdera, Teos' colony, when the Thracian king Kotys was litigating with Abdera over the ownership of territory, and the Senate had to arbitrate. This inscription was traditionally ascribed to the years immediately following the Third Macedonian War, but G. Chiranky has argued persuasively that the end

---

3. On this book (Paris, 1957), it suffices to refer to J. and L. Robert's remarks in *Bull. épigr.* (1959) no. 66.

4. J. Nicols, "Zur Verleihung öffentlicher Ehrungen in der römischen Welt," *Chiron* 9 (1979) 243–60; "Pliny and the Patronage of Communities," *Hermes* (1980) 365–85; "Tabulae Patronatus: A Study of the Agreement between Patron and Client-Community" *ANRW* 2.13 (1980) 535–61; "Patrons of Greek Cities in the Early Principate" and "Patrons of Provinces in the Early Principate: The Case of Bithynia," *ZPE* 80 (1990) 81–108.

5. *Hermes* 116 (1988) 304–24.

6. *Syll.*[3] 656. The text was improved by P. Herrmann, "Zum Beschluss von Abdera aus Teos Syll. 656," *ZPE* 7 (1971) 72–77.

of the second century provides a far better context.[7] An inscription found in the Heraion of Samos (another free city) honouring "Gnaeus Domitius son of Gnaeus, the patron assigned to the people by the Senate, and on behalf of the sanctuary of Artemis Tauropolos"[8] can be dated in the last third of the second century B.C.[9] It has recently been studied by Eilers,[10] with whom I agree that the patron (that is, the father of the Roman honoured) is the consul of 122 who had been legate in Asia in 129–126, and that *patroni datio ex s.c.* implies some legal proceedings involving Samos. Eilers suggests a *de repetundis* trial earlier than the Gracchan reform of 123/122, which is quite possible, but I would not exclude another possibility: that of a conflict between Samos and Roman *publicani* disputing the city's rights over the Ikarian sanctuary of Artemis Tauropolos. In any case, *patroni datio ex s.c.* should not be taken as an indication that the Senate imposed patronage on a reluctant Hellenic world. Samos evidently needed a patron to face the difficulties of Roman legal proceedings, and Cn. Domitius was probably appointed by the Senate both at the request of the city and with his own consent. Owing to the Senate's responsibility in this appointment, the city could hope that the patron would perform his duty, and the patron could hope that he would be less liable to *inuidia* while acting in the city's interest against a Roman senator or society of *publicani*.[11] The two decrees of the free city of Colophon discovered in Claros and recently published by Jeanne and Louis Robert can be ascribed to the period between the creation of the province of Asia and the First Mithridatic War: Menippos and Polemaios are both praised for becoming friends of Roman aristocrats and making them true patrons of the city.[12] Let us note that although these decrees were voted in honour of benefactor

7. G. Chiranky, "Rome and Cotys, Two Problems II: The date of *Sylloge*³, 656," *Athenaeum* 60 (1982) 470–81.

8. *IGR* 4.968: Γναῖον Δομέτιον Γναίου υἱόν, τοῦ δοθέντος ὑπὸ τῆς συνκλήτου πάτρωνος τῶι δήμωι, ὑπέρ τε τῶν κατὰ τὸ ἱερὸν τῆς Ἀρτέμιδος τῆς Ταυροπόλου; P. Herrmann, "Cn. Domitius Ahenobarbus, Patronus von Ephesos und Samos," *ZPE* 14 (1974) 257–58.

9. Delian statues of Antiochus Philopator before he laid claim to kingship (between 129 and 117) and of his *tropheus* Crateros were works of the same artist, Philotechnos of Samos: *I. Délos*, 1547–48.

10. C. P. Eilers, "Cn. Domitius and Samos: A New Extortion Trial," *ZPE* 89 (1991) 167–78.

11. See, for example, Liv. 43.2.3–6; Plin. *Epist.* 3.4.2–4 and 10.3a.1–2.

12. L. et J. Robert, *Claros I. Décrets hellénistiques* (Paris, 1989). Menippos, col. III, ll. 5–13 (p. 65): τοῖς μεγίστοις Ῥωμαίων συσταθείς […], τῆς τε πόλεως γνησίους πεποιηκὼς πάτρωνας ("commended to the greatest of the Romans, having made of them true patrons of the city"); Polemaios, col. II, ll. 24–31 (p. 13): ἐνέτυχεν μὲν τοῖς ἡγουμένοις Ῥωμαίοις καὶ φανεὶς ἄξιος τῆς ἐκείνων φιλίας τὸν ἀπὸ ταύτης καρπὸν

citizens and not of Roman aristocrats, patronage is clearly perceived in a positive way: not as a form of dependence, but as an instrument giving access to Roman authorities on behalf of the city. In these texts of the last third of the second century, patrons appear who use their influence in Rome, in senatorial debates or in legal proceedings.

Such situations, of course, occurred in earlier periods, and cities had patrons before the word *patron* was used in Greek inscriptions. In 189/8 Delphi conferred proxeny on T. Quinctius (Flamininus, cos. 198), L. Acilius (Balbus, praet. 197), and M. Aemilius Lepidus (praet. 191, cos. 187): the three names appear on a mere list of *proxenoi* with an indication of the date,[13] but the decree in honour of M. Aemilius Lepidus is fortunately preserved,[14] and the two proposers were on their way back from an embassy to Rome. In these circumstances, the traditional hypothesis that Flamininus, Acilius and Lepidus had helped them with advice and intervention in the Senate seems quite reasonable: these were services cities would expect from their *patrones* some decades later. Flamininus, Acilius and Lepidus had been preceded as *proxenoi* by Scipio Africanus at Delos in 193,[15] the same Africanus, his brother Lucius, another Scipio and L. Aemilius Regillus at Aptera in 189.[16] But Roman magistrates or senators are very rarely honoured or mentioned as *proxenoi* after 188: a descendant of L. Acilius is indicated by Daux as *proxenos* of Delphi in the second century,[17] but the inscription remains unpublished; a Cn. Aufidius, praetor and *proxenos* of Rhegion, is to be dated between 165 (since he does not appear in Livy's annual lists of praetors from 218 to 166) and the Social War.[18] More interesting, however, is a Rhodian inscription in honour of a citizen who was sent on missions to five Romans in the 90s and the 80s: two of them, L. Licinius Murena, imperator, and A. Terentius Varro, his legate, are called πρόξενος καὶ εὐεργέτης τοῦ δήμου.[19] As late as 83/81 the city of Rhodes did not think it was improper to honour as *proxenoi*

τοῖς πολείταις περιεποίησεν πρὸς τοὺς ἀρίστους ἄνδρας τῆι πατρίδι συνθέμενος πατρωνείας ("he approached the Roman leaders [probably on the occasion of one of his embassies to Rome] and, appearing worthy of their friendship, he made it fruitful for his fellow citizens, establishing for his fatherland bonds of patronage with the best people").

13. *Syll.*³ 585.

14. *FD* 3.4.427.

15. *IG* 9.4.712.

16. *IC* 2.3.5.

17. G. Daux, *Delphes au IIe et au Ier siècle* (Paris, 1936) 588.

18. *Syll.*³ 715.

19. *Syll.*³ 745. I shall study the identification of the first two magistrates of this list in my publication of the inscriptions found at Claros in honour of Romans.

a governor of Asia and one of his legates, although most of the cities reserved such a title for Romans of an inferior rank,[20] and it is probably not mere chance that the title *patron* is completely absent from Rhodian inscriptions, as it is also from Athenian ones. The proxeny conferred by Rhodes on Murena and Terentius Varro smacks of archaism, and it is quite possible that a few cities like Athens and Rhodes made it a point of honour to keep to Hellenic traditions. But many other cities, including free cities such as Samos, Teos or Colophon, *did* recognize Roman aristocrats as their patrons, or, more exactly, were eager to get them as their patrons.

The main difference between patronage and proxeny, to my mind, is that patronage is not only an honour awarded by the city, but also (and perhaps essentially, from the city's point of view) a commitment by the Roman aristocrat. As was shown by Wilhelm and later by Philippe Gauthier,[21] proxeny was never a real commitment; it was only a privileged status, by which a city rewarded a foreigner for his goodwill and demonstrated its hope that this foreigner would keep to his previous attitude. The specificity of patronage, already implied in the decrees found in Claros, is explicitly formulated in a letter of Q. Oppius to the city of Aphrodisias (ca. 85 B.C.), published by Joyce Reynolds: "the same ambassadors begged that you too should be allowed to enjoy my patronage. I accepted them because of my regard for your city and undertook the position of patron of your People."[22] The embassy of Aphrodisias and the answer of Oppius are quite in accord with the testimony of the *tabulae patronatus* found in the western part of the Roman world (e.g., "the decurions have decided that representatives from this order should be sent to T. Pomponius Bassus [. . .], instructed to obtain agreement that he would be pleased to accept our *municipium* into the *clientela* of his most eminent house and to be appointed patron").[23] As for patronage, the ultimate decision is that of the patron who agrees to commit himself, whereas if an embassy is sent after the vote of an honorific decree, it is only

20. E.g. Q. Calpurnius *eparchos*, commander of a garrison or *praefectus classis*, *proxenos* of Tenos at the end on the 2nd century (*IG* 12.5.841), or C. Cornelius, commander of a garrison and *proxenos* of Mesambria in 71 (*IGBR* I² 314a).

21. A. Wilhelm, "Proxenie und Euergesie," *Attische Urkunden* V, SBWien 220.5 (Vienna, 1942) 11–86; Ph. Gauthier, *Les cités grecques et leurs bienfaiteurs*, BCH Suppl. 12 (Athens, 1985), especially 131–49.

22. J. Reynolds, *Aphrodisias and Rome*, *JRS* Monograph 1, no. 3 (London, 1982) ll. 49–57: οἱ αὐτοὶ πρεσβεῖς παρεκάλεσαν ὅπως ἔξῃ τῇ [ἐ]μῇ πατρωνήᾳ καὶ ὑμεῖν χρῆσθαι. Τούτους ἐγὼ ἀνεδεξάμην, καταλογῆς ἕνεκεν τῆς ὑμετέρας πόλεως, ἐμὲ τοῦ δήμου τοῦ ὑμετέρου πάτρωνα ἔσεσθαι.

23. *ILS* 6106: *placere conscriptis legatos ex hoc ordine mitti ad T. Pomponium Bassum [. . .], qui ab eo impetrent in clientelam amplissimae domus suae municipium nostrum recipere dignetur patronumque se cooptari.*

to give the beneficiary notice of the decree and to urge him to maintain his benevolence towards the city (e.g., in a decree of the Amphictyonic League, honouring with proxeny Callistus of Cnidus, a friend of Caesar, in 48 B.C.: "that ambassadors should be appointed to give him notice of these honours and exhort him to keep the same benevolence towards all the Greeks").[24] Another Delphic inscription seems to be an exception to this rule. It was published as a decree of the city honouring a C. Sulpicius Galba with proxeny and citizenship in the years 20–5 B.C., but, according to J. Bousquet's supplements, an embassy was to be sent begging him to accept these honours: "that ambassadors should be appointed to exhort him to accept the honours voted for him."[25] Proxeny and citizenship, in this case, are nothing but supplements, and the whole decree probably requires new attention. It is not impossible that, in the age of Augustus, a decree conferring proxeny and citizenship on a Roman aristocrat would imitate some aspects of decrees begging Roman aristocrats to accept cities into their *clientela*. This would not invalidate the difference I emphasized between Greek traditional honours and typically Roman patronage. It is this difference that made it necessary for the Greeks to use the new words *patron* and *patroneia*. As for the frequent collocation *patron kai euergetes*, it was quite normal (for the Roman who agreed to become patron of a city was supposed to commit himself to being of some service), but of course it need not imply that *patron* and *euergetes* were one and the same thing.

Many inscriptions in honour of patrons are bases of statues erected while the patron was governor of the province (whether the city was part of the province or was a free city adjacent to the province). They begin to appear in the 90s B.C. and increase from the 60s. Of course, a city did not fail to honour its patron if he came to govern the province to which it belonged: when its patron M. Junius Silanus came as a governor of Asia in 76 B.C., the Carian city of Mylasa immediately dispatched an ambassador to meet him and persuade him to visit the city and see for himself its goodwill towards the proconsul and the Roman People.[26] But it cannot be doubted that cities frequently seized the opportunity of the provincial government of a Roman aristocrat to be included in his *clientela,* or tried to placate a

---

24. *Syll.*[3] 761A, ll. 23–25: ἑλέσθαι δὲ καὶ πρεσβευτὰς οἵτινες ἀποίσουσιν αὐτῷ τάσδε τὰς τιμὰς καὶ παρακαλοῦσιν αὐτὸν τὴν αὐτὴν διαφυλάσσειν πρὸς πάντας τοὺς Ἕλληνας εὔνοιαν.

25. *FD* 3.4.438B, ll. 5–8: [ἑλέσθαι δὲ] καὶ πρέσβεις [οἵτινες παρακαλέσουσιν αὐτὸν ταύ]τας δέξασθ[αι τὰς ἐψηφισμένας αὐτῶι τι]μάς. I adopt for these lines J. Bousquet's supplements, indicated in the apparatus criticus, rather than those of Cl. Vatin (*BCH*, 1972) 253–58, followed by J. Pouilloux.

26. *I. Mylasa* 109.

governor or a quaestor by begging him to become their patron. Inscriptions, unfortunately, cannot tell us whether a governor was approached just before he left his province by a city that had been able to test his benevolence and his efficacy, or whether the city thought it advisable to approach a new magistrate just after his arrival in the province. In this case, the original meaning of patronage was of course adulterated. The connection had a symbolic character or, rather, its pragmatic character decreased: the aim of the city was no longer to get powerful protectors to plead its cause in senatorial debates or judicial proceedings, but to limit the harm a magistrate might do during his proconsulship or quaestorship. It was a sort of short-term contract, since the client city, for its part, would hesitate to bear witness against its patron in a *de repetundis* trial. Such a development could make more understandable the paucity of inscriptions mentioning *patrones dia progonon*,[27] but perhaps we should admit that this precision was not systematically added on the bases erected for patrons, and, in any case, we should not rashly infer from such a scarcity that patronage was no longer hereditary in the Hellenic world. Let us read Cicero's letter to a governor of Asia: "Will you kindly regard the people of Nysa as specially recommended to your favour? Nero [the future father of Tiberius and of Drusus the Elder, who was to become quaestor two years later in 48] has the closest ties with them and is most active in championing their interests. So please let the commune understand that in Nero's patronage they have a most powerful protection. [. . .] With your backing, which I am sure will be and has already been forthcoming, he will be able to confirm the loyalty of the distinguished body of clients inherited from his ancestors and attach them by favours personal to himself."[28]

27. I know only eight *patrones dia* (or *apo*) *progonon* for the Republican and Augustan ages: L. Valerius Flaccus procos. (62 B.C.) in Claros (K. Tuchelt, *Frühe Denkmäler Roms in Kleinasien*, Ist. Mitt. Beiheft 23 [Tübingen, 1979] 164; I shall discuss the controversial identity of this Flaccus in my publication of these inscriptions from Claros); Sex. Pompeius Q. f. (son of Q. Pompeius Sex. f., known in 47–45 B.C. from Cic. *fam.*—13.49) in Thasus (J.-Y. Empereur and A. Simossi [*BCH*, 1994] 412–15); Cn. Domitius Ahenobarbus imp. (42–39 B.C.) in Ephesus (*I. Ephesos* 663); Cn. Domitius (? cos. 32 B.C.) in Samos (*IGR* 4.968; P. Herrmann, *ZPE* 14 [1974] 257–58); Messalla Potitus procos. (21–19 B.C.) in Magnesia ad Sipylum (*OGIS* 460; *IGR* 4.1338); Q. Aemilius Lepidus procos. (15–10 B.C.) in Halicarnassus (Le Bas-Waddington, 506); L. Calpurnius Piso (? cos. 1 B.C.) in Stratoniceia (*I. Stratonikeia* 1010); Drusus the Elder, brother of Tiberius, in Cnidus (*I. Knidos* 43), all of them members of the highest nobility.

28. Cic. *fam.* 13.64: *Nysaeos, quos Nero in primis habet necessarios diligentissimeque tuetur ac defendit, habeas tibi commendatissimos, ut intellegat illa ciuitas sibi in Neronis patrocinio summum esse praesidium. [. . .] Si te fautore usus erit, sicut profecto et utetur et usus est, amplissimas clientelas acceptas a maioribus confirmare poterit et beneficiis suis obligare* (trans. D. R. Shackleton Bailey).

Ti. Claudius Nero had inherited exceptionally large *clientelae* in the Hellenic world,[29] but the hereditary character of Asiatic *clientelae* is alluded to as a matter of course.

Identification of patrons is of course more difficult when there is no indication of a magistrature, but onomastic evidence leaves no doubt that in the Republican period they were members of senatorial families. One probable exception is L. Agrius Publianus Bassus, patron of Elaia,[30] who is generally identified with a L. Agrius, *eques Romanus*, mentioned by Cicero as bearing witness to the situation in Asia in 62 B.C. when L. Valerius Flaccus was governor, and with L. Agrius Publeianus honoured in Ephesus by *Italici quei Ephesi negotiantur*;[31] it is not mere chance that the city which chose as a patron this important businessman was the port of Pergamum. Interesting is also the use of πατρωνεύειν in inscriptions in honour of a L. Calpurnius L. f., a C. Cornelius C. f. or a L. Tillius L. f.;[32] these people, to my mind, acted in the interest of the cities in a way similar to that of a patron but had not the social status of a patron.

To conclude this first part of my paper, there was no desire by the Senate to substitute patronage for traditional Hellenic honours paid to benefactors. Patronage, unlike proxeny, was a real commitment, and for this reason, if the initiative came from the city, the final decision belonged to the Roman who agreed to take the city into his *clientela*. Patronage was added to the Hellenic system of services and honours, *euergesiai* and *timai*, without merging with it: every patron was necessarily a (real or virtual) *euergetes*, and received from the city honours usually paid to benefactors. But not all Roman *euergetai* were necessarily patrons (even *euergetai* receiving exceptional honours, like A. Aemilius Zosimus in Priene in the late 80s or 70s B.C.),[33] because patronage was largely reserved to magistrates or senators; other Romans had no opportunity to protect the interests of a city in a senatorial debate or to abstain from excessive harshness as provincial governors. Patronage was not rejected by the Hellenic world; at most, a few great cities like Rhodes or Athens avoided giving such a title to the Romans they honoured. The progressive disappearance during the reign of Augustus of patronage of

29. See E. Rawson, "The Eastern *Clientelae* of Clodius and the Claudii," *Historia* 22 (1973) 219–39, and "More on the *Clientelae* of the Patrician Claudii," *Historia* 26 (1977) 340–57 (= *Roman Culture and Society* [Oxford, 1991] 102–24 and 227–44).

30. *IGR* 4.271.

31. Cic. *Flacc.* 13.31; *I. Ephesos* 2058. See C. Nicolet, *L'ordre équestre à l'époque républicaine*, II: *Prosopographie des chevaliers romains*, BÉFAR 207 (Paris, 1974) 769, no. 15.

32. *I. Ephesos* 630b (80s B.C.); *IGBR* I² 314a (Mesambria, 74 B.C.); *SGDI* 2688 (Delphi, first decades of the 1st cent. B.C.).

33. *I. Priene* 112–14.

communities exercised by magistrates or members of the *nobilitas*[34] was a direct consequence of the monarchical character of the Principate. This character of the Principate was immediately perceived in the Greek world and ruined the foundations of a category of patronage that had been linked with the oligarchic character of senatorial government.

II. PATRONAGE AND ROMAN POLICY IN THE HELLENISTIC WORLD

Touloumakos puts forward as the first argument for his theory of a failure of patronage in the Hellenic world the fact that "the Greeks never term Roman power *patroneia*, whereas in Latin sources (Cicero, Livy) Roman power is called *patrocinium* of the oikoumene (*orbis terrae*) of the Greeks or other peoples."[35] The second part of this statement needs some qualification. Touloumakos refers of course to three well known texts of Cicero and Livy:[36]

> as long as the empire of the Roman people maintained itself by acts of service, not of oppression, wars were waged in the interest of our allies or to safeguard our supremacy; the end of our wars was marked by acts of clemency or by only a necessary degree of severity; the senate was a haven of refuge for kings, tribes and nations; and the highest ambition of our magistrates and generals was to defend our provinces and allies with justice and honour. And so our government could be called more accurately a *patrocinium* of the world than a dominion.[37]

34. Of course, that does not mean that patronage of communities disappeared. A new and important category of patrons were native magnates who became knights and then senators, that is, members of the imperial aristocracy. R. P. Saller (*Personal Patronage under the Early Empire* [Cambridge, 1982] 145–204) analyses patronage and provincials in North Africa during this period, but we should note that most of the inscriptions tabulated are related to the patronage of individuals, not of communities. However, as we shall see in the second part of this paper, patronage of individuals could be of great importance for communities also.

35. J. Touloumakos, *Hermes* 116 (1988) 318. On the Roman (including Ciceronian) real conception of empire, see P. A. Brunt, "*Laus imperii*," now reprinted in *Roman Imperial Themes* (Oxford, 1990) 288–323.

36. Other texts alluded to are irrelevant with respect to patronage: *Rhet. Her.* 4.13; Cic. *har. resp.* 19; *rep.* 3.35; Liv. 7.30.18; 9.20.10; 34.49.11.

37. Cic. *de off.* 2.27: *uerum tamen quamdiu imperium populi Romani beneficiis tenebatur, non iniuriis, bella aut pro sociis aut de imperio gerebantur, exitus erant bellorum aut mites aut necessarii, regum, populorum, nationum portus erat et refugium senatus, nostri autem magistratus imperatoresque ex hac una re maximam laudem capere studebant, si prouincias, si socios aequitate et fide defendissent. Itaque illud patrocinium orbis terrae uerius quam imperium poterat nominari* (trans. W. Miller).

The Roman people considers it an obligation imposed by its loyalty and consistency not to abandon that *patrocinium* of the liberty of the Greeks which it has taken upon itself.

You have undertaken to defend against slavery to a king the liberty of a most ancient people, most famed from the renown of its achievements or from universal praise of its culture and learning; this *patrocinium* of a whole people received into your *clientela* and loyalty it befits you to guarantee for ever.[38]

Cicero does not say that Roman power was modelled on patronage, but that it was so mild and just that it could have been named patronage rather than power: that implies a difference, more than a likeness, between patronage and power, and Ciceronian use of the word *patrocinium* is explicitly metaphorical. *Patrocinium* and *clientela*, in the Livian version of the Rhodian speech, are additions to his Polybian model (fortunately preserved: 21.22.5–23.12). J. Briscoe is misleading when he calls them "the slogan-words of Rome's attitude towards the Greeks."[39] The Roman slogan from 196 had been liberty, and there was no other. Moreover, in both Livian texts, *patrocinium* is used to evoke a Roman undertaking to protect Greek liberty, not a form of Roman hegemony; the *officium* alluded to is that of the *patronus*. That of the *cliens* is evoked in a famous text of the jurist Proculus explaining that the *maiestas* clause in a treaty does not exclude liberty, but only as a comparison (*quemadmodum . . . , sic . . .*).[40] These few texts do not prove that the Romans had a clear idea that their world power was largely modelled on the patronage system which existed within their own society, but contemporaries are not necessarily in the best position to analyse such complex behaviours as Roman imperialism, and modern historians might be perfectly correct in laying stress on the importance of a patronage model, whether or not it was already pointed out in ancient sources.[41] Reproaching A. N. Sherwin-

---

38. Liv. 34.58.11 (speech of Flamininus in front of Antiochus' ambassador in 193 B.C.): *populus Romanus susceptum patrocinium libertatis Graecorum non deserere fidei constantiaeque suae ducit esse*; 37.54.17 (speech of thc Rhodians in front of the Senate in 189 B.C.)*: gentis uetustissimae nobilissimaeque uel fama rerum gestarum uel omni commendatione humanitatis doctrinarumque tuendam ab seruitio regio libertatem suscepistis; hoc patrocinium receptae in fidem et clientelam uestram uniuersae gentis perpetuum uos praestare decet* (translations of E. T. Sage slightly modified).

39. J. Briscoe, *A Commentary on Livy: Books XXXIV–XXXVII* (Oxford, 1981) 382 (with reference to E. Badian, *Foreign Clientelae*, ch. 3).

40. *D.* 49.15.7.1: *hoc enim adicitur ut intellegatur alterum populum superiorem esse, non ut intellegatur alterum non esse liberum, et quemadmodum clientes nostros intellegimus liberos esse, etiamsi neque auctoritate neque dignitate neque uiribus nobis pares sunt* (corr. of Haloander for *uiri boni praesunt* of *F*)*, sic eos qui maiestatem nostram comiter conseruare debent liberos esse intellegendum est.*

41. Probably more damaging for these modern theories is the suspicion that the importance of *patrocinium* and *clientela* in Roman society has been largely overstated at the

White with what he called "the very misleading inference that, because 'clientela' is not a term of international law, it is, in the international sphere, only a metaphor," E. Badian added, "it is, at home and abroad, a habit of mind and a philosophy of society."[42] As a matter of fact, if patronage of Roman aristocrats over foreign communities is well attested, as we saw in the first part of this paper, the idea of patronage of the Roman people over these communities is, *pace* Badian, both quite unusual[43] and metaphorical. What is undeniable and important, in my opinion, are precisely the habit of mind and philosophy of society which Badian refers to, with the three main concepts of *fides, beneficium* and *officium*. For these concepts are not limited to patronage/clientship, and they played a major role in Roman imperial policy.

If Roman patronage had some specific qualities that explain why the Greeks, lacking a real equivalent in their own language, used *patron* and *patroneia* from the last third of the second century B.C., the habit of mind involved, or philosophy of human relationships (of which patronage was only one manifestation among others), was more extensive and less specifically Roman. Of course, Roman *fides* and Greek *pistis* were not the same thing. Differences appear most evidently in the Polybian narrative of the dialogue between the consul M'. Acilius Glabrio and the Aetolian Phaineas in 191 (20.9–10), though Polybius, probably under the influence of the Roman attitude towards Carthage just before the Third Punic War, interprets Roman *fides* in a somewhat schematic and reductive way.[44] But the Hellenistic ideas of *euergesia* and *eucharistia* were not so different from, nor less important than, Roman ideas of *beneficium* and *officium*: both Romans and Greeks accepted the principle that, even in the absence of any legal or formal commitment such as a treaty, receiving a benefit implied in exchange a dutiful gratitude that could infringe heavily upon real liberty. I referred in my book to some interesting Polybian texts.[45] Still more explicit are Strabo's remarks on the

---

expense of other forms of dependence: so P. Brunt, *The Fall of the Roman Republic* (Oxford, 1988) 382–442.

42. E. Badian, *Foreign Clientelae*, 42, n. 2.

43. For προστασία τῶν Ῥωμαίων in Polybius 22.3.1, "show of dignity" rather than "patronage," see F. Walbank, *A Historical Commentary on Polybius*, III (Oxford, 1979) 177.

44. See *Philhellénisme et impérialisme*, 72–81; and already E. S. Gruen, "Greek πίστις and Roman *Fides*," *Athenaeum* 60 (1982) 50–68.

45. Pol. 21.19.10 (speech of Eumenes in 189): Greek cities in Asia will think they owe the Rhodians their liberty, and obey them to show their gratitude; 22.7–8: the Achaeans decline money proposed by Eumenes to pay the council on the occasion of the federal meetings, because an acceptance would infringe the liberty of the koinon, or make it liable to censure for ungratefulness.

sources of royal power: "We say that kings have the greatest power. . . . They are potent in leading the multitudes whither they wish, through persuasion or force. Generally they persuade through kindness, for persuasion through words is not kingly; indeed, this belongs to the orator, whereas we call it kingly persuasion when kings win and attract men whither they wish by kindly deeds. They persuade men, it is true, through kindly deeds, but they force them by means of arms."[46]

Because of the emphasis they laid on the specific model of *patrocinium*, E. Badian and M. Errington underrated these similarities between Greek and Roman habits of mind in the philosophy of human relationships, and overrated an opposition between the Roman conception of extra-legal dependence of the weak on a strong protector and "the logical Greeks . . . [who] could not see beyond the law."[47] This idea of "the legalistically-minded Greeks"[48] is a generalization of the policy of Philopoemen and Lycortas when they opposed Achaean rights to Roman requests, but that policy does not necessarily mean that Philopoemen or Lycortas did not recognize the existence of extra-legal duties prescribed by gratitude. According to Polybius (24.10.9), their claim to *isologia* was founded on Achaean faithfulness to the Romans during the wars against Philip and Antiochus, and in 146, defending the memory of Philopoemen before Mummius and the ten Roman legates, Polybius reminded them of the Achaean decree of 192 declaring war on Antiochus and the Aetolians three months before the arrival of the legions and at a time when the other Greeks had deserted the Roman party (39.3.8). If Badian is right (as I think he is) in dating the *foedus aequum* between the Romans and the Achaeans to the winter of 192/1,[49] only a few months later, the origins of the disagreement can be defined in a more precise way: the Achaeans thought they had paid the Romans for their services, including the recovery of Corinth and Argos, whereas the Romans thought the Achaeans were bound to them by gratitude forever. The similarity with clientship (which does not necessarily mean that the Achaeans or others were clearly held to be clients of the Roman people) is precisely in this fundamental and

---

46. Strab. 9.2.40, p. 415 C.: μάλιστα τοὺς βασιλέας δύνασθαί φαμεν [. . .] Δύνανται δ' ἄγοντες ἐφ' ἃ βούλονται τὰ πλήθη διὰ πειθοῦς ἢ βίας. Πείθουσι μὲν οὖν δι' εὐεργεσίας μάλιστα. Οὐ γὰρ ἥ γε διὰ τῶν λόγων ἐστὶ βασιλική, ἀλλ' αὕτη μὲν ῥητορική, βασιλικὴν δὲ πειθὼ λέγομεν ὅταν εὐεργεσίαις φέρωσιν καὶ διάγωσιν ἐφ' ἃ βούλονται. Πείθουσι μὲν δὴ δι' εὐεργεσιῶν, βιάζονται δὲ διὰ τῶν ὅπλων (trans. H. L. Jones).

47. E. Badian, *Foreign Clientelae*, 42.

48. R. M. Errington, *The Dawn of Empire: Rome's Rise to World Power* (London, 1971) 190.

49. E. Badian, "The Treaty between Rome and the Achaean League," *JRS* 42 (1952) 76–80.

everlasting inequality: whatever service the client can render to his patron, it remains mere *officium* and does not restore (or create) equality between them. This fundamental inequality itself is founded on the Roman notion of *fides*, so that Polybius could say that, for the Romans, *in fide* and *in potestate esse* were one and the same thing (20.9.12): an excessive formula, of course, but significant. The Greek theory of *euergesia* and *eucharistia*, however, was not unaware of such inequalities; Aristotle notes that humans or children can never repay gods' or parents' kindness.[50] From this point of view cults of the Goddess Roma or of the Roman People, or the mere designation of the Romans as κοινοὶ εὐεργέται πάντων, frequent in inscriptions from the second half of the second century B.C., were explicit recognitions by the Greeks (expressed in their own system of honours) of this inequality that excluded any claim to *isologia*.

The unpleasant consequences of the *foedus aequum* concluded with the Achaeans probably explain why the Romans, as far as we know, did not conclude any other formally equal treaty until after the Third Macedonian War, when they established, to use Polybius' words, their *aderitos exousia*, and why they made use of it only with cities which could not misunderstand the meaning of these acts of courtesy (Maronea, Cibyra, Methymna, Callatis, Astypalaea).[51] Significantly, a clause with the obligation to have the same enemies as the Senate and the Roman people was included in the treaty Rhodes was compelled to implore in 164, and the same clause was even renewed in 51, although the city had been the most faithful ally of the Romans against Mithridates.[52] Rhodes still was, and remained until 42, an important naval power; as we have already noticed, it was also proud enough to honour the *imperator* Murena with proxeny, instead of begging him to become the patron of the city.

I would end my paper with some remarks on the famous embassy of the Achaean Callicrates in 180. According to Polybius, Callicrates was instructed to vindicate in front of the Senate the Achaean policy concerning Sparta, but he did quite the opposite: he taught the Senate how to enforce obedience, and came back with a threatening *senatus consultum* that ordered the Achaeans to settle Spartan and Messenian exiles. Elected *strategos* in

50. *EN* 8.11.1161a 10–19; 8.16.1163b 12–22.

51. See my study "Traités et domination romaine dans le monde hellénistique," in L. Canfora, M. Liverani and C. Zaccagini, eds., *I trattati nel mondo antico: Forma, ideologia, funzione* (Rome, 1990) 217–35.

52. P. Cornelius Lentulus Spinther, in Cic. *fam.* 12.15.2: *foedere quod cum iis M. Marcello Ser. Sulpicio ⟨coss.⟩ renouatum erat, quo iurauerant eosdem hostis se habituros quos senatus populusque Romanus*, with the commentary of H. Schmitt, *Rom und Rhodos* (Munich, 1957) 168–71.

179/8, he immediately carried out the *senatus consultum*, which was the beginning of the decline of the Achaean League (24.8–10). Polybius' account is biased because of his personal feud with Callicrates, whom he held responsible for his transportation to Rome in 167, and the importance of the embassy and its consequences are evidently overstated. Ernst Badian and Malcolm Errington inverted Polybius' analysis: Callicrates, to their mind, was more far-sighted than Lycortas and Philopoemen's other political heirs, admitted the real relationship between the two states, the real meaning of *clientela*, and wisely put an end to a dangerous legalistic policy.[53] Some years ago, I drew attention to another account of the embassy, that of Pausanias, who emphasizes the part played by some important protectors of the Spartan exiles.[54] I continue to think that Pausanias is right on this point, and to hold that the most influential of these protectors was Ap. Claudius Pulcher, who made acquaintance with some of the exiles in 195 during the war against Nabis (cf. Liv. 34.28.10), who brought them with him when he was ambassador to Achaea in 184 (Liv. 39.36.2), and whose brother Gaius, in 167, was to take a prominent part in the transportation to Italy of Callicrates' political enemies (Pol. 30.13.8; Liv. 45.31.9). If I am right, assistance by powerful *patroni* could have more impact, as early as 180, than Gruen is disposed to admit,[55] and the error of Philopoemen and Lycortas was less to ignore the duties of a client state than to ignore the strength of personal patronage in an aristocratic city such as Rome. Lycortas' son, Polybius, even if he hid this aspect of the embassy of Callicrates, drew a lesson from his father's failure: because he became a client of Scipio Aemilianus, he could not only outlive transportation to Italy, but also play an important political part in Greece after the Achaean War.[56] From the Spartan exiles of 184–180 B.C., from Callicrates and Polybius to Theophanes of Mytilene, Mithridates of Pergamum or Artemidorus of Cnidus, there is a third aspect of Roman political patronage in the Hellenic world: neither the impact of the pattern

---

53. E. Badian, *Foreign Clientelae*, 89–91; R. M. Errington, *Philopoemen* (Oxford, 1969) 195–205.

54. Paus. 7.9.6. See *Philhellénisme et impérialisme*, 299–306.

55. E. S. Gruen, *The Hellenistic World*, 164–66.

56. Cf. Plut. *Praec. ger. reip.* 18, p. 814 C–D: οὐ μόνον δὲ δεῖ παρέχειν αὑτόν τε καὶ τὴν πατρίδα πρὸς τοὺς ἡγουμένους ἀναίτιον, ἀλλὰ καὶ φίλον ἔχειν ἀεί τινα τῶν ἄνω δυνατωτάτων, ὥσπερ ἕρμα τῆς πολιτείας βέβαιον (αὐτοὶ γάρ εἰσι Ῥωμαῖοι πρὸς τὰς πολιτικὰς σπουδὰς προθυμότατοι τοῖς φίλοις), καὶ καρπὸν ἐκ φιλίας ἡγεμονικῆς λαμβάνοντα, οἷον ἔλαβε Πολύβιος καὶ Παναίτιος τῇ Σκιπίωνος εὐνοίᾳ πρὸς αὐτοὺς μεγάλα τὰς πατρίδας ὠφελήσαντας, εἰς εὐδαιμονίαν ἐξενέγκεσθαι καλόν. The continuity with the decree of Colophon in honour of Polemaios (n. 12) is obvious. As is well known, *philia/amicitia* is a frequent euphemism for *patrocinium/clientela*.

of patronage on Roman policy, nor the use of foreign *clientelae* in Roman political struggles, but the part that personal patron/client relationships between Roman and Greek politicians played in the vicissitudes of Greek cities within the Roman empire (status of cities, political struggles within cities, rivalries between cities). Perhaps this third aspect is no less important, even if the Romanocentric character of most of our sources rarely allows us a glimpse of it.[57]

57. I think it is worth while drawing historians' attention to a very interesting and puzzling text they might not know because of its origin. The new edition by T. Dorandi of *Filodemo, Storia dei filosofi: La Stoa da Zenone a Panezio (P. Herc.* 1018*)* (Leiden, 1994) 122, gives an improved version of what remains of column 72: [ἴ]διον μέρος καὶ σεσωκέναι τὴν πατρίδα κινδυνεύουσαν. Ὅθεν διὰ τὸ τῆς εὐεργεσίας μέγεθος δεύτερον κτίστη[ν] γενέ[σ]θαι. *Neos* or *deuteros ktistès* was to become a title given to citizens whose friendship with Roman magnates allowed their native city to recover freedom: Theophanes in Mytilene, or Mithridates in Pergamum (see L. Robert, "Théophane de Mytilène à Constantinople," *CRAI* [1969] 42–64, especially 50–52 = *OMS*, V [Amsterdam, 1989] 561–83). We have no information about the circumstances when Panaetius would have had the opportunity to be given such a title by the Rhodians (the text of Plutarch mentioned in the previous note and referred to by Dorandi is of no real help), and we cannot be sure that he is the man alluded to in column 72. He is still eulogized in col. 71, while his pupils are mentioned from col. 73 onwards: the hero of col. 72 must be Panaetius himself (Dorandi, *op.cit.*, 171) or one of his disciples (Comparetti, *RFIC* [1875] 542). The riddle of this text remains unsolved, but we should keep it in mind until new information, perhaps, gives us a solution.

SIX

Athens between Rome and the Kings: 229/8 to 129 B.C.

H. Mattingly

Athens liked to believe that it was a centre of moderation, civilisation and humanity in a sometimes irrational world. These are the very qualities that mark out Frank Walbank as scholar, colleague and friend. So I thought that this theme might be most suitable for this celebratory volume. I offer it as a small return for all that I owe him. His work is fundamental to it, as will soon appear—and so is that of Christian Habicht.[1] Athenian manoeuvring between the kings and Rome is worth close study, since it shows how a minor power could maintain the delicate balance. Only in 88 B.C., by a shift of policy quite out of character, did Athens finally court disaster. But even then, as Sulla noted (Plut. *Sulla* 14.5), the dead generations of Athens saved their descendants from the worst.

With one great Hellenistic monarchy in the first half of my period Athens had very few friendly dealings, until in 168 B.C. it was abolished by Rome after the Pydna victory. Freedom from Macedonian control in 229/8 B.C. led to a growing rapprochement with Egypt, the weakening of any ties with Pella. In 224/3 B.C. the tribe Ptolemais was created and the Ptolemaia festival, but the two Macedonian tribes were retained.[2] In a similar cautious spirit Athens approached Doson in the 220s through Prytanis of Karystos, an intimate of the king. Even as late as 210/9 B.C. an orator recalled attempted

---

1. Habicht's work can be conveniently studied in *Studien zür Geschichte Athens in hellenistischer Zeit* (Gottingen, 1982: henceforth *Studien*) and *Athen in hellenistischer Zeit* (München, 1994). *Athen* contains virtually only already published work, with a useful 1993 update (355–60). My references are to the original publications.

2. See Walbank in N. G. L. Hammond and F. W. Walbank, *A History of Macedonia* 3: 336–168 B.C. (1988) 340f.; W. S. Ferguson, *Hellenistic Athens* (1911) 205–12 and 237–40. For the date of the tribe Ptolemais see Habicht, *Studien* 103–12 and *ClAnt*11 (1992) 68–70.

Athenian mediation between Macedon and Aitolia ca. 220–217 B.C., designed to maintain friendship and peace with both parties. In 209 B.C. Athens joined Ptolemy IV, Rhodes and Chios in similar mediation, but to no effect.[3] Athens' non-aligned policy offended Polybios and seems to have irritated Philip V. In the end he lost patience and, picking a quarrel, he invaded Attika and caused widespread damage, though he failed to surprise Athens itself. This act of aggression drove Athens into alliance with Attalos I and Rome. Philip was now so hated that the two Macedonian tribes were abolished, all honours to the kings and their monuments were destroyed. A new tribe, Attalis, was created.[4] The bitter legacy of 200 B.C. meant that Athens was not reconciled with Philip, even after his defeat and new status as a Roman ally. When the Delphic Amphiktyony was reformed after the war with Antiochos and the Aitolians, Athens cooperated with the Thessalians in creating a new type of league. Its propaganda in the 180s talked of a union of democratic states and autonomous federations against those who threatened freedom. This looks anti-Macedonian, and some scholars have argued that the two Macedonian votes disappeared for a time and were not recovered till the start of Perseus' reign.[5] The very combination of Athens and Thessaly, formerly under strict Macedonian control, cannot have been exactly agreeable to Philip. Perseus seems to have had no success in rebuilding bridges with Athens, though he was assiduous in such attempts with other Greeks.[6] Athens' hostility towards Macedon had very deep roots. Since Antipater's intervention in 322 B.C. Athens had been repeatedly humiliated by Macedon—most notably by Antigonos Gonatas in the 260s, when after his victory in the Chremonidean War he imposed tough terms and a garrison. Doson's ambitions and Philip's increasingly aggressive behaviour strongly reinforced the old prejudices. But

3. For the Prytanis decree see B.D. Meritt, *Hesperia* 4 (1935) 515–18 and L. Moretti, *Iscrizioni storiche ellenistiche* (1967) I, no. 28, 60–63. For 210/9 see *IG* ii² 1304.5ff. (praise of Demainetos). Habicht skilfully sorted out the repeated embassies to the two sides in the war (*Studien* 134f.). For 209 B.C. see Pol. 10.25–26; Livy 27.29.4–17. Livy's 208 B.C. dating is wrong, as Walbank noted (*Commentary on Polybius* II, 15).

4. On the crisis of 200 B.C. see Walbank, *Macedonia* 3, 416–18; Pol. 16.25–26 with Walbank II, 533–35; Livy 31.14.6–10; Habicht, *Studien* 142–50.

5. On Athens and the Amphiktyony see Habicht, *Hesperia* 56 (1987) 59–71. On p. 60f. he vigorously supported the view of A. Giovannini (B. Laourdas and C. Makaronas, eds., *Ancient Macedonia* [Thessaloniki, 1970] 147–54) that Macedon never lost its votes; the list for 184 is very incomplete, whereas in 178 (*SIG*³ 636.5–7) 23 out of the original traditional votes are represented. They feel that after 196 B.C. Macedon could never seem a real danger to Greeks. But even if these points are allowed, the new league's propaganda must have sounded badly in Macedonian ears.

6. For Perseus and the Greeks see Livy 43.5.1–6; Pol. 27.5.1–8, and Livy 43.46.7–10 (Boiotia); Pol. 27.4.1–10, and Livy 43.45.8–46.1 (Rhodes); Walbank III, 289, 296–99.

with all the other Hellenistic kingdoms, even the minor ones, Athens had lively relations throughout my period. It is best to take them in turn.

I. ATHENS AND THE SELEUCIDS

Links between Athens and Antioch can be traced back at least as far as the last quarter of the third century. A certain Aristokreon son of Nausikrates— very possibly the nephew of the Stoic leader Chrysippos—was honoured at this time for his many services to Athens. Apparently he had first been crowned for help in 229/8 B.C., supporting Athens' bid for freedom and contributing to the defences of the harbours. He was subsequently crowned again when he came to Athens as a member of an embassy charged to renew the ancestral relations between his city and Athens. If that city was Seleukeia Pieria rather than Cilician Soloi, Chrysippos' home, this should help with the dating. Seleukeia was taken by Ptolemy III in the late 240s and kept by Egypt until Antiochos III recovered his port in 219 B.C.; in the peace of 217 B.C. it remained Seleucid, though Koile Syria went to Egypt. Only after 219 B.C. could Seleukeia have made its approach to Athens through the pro-Seleucid Aristokreon. On the occasion of his third honours Aristokreon was granted a further crown, the title of *proxenos* and the right of *enktesis*: both honours were to be hereditary. What his services were this time remains unclear.[7] Envoys from Alabanda/Antiocheia arrived in Greece ca. 203 B.C. and visited, doubtless among other places, Delphoi and Athens. In both these centres they were highly honoured, and in Delphoi one envoy expatiated at large on the virtues of Antiochos III as a royal

---

7. See *IG* ii² 786 and Diog. Laert. 7.185 with Plut. *Moralia* 1033 (Chrysippos summoned Aristokreon to join him in Athens). The decree was cut by a man active between 229/8 and ca. 203 B.C.: see Stephen Tracy, *Attic Letter-Cutters of 229 to 86 B.C.* (Berkeley, 1990: henceforth *ALC*) 46. Aristokreon's first visit fits in well with the probable date of Chrysippos' summons to his nephew. Though A. Wilhelm observed (ΕφΑρχ 1901, 50f.) that only Σ could be read in line 8, he still accepted Seleukcia as Aristokreon's home: with Köhler he felt that his mother could well have left Soloi and married into a leading Syrian family. There Aristokreon would have grown up and acquired status and influence. Habicht, however, takes Soloi as Aristokreon's home (*Studien* 61 with n. 11; *Chiron* 19 [1989] 13f. with n. 38). In the second passage he effectively disposed of H. Ingholt's attempt (*Berytus* 17 [1967/1968] 163–65) to identify Seleukeia and Antioch in the Aristokreon dossier as the Cilician cities of those names. L. and J. Robert (*Bull.Épig.* 1969, 448f., no. 184) had already taken the same line as Habicht. On Seleukeia in Pieria see Pol. 5.58–61 with Walbank I, 585–87; *RE* II A, coll. 1184–89. Many of its citizens were driven out by the Egyptians and fully reinstated by Antiochos III. The decree for Aristokreon typically concludes by envisaging further services to be followed by further honours (lines 13f. and 28–31).

patron and benefactor. He presumably did the same at Athens, but the relevant portion of the decree is lost. Antiochos was surely behind the city's initiative—seeking recognition of *asylia*—and he staked his prestige on their success. The city was granted Athenian citizenship among other honours.[8] For actual benefactions of Antiochos III to Athens we now have—thanks to Stephen Tracy's acumen—the evidence of the famous Attic decree for Pharnakes of Pontos from Delos. It must clearly be dated 196/5 and not 160/59 B.C., as had been almost universally believed.[9] The decree honours Pharnakes for services rendered and, noting Pharnakes' recent marriage to Nysa, the orator arranges for her honours too—since it was right to honour not just benefactors, but also their descendants. Now Nysa was the daughter of King Antiochos and his queen Laodike.[10] The dedications of Queen Laodike and an uncertain king, inventoried at Athens in 181/0 B.C., could well be among the benefactions of the royal pair implied in the Pharnakes Decree. Laodike was certainly keen to parade herself as a benefactor with her husband or in her own right.[11] Bronze statues of Pharnakes and Nysa were to be set up in Delos, and three men were chosen to carry out the decree. Their leader was a very distinguished Athenian, Leon son of Kichesias of Aixone. Born ca. 255 B.C. he is found in 192 B.C. blocking Apollodoros' attempt to draw Athens in on the side of Antiochos against Rome, and in 189 B.C. his eloquence helped persuade the Roman Senate to grant peace to the Aitolians. Clearly he was then regarded as completely reliable by Rome.[12] In 196/5 B.C., however, it was still possible for Athens to be friendly to Rome *and* to Antiochos. The king was sedulously cultivating good relations with other Greeks. He had offered one of his daughters—probably Nysa—to Eumenes II, but Eumenes prudently declined the honour, though Antiochos

8. See K. L. Pounder, *Hesperia* 47 (1978) 49–57; *OGIS* 234 (*FD* III, 4.163 especially lines 19–22); Habicht, *Chiron* 19 (1989) 10f.

9. For the correct date of *ID* 1497 bis (*IG* XI 1056) see Tracy, *AM* 107 (1992) 307–13. It was cut by a man active at Athens from 226/5 to ca. 190 B.C. (*ALC* 55–60). What remains of the secretary's name and demotic fits *IG* ii² 953 from Tychandros' archonship. Tracy had assigned *IG* ii² 953 to a cutter active from 169/8 to 134 B.C. (*ALC* 148). He was a pupil of a cutter active from 203 to 163 B.C. (*ALC* 82–88) and their hands are hard to keep apart. With good reason Tracy now assigns *IG* ii² 953 to the elder man (*AM* 1992, 311).

10. *ID* 1497 bis. 14–24.

11. *Hesperia* Suppl. 4 (1940)144f., line 8f.: Habicht, *Chiron* 19 (1989) 12f. On Laodike as a benefactor see P. Herrmann, *Anadolu* 9 (1965) 34–36, lines 35–55 (Teos: with her husband) and *SEG* 26, 1226 (Iasos: Laodike alone). For the Medusa at Athens (gift of a King Antiochos: Paus. 1.21.3) see later n. 30.

12. With Delos independent, Athens had to ask permission to set up the statues—hence the mission. See *ID* 1497 bis. 26–28 and 31–45. For Leon see Habicht, *Studien* 194f. and Tracy, *AM* (1992) 310; *IG* ii² 787.16 (ephebe in 237/6 B.C.); Pol. 21.29–31; Livy 35.50.4.

promised to restore cities and territories taken in 198/7 B.C.[13] Antiochos also
courted Rhodes, with rather better success. In 194/3 he was able to offer
the Rhodians as arbitrators between him and Smyrna and Lampsakos. A
decree from Kalymnos, honouring the Rhodian Menekrates as a friend of
Antiochos, seems to fit this context; in line 10 there is a tantalizing reference
to the Athenians.[14]

In the war between Antiochos and Rome Athens firmly took the Roman
side. But early in Seleukos IV's reign relations between Greece and Syria
could be re-established. Seleukos himself sent envoys in 186/5 B.C. to the
Achaian League to renew the old friendship and was well received.[15] Even
earlier, soon after Seleukos' accession, Athens honoured a trusty Seleucid
courtier in the familiar diplomatic language of the day. He is praised for
his care of the city's interests and of individual Athenians who came to
King Seleukos; for all this he was given Athenian citizenship.[16] Three years
later a certain Aristokreon was honoured at Athens. He too had helped
Athenians with business at Antioch and had earlier spent a profitable period
of philosophic study at Athens. His name at once recalls Chrysippos' nephew,
but it is not easily the same man—the full generation gap between the two
decrees is too long, and the later one shows no awareness of the many
honours recorded and granted in the first. Was this man a son or nephew
of the former *proxenos,* renewing his family's connections after a period of
estrangement between Athens and its Syrian friends?[17]

Towards the middle of his reign Seleukos was nearly seduced by his
brother-in-law Pharnakes into a technical breach of the Apameia treaty.
Pharnakes appealed for military help against Eumenes II, Ariarathes IV
and Prusias II, apparently dangling a five hundred talent bribe. Seleukos,
however, wisely refused to be drawn, and Pharnakes was soon compelled
to make an unfavourable peace.[18] Seleukos doubtless remained suspect
in Roman eyes. In 178/7 B.C. he sent his son Demetrios to Rome to
replace his brother Antiochos as a hostage: this was surely meant as a
conciliatory gesture. Antiochos promptly settled in Athens, where honours

13. Pol. 21.20.8–9 with Walbank III, 113; App. *Syr.* 5; Tracy, op. cit. (n. 12), 309.

14. Pol. 18.41a.1–3 and 52.4 with Walbank II, 603 and 623; Livy 33.20.7–13: *OGIS* 243.

15. Pol. 22.7.4 with Walbank III, 188.

16. *IG* ii² 925 + Agora I 2155 (187/6 B.C.): Tracy, *ALC* 119f.

17. *IG* ii² 785 (Charikles archon: 184/3 B.C.). Habicht thinks that 786 and 785 honour
the same man, Chrysippos' nephew; but he rightly notes that 785 shows no awareness
at all of the earlier decree. See *Chiron* 19, 13 with n. 36. This would be very strange
on his view.

18. See Diod. 29.24; Pol. frg. 96 and 26.2.14. For the peace of 180/79 B.C. possibly
brokered by Rome see later p. 138 and n. 83 and Pol. 25.2.2–15 with Walbank III, 271–74.

were immediately given him; he soon won such popularity by his generous bearing that two statues of him were set up in the Agora.[19] His brother's success at Athens was doubtless well received at Rome, and it apparently led Seleukos to assert himself. He offered his daughter Laodike to Perseus, and, since his fleet could not sail even as far as Rhodes, the Rhodian fleet undertook to convoy the princess to Macedonia; for this service Rhodes was liberally rewarded by Perseus. Roman displeasure was vented on the Rhodians, whose cause over their Lykian dependency suffered.[20] When Seleukos was assassinated in summer 175 B.C., Antiochos wasted no time. He swiftly passed over to Pergamon and was escorted by Eumenes and his brothers to the frontier of his kingdom. Athens welcomed his successful coup, as is shown by a famous decree honouring the Attalid initiative; it was to be published in Athens, Syria and Pergamon, but only the Pergamene copy has survived.[21] Rome evidently also acquiesced in the turn of events. Antiochos' long stay as a hostage had won him a wide circle of Roman friends, many in high places, and he had acquired genuine admiration and liking for the Roman way of life.[22]

In Seleukos' last years and at the start of Antiochos IV's reign a man from Laodikeia on the sea called Philonides had made himself so useful to Athens by helping those who came to see the kings that he and his two sons were given citizenship. His statue was set up in the precinct of Demos and the Graces, an unusual mark of honour. When he was later captured by pirates (?), Athens secured his release and, on his coming with his elder son to express his thanks, he and the son were publicly entertained at the Prytaneion.[23] The sons were made *proxenoi* at Delphoi, and for the younger Dikaiarchos we have the actual decree of 168/7 B.C.

19. For Demetrios see App. *Syr.* 45 and Walbank III, 284f. For Antiochos see Tracy, *Hesperia* 51 (1982) 60ff., no. 3 with Habicht's correction in line 7f., introducing the motif of ancestral goodwill to Athens (*Chiron* 19, 13 n. 33). For the statues see *OGIS* 248.55f. (in the Agora by 175 B.C.).

20. See Pol. 25.4.8 with Walbank III, 280f.; Livy 42.12.3; App. *Maced.* 11.2. The Delians dedicated a statue of Laodike after her marriage (*SIG*[3] 639). For Roman bullying of Rhodes see Pol. 25.4–6.

21. See *OGIS* 238. It was surely a decree of Athens—*pace* M. Fränkel (*Pergamum* VIII.I 85 no. 160), who argued for Antioch; language, institutions, sentiments all point to Athens.

22. Pol. 26.1a.1 and 1.4–6 with Walbank III, 284–86. E. Will (*Hist. polit. monde hellén.* ii [1966/1967] 256f.) believed in a plot between Rome, Antiochos and other enemies of Seleukos, which began with the exchange of hostages.

23. See *IG* ii[2] 1236: Habicht, *Studien* 85 and *Chiron* 19, 17f. The decree was cut by a man active from 199/8 to 176/5 B.C. (*ALC* 93). The decrees for Nikeratos of Alexandreia and Timarchos of Cypriot Salamis were set up in the 170s in the temenos of Demos and the Graces (*IG* ii[2] 908–909); for a later example see *IG* ii[2] 987 (Leontiskos of Patara).

which granted him the honour for his tireless service of the interests of both city and temple at the court of Antiochos.[24] Philonides the elder son was also influential with Antiochos and later Demetrios I; as a leading Epicurean he came to know the Academic Karneades and the Stoic Diogenes in Athens.[25]

Antiochos IV reciprocated Athens' support by unparalleled benefactions. His greatest gift was the promised completion of the temple of Zeus Olympios: significantly he entrusted it to an Italian architect, Cossutius.[26] But with Rome Antiochos was having less success. His spirited response to Ptolemaic aggression in Koile Syria caused Rome real concern, and, despite vigorous diplomacy by Athens and the Achaian League, the king and Rome moved steadily into confrontation. Finally in summer 168 B.C. after Pydna C. Popilius could deliver the Senate's famous ultimatum to Antiochos in his camp before Alexandria. The king had no option and was forced to withdraw his army from Egypt.[27] This was a real humiliation, and it could hardly be concealed. But Antiochos recovered remarkably and, after the grandiose pageant at Daphnai in 166 B.C., he turned his ambitions eastward where Rome could not reasonably interfere.

Indeed the Senate was in a conciliatory mood now and chose to overlook certain signs of Syrian rearmament in breach of Apameia.[28] At about this time Athens honoured Antiochos through a powerful military figure of his early years. It was probably in 166/5 B.C. in fact that Arrhidaios was praised for his care for Athens as a city and for individual Athenians who came to Syria—whether as envoys, heralds for the games or on other business.[29] Antiochos IV had been an unmatched benefactor of Athens. He also took

---

In 212/1 B.C., on the special request of Eurykleides and Mikion (founders of the precinct), the statue of Eumarides of Kydonia was moved to the temenos: see Habicht, *Studien* 162 and 84 on *IG* ii[2] 844.39–42.

24. See *OGIS* 241; *SIG*[3] 585, 103–105 and 212f. (corrected date).

25. For Philonides II see R. Phillipson, *RE* XX, coll. 63–73, no. 5; I. Gallo, *Frammenti biogr. da papiri* 2 (Rome, 1990) 38.

26. Pol. 26.1.11 with Walbank III, 287f.; Vitruvius VII praef. 15 and 17; Strabo 9.C 396; Livy 41.20.8. Work was broken off with Antiochos' death.

27. On Athens and the League in 169 B.C. see Pol. 28.19.2–4 and 20.1 with Walbank III, 354–56. The Greek envoys were sent on to Antiochos at Naukratis; he received them graciously and seems to have persuaded them of the justice of his cause. On 168 B.C. see Pol. 29.27.1–13 with Walbank III, 405f.; Livy 45.12.3–8: Habicht in *CAH* VIII[2] (1989) 343–45; E. S. Gruen, *The Hellenistic World and the Coming of Rome* (1984) 657–60.

28. See Habicht, *CAH* VIII[2] 350–53; Gruen, op. cit. (n. 27) 660–63.

29. See G. A. Stamires, *Hesperia* 26 (1957) 47–49, no. 7. L. Robert much improved both text and interpretation in *Hellenica* 11/12 (1960) 92–111. He showed that the archon's name was only 5/6 letters long, not 8 (Stamires). Charias is a possibility. The name

care to honour Delos with splendid altars and statues. Two Athenians set up statues of him there, one expressly given "for his goodwill towards the Athenian people."[30] Only when Antiochos was dead did the Senate allow a high-level embassy to enforce the Apameia disarmament terms. Antiochos V and his ministers could not resist the demands, but an Antioch mob lynched Cn. Octavius, the embassy's leader.[31]

Athens remained friendly to the Seleucids and in time even accepted Demetrios I's usurpation despite Roman reluctance. Certainly Menochares, one of his chief ministers, was honoured with a statue by an unknown Delian association.[32] When Alexander Balas, however, was recognised by both Rome and Pergamon as a legitimate son of Antiochos IV, Athens followed their lead. Alexander competed and won under this title at the Panathenaia of 150 B.C. This would have fallen soon after he had defeated and killed Demetrios I.[33] When Balas was deserted by Ptolemy VI and defeated by Demetrios II, Athens apparently followed Ptolemy and returned to backing the junior, but true, Seleucid line. Three Delian inscriptions seem to relate to Demetrios II rather than his father and should perhaps be dated to his first reign (146–140/39 B.C.). Two were set up by an Athenian, son of Lysias, who was governor of Seleukis; one was a statue of his son.[34] Another confidant of

---

could be doubtfully read ἐπὶ Χαρίου in *Hesperia* 3 (1934) 27–31 as of a recent archon, under whom a man honoured in 163/2 B.C. had served as taxiarch. Meritt later changed his reading to ἐπὶ 'Αχαίου (*Hesperia* 26 [1957] 73). By study of epigraphic hands Tracy has proved that Achaios must be the archon of 190/89 and not 166/5 B.C.: see *AJAH* 9 (1985) 43–47 and *ALC* 57 n. 3 (the cutter was active from 226/5 to ca. 190 B.C.). Tracy would return to Meritt's first reading, citing—as Meritt did in 1946—*Hesperia* 15 (1946) 221f., no. 49 (ΕΠΙ ΧΑΡΙ . . .) in support of this name; Charikles (184/3 B.C.) is too early for this stone. 166/5 B.C. is now vacant and Charias fits very well.

30. For the benefactions see Pol. 26.1.10f. and 29.24.13 with Walbank III, 287f. and 401; *ID* 1540–41; Livy 41.20.5–9. The Medusa *clipeus* over the theatre at Athens—mentioned by Pausanias with the oriental curtain at Olympia as given by a King Antiochos (1.21.3 and 5.12.4)—most likely came from Epiphanes, marked by his panache. But Habicht (*Chiron* 19, 11f.) and P. Callaghan (*BSA* 76 [1981] 59–70) have argued forcefully for Antiochos III.

31. See on this Habicht, *CAH* VIII² 353–56; Gruen, op. cit. (n. 27) 665f. and 227 with n. 115 (who implies that Cn. Octavius *may* have exceeded his brief).

32. Pol. 31.33.1 and 32.2.1–8; *ID* 1543 (—ochares).

33. For Balas see Diod. 31.32a; App. *Syr.* 67: Pol. 33.15.1–2 with 18.6–19; Justin 35.1.8–11; Strabo 13.C 684 and 16.C 751; *I Maccab.* 10–11: Joseph. *AJ* 13.35ff. and 119; *RE* I, coll. 1437f., no. 32. For the date of *IG* ii² 2317 (col.1.37 and 47: "— son of King Antiochos Epiphanes") see Tracy and Habicht, *Hesperia* 60 (1991) 218 and 230. The alternative (146 B.C.) seems ruled out: Balas was then locked in the decisive struggle with Demetrios II.

34. *ID* 1544f. (rightly assigned by the editors to the same man).

Demetrios II was honoured with a statue, whose base alludes to Antiocheia Mygdonis (Nisibis)—a city which was apparently not lost to Parthia until after Antiochos VII's defeat and death in 130 B.C.[35]

Antiochos VII was the last able Seleucid. One of his ministers— [Z]enodoros or [M]enodoros—was celebrated at Athens ca. 135 B.C., especially for his help while ambassador to Athens. The decree rehearses in glowing terms the many benefactions of the king and his forerunners, in particular Antiochos IV—whose stay at Athens in 178–175 B.C. is expressly noted and commended.[36] Kleopatra, wife of Demetrios II and Antiochos VII, had sent her son by Demetrios to Athens after Demetrios was captured in 140/39 B.C., and the future Antiochos VIII was still there when his father returned from Parthia and recalled him to Syria in 130/29 B.C. The New Style Attic tetradrachms of 131/0 B.C., with the elephant head symbol and the signature ANTIOCHOS were surely struck in honour of the young prince and his uncle, even if not actually by him as moneyer. The moneyer may have been an Athenian, whose name suggested the compliment. The issue of 134/3 B.C. with the Seleucid anchor and star symbol may have been another numismatic gesture to the Syrian royal house.[37] When Antiochos VIII assumed power with his formidable mother, he lost little time in making clear his feeling for Athens on his coinage: in 122 and 121 B.C. the royal pair struck bronze issues with the New Style reverse type of an owl on an amphora. Fresh New Style silver coinage must have travelled back to Syria with the young prince, and the type would have become familiar there.[38]

---

35. *ID* 1546. On Nisibis see *RE* XVII, coll. 727–30. Menodoros, a citizen of this Antioch, won an equestrian event at the Panathenaia of 166 B.C.: see Tracy and Habicht, *Hesperia* (1991) 187f., col.II, 24f.

36. See Meritt, *Hesperia* 36 (1967) 61–65, no. 6; Tracy, *GRBS* 29 (1988) 383–88 (improved text and correct date). Dedications of a King Antiochos were listed in an Asklepieion inventory (*IG* ii[2] 1019): see R. Hubbe, *Hesperia* 28 (1959) 187, no. 9 (138/7 B.C.?). Hubbe's date is suspect and the dedications may anyway have been old at the time of the list: see Tracy, *ALC* 142 n. 6. The cutter appears to belong to the late second century; the hand is assigned in *ALC* 242 to "the school of the ii[2] 1008 cutter," who was active from 118/7 to 97/6 B.C. (194–96).

37. For Antiochos VIII in Athens see App. *Syr.* 68. In *NC* 1969, 329f. with *Hist.* 20 (1971) 36 and *JHS* 91 (1971) 79 I argued that the prince himself was the moneyer. Habicht has contested this (*Chiron* 19, 20f. and 24) and he is probably right. He also wants to link the issue of 134/3 B.C. to Antiochos VII.

38. See G. MacDonald, *Catalogue of Greek Coins in the Hunterian Collection* III (1905) 98f., no. 16 and *BMC* "Seleucids," Pl. XXIII.5. Parts of a hoard have been appearing on the market lately, with Athenian New Style ending with mint specimens of the Antiochos/elephant issue and Syrian royal coinage of ca. 130 B.C., particularly tetradrachms of

Until the steady decline of Seleucid power from ca. 130 B.C. on Athens' interest in this kingdom had been lively, for good political and economic reasons—especially after the acquisition of Delos. The first real contacts apparently began under Antiochos III, who was led in due course to resume Seleucid claims on Asia Minor and Lysimacheia. This brought conflict with Rome, and from 192 to 187 B.C. Athens regarded Syria as its enemy too. Antiochos IV enjoyed great popularity at Athens for his quite exceptional benefactions, and the honours seem to cover his whole reign. Rome might have its passing difficulties with the king, but Athens was evidently allowed to go its own way. From 152 to 146 B.C., however, Athens studiously followed the Roman line on Alexander Balas. But they then felt free to support the cause of Demetrios II; after all, as Polybios noted (31.33.1–5 and 33.18.10f.), the legitimate Seleucids always had their supporters in the Senate. Despite Roman ambivalence Athens' attitude made sense, and with Antiochos VII from 138 B.C. on Rome and Athens were in full accord. Antiochos apparently repaid Athens hardly less generously than his great-uncle, and this was after all the deciding factor in Athens' dealings with most of the kings.

II. ATHENS AND THE PTOLEMIES

In 229 B.C., when Athens secured the withdrawal of the Macedonian garrison from the Peiraieus, Ptolemy III was the first dynast to offer friendly support. Already in 226/5 B.C. Kastor, a friend and minister of the king, was honoured at Athens for his goodwill and good services.[39] In 224/3 B.C. Athens in gratitude created a new tribe Ptolemais and instituted new games, the Ptolemaia. Habicht thinks that these honours elicited from Ptolemy a most munificent benefaction, the gymnasium that bore the dynastic name. But that was possibly the work of a later Ptolemy.[40] A notable minister of Ptolemy III and IV, Thraseas son of Aetos from Aspendos, governed Cilicia in the late 220s, as his father had done twenty years before. At some date after 224/3 B.C. he was made an Athenian citizen and enrolled in the

Kleopatra Thea and Antiochos VIII from 125/4. Note Harlan J. Berk's lists of Jan. 18 1994, nos. 105–42 (Attic); March 31, nos. 209–11 (Seleucid); July 13, nos. 267–75 (Attic) and 373–75 (Seleucid); Oct. 26, no. 169f. (Attic: Antiochos issue) and 233–35 (Kleopatra/Antiochos). The Athenian element of the Kessab hoard also ended with mint Antiochos specimens, but the Seleucid continued down to 105/4 B.C.: see H. Seyrig, *Trésors du Levant* (1972) no. 30, 96–103 with Pls. 34–37.

39. See *IG* ii² 838 and Habicht, *Studien* 102 and *ClAnt* 11 (1992) 76.

40. *Studien* 105–17.

tribe Ptolemais. Subsequently he was further honoured at Athens.[41] His son Ptolemaios served under Ptolemy IV in the war of 219–217 B.C. against Antiochos III, and Thraseas himself governed Koile Syria, certainly a few years after 217 B.C. and possibly ca. 209–204 B.C.[42] His help to Athens, the cause of his further honours, probably preceded his Syrian posting. He must at that time have been very influential at court and have had good connections both in Cilicia and in Koile Syria, where his fellow citizen Andromachos was Ptolemy IV's first governor. The help included a large consignment of hair, presumably designed—as with Sinope and Rhodes in the 220s—for making catapults. Athens needed to build up a stock of such defensive armaments, and in the crisis of 200 B.C. they surely proved their worth. It may be that the Cilician-Syrian area was the main source of supply for human and animal hair.[43]

Two Rhodians, Olympiodoros and (Did?)ymachos, were honoured at Athens under either Ptolemy IV or V. They were recognised as *proxenoi* and *euergetai*. The decree apparently treats the small island of Hydreia in the Saronic gulf as a Ptolemaic naval base. Certainly Methana/Arsinoe was such a base under these two kings. As late as 161 B.C. indeed we find Eirenaios of Alexandria responsible for troops at points in Crete, Thera and Arsinoe. A head of Ptolemy VI from Aigina may originate from the sanctuary of Isis at Arsinoe.[44] Early in Ptolemy V's reign the Athenian statesman Kephisodoros arranged the sending of an embassy to Alexandria, and another followed in 198/7 B.C., on which Asklepiades son of Zenon died.[45]

41. On Thraseas see *IG* ii² 836; *SEG* 39 (1989),1425 (Arsinoe, Cilicia) and 1576 (Tyre); C. P. Jones and C. Habicht, *Phoenix* 43 (1989) 317–46. Habicht acutely noted Thraseas' choice of the Ptolemais deme Phlya: see *ClAnt* 11 (1992) 76 n. 47. *IG* ii² 836 was cut by a man active from 229/8 to ca. 203 B.C. (*ALC* 46).

42. See Pol. 5.64.4, 65.3 and 87.6 (Andromachos sent to Koile Syria). Thraseas dedicated at Tyre (*SEG* 39.1576) a statue of Ptolemy IV without his queen; the king also appears alone on a dedication from Egyptian Thebes after the birth of Ptolemy V (ca. 210 B.C.). See *OGIS* 89. Arsinoe was apparently separated from Ptolemy in his last years, though she was not killed until after his death (Pol. 15.25.2–11 with Walbank II, 482f.).

43. For Rhodes supplying Sinope and Seleukos II supplying Rhodes see Pol. 4.56.2–3 and 5.88.8–9 with Walbank I, 512f. and 621.

44. See on *IG* ii² 1024 Habicht, *ClAnt* 11 (1992) 87–90. The cutter was active between 224/3 and 188/7 B.C. (*ALC* 62 and 66). For Methana/Arsinoe see Paus. 2.34.1; L. Robert, *Hellenica* 11–12 (1960) 157f. n. 5. For Eirenaios see *OGIS* 115. For the head of Ptolemy VI see J. Six, *AM* 12 (1887) 212–22.

45. See *SEG* 20.505 (215/4?) and *Berytus* 13 (1960) 138 no. 14; P. F. Callaghan, *BICS* 30 (1983) 33–35 (198/7 B.C.: Year 8 of Ptolemy V not IV). For Kephisodoros see Livy 31.9 and Paus. 1.33.3–5.

In 188/7 B.C. Alexandros, a prominent member of the Egyptian court, was honoured for help to Athenians travelling to Alexandria and Cyrene, in language typical of the period.[46] Three years later Zoilos was praised for similar help in Egypt, and, at the Panathenaia of 182 B.C., Ptolemy V won a chariot victory. Other Ptolemaic notables had competed successfully before this and continued to do so after their king's success.[47] Twenty years later Ptolemy VI and his sister matched their father. Like the Attalids as Athenian citizens the Ptolemies could compete either in the open events or in those limited to Athenians.[48]

Apparently in the minority of Ptolemy VI Nikeratos of Alexandria was rewarded at Athens for services rendered in Alexandria and Cyprus, where he enjoyed great influence with the governor Ptolemaios. He was given the titles of *proxenos* and *euergetes* and quite exceptionally the decree was to be posted in the precinct of Demos and the Graces. Probably in the same prytany a man from Cypriot Salamis was praised in almost the same words. Timarchos son of Timarchos was also hailed as *proxenos* and *euergetes*, and one copy of his decree was to be set up with Nikeratos' stele; a second was set up in Salamis.[49] The governor Ptolemaios may be the Megalopolitan, who was appointed to Cyprus in 197 B.C.; but it seems more likely that he was the Ptolemaios son of Makron, who is known to have been governor already in 172/1 B.C.[50]

The king of Egypt most favoured at Athens after Ptolemy III was undoubtedly Ptolemy VI. Under him Ptolemaios son of Ptolemaios was highly honoured at Athens. He must certainly have been an important personage, though not of royal stock. Apart from the usual gold crown he was given the extraordinary honour of an equestrian statue on the Akropolis, near the old Polias temple. Set up in such a spot it was meant to be seen by

46. Another nameless Ptolemaic official was honoured in the same year (*IG* ii[2] 893a). Tracy rightly detached frgs. b and c, which concern [—]archos of Eretria, from this decree.

47. *IG* ii[2] 897. Zoilos may be the man who was high priest of Alexander in 196/5 B.C.: see Habicht, *ClAnt* 11 (1992) 72 with n. 53. The orator also proposed the decree for Alexandros (891.4f.). For Ptolemy V's victory see *IG* ii[2] 2314.41 with Tracy and Habicht, *Hesperia* 60 (1991) 216 with n. 119 and 218–20 (date). For other prominent Egyptian victors see Habicht, *ClAnt* 11 (1992) 78 f.

48. See *Hesperia* 60 (1991) 189f., lines 21f. and 31f., and 216. Ptolemy VI won a second victory in 158 B.C.: see *IG* ii[2] 2316.45 with *Hesperia* 60, 218 and 232f. Philetairos is called an Athenian on the Athenian dedication at Olympia (*SIG*[3] 641).

49. See *IG* ii[2] 908 (*ALC* 101: 194/3 to 148/7 B.C.) and 909 (*ALC* 115: 189/8 to 178/7 B.C.).

50. For the earlier Ptolemaios see Pol. 18.55.4–6 with Walbank II, 627: for the second see *SIG*[3] 585 (his father's Delphic proxeny, 188/7 B.C.) and Pol. 27.13.1–4 with Walbank III, 311f.

all who came from Egypt, as a clear record of Athens' gratitude for his services.[51]

Many scholars think that Ptolemy VI was the founder of the famous gymnasium at Athens, but Habicht strongly dissents. Unluckily the site of the gymnasium has not yet been found, so that its ruins cannot be tested archaeologically.[52] If the builder *was* Ptolemy VI, he may well have been consciously competing with Antiochos IV's temple of Zeus and the Stoas of Eumenes and Attalos II.[53] The gymnasium may not have been finished until ca. 150 B.C., and the quite exceptional celebration of the Ptolemaia in 149/8 B.C.—with over sixty distinguished *hieropoioi*—could have marked its dedication. By the 120s it was much used by philosophers for their lectures, which were by then zealously followed by the ephebes.[54] Significantly the *hieropoioi* of 149/8 B.C. included two leading Stoics—Panaitios of Rhodes and Mnasagoras of Alexandria Troas—and probably one of their Roman followers, Sp. Mummius.[55]

At Delos Athens permitted a body of Cretan mercenaries in 154 B.C. to set up statues of Ptolemy VI and his general Aglaos of Kos. The king had been labouring under severe Roman displeasure, and Rome even backed his brother's ill-fated attack on Cyprus. But when this failed and Ptolemy showed magnanimity and restraint, Rome's attitude began to change too—as the wording of the Cretan decree indicates.[56] Probably about the same time a private Athenian citizen dedicated at Delos a statue of Chrysermos of Alexandria. He is described as a kinsman of Ptolemy and he was then director of the Alexandria Museum. His grandfather had been a favourite of Ptolemy IV, and the whole family was clearly one of great distinction.[57]

51. *IG* ii² 983. Habicht showed that he could not be royal, since even his father was not given the title, refuting—among others—Kirchner in *IG* ii² (*ClAnt*11 [1992] 82).

52. For Habicht's attribution to Ptolemy III see *Studien* 112–17. For the archaeological problems see J. Travlos, *Pictorial Dictionary of Ancient Athens* (1971) 233–41 (following Homer Thompson in seeing Ptolemy VI as the founder).

53. The Stoa of Attalos seems to have been completed before ca. 150 B.C. See Meritt, *Hesperia* 26 (1957) 83–87 and Travlos, op. cit. (n. 52) 505–21.

54. See *IG* ii² 1938 (*hieropoioi*); 1006 (123/2 B.C.), lines 18–20 and 62–65 (ephebes and philosophers); Apollodoros frg. 59 in *FGH* II B, no. 244 (a philosopher: perhaps Charmadas).

55. See *IG* ii² 1938.25.8 and 40. For Spurius Mummius see Cic. *Brut.* 25.94.

56. *ID* 1518 and 1517. On the Cyprus episode see Pol. 33.11.7 and 39.7.6 with Walbank III, 554f. and 738f. For Ptolemy's care to placate Rome see *ID* 1518.9–11 and Diod. 31.33.

57. *ID* 1525. Chrysermos' father was made *proxenos* of Delphoi in 188/7 B.C. (*SIG*³ 595.136f.). For the grandfather see Plut. *Kleomenes* 36f.

After the death of Philometor, intervening in the civil war between Balas and Demetrios II, Athens' relations with Egypt are harder to chart and they may have cooled. But Habicht is surely right in maintaining that there was no such complete diplomatic rift between ca. 145 and 110 B.C. as Ferguson envisaged. All the same the expulsion of the intellectuals by Ptolemy VIII in 145 B.C. must have had some effect, especially as some found their way from Alexandria to Pergamon or Athens. Under Ptolemy IX Soter, at any rate, cordial relations were resumed.[58]

Athens' friendly relations with Egypt had been reinforced in the Chremonidean War in the 260s, when Ptolemy II helped the allies against Antigonos Gonatas with money and a fleet. Ptolemy III pursued similar anti-Macedonian policies in Greece and he was suitably honoured at Athens, though financial help was now going to the Achaian League and Kleomenes of Sparta. Athens did not count enough militarily in this game. Close ties continued under his successors, of whom Ptolemy VI seems to have been the most popular. Though under Roman displeasure from 162 to 154 B.C., he always had his supporters in the Senate, and it is possible that Athens was allowed to pursue its own interests throughout his reign without being leaned on by Rome. Once again, as with Syria, Delos must have played a significant role, and Athens will have been well repaid by royal favour, perhaps by the gift of the famous Gymnasium. Athens cleverly exploited the keen competition between the kings for the approval of the world's premier cultural centre. A century and more after the Chremonidean War Athens was still worth courting by a Ptolemy.

III. ATHENS AND THE ATTALIDS

The earliest relations between Athens and Pergamon rested on shared philosophical interests. But the purchase of Aigina by Attalos I in 209 B.C. showed the shape of the future. Pergamon would become increasingly involved in Greek affairs. Athens' mediation between Philip V and the Aitolians in that very year may be partly explained by this new political factor.[59] When Attalos visited Athens with Roman envoys in the crisis of 200 B.C., he reminded them of past benefactions, made impressive promises

---

58. See W. S. Ferguson, *Klio* 8 (1908) 341–45 and *Hellenistic Athens* (1911) 369; Habicht, *ClAnt* 11 (1992) 83–85.

59. Diog. Laert. 4.30.37f., 60 and 5.67; Habicht, *Hesperia* 59 (1990) 561f. On Attalos and Aigina see Pol. 11.5.8 and 22.8.9–10 with Walbank III, 189f.; Livy 27.30.11 and 33.4 with 28.5.1 and 31.14.11. From early in the Attalid occupation probably comes *IG* ii[2] 885, a decree of Aigina rather than of Athens. See on this the convincing article by R. E. Allen in *BSA* 66 (1971) 1–12; Tracy, *ALC* 227 n. 7 and 239. The hostile Achaian view of

and received honours to match. A new tribe with its priest was created in his name and a new deme in it was named after his wife Apollonis.[60] In 196/5 B.C. a prominent Pergamene was honoured for his services to Athens and to Athenians visiting Pergamon. He had for some time stood high in Eumenes' favour, and now that Eumenes had become king more was clearly expected of him.[61]

In 193/2 B.C. another Pergamene was singled out for services in both Pergamon and Athens, where he had stayed for a while and studied philosophy in the school of Euandros. He had apparently been a minister of Attalos and encouraged him to support Athens' cause against Philip V.[62] In this year probably an unusually long list of prytany officers was honoured by the Ptolemais prytany, including the priest of Attalos Anthemion Perithoides. He had been an ephebe in 204/3 B.C. and so would have been very young as a priest—yet the date seems sound. Why Attalos' priest was specially honoured this year is unclear, but it could have been because of Eumenes' visit to Athens in 192 B.C.[63] In 190/89 B.C. Menandros of Pergamon was honoured for his services at Eumenes' court and his help collectively and individually to Athenians. Another Pergamene was praised similarly this same year. Two decrees are inscribed on this stone, the first perhaps of an earlier date. This has caused much debate. The first decree celebrates the son of Theophilos, who received the usual gold crown, the title of *proxenos* and right of *enktesis*. The second decree extols Theophilos son of Theophilos of Pergamon in glowing terms for his use of his influence with Eumenes on Athens' behalf. It then unluckily breaks off. But it seems a reasonable

---

Attalos and Aigina is clearly not the whole story. For Athenian mediation in 209 B.C. see Pol. 10.25.1–5; Livy 27.30.4–17.

60. Pol. 16.25f. and Livy 31.14f.

61. *IG* ii² 953 (archon Tychandros). On the established 160/59 B.C. dating, the phrase about the *arche* in line 10 was taken to mean either that Eumenes had created a joint regency for Attalos or that he had left him his kingdom on his death. See for this interpretation R. E. Allen, *The Attalid Kingdom* (1983) 117 and 223 n. 18. Tracy (*AM* 107 [1992] 311f.) supports the view implied in my text that Eumenes had lately taken over the *arche*.

62. *IG* ii² 886: 6–17 recall the years 200–197 B.C. The honorand inherited goodwill to Athens from a forebear (line 7).

63. See *Agora* XV, 259 (97/6 B.C.) and for the correct dating Mattingly, *Hist.* 20 (1971) 26–28 and M. Piérart, *BCH* 100 (1976) 443–47; Tracy, *ALC* 63 (the cutter operated between 224/3 and 188/7 B.C.). For Eumenes in Athens in 192 B.C. see Livy 35.39.1–2. Athenodoros Konthyleus, a Councillor in *Agora* XV, 259, was an ephebe in 210/9 B.C. and *proedros* in 184/3 (archon Charikles). See *Agora* XV, 166 with *Hesperia* 34 (1965) 90, no. 3, line 14. The evidence taken together favours the archon Phanarchides for *Agora* XV, 259 against Hippias (181/0 B.C.), the one alternative.

suggestion that *both* decrees concern Theophilos son of Theophilos of Pergamon and that the second gave him Athenian citizenship; we know that his sons were demesmen of Halai.[64] Two years later Athens honoured another man who had worked on Attalos in Athens' interest during the years of crisis.[65] About this time yet another friend of Eumenes, Pausimachos son of Philostratos, received an honorary decree in the customary terms. He was given Athenian citizenship like Theophilos.[66]

In 175/4 B.C., the year when the Attalids escorted Antiochos IV to his kingdom to Athenian delight, Athens honoured Eumenes' brother Philetairos for his inherited goodwill to the city. The language recalls the praise of the future Antiochos IV in 178/7 B.C. An Athenian dedication of a statue of Philetairos at Olympia may belong to the same context.[67] It was probably in the 170s that Hikesios of Ephesos, Eumenes' governor of Aigina in the 190s, was praised at Athens and given citizenship.[68] Also in the 170s, it would seem, Athens honoured a man of Kyzikos well connected with Pergamon. He may have been the Philotes who was honoured at Larissa in 170 B.C. with his fellow-envoy Asklepiades of Pergamon; both had done good service with the consul P. Crassus in the previous year.[69] An Athenian Kalliphanes son of Kalliphanes Phylasios, who had fought with the Romans, Attalos and Athenaios at Pydna, was the first to bring news of

---

64. *IG* ii[2] 946 and 947. For a thorough discussion of the problems of 947 see Habicht, *Hesperia* 59 (1990) 565–67. His conclusion is close to mine. For Halai as Theophilos' deme see *ID* 1554.4 (Apollonides Theophilou Halaieus) and *Hesperia* 23 (1954) 252 no. 33 ([Th]eophilos The[ophilou Hal]aieus). Apollonides was also honoured at Pergamon without his demotic (*OGIS* 334 = *Inschr. Perg.* 172).

65. See *IG* ii[2] 894 (188/7 B.C.) and Habicht, op. cit. (n. 64) 568. The first decree on the stone is from an earlier year; it goes back to Attalos and the crisis years (lines 1–5).

66. See *IG* ii[2] 954; M.J. Osborne, *Naturalization in Athens* (1981), I, 209–11, D 100 (a new edition); Tracy, *ALC* 101 (cutter of 194/3 to 148/7); Habicht, op. cit. (n. 64) 569 (190/89 B.C.?). Osborne demonstrated that the name of the archon Hippias (181/0 B.C.) would fit the space available as well as Achaios.

67. See *IG* ii[2] 905 and Habicht, op. cit. (n. 64) 569f. For Antiochos IV see Tracy, *Hesperia* 51 (1982) 6off. with the correction by Habicht (*Chiron* 19, 11f. n. 33) in line 7f. For Olympia see *SIG*[3] 641. Philetairos is there an *euergetes* and citizen. Habicht thought that the Olympia statue was probably voted in the lost part of *IG* ii[2] 905.

68. *IG* ii[2] 922; Osborne, *Naturalization* I, 219–21, D 106 (new edition). Hikesios was praised at Megara ca. 190 B.C. soon after Megara joined the Achaian League (*IG* IV 15 = *SIG*[3] 642).

69. See *IG* ii[2] 955 and the new decree from Larissa published by K. I. Gallis in *AAA* 13 (1980) 246–49; B. Helly comments on its historical aspects, ibid. 296–301. See also *SEG* 31 (1981) 575 and Habicht, *Tyche* 2 (1987) 27 n. 27. Both envoys had been with Eumenes and Attalos as well as the consul.

the decisive victory to Athens in summer 168 B.C. and was highly honoured as a result.[70] After Pydna a Pergamene Diodoros was praised for his use of influence with Eumenes and his brothers, especially for Athenian embassies.[71] It was just at this time that Roman distrust of Eumenes turned to barely disguised displeasure. This did not prevent the eastern Greeks from offering Eumenes lively sympathy and support; but Athens had to proceed a little more carefully. As with Rhodes in Lykia, Athens had in Delos and Lemnos areas where Athenian interests could easily be damaged by Rome.[72] In a famous letter to the high priest at Pessinos ca. 154 B.C., Attalos II showed that he had still not forgotten the lesson of his brother's fall from grace, proclaiming *his* intention to observe Roman interests at all times.[73]

Like the Seleucids and the Ptolemies, the Attalids participated in the Panathenaia. In 178, 170 and 162 B.C. Eumenes won chariot victories, whilst Attalos II won in 178 and 170, Philetairos and Athenaios in 178 only.[74] Attalos was also noted for his benefactions to Athens. Eumenes had given the great Stoa that bore his name. Attalos' greatest gift was a second Pergamene Stoa, probably completed before 150 B.C. Its dedicatory inscription names it the gift of "King Attalos son of King Attalos and Queen Apollonis."[75] The same royal style is used on the base of a statue to the king's friend Theophilos son of Theophilos Halaieus, which probably stood in front of the Stoa near a chariot-group involving Attalos himself. At the same time probably Attalos dedicated a statue at Delos of Theophilos' brother Apollonides.[76]

---

70. B. D. Meritt, *Hesperia* 3 (1934) 18–21, no. 18 and 5 (1936) 429f., no. 17; L. Moretti, *ISE* I, no. 35.

71. *IG* ii[2] 945 = *SIG*[3] 651. The lettering is unique. The decree is one of a small group—like *IG* ii[2] 922—specially commissioned for men close to kings: see Tracy, *ALC* 135 and 227 n. 27.

72. For Eumenes' disgrace see Pol. 29.6.1–9, 13 and comment by Walbank, III, 365f. and Pol. 31.6.1–6 (C. Sulpicius Galus in Asia, 163 B.C.): Livy 44.24.9–26.2. Polybios noted that Rome simply made Greeks more friendly to Eumenes (31.6.6). See Eumenes' letter of thanks to the Ionian League's honours in 167/6 B.C. (*OGIS* 763; M. Holleaux, *Études* 2 (1938) 153–78). Rhodes also became reconciled to Eumenes at this time (Pol. 31.31.1–3).

73. *OGIS* 315 C VI.52–66.

74. See *IG* ii[2] 2314 col.II.83–90 with Tracy and Habicht, *Hesperia* 60, 188f. col. I.37f. and 47f. with III.23f. (as a citizen of tribe Attalis). For the dates of the new lists see 192f. and for 2313–17 see 217–21.

75. See Meritt, *Hesperia* 26 (1957) 83–88 and H. A. Thompson, ibid., 103–107.

76. See Meritt, *Hesperia* 23 (1954) 252; *ID* 1554. The same style was earlier used for Philetairos at Olympia (*SIG*[3] 641). This was probably in 175/4 B.C., as already noted; Philetairos is last mentioned in 170 B.C. (Livy 42.35.7), and only the other three brothers congratulate Rome in summer 168 B.C. (Livy 45.13.12).

For the short reign of Attalos III documentation from Athens and Delos fails us. It would be strange if relations had not remained harmonious. But the early death of the king, childless, and his will in favour of Rome changed everything. Athens had to come to terms with the new, disconcerting situation created by Rome's acceptance of the Attalid legacy.[77]

Athens had shown perhaps rather more independence with the Attalid dynasty than with the two major kingdoms. From 200 B.C. they basically followed the Roman line, though in 175 B.C. enthusiasm may have led to slightly bold anticipation of Roman policy. Rome's coolness towards Eumenes in the 160s seems to have had no discernible effect on Athens' attitude, and Attalid benefactions—again an important factor—seem to continue. Under Attalos II and III Rome was once more friendly to Pergamon, and Athens had no need even to tread warily. Pergamon was a cultural and educational centre inferior only to Athens and Alexandria, and shared interests—especially in philosophy—strengthened the ties fostered by economic and political mutual advantage.

IV. ATHENS AND THE LESSER KINGS

It is now clear that Pharnakes ascended the throne of Pontos ca. 197 B.C. and not in the mid 180s. He was at once involved with Athens through financial obligations possibly incurred by his predecessor.[78] Athens had a long tradition of interest in the Black Sea area, not least from the need to ensure regular and reasonably priced shipments of corn. *IG* ii^2 903 shows that this concern was still lively in the 170s. In Hippakos' archonship a merchant active in the Black Sea trade was highly honoured for his help to Athens in shortages of both wheat and oil.[79] In 196/5 B.C. Athenian envoys had visited Pharnakes, who was financially embarrassed at the start of his reign, and they received some of what he owed Athens—in money or in corn—and were promised the rest in instalments.[80] After the envoys'

77. On the Attalid legacy see now Habicht, *CAH* VIII^2 376–80.

78. On *ID* 1497 bis Tracy (*AM* 107 [1992] 307–13) is absolutely decisive, and I have already used his new date in a Seleucid context.

79. The honorand, whose name is lost, sold wheat cheaply at Athens rather than profiteer and redirected a large consignment of oil from the Pontic trade to Athens in 176/5 B.C. See Ph. Gauthier, *REG* 95 (1982) 275–90 for an improved text and new interpretation.

80. Tracy is surely right in taking *ID* 1497 bis. 3–7 as showing a young king not yet settled in power. These lines made little sense in the old 160/59 B.C. context, when Pharnakes would have had well over twenty years on the throne. See op. cit. (n. 78) 312.

return to Athens the Council learned of Pharnakes' marriage to Nysa and included her in the honours voted to the king. One of the three-man mission appointed to carry out the decree was to travel to Pontos with a copy of it and talk frankly to the king about Athens' needs.[81]

After this remarkable beginning we hear little about Athens and the kings of Pontos for a long time. In the war between Eumenes II and Pharnakes from 183 to 179 B.C., Athens, though sympathetic to Eumenes, was neutral— unlike Seleukos IV, who was nearly tempted to intervene militarily.[82] The Romans apparently in the end brokered a peace unfavourable to Pharnakes, who had to pay heavy indemnities to his enemies and lose all his gains except for Sinope.[83] A treaty made soon after the peace between Pharnakes and Chersonnesos stressed that both parties were bound to consider carefully the interests of Rome.[84]

Pharnakes' sister Laodike was honoured at Delos, while he was king, by a Rhodian and two other individuals who may also be from Rhodes. Rhodes had championed Sinope against both Pharnakes and his father, so that Rhodians were unlikely to honour the Pontic royal house until a decent interval after 183 B.C. had passed. Thus, if, as Tracy now believes, this dedication belongs to the time of Delian independence, it probably falls near its end.[85] Pharnakes and Nysa evidently had a son called Mithradates, who would succeed to the throne eventually and become known as Euergetes— but not before his uncle Mithradates had had a short and uneventful reign.[86]

---

81. The honours to Nysa read like an afterthought, and careful study of the decree's wording supports the view in the text. Nothing unluckily is known of Philoxenos Peiraieus, who was given the tricky Pontos task (line 42f.).

82. On Seleukos see Diod. 29.24; Pol. frg. 96 and 26.2.14.

83. Walbank probably rightly saw Rome's hand here, though the last embassy left before serious negotiations began. See III, 271–74 on Pol. 25.2.1–14.

84. See *IPE* I^2 402: Walbank, III, 20 and 273f. (date). It is dated in the 157th year of Pharnakes' era. Later Pontic kings used the same era as Bithynia, which cannot be meant here; it would yield an impossibly late year. Pharnakes' era seems to have begun with the accession of Mithradates I at Kios in 337/6 B.C. (Diod. 16.90.2), and Year 157 would work out as 180/79 B.C. S. Burstein suggested (*AJAH* 5 [1980] 1–12) that Pharnakes used the Seleucid era, the 157th year of which would be 156/5 B.C. It is hard to see why Pharnakes should have chosen the Seleucid era—hardly as having a Seleucid wife—and 156/5 B.C. seems impossibly late now.

85. *ID* 1555f. and Tracy, op. cit. (n. 78) 309f. If the dedicants were Athenians, one would expect the ethnic at this time. Asklepiades and Hermogenes are known Rhodian names (editors *ad loc.*). For Rhodes, Sinope and Pontos in 183 B.C. see Pol. 23.9.2 and compare Pol. 4.56 with Walbank I, 511–13 (the 220s).

86. Mithradates V was presumably not yet of age when his father died. Apart from his fine coinage Mithradates IV is known only for his intervention for Attalos II against Prousias II (Pol. 33.12.1).

Pharnakes probably also had a daughter Nysa, who married Ariarathes V
of Cappadocia some time after 160 B.C. While Ariarathes was still un-
married, Demetrios I of Syria offered him his sister Laodike in marriage;
but Ariarathes prudently declined and broke off his friendship in view
of Rome's known disapproval of Demetrios.[87] Mithradates V Euergetes
was honoured by an Athenian Aischylos son of Zopyros at Delos, and in
129/8 B.C. the gymnasiarch Seleukos of Marathon set up another statue
of the king. Mithradates had recently fought valiantly for Rome against
Aristonikos and received Greater Phrygia as his reward. One of his ministers Dionysios son of Boethos, an Athenian, was honoured at Delos by
Chaireas of Amisos.[88] After this we hear little until the rich crop of honours
for Mithradates VI and his court at Delos—culminating in 102/1 B.C.—
and the steady movement of Athens into the king's camp against Rome
in the 90s.[89]

With the Cappadocian kingdom Athens' relations are almost harder
to chart, but appear friendly. Ariarathes IV's daughter Stratonike was
honoured with a statue at Delos for her virtue and goodwill—but without
mention of either of her two Pergamene husbands. It may date from the years
of her widowhood (138–134 B.C.).[90] Ariarathes V had philosophic interests
and corresponded with Karneades. He may have stayed at Athens during
his virtual exile in the early 150s, when Orophernes, backed by Demetrios
I, nearly seized Cappadocia from him. Still in the 150s, possibly, the guild of
the Athenian Dionysiac *technitai* honoured Ariarathes and his queen Nysa as
generous royal benefactors. The leader of the guild was probably a *hieropoios*
at the Ptolemaia of 149/8 B.C. and a *theoros* at the Pythais of 138/7 B.C.[91]
Ariarathes died a hero's death fighting against Aristonikos in 130 B.C. and
his sons received Lykaonia as a reward. At first Nysa acted as regent
for the eldest son Ariarathes VI. Later his uncle Mithradates V overran
Cappadocia, pursuing dynastic claims, but was forced to relinquish it under

87. It is clear from *OGIS* 352 II.69 that Nysa's father was a king, but the name is lost.
On Ariarathes V's refusal of Perseus' widow see Diod. 31.28.

88. *ID* 1556–58. For Aristonikos see Eutrop. 4.20; Justin 37.1 and 38.5; App. *Mithr.* 13
and 57. Phrygia was taken away from Mithradates VI in 119 B.C. (*OGIS* 436), as Justin and
Appian record.

89. See *ID* 1559 and 1560–74. Many were set up in the Kabeireion by the priest
Helianax Asklepiadou.

90. *ID* 1575. See the editors' note on p. 56.

91. See Pol. 32.10.2–8 with Walbank III, 530f.; App. *Syr.* 47; Diod. 31.32 b
Ariararathes given refuge by Attalos). For Karneades see Diog. Laert. 4.64. For the
technitai see *OGIS* 352 and for Menelaos Aristonos see *IG* ii² 1938.46; *FD* III
2.47.8.

Roman pressure. Presumably through all these vicissitudes Athens followed the Roman lead.[92]

Mastanabal son of King Massinissa came to Rome after Pydna to congratulate the Senate. There he probably met the young Nikomedes brought thither on the same mission by Prousias II of Bithynia. Certainly the two princes became firm friends, and as king, Nikomedes dedicated at Delos statues of King Massinissa and King Mastanabal in 149 B.C., after Massinissa's death. A statue of Mastanabal's brother Gulussa may fit the same general context. Massinissa himself had been honoured at Delos as early as 178 B.C. with statues and other distinctions for generously supplying corn.[93] Nikomedes' son received a statue as patron of the ephebes in 159/8 and later as king in 127/6 B.C. another statue from the gymnasiarch Dioskourides.[94] Nikomedes II had also fought to great effect against Aristonikos, and these Delian honours for him and his son would have been well received in Rome.[95]

With these lesser kings—even with Mithradates V of Pontos—Athens had less need to observe Rome's interests and could pursue its own with little fear. These kings were often willing to be very generous to Athens and they were all well worth courting for some advantage which Athens might gain from them—perhaps in terms of favourable trade for Athenian citizens. The honorary decrees reveal that this was often the point at issue. As Polybios sourly remarked (5.107.7f.), Athens flattered all the kings alike without discrimination in hopes of royal generosity. These hopes were rarely disappointed.

V. ATHENS AND ROME

Relations were normally positive and friendly. Athens was grateful for Roman help in the crisis of 200 B.C. and loyally backed Rome in all the wars that followed. The Athenians greeted the Pydna victory with special fervour, and their long good faith was rewarded by the gift of Delos, Skyros, Lemnos and the territory of Haliartos. As Polybios dryly noted, Delos and Lemnos were to prove a somewhat *damnosa hereditas*.[96]

92. For Ariarathes V and Lykaonia see Justin 38.1.2; Mark Hassall, Michael Crawford and Joyce Reynolds, *JRS* 64 (1974) 206f. and 211 (new evidence from the Knidos copy of the law on the eastern provinces: col. III. 22–27). For Mithradates V see J. G. F. Hind, *CAH* IX[2] (1994) 132f.

93. *ID* 1577 and 1577 bis: Livy 45.13.12–17 (Masgaba!); *ID* 1578 (Gulussa: not from the same monument); *ID* 442 A.100–104 (178 B.C.).

94. *ID* 1580 and 1579. Nikomedes II still ruled in 128/7 B.C. (*Inschr. Prien.* 53).

95. See Eutrop. 4.20.

96. See Pol. 30.20.1–9 with Walbank, III, 443f.; Livy 33.30.

The Delians were forced to leave Delos in 167 B.C. to make way for Athenian settlers; the few inhabitants who were allowed to stay henceforth call themselves Rhenaioi. The Senate allowed the exiles to take all their movable wealth with them and apparently envisaged some form of compensation for the rest. Some Delians settled within the territories of the Achaian League and may have become citizens. They certainly put pressure on the League to support their claims at Rome, since Athens had allegedly not kept the bargain. In 159/8 B.C. envoys from the League and from Athens came before the Senate. One of the Achaian representatives was Polybios' brother Thearidas, who had evidently not been barred from a political career. The Senate decided for the Achaians, ruling that the agreements of 167 B.C. should be respected.[97] The success of this démarche may have encouraged others. This could well be the context of an appeal by a certain Demetrios of Rhenaia against the Athenian settlers and the governor. They had been impeding his service of Sarapis in a private shrine. Though there was a long discussion in the Council, Athens had no option but to instruct the governor to obey Rome, insisting on Demetrios' rights.[98] The date of this affair is debatable. The praetor Q. Minucius Q.f., who introduced the matter in the Senate, cannot be closely identified. One of the three witnesses to the decree, however, gives more help. Ti. Claudius Ti.f.Crust. was clearly given his tribe to distinguish him from a Ti. Claudius Ti.f.Nero Arnensis. He must be an Asellus, son of the praetor of 205 and father of the notorious tribune of 140 B.C. This man was allegedly poisoned by his wife about the same time as the consul L. Postumius Albinus suffered the same fate in office in 154 B.C.[99] In the *SC de Tiburtibus* of ca. 159 B.C. the three witnesses are still recorded without tribes in the old fashion, as the other two in the *SC de Delo*. By the late 140s tribes were added routinely for all witnesses. A dating for the *SC de Delo* in the period 158–154 B.C. would suit all the evidence.[100]

About this time Athens was putting pressure on independent Oropos, long an irritation to Athenian pride. Oropos appealed to Rome in autumn 157 B.C. and the Senate referred the matter to Sikyon for arbitration. When Athens refused to appear, Sikyon imposed a five hundred talent fine by default. Athens then appealed to Rome, and in 155 B.C. the famous three philosophers'

97. Pol. 32.7.1–5 with Walbank III, 525f.

98. See *SIG*[3] 664 = *ID* 1510 and R. Sherk, *Roman Documents* no. 5, pp. 37–39; P. Roussel, *Délos colonie Athénienne* (1916) 120f.

99. For Arnensis and the Nerones see Livy 29.37.10. For the murders of Albinus and Asellus see Val. Max. 6.3.8 and Livy *Epit.* 48. The epitome sets the trials in 150 B.C.; perhaps the suspicions reached certainty only a few years after the respective deaths.

100. For the Tibur document see *CIL* I[2] 586 and for the point about the normal usage before the 140s see my argument in *NC* (1969) 193f.

embassy presented the Athenian case. The Senate then reduced the fine
to one hundred talents, but Athens managed to evade paying even that.
The Senate now appeared to lose interest in the affair.[101] Athens then
somehow contrived to win over Oropos, and an agreement was reached
under which Athens put in a garrison and Oropos gave hostages. Not much
later members of the garrison began harassing the Oropians and the anti-
Athenian party probably had to leave with their dependents. When an appeal
to Athens failed, Oropos turned to the Achaian League, which, however,
proved reluctant to forfeit Athens' friendship. But in 151/0 B.C. Menalcidas
as general, backed by Kallikrates, induced the League to approve military
action on behalf of Oropos. Athens reacted swiftly, invading Oropian
territory and removing the garrison. Menalcidas and Kallikrates now
proposed an invasion of Attika, but they were overruled by their colleagues.
An inscription from Oropos praises Hieron of Aigeira who had urged
vigorous intervention on the League, using as one argument the unshaken
loyalty of Oropos to Rome. This consideration surely helped persuade
Athens to cut its losses. But the lesson was lost on the new League leaders,
who were soon in open and disastrous opposition to Rome. There could
be only one outcome, though it was delayed till 146 B.C.[102]

Athens' temporary difficulties with Rome in the 150s seem to have led
to at least one interesting development. Already in 159/8 B.C. at Delos
the former priest Euboulos of Marathon was praised for carrying out all
his duties efficiently "for the Athenians and the Romans."[103] In 152/1 B.C.
at Delos a priest of Hestia, Demos and Roma was added to the existing
nine. The priest is recorded again in 129/8 B.C., but by ca. 100 B.C. the
title was shortened to priest of Roma. The creation of the new priesthood
at this point suggests a firm desire to assure Rome of Athens' continued
devotion.[104]

101. See Pol. 32.11.4–5 with Walbank III, 531–33; Paus. 7.11–14; Cic. *Acad.* 2.137 with
Gell. 6.14.8–10 and Plut. *Cato Maior* 22 (the philosophers' embassy).

102. *SIG*³ 675 neatly supplements Pausanias. For Oropos and Rome see lines 8–12.
Pausanias saw the point about Achaian folly, and his account of Oropos leads directly
into the war between the League and Rome.

103. *ID* 1498.17–22.

104. *ID* 2605.9. The restoration of Demos after Hestia is justified by *ID* 1877. For
Roma alone see *IG* ii² 2336.45 and 124f. For nine priests in 153/2 B.C. (Phaidrias archon)
see *ID* 1499.15–22. *ID* 2605 has the ruined names of administrators corresponding to
what survives in *ID* 1432 Aa.13f. (accounts of Phaidrias' year) of the administrators of the
next year. The dating 158/7 B.C. found at *ID* 2605 and adopted by other scholars (as by
Habicht, *Hermes* 119 [1991] 197) rests on the belief that the tribal cycle for the Great Gods
known from the 120s (one year ahead of the secretary cycle) went back before 150 B.C. On

On the troubles that Lemnos caused Athens we are less well informed than on Delos or Oropos. But in the 140s serious difficulties had certainly arisen, requiring appeal to the Senate in 140 B.C. and a judgement satisfactory both to Athens and to the colonists in Lemnos. We have a decree from those in Myrina, which shows that the matter was settled when C. Laelius presided in the Senate, presumably as consul; his praetorship in 145 B.C. was largely spent fighting rebels in Further Spain. The decree is dated on the Athenian side by Herakleitos Poseidippou, hoplite general for the second time—a man who was clearly very prominent in the 140s from our other evidence.[105] The colonists from Herakleia passed a similar decree, honouring an Athenian Epikles Acharneus for his valiant efforts on their behalf. He won a chariot victory at the Great Panathenaia as early as 166 B.C. The decree for him has very close verbal links with another of ca. 145–135 B.C.; both unusually give the name of the Military Treasurer.[106]

Surprisingly, Delos under Athens has not provided much evidence of dedications by or to Romans from 167 to 129 B.C. Most of the known offerings by Roman generals and other officers date to the period of independence. But the Athenian temple accounts do record a dedication by Cn. Octavius, the consul of 165 B.C.[107] The Athenian people for their part set up a statue of the consul L. Caecilius Q.f.Metellus for his goodwill. Is this the consul of 142 or 117 B.C.? There is much to be said for the earlier date. The consul of 142 B.C. accompanied Scipio Aemilianus and Sp. Mummius on the famous eastern embassy. There is a good case for dating this 144/3 B.C. In summer 143 the envoys would have travelled from Rhodes to Pergamon, Delos, Athens and Rome. This would have given L. Metellus an excellent chance to show his sympathy and readiness to help Athens in his hoped for consulship.[108] The Cn. Octavius Cn.f. honoured at Delos as praetor could well be the consul of 128 B.C., as Badian acutely saw—son of the man

---

this theory Ariston Aristonos Steirieus (III) with archon Mikion (*ID* 1899) ought to go in 144/3 B.C.; but in fact that year is firmly taken by the archon Theaitetos. The priest of *ID* 2605 Seleukos Diokleous Pergasethen (I) can no longer be fixed in 158/7 B.C. as by P. Roussel (*DCA* 349f.).

105. See *IG* ii² 1224. On Laelius see Broughton, *MRR* I, 469. On Herakleitos see Tracy, *ALC* 155 and 160; *IG* ii² 2445.4 and 2334.6–9 (ca.150–140 B.C.).

106. *IG* ii² 1223. With lines 17–19 compare *IG* ii² 853 (ca.140 B.C.: A. S. Henry, *Chiron* 14 [1984] 94) 13f. and 15–17. Tracy ascribes 853 to a cutter active from 169/8 to 135/4 B.C. (*ALC* 148).

107. *ID* 1429 A I.12.

108. See *ID* 1604 bis with E. Badian, *Chiron* 20 (1990) 401 (n. 7), who inclines towards 117 B.C. For the date of Scipio's embassy see my article in *CQ* n.s. 36 (1986) 491–95.

who made the earlier dedication there. He was perhaps commander of the Roman fleet against Aristonikos in 131 B.C.[109]

The evidence is indeed thin from this source. But there can be no doubt that by 140—after the shock of Mummius' victory, tempered by a moderate settlement shaped by Polybios—Athens remained loyal and friendly to Rome and was back in full favour. Nothing occurred to disturb this harmony until the fatal madness that seized some Athenian politicians and led to the calamitous alliance with Mithradates VI from 88 to 86 B.C. against the might of Rome. My paper has, I think, shown how out of character this aberration was. The troubles of the 160s and 150s were passing phases, and Rome, rather than Athens, seems to have been responsible. Athens was clearly careful to distance itself from the Achaian League's folly, even though it had received some not dissimilar provocation from Rome. The city had always known just how far it could safely go. Even with the strongest, most ambitious, most generous and friendly of kings Athens had never before compromised itself in the eyes of the most powerful patron of all.

109. See *ID* 1782 with Badian, op. cit. (n. 108) 405f. (n. 22). Badian's suggestion about the fleet seems particularly happy as giving a reason for Octavius' presence and his honour; we know only about a few of the lesser military officers on land in this war, nothing of the fleet.

SEVEN

Poseidonios and Athenion:
A Study in Hellenistic Historiography

Klaus Bringmann

Poseidonios was a Stoic philosopher and historian. As a philosopher, he held a particular theory on the origins of man's actions and regarded history as a source of material to support his views on the psychological causes of human error. He saw history through the eyes of a philosopher and moralist, and his version of an episode from the history of Athens in 88 B.C., the so-called Athenion episode, illustrates the problems to which this could lead. In it Poseidonios conflated the reigns of two successive tyrants and gave the first, Athenion, who made only a brief appearance upon the political stage in summer 88, characteristics which were drawn from the story of the second tyrant, Aristion, who ruled the city from autumn 88 until March 1 of 86.

This theory is based upon two assumptions: (I) that Athenion and Aristion were not one and the same but two different persons from Athenian history, and (II) that Poseidonios' *History* ends in the summer of 88. The arguments underlying each of these assumptions will be presented in turn, and finally (III) an attempt will be made to interpret the events in the light of Poseidonios' concept of historical causality.

—I—

The only information we have on Athenion, who led Athens into the camp of Mithradates in that critical year 88 B.C. and so paved the way to disaster, comes from Poseidonios, and then only because Athenaios made use of his detailed account, partly quoting it word for word, partly paraphrasing it. It is the largest and most productive fragment from Poseidonios' *History* to have

For the English translation I am indebted to Dr. David Wigg of Frankfurt.

survived.[1] The part that deals with the tyrant's violence in Athens has given rise to the view that Athenion is in fact none other than Aristion, who is well known from the sources and whose reign of terror was brought to an end when the Romans captured the city.[2]

However, we know from Strabo 9.1.20 that during the Mithradatic War not only Aristion, whom he mentions by name, but at least one other tyrant successively ruled Athens in the King's name: ἐπιπεσὼν δ᾽ ὁ Μιθριδατικὸς πόλεμος τυράννους αὐτοῖς κατέστησεν, οὓς ὁ βασιλεὺς ἐβούλετο. In the last century, B. Niese managed to prove that the first of these was Athenion, the second Aristion.[3] He demonstrated that they came to power during separate but consecutive phases of the history of Athens during the Mithradatic War. Athenion returned from a long stay as ambassador at the court of Mithradates in spring 88, was elected strategos of the hoplites and placed his own people in the other offices. The city then went over to the Pontic King's side. The Romans responded by taking Delos, the most important Athenian overseas territory, and Athenion's attempt to recapture it failed. The Athenian expedition led by Apellikon was repulsed, and Rome was able to keep control of the island. Later, however, in the autumn of 88, Archelaos, Mithradates' general, took it and slaughtered the Romans there. Delos was returned to Athens, and it was in this context that Aristion began to play a part. On the King's orders he brought the Athenians the Delian temple treasure. He was accompanied by a two-thousand-strong Pontic unit, and usurped power in Athens with the help of this bodyguard. He was to stay in power until the bitter end, when Sulla took the city on March 1 of 86.

So far so good. But the episode of Athenion poses more questions than it answers. If we follow Poseidonios' version of the story, then Athenion's assumption of power was by no means a violent coup d'état, but was

1. Athenaios 5.211e–215b = fr. 253 E.-K. (L. Edelstein and I. G. Kidd, eds., *Posidonius*, vol. 1, *The Fragments*[2] [Cambridge, 1989], and I. G. Kidd, ed., *Posidonius*, vol. 2.1 and 2, *The Commentary* [Cambridge, 1988]; fr. 253: 2.2, 863–87).

2. The scholars who believe that Athenion and Aristion are one and the same are listed most completely by G. R. Bugh, "Athenion and Aristion of Athens," *Phoenix* 46 (1992) 111 n. 8. J. Malitz, "Die Historien des Poseidonios," *Zetemata* 79 (München, 1983) 342f. straddles the fence between postulating identity and the assumption that there were two tyrants.

3. B. Niese, "Die letzten Tyrannen Athens," *RhM* 42 (1887) 547–81; G. R. Bugh, op. cit. (n. 2) 111 n. 8 lists the scholars who follow Niese. Niese's convincing conclusion was reached by a comparison of Poseidonios in Athenaios (see n. 1) on the one hand, and Strabo 9.1.20 and Appian, *Mithr.* 28–29 on the other. The approximate dates used in the following text are drawn from E. Badian, "Rome, Athens and Mithradates," *AJAH* 1 (1976) 108–11.

supported by a population blinded by enthusiasm. There is no reason to believe that Athenion had to deal with any opposition from the political elite of Athens. On the contrary, the surviving list of archons for 88/87, *IG* 2².1714, shows that Athenion's candidates, who were elected in early summer 88, belonged to the established political class.[4] Most of them had previously held important office. Oinophilos, the Archon Basileus, and son of Amphias of Aphidna, belonged to one of the most prominent families and was even allied to Medeios, who was Archon eponymos for three years prior to Athenion's rise to power, from 91/90 to 89/88.[5] Everything points to the political elite's having supported the new foreign policy of the city in the summer of 88.

So much the more surprising is Poseidonios' observation (l.111f. E.-K.) that it was only a few days after his rise to power before the philosopher proved himself to be the worst possible of tyrants. He does not say explicitly why Athenion visited the city with such terror, and instead of seeking an explanation he resorts to cliché, observing that it lies in the nature of tyranny to remove any well-meaning parties. The explanation must be gleaned from the account of the individual episodes in the reign of terror.[6] One of the basic assumptions is that a wave of inhabitants tried to leave the city. The tyrant tried to prevent this, but his only achievement was that many, out of fear "of what was to come," let themselves down from the city walls by night and fled. Those who were caught were brought back into the city and accused of pro-Roman sympathies.[7] There is also talk of Athenians who remained in the city being tried for treason on the grounds that they were plotting for the return of those who had fled (and therefore were plotting the downfall of the regime). It stands to reason that such a sudden change of mood, from overwhelming optimism to sudden defeatist

4. Cf. E. Badian op. cit. 112f. with n. 30. The name of the eponymous archon is missing from the list. Chr. Habicht has made the tempting suggestion that the person involved, who fell foul of a perpetual *damnatio memoriae*, was none other than King Mithradates: "Zur Geschichte Athens in der Zeit Mithradates VI: Der eponyme Archon im Jahr der 'Anarchie' (88/87)," *Chiron* 6 (1976) 127–35 = idem, *Athen in hellenistischer Zeit* (München, 1994) 216–23.

5. *IG* 2².1713 col. II. Medeios and Oinophilos were honoured together by the Council: B. D. Meritt, *Hesperia* 33 (1964) 193, no. 43.

6. l.120–45 E.-K. I will not go into the much-discussed question of whether the extant texts contain doublets, and how they might be explained. Since I. G. Kidd doubted their existence (*Posidonius* 2.2, 879–82), it is probably necessary to follow G. R. Bugh op. cit. (n. 2) 114 when he maintains that "One person's doublets are another's rhetorical variatio."

7. The emendation suggested by J. Touloumakos, "Zu Poseidonios Fr. 36 (Jac.)," *Philologus* 110 (1966) 141 has rightly been incorporated in l.125–26 E.-K.: τὰ Ῥωμαίων φρονεῖν προσεποιεῖτο ⟨τοὺς ληφθέντας⟩.

panic, cannot have so altered the former consensus between ruler and ruled within just a few days. The surviving account does not say what actually caused this transition, but the details of the individual episodes allow a reconstruction. The missing link is, simply, the appearance of Sulla in the theatre of war in Greece. The dangerous consequences of supporting Mithradates became apparent when war reached Athens and Attica. Instead of the promised wealth and democracy, the city found itself engaged in a struggle for life and death. The razed remains of Corinth provided a salutary reminder, and in the moment of truth the mood changed. Many began to flee,[8] trying to save what they could by changing sides. The tyrant, whose fate was linked to that of Mithradates to the bitter end, reacted in the only way he could: he resorted to terror in order to prevent desertion and "betrayal."

There are other indications which support this interpretation. Poseidonios places the blame for a famine in the city at Athenion's door,[9] and notes that the tyrant provided the Athenians with only barley and a little wheat. In the end, he writes sarcastically, the Athenians received no more than rations fit for chickens as the rewards of their rashness: Ἀθηνίων ... χοίνικα κριθῶν εἰς τέσσαρας ἡμέρας διεμέτρει τοῖς Ἀθηναίοις ἀνοήτοις, ἀλεκτορίδων τροφὴν καὶ οὐκ ἀνθρώπων αὐτοῖς διδούς. The satirical comment does not apply to the type of grain (barley), but rather to the amount. The normal daily ration consisted of a choinix, approximately one litre according to the Attic system of measures,[10] but the Athenians had to make do with a quarter, that is they were fed like chickens. There is no answer to the obvious question, why Athenion should have subjected the Athenians to these hunger rations in the summer of 88, as they make sense only during Sulla's siege of the city, when there definitely was a dramatic shortage of food, as is well-attested,[11] and is only to be expected in the circumstances. The conclusion appears to be unavoidable, that the picture of Athenion is painted with colours actually appropriate to the story of Aristion.

---

8. Those refugees whose names are known are Philon, the head of the Academy, who taught in Rome during the Mithradatic War (Cicero, *Brut.* 396), as well as Medeios and Kalliphron, who witnessed the siege in Sulla's camp (Plutarch, *Sulla* 14.9). Medeios was probably the son of the eponymous archon of 91/90–89/88 of the same name, and was himself archon in the 60s (*PA* 10099); Kalliphron was archon in 58/57 (*PA* 8231).

9. Cf. l.138–40 and 158–61 E.-K.

10. Cf. e.g. Herodotos 7.187.2; Diogenes Laertios 7.18; Thucydides 4.16.2 (the Spartans receive two, their slaves one choinix per day). For the ancient evidence and its interpretation, cf. L. Foxhall and H. A. Forbes, "Σιτομετρεία: The Role of Grain as a Staple Food in Classical Antiquity," *Chiron* 12 (1982) 51–82.

11. Cf. Appian, *Mithr.* 35; Plutarch, *Sulla* 13.

G. R. Bugh recently found a further indication of this in l.122–25 E.-K.[12] καὶ ὁ Ἀθηνίων ἱππέας ἐπαποστείλας οὓς μὲν ἐφόνευσεν, οὓς δὲ καὶ δεδεμένους κατήγαγε, δορυφόρους ἔχων πολλοὺς τῶν καταφρακτικῶν. Bugh argues convincingly and carefully that Kaibel's emendation καταφρακτικῶν is better than the contradictory tradition ἀφρακτικῶν A: φρακτικῶν C. The word is a technical term for the heavily armoured cavalry which the rulers of the eastern dynasties, including Mithradates, employed in large numbers. From Appian we know that Aristion came to Athens accompanied by Pontic troops. It was with their help, Appian adds in *Mithr.* 28, that he usurped power and had Roman sympathisers either executed or sent to the King. In other words, if Poseidonios, according to Athenaios, has the tyrant sending out heavy cavalry which was serving in his bodyguard to hunt down fugitive Athenians, then this can apply only to the cataphracts which Aristion had brought to Athens, for neither did the Athenian cavalry have any, nor had Athenion returned to Athens from the court of Mithradates with Pontic troops.

But even if the situation is quite clear, it has been variously interpreted. It forms the basis for the identification of Athenion with Aristion, but this is incorrect, as been shown above. U. von Wilamowitz sought another way out.[13] He places the blame for the confusion of the two tyrants on Athenaios. He suggests that the first part of the fragment, which is quoted word for word, comes from the story of Athenion, but that the second part is a patchwork paraphrase of a collection of excerpts, which at least in part have their origin in Poseidonios' description of Aristion's reign of terror. Thus it is Athenaios who taints the first tyrant with terror. G. R. Bugh has resurrected Wilamowitz' proposition, expanding and modifying it with new arguments. Like Wilamowitz, he recognises that 146–80 E.-K., that is, the final paragraph of the second section, which describes the failure of Apellikon's expedition to Delos, belongs to the story of Athenion. The conclusion of this analysis is that Athenaios has included sections from the description of the later tyranny of Aristion in the episode of Athenion (l.12–111 E.-K. and 146–80 E.-K.).[14]

But this suggestion is not acceptable either. In the narrative the expedition forms the pinnacle of the tyrant's violent deeds. l.130–32 E.-K. talks of extensive confiscations and several cisterns being filled with the stolen money. But the expedition to Delos is considered even worse, for Athenion no longer satisfied himself with robbing the citizens, he now turned his attention to

---

12. G. R. Bugh, op. cit. (n. 2) 114–19.

13. U. von Wilamowitz, "Athenion und Aristion," *SB* (Berlin, 1923) 43, 48–50 = idem, *Kleine Schriften*, 5.1 (Berlin and Amsterdam, 1971) 210, 216–19.

14. G. R. Bugh, op. cit. (n. 2) 123.

foreigners by trying to get his hands on the temple treasure of Delos (1.146–48 E.-K.). Furthermore, the passage concerning the story of Apellikon contains a reference to the Athenians' receiving emergency rations (1.158–61 E.-K.) which is twice tied into the context. Not only is the hunger in Athens contrasted with the sumptuousness of the Athenian expeditionary corps on Delos, but Athenion and Apellikon, the commander of the expedition, are also compared. Apellikon, it is said, joined Athenion because he adhered to the same philosophical school, the Peripatos, but Athenion had forgotten the teachings of the Peripatos, doing no good deeds for his fellow citizens, and instead putting them on emergency rations (1.157–61 E.-K.).

But even Bugh cannot explain why Athenaios should have attributed Aristion's reign of terror to the ephemeral tyrant Athenion. On the authority of A. Tronson,[15] he contents himself with an observation which was made when checking quotations in surviving prose works. In order to enhance his argumentation Athenaios is supposed to have abridged the texts he used, or even changed their sense. Bugh claims that this has happened in the Athenion fragment, and that Athenaios deliberately confused the two tyrants:[16] "I believe that Athenaios knew that there were two tyrants in Athens in this period and purposely conflated the two careers." But even if we cannot check the original passages quoted by Athenaios, Bugh still has not managed to answer the question of what intention Athenaios was pursuing when he did so.

His intention can in fact be gleaned from the context into which the extensive fragment from Poseidonios' *History* is inserted.[17] The theme of the section into which it is incorporated is the contradiction between the teachings and the actions of philosophers. A short reference to an otherwise unknown Epicurean, Lysias, who became tyrant in Tarsos (215 B–C), follows the long excerpt from Poseidonios (211 D–215 B), which is, in turn, followed by a long and sarcastic discussion of the Platonic portrait of Socrates (215 D–220 A). The conclusion is provided by an appendix on the other Socratics (220 A–221 A). Nobody would fit better into this gallery of pseudophilosophers than

15. A. Tronson, "Satyrus the Peripatetic and the Marriages of Philip II," *JHS* 104 (1984) 124f.; cf. R. W. Sharples and D. W. Winter, "Theophrastus on Fungi: Inaccurate Citations in Athenaeus," *JHS* 103 (1983) 154–55. An examination of the forty-two quotations and passages from Herodotos, on the other hand, revealed that apart from textual variations and abridgements the sense of the original was severely distorted only in one single passage, Herodotos 2.51 in Athenaios 6.231d. P. A. Brunt, "On Historical Fragments and Epitomes," *CQ* 30 (1980) 480–82 concludes: "We may assume then that in general Athenaeus is fairly reliable" (481).

16. G. R. Bugh, op. cit. (n. 2) 120.

17. Cf. the description of the context by I. G. Kidd, *Posidonius* 2.2, 863f.

Aristion. To be sure he was an Epicurean, and Appian used this as an excuse for augmenting his description of his reign of terror with an excursus on philosophers, the tone of which closely corresponds to the attack on philosophers in Athenaios' fifth book.[18] But why did Athenaios pass up the opportunity of attacking such a prominent figure as Aristion, turning his pen on Lysias, who was virtually unknown, instead? There is no obvious reason. J. Malitz comments, "Athenaios müßte die Historien sehr flüchtig gelesen haben, wenn ihm die Kapitel über den Epikureer Aristion tatsächlich vorlagen, ihm aber bei der Niederschrift des 'Sophistenmahls' als Epikureer aber nur Lysias von Tarsos eingefallen ist."[19] If, then, we may not assume that it was Athenaios who filled out Poseidonios' account of Athenion with excerpts from the story of the terror regime of Aristion, then it must have been Poseidonios who was responsible for this contamination of the two tyrants. But again, no satisfactory answer has yet been found to the question of why the author inserted a description of the suffering and terror during the later wartime dictatorship of Aristion into the episode of Athenion. I. G. Kidd assumes that he centred his attack on philosophers who turned into tyrants on the figure of Athenion, and therefore excluded the aspects of tyrannical rule in the later story of Aristion.[20] But how could a historian have written about Aristion without including desertion, plots, hunger and terror, which were an integral part of his regime while the city was being besieged? An answer to this paradox would be at hand if Athenaios found in the histories of Poseidonios a detailed description of the "tyrant" Athenion, but Aristion and his reign of terror were not mentioned. Until recently this has not been suggested, and Kidd merely states defensively, "No doubt he [sc. Poseidonios] then went on to give an account of Aristion, the campaign in Greece, and the capture of Athens by Sulla."[21] However, recently E. Ruschenbusch has plausibly demonstrated that Poseidonios' *History* ended in the year 88.[22]

— II —

Ruschenbusch bases his assertion on Felix Jacoby's discovery that the fragment about the end of Marius, Plut. *Mar.* 45.3–6 (*FGrHist* 87 fr. 37 = fr. 255

18. Appian, *Mithr.* 28: cf. G. R. Bugh, op. cit. (n. 2) 119.

19. J. Malitz, op. cit. (n. 2) 343.

20. I. G. Kidd, *Posidonius* 2.2, 885: "Besides, Posidonius in his *History* probably concentrated his attack on the philosopher-tyrant on Athenion, and did not repeat and dwell on this aspect in his subsequent account of Aristion and the siege and capture of Athens."

21. I. G. Kidd, *Posidonius* 2.2, 187.

22. E. Ruschenbusch, "Der Endpunkt der Historien des Poseidonios," *Hermes* 121 (1993) 70–76.

E.-K.), belongs to an appraisal, the original of which, that is Poseidonios, is related not to his death (January 13 of 86) but to his conflict with Sulla over the supreme command against Mithradates in 88. Jacoby compares the fragment with Diodorus 37.29–30 and notes "zusammenfassende würdigung des Marius ... Diod. XXXVII 29, 2–5, die bei Dindorf richtig zwischen die beiden perikopen *Exc. De sent.* 400, 10ff. = Diod. 29, 1; 30 gestellt ist. die vorlage gab sie nicht im todesjahre des Marius, sondern skizzierte beim kampfe um den oberbefehl gegen Mithridates vorgreifend die letzten schicksale des Marius und der Marianer. das zeigt der vergleich von Diod. 29, 1 ... mit dem vollständigeren, aber der gleichen quelle schöpfenden Plut. *Marius* 34, 5–6."[23] Ruschenbusch is right in perceiving that this means that Poseidonios did not include the events of 86 in his chronological narrative, and therefore his *History* ended with the year 88. In this context it is important to note that for events after 88 Athenaios no longer used Poseidonios, but Nicolaus of Damascus who continued his work (*FGrHist* 90 fr. 74–80 and 94–95). The join between the two histories is indicated by *FGrHist* 90 fr. 95: Νικόλαος ... καὶ Ποσειδώνιος (*FGrHist* 87 fr. 38 = fr. 51 E.-K.) ... ἐν ταῖς Ἱστορίαις ἑκάτερος τοὺς Χίους φασὶν ἐξανδραποδισθέντας ὑπὸ Μιθριδάτου τοῦ Καππάδοκος παραδοθῆναι τοῖς ἰδίοις δούλοις δεδεμένους ... It is significant that Athenaios names Nicolaus as his main authority for the events of 86, and Poseidonios is relegated to second place. The reason for this is that Nicolaus mentions the Chians' deportation to Colchis in the context of the events of 86, while Poseidonios refers to this event in advance, just as he did with the death of Marius and the fate of the Marians.

Ruschenbusch also discovered the reason why the deportation of the Chians was mentioned so early. During Mithradates' blockade of Rhodes there was a sea battle between the royal and the Rhodian fleets. In the heat of the engagement a Chian ship, which was of course allied with Mithradates, inadvertently rammed the royal flagship. Appian describes his reaction in *Mithr.* 25: ὁ βασιλεύς, οὐδὲν τότε φροντίζειν ὑποκρινάμενος, τὸν κυβερνήτην ὕστερον ἐκόλασε καὶ πρωρέα, καὶ Χίοις ἐμήνισε πᾶσιν. Appian *Mithr.* 45 further indicates that the King's anger was one of the deeper reasons for the deportation two years later: Χίοις δὲ μηνίων, ἐξ οὗ τις αὐτῶν ναῦς ἐς τὴν βασιλικὴν ... ἐνέβαλε ... Accordingly, it was the naval battle of the summer of 88 that led Poseidonios to refer to the subsequent results of Mithradates' anger.

What we know of the scope and extent of the *History* fits well with the end-date suggested here. In Suidas (2107–2109) we read s.v. Ποσειδώνιος:

23. F. Jacoby, *FGrHist* II C, 188.

ἔγραψεν ἱστορίαν τὴν μετὰ Πολύβιον ἐν βιβλίοις νβ' ἕως τοῦ πολέμου τοῦ Κυρηναϊκοῦ καὶ Πτολεμαίου. Poseidonios took up where Polybios had left off, that is in 145. We cannot reconstruct his exact arrangement, but at least it is clear that it was basically chronologically organised and divided up between the various theatres of war within fairly short periods, thus resembling the work of his predecessor Polybius. In Book 7, for example, Scipio the Younger's visit to the court of Ptolemy VII Physkon in Alexandria (140/39) was described,[24] in Book 16 the Parthian campaign and disaster of Antiochos VII Sidetes (130/29),[25] and Book 49 contained a portrayal of the character of the Roman Apicius, who in 92 acted as accuser of P. Sulpicius Rufus.[26] So the first sixteen books seem roughly to have followed the rule "one year per book," and the following thirty-three (17–49) vary only slightly (thirty-seven years: thirty-three books). On the other hand, if we accept on average 12 to 14 months for each book, then the generally accepted view that Poseidonios' *History* continued to 86, or even the middle of the 80s,[27] becomes difficult to hold. It seems quite unlikely that so eventful a period as the years covering the Social Wars, the conflict between Marius and Sulla and the Mithradatic War could have been packed into three books. However, if we accept that Book 50 began with the events of the summer of 91, then the probability that the last book ended with the year 88 is high. This would also correspond well with the details of the end of the work provided by Suidas, which W. Theiler has emended to ἕως τοῦ πολέμου τοῦ Κυρηναϊκοῦ καὶ Πτολεμαίου ⟨ Ἀλεξάνδρου⟩.[28]

Ptolemy X Alexander, who was suspected of murdering his mother, Cleopatra III, was, as Poseidonios mentions in Book 47, universally hated. In 88 he was expelled by the Alexandrians and perished in the same year in a sea battle near Cyprus against his brother, Ptolemy IX Lathyros.[29] It is generally accepted that the royal name Ptolemaios has to be qualified by a distinguishing name, and even I. G. Kidd is of the opinion that Ptolemy X Alexander would fit in well with the rest of the tradition, with the reservation

24. Fr. 58 E.-K. = *FGrHist* 87 fr. 7.

25. Fr. 63–65 E.-K. = *FGrHist* 87 fr. 11–13.

26. Fr. 78 E.-K. = *FGrHist* 87 fr. 27.

27. Cf. J. Malitz, op. cit. (n. 2) 63 and 70f.; I. G. Kidd, *Posidonius* 2.1, 280: "On the whole the balance of evidence still points to the mid-eighties for the end-point."

28. W. Theiler, *Poseidonios. Die Fragmente*, vol. 1, *Texte* (Berlin and New York, 1982) T 1a, 8.

29. Fr. 77 E.-K. = *FGrHist* 87 fr. 26. On the date and circumstances of his death cf. A. E. Samuel, *Ptolemaic Chronology*, Münchener Beiträge zur Papyrusforschung und antiken Rechtsgeschichte 43 (München, 1962) 152 and idem, *Chronique d'Ég.* 40 (1965) 376ff.

that "his death is rather early for the finish of the *History*."[30]   But this objection is based on the assumption that Poseidonios mentioned the death of Marius and the deportation of the Chians at their proper place within the chronological framework, which now collapses given their earlier inclusion in connection with the events of 88.

   88 is also consistent with what we know about the Cyrenaean War, which is mentioned in a note in Suidas. When Lucullus arrived in Cyrene on Sulla's orders in the winter of 87/86, he found the situation chaotic after a series of tyrannies and wars,[31] and restored internal order in the city. This provides us with a terminus ante quem, for when Lucullus arrived war and tyranny had come to an end, but the city was still suffering from the consequences and the situation had not been stabilised. Further details about the war and the tyrannies are included in Plutarch *Mor.* 255 E–257 E, which deals with the courageous determination of a Cyrenaean woman to free her native city from tyranny. First of all Aretaphila succeeded in persuading Leander to remove his brother Nicocrates as tyrant, but when he succeeded him on the throne she managed to involve him in a major war with the Libyans, which ended in his capture and death. Plutarch *Mor.* 255 E dates these events to the critical phase of the Mithradatic War: Ἀρεταφίλα δ' ἡ Κυρηναία παλαιὰ μὲν οὐ γέγονεν, ἀλλ' ἐν τοῖς Μιθριδατικοῖς καιροῖς. However, since in winter 87/86 Lucullus no longer found war and tyranny, merely the aftermath, the events described by Plutarch must belong to the first phase of the Mithradatic War, and there is no reason for not supposing that Poseidonios included the Cyrenaean War in his description of the critical year 88 which ended his work.

— III —

The fact that his *History* ended in 88 would explain why Poseidonios names and grants a key role to an ephemeral tyrant who is not even mentioned by Strabo, Plutarch or Appian. Poseidonios was not interested in portraying a key moment in Athens' path to disaster, but rather in using the story of Athenion as a general moral example by portraying him as the prototypical political seducer, the opposite of the Platonic Philosopher King.[32] He probed

---

   30. I. G. Kidd, *Posidonius* 2.1, 280.

   31. The decree of Aleximachos, which was published by J. M. Reynolds, "A Civic Decree from Tocra in Cyrenaica," *ArchCl* 25/26 (1973/74) 623–30, also refers to the war with the Libyans; see also Moretti, "Un decreto di Arsinoe in Cirenaica," *RFIC* 104 (1976) 385–418 (= L. Robert, *REG* 90 [1977] 444 no. 594 and 91 [1978] 506 no. 561).

   32. For the interpretation of the fragment cf. the commentary by I. G. Kidd, *Posidonius* 2.2, 865–87 as well as the summary in idem, "Posidonius as Philosopher Historian," in M. Griffin and J. Barnes, eds., *Philosophia Togata: Essays on Philosophy and Roman Society* Oxford,

the inner relationship between seducer and seduced, and used Athenion as an example of the principal causes and the intermediate circumstances that led to tyrannical rule. His interest in what actually happened, that is, in facts and chronology, took second place. Indeed it was the fact that Aristion had disappeared from the stage that made it possible to use Athenion as the prototype of the tyrannical man. The reign of terror as a phenomenon was removed from its context of war and siege, and it is not the practical necessities of a war-time dictatorship which receive the focus of attention in the portrayal, but the psychological makeup of the tyrant and the irrational masses.

As a historian Poseidonios was mainly interested in the reasons behind human actions,[33] and he differentiated between the chain of intermediate, proximate causes and the principal ones, which lie in the makeup of the individuals involved. According to Poseidonios, it was the job of the philosopher, or more properly of the psychologist, to ascertain the principal causes, and this was the foundation of ethics. As a philosopher he differentiated among the three faculties of the soul, as Plato had: a rational one, the δύναμις λογιστική, and two irrational ones, the θυμοειδές and the ἐπιθυμητικόν.[34] He defined the emotional states caused by the irrational capacities as overwhelming impulses, πλεονάζουσαι ὁρμαί, which tended to excess, just as the momentum of a sprinter flings his body over and beyond the finishing line.[35] From this followed the demand that the irrational capacities be kept in check by the rational, otherwise humans would be incapable of using their resources, which, although they are morally indifferent, are that towards which the emotional states are directed, in harmony with nature and under the direction of the δύναμις λογιστική. In this case the resources are wealth and power, which represent the means of satisfying the desire for sensual pleasure, ἥδεσθαι, and power over others, κρατεῖν.[36] Therefore moral education aims to soothe the irrational faculties of the soul, so that they follow the rule of common sense, and analogously, it is the job of the statesman to bring the emotions of the masses under the control of the δύναμις λογιστική.

1989) 39–46. I had no access to: F. J. Gómez Espelosin, "Filósofos al poder o algunas consideraziones sobre las tiranías atenienses del 88 a.C.," *Polis* 2 (1990) 85–97.

33. On the following see esp. I. G. Kidd, op. cit., (n. 32); D. E. Hahm, "Posidonius' Theory of Historical Causation," *ANRW* 36.2 (Berlin and New York, 1989) 1325–63 (with a detailed bibliography) and K. Bringmann, "Geschichte und Psychologie bei Poseidonios," *Entretiens Fondation Hardt* 32 (Vandœuvres-Genève, 1986) 29–59.

34. Fr. 32 E.-K. = fr. 422b Theiler (n. 28).

35. Fr. 34 E.-K. = fr. 407 Theiler.

36. Fr. 169 E.-K. = fr. 416 Theiler.

Athenion failed to fulfill what was demanded of the statesman, and the main reason for his failure lay in the makeup of his character, since he succumbed to the temptation of striving for power and wealth and did not shy away from resorting to deception and fraud in order to satisfy his lust. Accordingly the Athenion episode begins with an exposition of a negative character: "Athenion, an assiduous attender at the school of the Peripatetic Erymneus, bought an Egyptian slave girl with whom he had sex. Her child, whether by Athenion or another, also named Athenion, was brought up in the master's house. The boy was taught to read, would help his mother prop the old man up when he went out, became his heir, and was slipped illegally into the citizen roll to become an Athenian citizen. He married a shapely wench with whose help he set off on the hunt for young pupils in the life of a professional teacher. Having made his pile as a sophist in Messene and Larissa in Thessaly he returned to Athens."[37] The pseudophilosopher, who merely saw philosophy as a lucrative means of earning money, managed to attain a position of power when Rome's might in Asia Minor collapsed. As Athens' ambassador at the court of Mithradates he flattered his way into the King's favour, was rewarded with the title of "Friend," and began to shower the Athenians with messages which were intended to spur their greediness: "So he began to buoy up the hopes of the Athenians with letters, leading them to believe that, as he had the greatest influence with the Cappadocian, not only would they be freed from their pressing debts and live in concord, but recover the democracy, and obtain huge gifts, both individually and nationally. The Athenians started to brag about this, convinced that the Roman supremacy was broken."[38] This produced an atmosphere in which the demagogue's words were received as the tidings of a saviour, and once the wave of enthusiasm had brought him the rank of strategos of the hoplites he revealed his true character. The thirst for power drove him beyond the finishing line, he became a tyrant, and violence and terror became means to their own ends.

Nobody can doubt that Poseidonios produced in the Athenion episode an impressive demonstration of his view of historical causality. But the road to terror also encompassed various secondary causes: public and private debts, the constitutional problem which was still awaiting a ruling in the Senate,[39] the rising star of Mithradates and the impending collapse of

---

37. Z. 12–23 E.-K. The translation is from I. G. Kidd, *Posidonius* 2.2, 865.

38. Z. 26–32 E.-K. The translation is from I. G. Kidd, *Posidonius* 2.2, 866.

39. The constitutional problem referred to by Athenion in his speech is not explained, but probably is related to the fact that Medeios held the office of eponymous archon three years in succession; cf. E. Badian, op. cit. (n. 3) 108.

Roman power. But in the eyes of the philosophising historian none of these circumstances had the quality of the determining cause. This lay above all in the psychological disposition of the false philosopher, who was driven by a lust for power, and secondly in the availability of the "irrational" masses. For this reason it is Athenion's character, and not the pragmatic context into which his actions fitted, which is the centre of the historical narrative. He gained citizenship, and, it is implied, perhaps his inheritance also, through fraud; philosophy was just a way of getting rich; at the court of Mithradates it was flattery that ingratiated him with the monarch; and he understood how to awake hopeless expectations in Athens. On his return to Athens he whipped up the hysterical masses, gained power and misused it. The false philosopher became a tyrant. This picture is drawn with paradigmatic sharpness—indeed overdrawn. By giving the tyranny of Athenion details which were later to characterise Aristion, it was possible to present an even clearer expression of the soul of the tyrant succumbing to his lust for power than would have been possible had he only made the connection between the demands of war and siege on the one hand and the reaction—terror and suppression—on the other.

But however impressively the Athenion episode documents the qualities of the historian, it also shows the high price that was paid for the obvious advantages. Poseidonios was not afraid of discrediting the origin of his antihero with scandal and insinuation: "It is hardly historical objectivity, but clearly it is not meant to be. It is the style of Attic rhetorical invective against an opponent," I. G. Kidd commented, drawing on the work of U. von Wilamowitz and K. Reinhardt.[40] J. Malitz was right when he supposed that Poseidonios' description of Athenion's origins and career bore little relation to historical reality.[41] The description of his reign of terror has anachronistic elements, as was shown above. Even in the masterly narrative of Athenion's reception and conduct in Athens anachronistic exaggeration is not avoided. In the demagogic speech which Poseidonios places in the mouth of his protagonist, he boasts to the Athenians that ambassadors, not just from the Italians, but from the Carthaginians too, have arrived at the King's court in order to form an alliance to destroy Rome.[42] Theodor

40. I. G. Kidd, *Posidonius* 2.2, 866.

41. E. Badian, op. cit. (n. 3) has no doubts on the matter: "And we must, of course, rid our minds of any scrap of belief in Posidonius' story of Athenion's murky origins: it belongs to a class of topoi known from Aristophanes through Demosthenes to Cicero and well beyond. . . ."

42. l. 89–92 E.-K. According to C. Nicolet, Tyrian merchants are meant: "Mithradate et les ambassadeurs de Carthage (et Posidonius fr. 41)," in *Mélanges A. Piganiol*, vol. 2 (Paris, 1966) 807–14; such salvage attempts are not convincing.

Mommsen comments ironically, "ein vortrefflicher Peisthetaeros, der durch eine glänzende Karriere, die bei Hof gemacht, den Pöbel zu blenden ihm mit Aplomb zu versichern verstand, daß aus dem seit beiläufig 60 Jahren in Schutt liegenden Karthago die Hilfe für Mithradates schon unterwegs sei."[43] In other contexts it has been observed that Poseidonios can on occasions be quite free with chronology and facts. In Diodorus' analysis of the causes of the first Sicilian Slave Revolt (136–133), which draws on Poseidonios' *History*, we read, "The Praetors did not dare to take measures against the bands of slaves who had been armed by their masters, because the land-owners were mainly Roman Knights—and they sat in judgement over the provincial governors."[44] K. Reinhardt appositely remarked on this: "Es ist nicht zu verkennen, wie alles darauf angelegt ist, um auf diese Pointe hinauszulaufen."[45] Yet the courts involved were not transferred to the Knights until the *lex Acilia* of 123 or 122.

There was also this point, it would seem, in giving Athenion the characteristics of Aristion: Athens' history ended with the admonitory example of a tyranny that did not arise from the external circumstances of a struggle for life or death, but as a final and direct consequence of the psychological disposition of a false leader and of the "irrational" Athenians.[46]

---

43. Th. Mommsen, *Römische Geschichte*, vol. 2^2 (Berlin, 1889) 288.

44. Diodorus 34/35.2.3 and 31 = *FGrHist* 87 fr. 108 (respectively p. 287, l. 26ff. and *Exc. De virt.* I. p. 302, 37ff.).

45. K. Reinhardt, s.v. Poseidonios, in *RE* 32.1 (1954) 633f.

46. Poseidonios' political attitude towards the Athenian masses in some ways resembles that of Polybius; cf. now F. Walbank, "Polybius' Perception of the One and the Many," in I. Malkin and Z. W. Rubinsohn, eds., *Leaders and Masses in the Roman World* (Leiden, New York, and Köln, 1995) 203–204.

EIGHT

The Middle Stoics and Slavery

Peter Garnsey

I. INTRODUCTION

Two contrasting conceptions of slavery emerged in Greece in the Classical and early Hellenistic periods. Aristotle in the *Politics* justified legal slavery with the argument that some people, being deficient in reason, were naturally fitted to serve as slaves of others who were by nature free, and that their best interests lay in doing so.[1] For the Stoics, on the other hand, slavery was a moral condition characteristic of people who allowed themselves to be dominated by passions and emotions. Most people were in this state, most were "bad" or "inferior," while the "good" and "wise" were very few. By comparison with the slavery that was a condition of the soul, legal slavery was of marginal importance. It was an external—like health and illness, wealth and poverty, high and low status—over which we had no control. As such, it was neither good nor bad but, rather, indifferent.[2] These rival doctrines correlate interestingly with two common

This paper has benefited from the helpfully critical comments of Prof. I. Kidd, Prof. D. Sedley and Paul Cartledge. I am delighted to be able to record here my debt, both personal and academic, to Frank Walbank.

1. For Aristotle's view, see e.g. Smith (1983); Schofield (1990); Brunt (1993) 343–88. The Aristotelian theory has a Platonic base: see e.g. *Rep.* 590c–d; *Laws* 966b; cf. *Rep.* 469b–c; Vlastos (1973) 147–63; Morrow (1939) 30–46. The subject of this paper and related matters are treated in greater detail in my book *Ideas of Slavery from Aristotle to Augustine* (Cambridge, 1996).

2. In assessing the treatment of slavery by the Old Stoa, I am more inclined towards the cautious, minimizing approach of Schofield (1991) than the imaginative reconstructions of Erskine (1990). Literature relevant to the Middle Stoics includes: Capelle (1932); Strasburger (1946); Pohlenz (1959); Milani (1972); Griffin (1976); Malitz (1983); Atkins

motifs of non-philosophical literature, both designed in their different ways to provide ideological support for the slave-system: on the one hand, slaves were stereotyped as rascally, prone to excesses of drinking and eating, and dumb, and on the other, slaves were reminded that while unfree in law they could be free in spirit if they were virtuous.

This brief summary leaves open some large gaps. For example, nothing has been said about a Stoic view, or Stoic views, on natural slavery as defined by Aristotle, or about attitudes of Stoics as a group, or of individual Stoics, to institutional slavery as practised in their time. There is something to be said under both heads, but in inquiring into these and other matters we quickly encounter major obstacles. Stoicism was founded in Athens by Zeno of Citium around 300 B.C. and lived on through the Hellenistic and Roman periods of antiquity. It must be considered doubtful whether an "orthodox" position on slavery could have been sustained over such a long period— supposing there was such a thing. But if (legal) slavery was as marginal to Stoic concerns as I believe it was, then no canonical doctrine is likely to have been laid down on the subject by the founding fathers.

The first problem is that there are no surviving treatises or extended discussions from a professed Stoic philosopher before the middle of the first century A.D., that is to say almost four hundred years after the movement began—the key figures of the late period being the younger Seneca, Musonius Rufus and Epictetus, followed by Marcus Aurelius. Four to five hundred years is a long time for a system of beliefs to remain unified and stable. In any case, access to that system, insofar as it was ever a coherent whole, is difficult. We have only fragments of the works of the early Stoics (Zeno and his immediate successors, Cleanthes and then Chrysippus). Nor do we have much first-hand knowledge of the so-called Middle Stoics, whose leading representatives, Panaetius and Posidonius, flourished in the later second century B.C. and the first half of the first century B.C. respectively. Again, their works are not extant.

One brief example will bring home the size of the problem. The well-known Stoic paradox "Every good man is free, every bad man a slave" was probably formulated by Zeno—at any rate, it dates from the early Stoa and presumably received a number of treatments in the following period. Zeno would not have been amused had he been able to foresee that the only versions that survive in the twentieth century are from a Roman eclectic,

(1989); Dumont (1989); Ferrary (1974) (1977) (1988) (1995). Long and Sedley (1987) is an invaluable selection of documents with translation and commentary, drawn from von Arnim (1903–1905). For Posidonius' historical fragments, see Jacoby (1926) II.A and C; Edelstein and Kidd (1972) (text); Kidd (1988) (commentary).

Cicero, a Hellenized Jew, Philo of Alexandria, and a Christian bishop, Ambrose of Milan.[3]

The Stoic attitude to natural slavery is a rather different issue. There is neither any sign nor any likelihood that the Stoics aligned themselves with one or other position in the debate as it surfaces in the pages of Aristotle, nor even that they confronted the question at all. My position (which I do not intend to argue for in detail here) is that, while the matter did not engage their attention directly, certain doctrines of the Stoa are incompatible with the theory of natural slavery.

As for legal slavery, this held little philosophical interest for Stoics, and they did not discuss it in any detail. Very few of the surviving texts from the early Stoa touch on the subject, while Cicero, who preserves a certain amount of Stoic thought (generally believed to have been derived from Stoics of the middle period), mentions slavery only rarely in the relevant works, notably in *De officiis*.[4]

That is not to say that individual Stoics did not from time to time touch on the subject of legal slavery in their writings. If Philo's Stoicizing treatise *Every Good Man is Free* (alluded to above) can be taken as a pointer to earlier, mainstream Stoic discussions, some space would have been taken up in proving that true slavery was not slavery as conventionally interpreted, that is to say, legal slavery, but rather slavery of the mind or soul. A more direct treatment of legal slavery by a philosophical writer is Seneca's *De beneficiis* Book 3.18ff. and *Epistulae* 47. Here philosophical arguments, and especially the doctrine that all men, wherever they stand in the existing social hierarchy, are equal in the spiritual realm, or the cosmic world, are employed to convince masters to eschew cruel treatment of their slaves.

The purpose of this paper is to ask what, if anything, can be recovered of the thoughts and reflections of Middle Stoics. Of Panaetius' views on slavery, there is virtually nothing that can be said, especially if (following Atkins) we should now be less willing than earlier scholars have been to assume that

3. See Cicero *Stoic Paradoxes* 5; Philo *Every Good Man is Free;* Ambrose *Ep.* 7 (in *Corp. Sel. Eccl. Lat.* 82.10.1).

4. Cicero *De off.* I.41: *est autem infima condicio et fortuna servorum, quibus non male praecipiunt, qui ita iubent uti, ut mercennariis, operam exigendam, iusta praebenda*; cf. Seneca *De ben.* 3.22.1 (Chrysippus: *servus perpetuus mercennarius est*) and Athenaeus 6.274c–d (Rutilius Rufus paid his slaves for merchandise). See also the less benign *De off.* 2.24: *sed iis, qui vi oppressos imperio coercent, sit sane adhibenda saevitia, ut eris in famulos, si aliter teneri non possunt; qui vero in libera civitate ita se instruunt, ut metuantur, iis nihil potest esse dementius.* Note that *De off.* 2.26–27 on the justification of Roman imperialism, unlike the more celebrated text *De Re Publica* 3.36–37, makes no use of the language of slavery.

Panaetius was directing Cicero's pen in *De officiis*.[5] In any case (as I have already observed), thoughts on slavery appear only rarely in that work and do not amount to much. This leaves, essentially, Posidonius.

A preliminary observation is that, in our search for the thoughts of Posidonius on slavery, at best we have to deal with his historical, not philosophical, work. We are viewing Posidonius as the successor of Polybius, beginning his *History* where Polybius left off (in 145 B.C.), rather than as a follower of a Stoic philosopher, Panaetius or Antipater. The best that a student of his philosophy can hope for is that Posidonius will offer thoughts of a philosophical kind on this or that historical event as it comes into his sights.

The evidence, such as it is, is of two kinds. The first consists of passages that are attributed to Posidonius (or that are regarded as of Posidonian origin) by modern authorities, not by the ancient sources themselves. A second category consists of citations of Posidonius preserved by Athenaeus from Naukratis in Egypt, who compiled a large, eccentric work, the *Deipnosophistai*, in the early third century A.D. One, concerning the Mariandyni and Heracleots, is important, problematic, and, as it happens, philosophically interesting (and will receive the lion's share of attention in what follows). Another, on the Chians, is a mere snippet and reveals very little. A third, a scrap from Posidonius' discussion of the first slave revolt in Sicily, is not much more informative; its main function and use have been to encourage scholars to attribute the whole of Diodorus' narrative of the revolt to Posidonius. A fourth quotation, this time from a letter of Seneca, does not refer specifically to slavery, but is relevant to the discussion of the Mariandyni and Heracleots. With such a meagre harvest of information at our disposal, it should be only too obvious that "a tidy and rounded" assessment of Posidonius' views on slavery is beyond our grasp.[6]

II. POSIDONIUS AS AN INTERMEDIATE SOURCE

There is no good reason for seeing the hand of Posidonius behind part of the third book of Cicero's *De Re Publica*. This is the speech of Laelius (in reply to Philus), offering a justification of the rule of Rome over her

---

5. Atkins (1989). Recent scholarship is in agreement in denying, against Capelle (1932) and others, the Panaetian origin of Cicero *De Re Publica* 3.35–36. See bibl. in Ferrary (1988) 363. Note the comment of Strasburger (1946) 45, n. 1: "There is preserved not the tiniest scrap of Panaetius' political doctrines."

6. This has not prevented numerous scholars from positing connections between ideas expressed in disparate fragments, some not obviously (or plausibly) Posidonian. See Gruen (1984) I 351–52 (whose words are quoted in the text).

subjects, to which we have partial access through later writers, in particular Augustine, *De Civitate Dei*. The negative case has been argued successfully by others and need not be rehearsed. There would be profit in attempting a reassessment of the key fragments, but that should be postponed to another occasion.[7]

Posidonius may legitimately be taken as a prime source for Diodorus on the slave revolts of Sicily, or at least the first revolt, that of the 130s B.C.[8] Diodorus was, however, influenced by other writers as well, and, one fragment apart, it is something of an act of faith to claim that any particular passage is wholly or substantially Posidonian.

The fragment in question runs as follows (the writer is Athenaeus):

> Posidonius in Book 8 of the *History* says of the Sicilian Greek Damophilus, who caused the outbreak of the slave war, that he was addicted to (a familiar of: *oikeios*) luxury, and writes just as follows: "So he was a slave *(doulos)* to luxury and malpractice, driven through the country in four-wheeled chariots at the head of horses, luscious attendants, and a concourse of bumsuckers and soldier-slaves. But later he came to a violent end with his whole household, treated with extreme violence by the slaves." (Athenaeus *Deip.* 542b [= Edelstein and Kidd F59, Jacoby F7])

7. In particular, the contributions of Augustine, Carneades (who argued both sides of the case), and Cicero need to be reevaluated, and the philosophical content analysed afresh. For the critique, see especially Ferrary (1988) 363–64, 376, 381. On the content, a full recent discussion is Dumont (1989), but I am not convinced that the texts justify his distinction between an Aristotelian "esclave par nature" and a Ciceronian "esclave par perversité" (715), where the slave is "criminel" but has an "aptitude au bien et à la rédemption," and has "des virtualités d'homme libre et de citoyen romain" (724).

8. Scholars are virtually unanimous, though Dumont (1989) both introduces other writers alongside Posidonius (e.g. 203–13), and believes that Posidonius was merely transmitting thoughts originating in discussions and debates among Roman senators contemporary with the events (104, 239–41). More representative of recent historiography is Kidd (1988) 294–95, commenting on Athenaeus 542b (= F59) quoted in the text: "This sentence forms the only secure link between Diodorus Book 34 and Posidonius. Nevertheless, the strong likelihood remains that Diodorus used Posidonius for his whole account of the first Sicilian slave war." He admits, however, that "there is still no control over the possible extent and fidelity of this use." As for the second war, Kidd (1988) 905 (on F262) is more hesitant, but still concludes: "Since there is secure evidence that Diodorus used Posidonius for at least part of his account of the first slave war . . . it is likely that he also used him for the second. But here the case for plain recognition is weaker: there is no positive link between the two authors, DS 36.1–11 shows little sign of Posidonian features, and there is no control to gauge any possible extent or fidelity of usage. We cannot assume that Diodorus simply reproduced Posidonius here, even though he may well have used him as a main source."

The parallel passage in Diodorus (34.2.34) from the tenth-century excerptor shows considerable rewriting, and incidentally omits the description of Damophilus as a (moral) slave—the only Stoic element in the piece (characteristically, but not exclusively Stoic, however). Athenaeus himself has substituted the anodyne *oikeios*, "familiar." One wonders how much else was filtered out of the Posidonian text by Diodorus and later writers. For what is "left" is evenhanded judgment on the causes of the revolt (the cruelty of masters), the nature of the slave system in Sicily, and the attitude of the slave rebels (who are exonerated from blame for the war and pictured as capable of repaying good treatment with mercy)—but without any philosophical underpinning.[9] We may compare, for example, the different ways in which the humane treatment of slaves is advocated in Diodorus and in Seneca. The former writes:

> Not only in the exercise of political power should men of prominence be considerate towards those of low estate, but so also in private life they should— if they are sensible—treat their slaves gently. For heavy-handed arrogance leads states into civil strife and factionalism between citizens, and in individual households it paves the way for plots of slaves against masters and for terrible uprisings in concert against the whole state. The more power is perverted to cruelty and lawlessness, the more the character of those subject to that power is brutalized to the point of desperation. Anyone whom fortune has set in low estate willingly yields place to his superiors in respect of gentility and esteem, but if he is deprived of due consideration, he comes to regard those who harshly lord it over him with bitter enmity. (Diod. 34/35.2.33)

Seneca too can sound like a relatively benign pragmatist:

> I do not wish to involve myself in too large a question, and to discuss the treatment of slaves, towards whom we Romans are excessively haughty, cruel and insulting. But this is the kernel of my advice: Treat your inferiors as you would be treated by your betters. And as often as you reflect how much power you have over a slave, remember that your master has just as much power over you. "But I have no master," you say. You are still young; perhaps you will have one. Do you not know at what age Hecuba entered captivity, or Croesus, or the mother of Darius, or Plato, or Diogenes? (*Ep.* 47.11–12)

But in the opening of this celebrated letter he strikes a quite different note:

> I am glad to learn, through those who come from you, that you live on friendly terms with your slaves. This befits a sensible and well-educated man like yourself. "They are slaves," people declare. Nay, rather they are

---

9. See e.g. Diod. 34/35.2.25–28, 32–37, 39–41. Eunus, the slave-leader, is not sympathetically treated. See e.g. 34.2.23.

men. "Slaves!" No, comrades. "Slaves!" No, they are unpretentious friends. "Slaves!" No, they are our fellow-slaves, if one reflects that Fortune has equal rights over slaves and free men alike. (*Ep.* 47.1)

Diodorus at least grants that slaves were not innately *savage:*

> Although the rebellious slaves were enraged against the whole household of their masters, and resorted to unrelenting abuse and vengeance, there were yet some indications that it was not from innate savagery (οὐ δι᾽ ὠμότητα φύσεως), but rather because of the arrogant treatment they had themselves received that they now ran amuck when they turned to avenge themselves on their persecutors. (Diod. 34/35.2.40)

In sum, the reflections of Diodorus/Posidonius (?) are interesting and balanced. The treatment of the contemporary slave system (at its worst), and the message about how masters should deal with their slaves, are marked by a greater humanity than, for example, Plato's discussion in the *Laws*.[10] But they are not distinctively Stoic, and in any case fall far short of the best that Stoicism had to offer.

III. POSIDONIUS ON THE CHIANS

> The first Greeks, so far as I know, who made use of purchased slaves were the Chians. This is recorded by Theopompus in the seventeenth book of his *Histories:* "The Chians were the first Greeks, after the Thessalians and Lacedaemonians, to use slaves, but they did not acquire them in the same way. For the Lacedaemonians and Thessalians, as will be seen, constituted their slave-class out of the Greeks who had earlier inhabited the territories which they themselves possess today, the Lacedaemonians taking the land of the Achaeans, the Thessalians that of the Perrhaebians and Magnesians. The people reduced to slavery were in the first instance called Helots, in the second Penestai. But the slaves whom the Chians own are derived from non-Greek peoples, and they pay a price for them." This, then, is the account given by Theopompus. But I believe that the Deity (*to daimonion*) became angry at the Chians for this practice, since, at a later time, they were disastrously involved in war on account of their slaves.[11]

> I imagine that none of you is ignorant, either, of the story told by the noble Herodotus concerning Panionius of Chios and the just deserts which he

10. Plato *Laws* 776c-778a (containing criticism of Spartan helotage and general advice about slave-treatment—with which Aristotle finds fault; cf. *Pols.* 1260b5–8.)
11. There follows a lengthy narrative of the Chian slave revolt led by one Drimacus purporting to be cited from the *Voyage in Asia* by Nymphodorus of Syracuse.

suffered for having made eunuchs of freeborn boys and selling them. *Nicolaos the Peripatetic and Posidonius the Stoic both say in their Histories that the Chians were enslaved by Mithridates the Cappadocian and handed over in chains to their own slaves, to be transported to Colchis.* So truly did the Deity (*to daimonion*) vent his wrath upon them for being the first to use purchased slaves, although most people did their own work when it came to menial services. (Athenaeus *Deip.* 265b–266f.)

This is truly a tiny scrap, and no more should be made of it than it merits. It would no doubt be pleasing if we could set Posidonius' "reflections" on the slave-market alongside his "reflections" on a different, earlier form of servitude (see next section). But we cannot. Only the italicized sentence remains of Posidonius' treatment of the Chians, and it is shared with Nicolaos. Posidonius no doubt said rather more than this. He may have echoed the rather more meaty testimony of Theopompus, that the Chians inaugurated the slave-market; he may have said "serve you right" to the Chians; and he may have introduced or taken over the theme of divine retribution. But the passage does not justify these inferences. The invocation of the Deity, as the text stands, can only be attributed to Athenaeus (via his spokesman on this occasion, one Democritus). This seems proven by the sentence that follows the citation of Theopompus, where the Deity—also here termed *to daimonion*—makes its first appearance, but on the express "invitation" of Athenaeus' spokesman: "But I believe that the Deity became angry at the Chians for this practice ..."[12] One might add that *to daimonion* (as distinct from *ho daimôn*) is not a normal Stoic term for the divine.[13]

IV. POSIDONIUS ON THE MARIANDYNI AND HERACLEOTS

Posidonius (he of the Stoa) says, in the eleventh book of his *Histories*: "Many persons being unable to manage themselves on account of the weakness of their intellect, give themselves voluntarily to the service of more intelligent men, in order that they may secure from them provision for their daily needs, and in turn may themselves render to their patrons, through their own labours, whatever they are capable of in the way of service. And so in this manner the Mariandynians put themselves in subjection to the Heracleots, promising to serve them continuously so long as the Heracleots provided for their needs, though they stipulated in addition that there should be no selling of any of

---

12. Cf. Kidd (1988) on F51, 276–77, with whom I entirely agree.

13. *To daimonion* also makes some appearances in Diodorus' narrative of the First Sicilian Slave Revolt. See 33/34.2.24b (*daimonion/theoi*); 34/35.9 (*daimonion/theoi*). Cf. 33/34.2.47 (*to theion/theoi/theos*). I do not see the hand of Posidonius here.

them beyond the Heracleot territory, but that they should stay right in their own territory." (Athenaeus *Deip.* 6.263cd)

The fragment concerns an obscure event in the past, the subjection of the Mariandyni (perhaps Thracian but in any case non-Greek) by the Greek colonists of Heracleia Pontica, who had settled on or near their territory in perhaps 554 B.C. The reduction of the Mariandyni following a substantial expansion of the territory of the city was perhaps subsequent to the initial colonisation by around a hundred years—a century apparently marked by intermittent warfare between the two peoples.[14] In our fragment, the event is given a tendentious and highly improbable interpretation, voluntary submission of the Mariandyni as opposed to conquest by the Heracleots. And the fragment begins with a historical or pseudo-historical generalization purporting to explain the allegedly voluntary surrender of the Mariandyni. It happens that the generalization contains the suggestion of a psychological doctrine which has reminded a number of commentators of Aristotelian slave theory.[15] Read alongside a passage in Aristotle's *Politics*, "The art of war is a natural art of acquisition, for the art of acquisition includes hunting, an art which we ought to practise against wild beasts, and against men who, though intended by nature to be governed, will not submit; for war of such a kind is naturally just" (1256b20–25), it is easily interpreted as implying that the Mariandyni were Aristotelian natural slaves who behaved in precisely the way that Aristotle thought natural slaves should behave, saving the Heracleots the trouble of subduing them in a "just" war. And yet the whole is assigned by Athenaeus to a writer whom he identifies as a Stoic. Just what was Posidonius, "he of the Stoa," doing?

The passage is a fragment, one of thousands that make up the monstrous compilation which is the *Deipnosophistai* of Athenaeus. Athenaeus, a scissors-and-paster on a monumental scale, was interested (in the most superficial way) in the content of the passage, not in the origin of the views expressed therein. It was his custom to cite his sources, but essentially in order to parade his learning (ostensibly that of the participants in his dinner-table

---

14. Mariandyni: the best discussions are by Vidal-Naquet (1972) and Burstein (1976). See also Asheri (1972); Burstein (1979); Alexandru (1984); Garlan (1988) 102–106; Ferrary (1988) 379–80. A different version appears in Strabo 12.3.4 p. 542 (see below n. 23). Partial parallels: *FGrH* 2A 90F8 (Ephorus, Sparta); *FGrH* 3B 424F1 (Archemachus, Thessaly). Plato compares Mariandyni with Helots and Penestai in *Laws* 776cd. See Ducat (1990) (1994); de Ste. Croix (1981) 149–50.

15. See, e.g., Milani (1972) 179–80; cf. Ferrary (1988) 379–80: "On retrouve là, incontestablement, un écho de la description aristotélicienne des rapports entre l'esclave par nature et son maître. . . . Les M. sont le type même des esclaves naturels. . . ."

conversation of the erudite). Lacking any hint as to the context, we cannot even be sure that Posidonius was not quoting someone else. If (in order to get the argument off the ground) we grant that he was in fact speaking for himself, we may still nurse doubts as to whether the fragment represents the considered thoughts of Posidonius on slavery.

Three questions might be asked in this connection. (1) *Is* there enough in the fragment to represent the "considered thoughts" of Posidonius (or of *anyone*)? The answer to this must be no. What we have is the briefest of assertions, not argument. (2) Did Posidonius personally approve of the explanation given of the behaviour of the Mariandyni? The answer is yes, but the issue is not cut and dried. We might compare another fragment of Athenaeus:

> Plato, in the second book of the *Republic*, thus portrays his new citizens at dinner when he writes: "It would appear," he said, "that you represent your men as feasting without any relish." "Quite true," I said; "I forgot that they will have a relish also, such as salt, of course, and olives, and cheese; and they will cook bulbs and green vegetables, the sort of which they make boiled dishes in the country. And we will set before them dessert, I suppose, figs and chick-peas and beans, and they will toast myrtleberries and beech-nuts before the fire, sipping their wine in moderation the while. Thus will they spend their lives, peacefully and healthily, and in all probability will die in old age and transmit a similar mode of life to their offspring." (Athenaeus *Deip.* 138a–b, citing *Rep.* 372c)

If we had nothing more of the *Republic* than this text, we would still be in a strong position to claim that Plato approved of the lean fare of the first citizens of his ideal state (but we would not know that Glaucon was scornful of it). The reader of the fragment of Posidonius is not so well placed. It contains no prescriptive element, no nod of approval. Still, it is unlikely that Posidonius was simply passing on a received, conventional explanation of the behaviour of the Mariandyni; the natural interpretation is that he composed the generalization *and in so doing* was endorsing the thought it contains. The third question bears on the same matter, but is a larger issue which requires more extended discussion.

(3) Does the fragment contain anything that suggests Stoic, or specifically Posidonian, doctrine? As we saw, the passage is normally classified as Aristotelian in pedigree. In support of this supposition, the following arguments might be adduced. First, intellectual incapacity is certainly a characteristic of the Aristotelian natural slave, even if Aristotle does not use the terminology employed by Posidonius to describe it. Secondly, if the implication of the text is that the incapacity was congenital (but see below), this too is compatible with Aristotelian doctrine. Thirdly, there is an assumption of mutual benefit, a hallmark of the natural master/natural slave relationship in

Aristotle (though he conceded that most benefit fell to the master). Fourthly, insofar as the passage makes the transition from the mental or intellectual realm to the social and political world, it is in step with Aristotle. Aristotle held that a natural slave should be a legal slave.

There is, however, a core of Stoic doctrine in the fragment. *Astheneia* of the *dianoia* ("weakness of the intellect") is Stoic terminology:[16] it evokes the extensive Stoic literature on the soul, and the different intellectual and moral responses of the wise man and the inferior man, or fool (*phaulos*), to the pull of the passions. The wise man's stability, strength and "tension" (*eutonia*) are contrasted with the inferior man's inconstancy, weakness and "lack of tension" (*atonia*). In a number of similes, the soul of the inferior man is compared to a body that is prone to any "slight or chance" disease, to fighting children, to the rider of a disobedient horse, and to the subjects of a tyrant.[17] Posidonius was fully engaged in this discussion (in which he vigorously opposed Chrysippus' unitary view of the soul), introduced his own terminology and added to the store of similes.[18]

The Mariandyni (and their like) would appear then to be Stoic *phauloi*. A Stoic *phaulos*, however, is not an Aristotelian natural slave, and there is nothing in the wording of this text to suggest he is. To attribute to the *phaulos* a weakness in respect of his reasoning powers is not enough *in itself* to earn

---

16. See indices of von Arnim, *SVF* 3.177, 471, 473, etc. (*astheneia*); 1.148, 202; 2.840; 894, etc. (*dianoia*). A sample Stoic text is *SVF* 3.548 = Stobaeus 2.111.18–112.8 = *L&S* 41G (in part): "They (the Stoics) say that the wise man never makes a false supposition, and that he does not assent at all to anything incognitive, owing to his not opining and his being ignorant of nothing. For ignorance is changeable and weak assent. But the wise man supposes nothing weakly, but rather, securely and firmly; and so he does not opine either. For there are two kinds of opinion, assent to the incognitive, and weak supposition, and these are alien to the wise man's disposition. So precipitancy and assent in advance of cognition are attributes of the precipitate inferior man, whereas they do not befall the man who is well-natured and perfect and virtuous." See also *SVF* 3.378 = Stobaeus 2.88.22–89.3 = *L&S* 65C (in part): "In the case of all the soul's passions, when they (the Stoics) call them 'opinions,' 'opinion' is used instead of 'weak supposition,' and 'fresh' instead of 'the stimulus of an irrational contraction or swelling.' " For weakness in Posidonius, see next note.

17. For the comparisons, see Galen *On Hippocrates' and Plato's Doctrines* 5.2.1 (= *L&S* 65R); Plutarch *On Moral Virtue* 446F–447A (= *L&S* 65G); Stobaeus 2.88.8 and 2.90.6 (= *L&S* 65A). For Posidonius on weakness, as preserved in Galen *On Hippocrates' and Plato's Doctrines*, see Frs. 164–69EK, with Sedley (1991) 148–50. The term *euemptosia* (= "proneness") is distinctively Posidonian, and the horse simile is apparently his.

18. Perhaps Posidonius should have asked himself (a) whether the Heracleots are convincingly cast as Stoic wise men, and (b) how it was that the Mariandyni "fools" were wise enough to entrust themselves to their betters.

him the designation of natural slave: in the Stoic thought-world, it made him inferior, that is all. There is no trace in Stoic literature of a doctrine that *phauloi,* or some *phauloi,* were irredeemably flawed, vicious or subrational beings.[19] The Stoic doctrine of the (very few) wise who alone are free and of the (very many) fools who are slaves is not a doctrine of people who by nature are disposed one way or the other.

The Mariandyni, in Posidonius' eyes, were inferiors who had submitted to people they judged to be cleverer than they. The voluntary submission of inferiors to superiors was not in principle unacceptable to Stoics. Indeed such a relationship was a central feature of the Golden Age society envisaged by Posidonius in a fragment from an unnamed work passed down by Seneca, and it is characterized as entirely natural.[20] Posidonius, according to Seneca, envisaged a community without political institutions, laws and courts, in which people "still uncorrupted, followed nature," entrusting themselves voluntarily to their betters, the wise. For "nature has the habit of subjecting the weaker to the stronger." The attitude of the wise rulers is described in this way:

> They kept their hands under control and protected the weaker from the stronger. They gave advice, both to do and not to do; they showed what was useful and what was useless. Their forethought provided that their subjects should lack nothing; their bravery warded off dangers; their kindness enriched and adorned their subjects. For them ruling was a service, not an exercise of royalty. No ruler tried his power against those to whom he owed the beginnings of his power; and no one had the inclination or the excuse to do wrong. (Sen. *Ep.* 90.4–5)

Slavery is not mentioned: men in their original state followed their natural leaders without duress; there was no need to enslave them. This is not surprising. In Plato's ideal state too, before it begins to degenerate (as pictured in *Republic* Book 8), the relationship of rulers to ruled is not described

19. Moreover, such a doctrine would be hard to reconcile with Cleanthes in *SVF* 1.566 = Stobacus 2.65.8 = *L&S* 61L: "All men have natural tendencies to virtue," or Chrysippus et al. in Diog. Laert. 7.91 = *SVF* 3.223 = *L&S* 61K: "Virtue is teachable . . . as is evident from the fact that inferior men become good." The discussion of Scott (1988), esp. 142–47, is pertinent to the issue. Certainly it was acknowledged that there are differences among inferiors in terms of their "initial natural make-up" (cf. Chrysippus in Aulus Gellius 7.2.6–13). But there is no evidence for any Stoic taking a stance on the irremediability of some people's vice.

20. Seneca *Ep.* 90.4 reads: *sed primi mortalium quique ex his geniti naturam incorrupti sequebantur, eundem habebant et ducem et legem, commissi melioris arbitrio. Naturae est enim potioribus deteriora summittere.*

as that of slavery.[21] This example is not idly chosen, for the influence of Plato on Posidonius is marked. In particular, whereas Chrysippus (and probably Zeno before him, and mainstream Stoicism as a whole) defined passion in intellectual terms as "weak opinion," and saw emotional conflict as a product of the fluctuation or perversion of the reasoning faculty, Posidonius returned to the Platonic doctrine of the divided soul, according to which reason and passion operate as separate forces (and he unconvincingly claimed that Chrysippus had abandoned the doctrines of Zeno).[22]

But were not the Mariandyni slaves, even if they were not natural slaves? What Posidonius *says* is that they negotiated a contract which involved an exchange of service (*hypêresia*) for the provision of their essential needs—and that they would not be sold abroad, out of their homeland. The status of the Mariandyni is left vague. What is clear is that they were determined not to be chattel slaves, who were quintessentially uprooted from their native environment and sold abroad. If we stay within the logic of the passage, as we must if our aim is to recover the thoughts of the author, then the implication is that they were not, in Posidonius' view, slaves at home. Posidonius might have said, as Strabo writing not long afterwards did, that "*they sold them* but not beyond the boundaries of their country." He did not, and in not doing so was implicitly rejecting this detail, which later figures, among others, in Strabo's account.[23]

21. Legal slavery enters Plato's ideal polis when the polis begins to degenerate in *stasis:* "The violence of their opposition [sc. between the two elements of the governing class] is resolved in a compromise under which they distribute land and houses to private ownership, while the subjects whom they once ruled as freemen and friends, and to whom they owed their maintenance, are reduced to the status of serfs and menials, and they devote themselves to war and holding the population in subjection" (*Rep.* 547b–c). Note that slavery is not mentioned in Seneca's (very brief) evocation of the corrupt city of Posidonius.

22. See Galen *On Hippocrates' and Plato's Doctrines* 4.3.2–5 (= *L&S* 61K); 5.5.8–26 (= *L&S* 65M). Posidonius knew, and was influenced by, some of Aristotle's works, especially those of a scientific kind. See Edelstein and Kidd T85 = Strabo 2.3.8 (alluding to Posidonius' interest in aetiology), with Kidd (1988) 84–86, drawing on Sandbach (1985). But there is no sign that Posidonius knew the *Politics*, and in any case he was more familiar with Plato.

23. Namely, the forcible subjugation of the Mariandyni, and the overt comparison with helotage. Strabo 12.3.4, p. 542 runs: "This too has been said, that the Milesians who were first to found Heracleia forced the Mariandyni, who held the place before them, to serve as Helots (*heilôteuein enagkasan*), so that they were sold by them (*hôste kai pipraskesthai hup' autôn*), but not beyond the boundaries of their country (for the two peoples came to an agreement on this), *just as the Mnoan class as it was called were serfs (ethêteuen hê Mnoïa) of the Cretans and the Penestai of the Thessalians.*" For the Hellenistic tradition that included the Mariandyni among those "between slave and free," see also

To sum up: for a reason that totally escapes us and cannot be recovered, Posidonius in his *Histories* was reviewing the case of the Mariandyni. He had received the tradition that this tribe, some five hundred years in the past, had voluntarily committed themselves to serve the citizens of a Greek polis newly established on their territory. Instead of subjecting the tradition to critical examination (and deciding that he had before him an *ex post facto* justification of subjection by force), he tried to work within it and make sense of the behaviour of the tribesmen as it stood. He decided that their behaviour was intelligible, and perfectly natural, insofar as they were inferiors submitting to the direction of their intellectual superiors. What Posidonius thought he had found was a historical example of a voluntary agreement between a ruling and a subject community, which involved control but fell short of slavery. Aristotle was far from his mind. This is a Stoic philosopher at work—and a historian who has suspended his critical faculties.

What is revealed about his attitude to slavery? Very little. Posidonius provides an interpretation of the action of the Mariandyni as it is represented in the tradition, but he does not moralize or pass judgment: he does not applaud them, criticize them for naivety, or urge others to model themselves on them. He passes no straightforward comment on slavery. He might be represented as implying that the Mariandyni were behaving sensibly; but an aspect of this was that they believed that they were protecting themselves from "real" slavery, the slavery that would make them commodities to be bought and sold. Slavery of that kind was not a condition that any free man would enter into willingly. If Posidonius believed this, then he was in line with the rest of the human race.

V. CONCLUSION

Middle Stoic views on slavery remain elusive. What we have suggests that there was no significant deviation from early Stoic thinking, itself known only from a handful of fragments. The philosophical works of Panaetius and Posidonius, of which we have inadequate, partial knowledge, yield nothing; we are left with some fragments from Posidonius' *Histories*, and some passages in Diodorus that may go back to Posidonius.

This is not a promising body of material to be working with. At best, we might be offered theoretical comments provoked by historical events, but they are bound to be isolated and discrete, and to amount to rather less, in

---

Kallistratus 348F4; Pollux 3.83, with Lotze (1959); Finley (1964); Vidal-Naquet (1972); and n. 14 above.

each case, than a systematic, philosophical argument. At worst, we have, as in the case of Diodorus, a text which comes down in the form of substantial fragments from Byzantine compilations, a text which was originally put together by a historian with no known philosophical proclivities, and which probably drew from a number of sources. The likelihood of our obtaining access to the philosophical position of one of those sources, even if he happened to be the main one, must be slim. Not a single text in Diodorus is attributed to Posidonius. The characterization of Damophilus as a "slave of luxury and malpractice" (for what it is worth) would have been lost if Athenaeus had not cited Posidonius' actual words.

There is the other danger, that we might be misled into thinking that, because Posidonius the historian was drawn into fairly extensive narrative of slave revolts, as he was, *qua* Stoic philosopher he was systematically interested in legal slavery as such. There is the further temptation to believe, on the basis of the Chian and Mariandyni/Heracleot fragments, that Posidonius was critical of chattel slavery as such, and that he returned to the Aristotelian position that legal slaves should be natural slaves, who ideally surrendered themselves to their natural masters.

These issues may be dealt with in reverse order. First, Posidonius did not put an Aristotelian hat on, even for a moment. His Mariandyni were Stoic inferiors, not Aristotelian natural slaves, and in voluntarily submitting to their superiors they were behaving like the uncorrupt (not yet vicious) citizens of Posidonius' Plato-inspired Golden Age. Nor do the fragments support the supposition that Posidonius was in favour of one way of entering slavery (voluntary submission) and opposed to another (the slave market).

Posidonius may be credited with criticism of the worst abuses of the existing slave system in Sicily—mass enslavement of free men, overstocking of households and properties with slaves, inadequate supervision of slaves, cruel and brutal treatment—but his strictures had already been voiced by a section of the Roman political class before him, and they do not, and were not intended to, undermine slave institutions as such, including the operation of the slave market.

In this, Posidonius' position was no different from that of Seneca, who was fiercely critical of cruelty to slaves. But, as we saw, the generalisations of Diodorus/Posidonius (?) are marked by pragmatism rather than egalitarianism. The call for mild treatment of slaves is not supported in Diodorus, as it is in Seneca, by a reminder either of the common humanity of slaves and masters, or of the benefits beyond the call of duty that faithful slaves can bring to their masters.

As to attitudes to legal slavery as such, here I suspect the remarks of Philo in his treatise on the Stoic paradox are valid for Posidonius, as for other Stoics:

Slavery then is applied in one sense to bodies, in another to souls; bodies have men for their masters, souls their vices and passions. The same is true of freedom; one freedom produces security of the body from men of superior strength, the other sets the mind at liberty from the domination of the passions. No one makes the first kind (sc. of slavery/freedom) the subject of investigation. For the vicissitudes of men are numberless, and in many instances and at many times persons of the highest virtue have through adverse blows of fortune lost the freedom to which they were born. Our inquiry is concerned with characters which have never fallen under the yoke of desire, or fear, or pleasure, or grief; characters which have as it were escaped from prison and thrown off the chains which bound them so tightly. Casting aside, therefore, specious quibblings and the terms which have no basis in nature but depend upon convention, such as "homebred," "purchased," or "captured in war," let us examine the veritable freeman, who alone possesses independence, even though a host of people claim to be his masters. (*Every Good Man* 17–19)

Stoics did not bother themselves with arguments about legal slavery, for example, in differentiating between the various ways of entering into that condition (perhaps in terms of relative levels of justice), but instead gave their attention to true slavery, which was a property of the mind or soul, and how to liberate oneself from it—because they held that moral slavery, unlike legal slavery, is within our control. The Stoicizing treatises of Philo and Cicero, in his capacity as author of *Paradoxa Stoicorum* 5, are concerned with moral, not legal slavery, and in this respect are as reliable a guide as we can hope to have to the character and content of Middle Stoic thought on slavery.

NINE

Physis and *Nomos*:
Polybius, the Romans, and Cato the Elder

A. M. Eckstein

The historian Polybius is the earliest Greek intellectual to have left us a detailed impression of the Romans and their society, having known them at close hand during seventeen years of living in Italy (167–150 B.C.). It is sometimes argued that Polybius thought of the Romans as recognizably ordinary human beings, not different in nature from the Greeks; but this view turns out to be quite controversial—especially in regard to military affairs.[1] The purpose of the present paper is to offer new arguments and evidence that Polybius did indeed think of the Romans as recognizably ordinary human beings. Yet if they were ordinary human beings, what then accounted for the Romans' absolutely extraordinary military-political success? The origin of this success was the question Polybius posed to his audience right at the beginning of his *Histories* (1.1.5). Polybius' answer, I will argue, was that the constellation of good social systems the Romans inhabited—not their special nature—was what provided these "ordinary men" with the ability to conduct outstandingly courageous and virtuous action. In other words, Polybius thought that the Romans did share the same human weaknesses as the Greeks; but he also believed that the systems evolved over time

This paper has been much improved by the comments of the anonymous referees. I would also like to thank Paul Burton for discussion of Cato and ancient rhetorical theory. It will be evident, too, that the paper has greatly benefited—as is true of so many studies in Hellenistic history—from the work of Frank Walbank.

1. For the first view, see A. Momigliano, *Alien Wisdom: The Limits of Hellenization* (Cambridge, 1975) 22–24; *contra*: see now esp. W. V. Harris, *War and Imperialism in Republican Rome* (Oxford, 1979) 53, and E. Rawson, "The Expansion of Rome," in J. Boardman, J. Griffin, and O. Murray, eds., *The Oxford History of the Classical World* (Oxford, 1986) 423. Cf. below, pp. 179–86.

within Roman culture and society prevented such weaknesses from being as destructive as they were in the Hellenic world.

The primary example of such a "system" can be found in Polybius' view of the Roman army. But it should be stressed that if Polybius in fact perceived the Romans as "ordinary men" in military respects, this was not—and is not—the universal view. The Romans themselves often proclaimed and extolled their natural courage: *Fortes Romani sunt tanquam caelus profundus,* Ennius said (*Ann.* 470)—a sentiment echoed persistently in Livy.[2] And the same idea appears often enough in modern commentary. Thus according to Kromayer-Veith, "The Roman was a natural soldier, whereas the Greek was, in his innermost character, unsoldierly."[3] Similar opinions—emphasizing the specialness of the Romans as a people in terms of their natural ferocity, violence and/or love of war—can be found in a whole range of other modern scholars.[4] On this hypothesis, of course, the eventual Roman conquest of Polybius' Hellenes would seem a foregone conclusion.

Now, setting aside for the moment what Polybius thought of the Romans, it is certainly true that he thought of his Greek contemporaries as basically "unsoldierly" in character—as a short discussion of examples from the *Histories* will serve to prove. For convenience, one may assemble Polybius' criticisms under three headings: the common soldiery of the Hellenistic Greek states had a strong tendency toward laziness and self-indulgence; they were often greedy for loot, sometimes to the point of self-destruction; and, most importantly, they suffered from extremely fragile morale when faced with actual battle.

2. See, e.g., Livy 3.61.11–62.3; 7.13.5 and 34.6; 8.38.4; 29.30.9; 37.30.6. On the ideology at work here, see L. R. Lind, "Concept, Action and Character: The Reasons for Rome's Greatness," *TAPA* 103 (1972) 236–39; and now N. Rosenstein, "Competition and Crisis in Mid-Republican Rome," *Phoenix* 47 (1993) 333 and n. 62.

3. "Der Römer war an sich Soldat, der Grieche . . . im innersten Wesen unsoldatisch": J. Kromayer and G. Veith, *Heerwesen und Kriegführung der Griechen und Römer* (Munich, 1928) 1.

4. Thus T. Africa, *The Immense Majesty: A History of Rome and the Roman Empire* (New York, 1974) 67, emphasizes the Romans' "aggressive masculinity"—both on the battlefield and in the bedroom; H. C. Boren, *Roman Society* (Chapel Hill, 1977) 33–34, underlines the inherent ruggedness, courage, and military virtue of the Romans; W. Eder even speaks of "pathologische Züge" (*Gnomon* 54 [1982] 550); and D. B. Nagle and S. M. Burstein, *The Ancient World: Readings in Social and Cultural History* (Englewood Cliffs, N.J., 1995) 195f., have an entire section labeled "Ferocity." A classic exposition of this thesis is Harris, *War and Imperialism* 41–53: he stresses the extraordinary willingness of ordinary Romans to go into army service (pp. 45, 46, 48), specifically warns against assuming that ordinary Romans were unwarlike (p. 47), and concludes that the Romans were more ferocious and violent than other advanced peoples of the Mediterranean (p. 53).

Self-indulgence. When the Seleucid general Xenoetas captured the camp of the pretender Molon in 222, he allowed his troops a period of relaxation after this success; the men then went utterly wild with food and drink. When Molon counterattacked, most of Xenoetas' army was already too drunk even to offer a defense, and the result was total disaster (Polyb. 5.46.4–48.5). These, by the way, were picked troops (5.46.11).[5] In Polybius' *Histories*, negligence, sleepiness, and/or drunkenness among the soldiery also lead to disaster for the Syracusans (8.37), Aetolians (Livy [P] 31.41), Macedonians (Polyb. 29.15.1–2), and even Spartans (Livy [P] 35.37.2).[6]

Self-destructive greed. The temptation toward undisciplined looting was a characteristic of all Hellenistic Greek armies, according to Polybius. Aetolian soldiers could not control themselves—even pillaging friendly communities (4.6.10 and 12); Seleucid armies suffered from the same problem (cf. 5.57.7–8); and everyone knew that the troops of Antigonid Macedon constituted a formidable looting machine.[7] Indeed, Polybius offers it as a basic rule of international life that it is almost impossible to keep any Greek soldiers from undisciplined looting—even if the men thereby risked serious damage from surprise counterattack (10.17.1–4).

Physical cowardice. Modern scholars sometimes assert that Hellenistic Greek armies were better fighting forces than the amateur citizen-levies of the Classical age, because of the intensification of drill and the presence in most armies of at least some true professionals (mercenaries).[8] One could not, however, tell this from Polybius. To begin with, he does not hide the truth

5. B. Bar-Kochva, *The Seleucid Army: Organization and Tactics in the Great Campaigns* (Cambridge, 1976) 98, suspects political bias is at work in Polybius' presentation of this incident, since he and his sources were hostile to Hermeias, the chief advisor of the young Antiochus III, and Xenoetas was one of Hermeias' allies. But Polybius' point here is not really about Hermeias and his allies but about the fragile character of Hellenistic armies (as is proven by the generalizing statement about self-indulgent soldiery at 5.48.1). Polybius, a citizen of the Achaean League, does not hide the fact that Xenoetas was himself an Achaean (5.46.6).

6. For Livy 31.41 and 35.37 as deriving from Polybian material, see J. Briscoe, *A Commentary on Livy, Books XXXI–XXXIII* (Oxford, 1973) 1–2 and 115 (for 31.41), and *A Commentary on Livy, Books XXXIV–XXXVII* (Oxford, 1981) 2 and 181. Cf. also frg. 40 B-W: another reference to drunken and disorderly soldiers unable to hear a word of command or take thought for the future. The context is unclear; but see F. W. Walbank, *A Historical Commentary on Polybius* III (Oxford, 1979) 746.

7. On Macedonian looting, see Polyb. 4.65.1 (Oeniadae); 4.72.1 (Psophis); 4.84.5, cf. 64.1 (Elis); 5.19 (Laconia); and 5.8.6–9 (Thermum, the capital of Aetolia, where the booty included 15,000 beautifully decorated suits of armor dedicated to the gods).

8. See, recently, P. Culham, "Chance, Command and Chaos in Ancient Military Engagements," *World Futures* 47 (1989) 191–205.

about his own Achaeans: the men of the Achaean League had a tendency to flee shamefully from battle, whether in the 220s, the 190s, or the 140s.[9] Strong personalities, if given years to work on it, might be able to whip these men into some sort of shape (as Polybius' hero Philopoemen did, between 210 and 207); but here the problem was that the Achaean officer class tended to be made up of incompetents, fops, and cowards.[10] These problems were in fact characteristic of almost every Greek army: Antiochus III, the Seleucid king, was himself a formidable warrior—but he thought his army consisted mostly of worthless cowards, whether in 217 (Polyb. 5.85.13, cf. 87.2), or 191 (cf. Livy [P] 36.15.5–16.3), or 189 (Livy [P] 37.39.6).[11] Acarnanian troops fled from even the prospect of real battle (Polyb. 5.96.3), as did the men of Elis, twice (5.69.4–8, 95.8–9). Most of the Aetolian army simply refused to take the field for the crucial campaign of 191—despite the pleas and threats of their generals (Livy [P] 36.15.4–5).[12] As for the soldiers of Ptolemaic Egypt, they too were thought to be worthless—lazy as well as cowardly (Polyb. 5.63.11–65.10).

In Polybius, then, the Greeks are indeed presented as inherently unsoldierly in character. But the question is whether the Romans—as Polybius presents them—are inherently all that much better. And here we are immediately confronted by the fact that not only do many modern scholars believe that the Romans *were* more ferocious and violent than other advanced peoples of the Mediterranean (see above, p. 176 and n. 4), but that some scholars have argued that Polybius believed this, too—and indeed have based their own conclusions about the Romans in part on what they take to be Polybius' opinion. Thus William V. Harris argues for the inherent ferocity, violence, and warlike character of the Roman people by pointing to Polybius 1.37.7–10, where the Greek historian remarks that the Romans

9. On Achaean fecklessness in the 220s, see Polyb. 2.47.8; 4.7.6–7; 4.12.8–12. In the 190s: see Livy [P] 33.14.6 and 35.26.9 (Polybian derivation: Briscoe, *Commentary* I 275; *Commentary* II 181). In the 140s: see Paus. 7.15.2–4 and 10, and 7.14.3, apparently based on Polybian material; cf. E. S. Gruen, "The Origins of the Achaean War," *JHS* 96 (1976) 65–69.

10. Philopoemen's efforts to make the Achaean army battle-worthy, over a period of years between 210 and 207 B.C.: see Polyb. 10.22–24 and 11.8–10; cf. Plut. *Phil.* 9.2. Polybius in fact once defined the essence of generalship as the imposition of useful order, through purposeful training, on what was at the beginning merely "a disorganized mob" (πλῆθος ἄτακτον: cf. Ael. 3.4, a quotation from Polybius' lost *Treatise on Tactics*). But that achievement required a certain type of officer: for the Achaean officer class as incompetent, cowardly fops, see esp. Polyb. 11.8–9 (excoriating).

11. On the Polybian derivation of Livy 36.15–16 and 37.39, see Briscoe, *Commentary* II 241 and 343.

12. For Livy 36.15 as deriving from Polybian material, see Briscoe, *Commentary* II 241.

tend strongly to believe that their βία (which Harris translates simply as violence) will conquer anything.[13] And Elizabeth Rawson is similar: she stresses the ferocity of the Roman soldiery as they appear in Polybius as part of her explanation of the roots of Roman imperialism—basing her opinion on Polybius 10.16–17, the historian's famous account of how the Romans sack cities.[14]

But neither of these passages can bear the weight being put on it. Polybius 1.37.7–10 is an account of how the Romans wrongly trust in willpower and effort in the face of inclement weather (severe storms at sea).[15] And while the βία referred to at 1.37.7 may mean "violence" in a certain sense, later in this same sentence Polybius specifically equates this βία with ὁρμή (ibid.)— that is, "spirit" (in this case, the spirit of determination). In other words, Polybius does not seem to be speaking here of sheer love of physical violence (savagery, ferocity, warlikeness) as a characteristic of the Romans, let alone as the characteristic that sharply separates them from all other people. As for Polybius 10.16–17, the point being made by the historian in that passage is *not* that the Romans are more violent than other men in the sacking of cities—indeed, he presents the Greeks as tending to be far wilder and more out of control (10.17.1–4, explicit). Rather (and precisely), Polybius' emphasis is overwhelmingly on Roman discipline, and (among the officer-class at least) self-discipline (10.16 *passim*, cf. 17.6).[16]

Moreover, balanced against the thinness of the evidence adduced to support the idea that Polybius thought of the Romans as specially violent and inherently adapted to military life is a plethora of passages where Polybius depicts the Roman soldiery as suffering from serious defects quite similar to those of ordinary Greek soldiers. These passages demonstrate just how deeply Polybius' opinion on the question of Romans as "natural soldiers" (different from the Greeks) is in conflict with the opinion of many modern scholars.

For instance, *self-indulgence*: a strong tendency among Greek troops, it was equally strong among the Romans. The classic case here is Scipio Africanus' mistake in granting a period of relaxation to his soldiery following the great victories won against the Carthaginians in Spain (206). Polybius says that the troops of Scipio's army soon became "disturbed and seditious"

13. *War and Imperialism* 53; the reference to Polyb. 1.37 is in fact the culminating argument in Harris' discussion of Roman warlikeness and ferocity (41–53).

14. "The Expansion of Rome," 423.

15. F. W. Walbank, *A Historical Commentary on Polybius* I (Oxford, 1957) 97, rightly notes that Polybius' discussion here is really meant to be focused on Rome's naval efforts.

16. For detailed discussion of Polybius' emphasis in 10.16–17, see below, pp. 184–86.

because he was allowing them too much leisure, and even (as with Xenoetas' troops) too much food (11.25.7). And this relaxation of discipline soon led to outright mutiny—a widespread and very dangerous mutiny over pay. Order was restored only by the public execution of dozens of ringleaders (11.25–30). Polybius employs this incident in particular to proclaim in detail his *general* rule that one should never allow ordinary soldiers too much rest or idleness, or too much luxury and plenty (11.25.7). That is, in this respect he is explicit in not seeing Roman soldiers as different from all others.

Self-destructive greed. The fact is that Roman troops as Polybius presents them—if left to their own devices—are just as greedy for pillage as are the Greeks. Thus at Astapa in Spain in 206, Roman soldiers were so eager for the gold and silver of the town (which the inhabitants had put to the torch) that they rushed into the enormous pyre of flaming metal, trying to grab up pieces; many in this way were burned to death (Polyb. 11.24.11).[17] A similar situation occurred in the Greek city of Phocaea in 190: despite the formal surrender of the city, and the Roman commander's consequent promise of good treatment, he was simply unable to control his men—who went wild with looting (Livy [P] 37.32.8–14).[18] Of course, Polybius' point in 10.16–17 was that Roman soldiers (unlike Greek ones) were normally kept under better control by their officers; Phocaea—like Astapa—was thus unusual.[19]

Finally, *physical cowardice.* It is true that Polybius thought the Romans, especially when defending their Italian homeland, to be good soldiers in battle (6.52.6–10); and he certainly recorded outstanding instances of Roman bravery.[20] Yet if Polybius considered the Romans good soldiers, that only reveals the low quality of the standards he was applying—for often enough he depicted these same Roman troops as wavering seriously, or panicking. Roman armies suffered from low morale after Lake Trasimene (3.90.3–4), and before the battle of Cannae (3.107.4–5). During the Second Macedonian War there was widespread mutiny at Apollonia in Greece, caused by

17. For the connection between the Polybian fragment 11.24.11 and the Roman sack of Astapa (Livy 28.23), see rightly F. W. Walbank, *A Historical Commentary on Polybius* II (Oxford, 1967) 305.

18. For Livy 37.32 as deriving from Polybian material, see Briscoe, *Commentary* II 2.

19. For the greed of ordinary Roman soldiers in Polybius (which normally was kept under discipline) see also 2.31.4; 3.76.13; and cf. Livy [P] 36.34.7 (Polybian derivation: see Briscoe, *Commentary* II 2; 226; 241).

20. See, e.g., the spirited Roman assault on the walls of New Carthage, a very difficult operation (10.13.6–10); or, from the legendary period, the description of Horatius at the bridge (6.55).

war-weariness (Livy [P] 32.3).[21] The Roman heavy infantry gave way before the Macedonian phalanx at Atrax in 198 (Livy [P] 32.17.11–18.1), and at Cynoscephalae in 197 (Polyb. 18.25.2–4); the former battle decisively ended the year's campaigning, while in the latter case a counterattack by Roman reserves against another part of the Macedonian line managed to save the day.[22] The entire Roman left wing panicked at the crucial battle of Magnesia in 189—though again the situation was saved, this time by the bravery of individual officers (Livy [P] 37.43.1–3).[23] During the Third Macedonian war, Roman army morale plummeted after Perseus' initial victories (Livy [P] 42.61.5, cf. 60.6)—and later, Roman troops panicked in three separate engagements.[24]

The last examples have come mostly from Roman encounters with the Macedonians; and indeed in Polybius there is only one army that is presented as consistently free from disgraceful conduct in combat, one army that is as valiant on land as it is (fighting as marines) at sea, as valiant in defense as in offense: not the army of Rome but the army of Macedon. The Macedonians, Polybius tells us, enjoy war as if it were a banquet (5.2.6)—something he never comes close to saying about Roman troops; the Roman general Flamininus thought his own men inferior in quality (Livy [P] 32.18.1).[25] It appears, further, that Polybius offered at least a partial explanation for the

21. On the Polybian derivation of this passage, see Briscoe, *Commentary* I 172, arguing strongly against H. Nissen, *Kritische Untersuchungen über die Quellen der vierten and fünften Dekade des Livius* (Berlin, 1862) 132 (who thinks it is annalistic in origin).

22. On the crucial strategic importance of the Roman defeat at Atrax for the campaign of 198, see A. M. Eckstein, "T. Quinctius Flamininus and the Campaign against Philip in 198 B.C.," *Phoenix* 30 (1976) 131–36. On the Polybian derivation of Livy 32.17, see Briscoe, *Commentary* I 2. On the battle of Cynoscephalae as Polybius presented it, see now A. M. Eckstein, *Moral Vision in the Histories of Polybius* (Berkeley, 1995) 183–92 (on Flamininus' counterattack, esp. 187–91).

23. For Livy 37.43 as deriving from Polybian material, cf. Briscoe, *Commentary* II 303.

24. For the Roman panic at Phalanna in 171, see Livy [P] 42.64.6; for the Roman panic at Cassandreia in 169, and again at Meliboea soon after, see Livy [P] 42.12.3 and 13.6. For the Polybian derivation of Livy 42.60–61 and 65, and 44.12–13, see Nissen, *Kritische Untersuchungen* 250 and 254–55.

25. Polybius at 5.2.6 is actually quoting a famous line from Hesiod (concerning the sons of Aeaces), and applying it to the Macedonians. For discussion, see Walbank, *Commentary* I 539–40. Flamininus' opinion of the relative worth of his own men compared to Macedonian fighters as Polybian in derivation: see Briscoe, *Commentary* I 2. The consul A. Hostilius Mancinus, 25 years later, seems to have held the same opinion—and refused a Macedonian challenge to set-piece battle: see Plut. *Aem.* 9.3. Polybian depictions of Macedonian valor in each and every situation: see 4.60.4–8; 5.100.6; 8.14.9; 16.3.8, 3.11, and 4.13; Livy [P] 32.17.4–18.1; 36.25; 42.54 and 59.1–6; 43.18; 44.37.9–10 and 42.7.

special Macedonian fierceness in war: the harshness and poverty of much of Macedon itself, combined with its exposure to the destructive raids (and brutalizing cultural influence) of barbarian neighbors. A good portion of the Macedonian population, then, was simply "more ferocious" than ordinary men (*ferociores*: Livy [P] 45.30.7).[26]

Yet the Romans in the end defeated even the Macedonians—not to mention all the other Hellenistic Greek powers; and the Romans, according to Polybius, had failings much like those of ordinary men. If one discarded (as Polybius evidently did) the idea that the Romans were inherently more ferocious than other peoples, how was this startling Roman success then to be explained? We have returned once more to the question Polybius posed to his audience at 1.1.5.

One alternative answer, widespread among Polybius' contemporaries (cf. Polyb. 1.63.9), was that the Romans had simply benefited from an extraordinary run of good luck. Like the hypothesis of special Roman ferocity, this hypothesis too has its modern supporters. For instance, Michel Roux, in his recent study of Roman and Hellenistic Greek armies, concludes that on balance their military technique was about equal (the Romans being ahead in some areas, the Greeks in others); what won for the Romans was the superior generalship that specific Roman commanders happened to display on specific (and varied) battlefields.[27] Now, Polybius himself was willing to allow a role for *Tyche* (Fortune) in the destruction of Macedonian power—and he allowed a role as well for the personal deficiencies and misjudgments of Philip V, and then of Perseus.[28] But he also strongly warned against giving too much weight to the idea of luck in the rise of Rome (see the emphatic statement at 1.63.9).[29] In fact, the Greek historian avoids the temptation of assigning the success of the Romans either to inherent and natural differences

---

On the Polybian derivation of the various Livian passages cited, see (in order) Briscoe, *Commentary* I 2; II 2 and 225–26; Nissen, *Kritische Untersuchungen* 254, 258, and 264.

26. On the Polybian derivation of Livy 45.30, cf. Nissen, *Kritische Untersuchungen* 276. Note how the passage strikingly resembles Polybius' extant discussion of the harsh physical environment of his own native Arcadia, and the effect this has on Arcadian culture and character (4.20–21). The crucial difference, however, is that the Arcadians have taken steps to mitigate the harsh effect of their environment, by means of education (4.21)—whereas the Macedonians clearly have not.

27. See M. Roux, "Recherches sur les aspects militaires de la conquête du monde gréco-hellénistique par Rome au IIᵉ siècle avant Jésus-Christ," *REA* 95 (1993) esp. 443 and 456–57.

28. See, in general, the classic study by F. W. Walbank, "Φίλιππος Τραγῳδούμενος: A Polybian Experiment," *JHS* 58 (1938) 55–68.

29. See the remarks of Walbank, *Commentary* I 129–30.

between the Romans and other peoples, *or* to the impact of sheer good luck. For him, the answer lay elsewhere.

As far as the strictly military aspect of Roman success went, Polybius concentrated the attention of his audience on the various artificial *systems* the Romans had evolved to make their soldiers more orderly and effective. The legion is one such system, of course, and its tactical advantages in battle are discussed by Polybius at length in a famous passage in Book 18 (18.29.1–30.4). Similar is his praise of the Roman tradition of always keeping back a good part of the army in reserve during battle—unlike, especially, the conduct of Macedonians (18.32.3–6). But an earlier discussion, in Book 6, is more directly relevant to the purpose of this paper—which (again) is to emphasize how much Polybius saw the Romans as ordinary human beings. Book 6 deals explicitly with the reasons for the enormous success of Rome, and an important place in it is given over to the system of military punishment and reward meted out to individual Roman soldiers. It is clear why: Polybius believed it was this complex system of punishments and rewards that was most responsible for bringing ordinary men (as he thought the Romans generally were) up to a level of steadiness and courage on campaign and in battle which—though not super-human—was well above average.

The various *Greek* systems of military punishment and reward stand in the background to Polybius' discussion. Our evidence strongly indicates that by Roman standards, Greek punishments were extremely lax and the Greek system of rewards haphazard.[30] Polybius seems well aware of this: he had, of course, been hipparch of the Achaean League, and he makes an implicit comparison between the Romans' system and the Greek system (to the detriment of the Greeks) at 6.39.11. Moreover, he underlines the problems Greek commanders face when (for instance) he notes how difficult it was for the Achaean hipparch to impose military discipline upon his fellow-citizens (10.23.9).[31]

By contrast, the Roman system both of punishment and reward wins Polybius' praise in a long and detailed exposition (6.35–39). The Romans provided their soldiers with an extensive list of specific military delicts, such as laxity on sentry-duty (6.35.8–37.7), or throwing away one's weapons in battle (evidence of fear: 37.11). And the penalties for these delicts were all assigned immediately, by courts-martial in camp (37.1): very different from the systems prevailing in the Greek city-states, where the defendant had

---

30. For discussion of discipline in Greek armies, see esp. W. K. Pritchett, *The Greek State at War* II (Berkeley, 1974) 232–45. On the haphazard character of Greek military awards, see Pritchett, 290.

31. Cf. the remarks of Walbank, *Commentary* II 225.

far more rights (including a civilian trial).[32] Officers—to Polybius' obvious approval—were subject to the same severe punishments as their men (6.37.5–6). Moreover, Polybius says that for many offenses, the penalty assessed in the Roman camp amounted to death—the running of a gauntlet of cudgels and stones which it was theoretically possible to survive, but which few men did (37.2–3).[33] If whole units were found guilty of dereliction of duty in battle, they suffered immediate decimation (execution of one-tenth of their personnel)—even though these men were citizens (cf. Polyb. 6.38.1).

This stern regimen of punishment certainly was no total guarantee of Roman behavior in battle as Polybius described it: incidents of Roman failure, fecklessness, and panic are a quite prominent feature of the *Histories* (see above). But to the historian it did seem admirably designed to *minimize* "unmanly and shameful conduct" (ἀνανδρία, αἰσχύνη: 6.37.10). One may note that Polybius is thus explicit that such conduct is perfectly possible among Roman soldiers—a possibility missing from his descriptions of the Macedonians. And he is also impressed with how the Roman system of elaborately-supervised sentry-duty, with accompanying punishments, prevents negligence and sleepiness among either men or officers (6.36–37, a very detailed account)—a type of failing that, this time, both Romans and Macedonians shared.[34]

The harsh system of Roman military punishments, Polybius says, was paralleled by an equally extensive and emphatic list of public commendations, rewards, and decorations for specified acts of valor: for example, being the first to mount the wall of an enemy city, or saving the life of a comrade (6.39.5–6). Further, the historian stresses how the recipients of such rewards were honored continually throughout the rest of their lives, even after demobilization, and especially in religious processions (39.9). As with the heavy Roman punishments for military delicts, Polybius is explicit that the elaborate Roman system of public rewards is "an admirable method for encouraging soldiers to face danger on the battlefield" (39.1). He concludes that this careful system of rewards and punishments is a crucial factor in Rome's overall military success (39.11).

If the Romans have developed a *system* through which to overcome their weaknesses—the weaknesses of relatively ordinary men—on the battlefield,

32. See Pritchett, *Greek State at War* II 233–34 and 238–45.

33. For discussion of the institution described at Polyb. 6.37.2–3, see Walbank, *Commentary* I 720.

34. On Macedonian negligence and sleepiness on guard-duty, see Livy [P] 31.23.1–4 (an incident of 200 B.C.; Polybian derivation: Briscoe, *Commentary* I 1–2, cf. 115); and Polyb. 29.15.1–2 (an incident a generation later).

Polybius also emphasizes that they have developed a *system* through which to overcome the dangers inherent in undisciplined looting. It is not that Roman soldiers are not tempted by booty; on the contrary, in this they are recognizably like Greeks (see above). But—in the famous passage appended to his account of the Roman sack of New Carthage in Spain in 209—Polybius explains to his readership the virtues of this other Roman system (10.16–17).

In this passage Polybius is quite overt in comparing Romans and Greeks—but not as different types of human beings: rather, as the products of differently structured social circumstances. Greeks, the historian says, engage habitually in anarchic looting; this is because by tradition, every Greek soldier gets to keep whatever he can personally steal and conceal. And the result of such anarchy can be disastrous if the enemy manages a counterattack against the now-disorganized troops (10.17.2–4, cf. 16.8–9). Yet while most men cannot pass up the chance for looting, no matter *what* the military risk (17.1)—and it is clear that Polybius is including Romans in his thinking—the fact is that the Roman approach is far more organized, careful, and steady. They never employ more than half their available men in looting, reserving the others to stand guard against counterattacks (10.16.2–4 and 8–9); note once more the Roman emphasis on keeping a reserve (cf. p. 183, above, on battle-management). And the delegated looters do not act on the basis of each-man-for-himself (as the Greeks openly do): rather, they dutifully bring the collected booty to their officers, who then sell it, and divide the proceeds equally among *all* the men, i.e., looters and guards (16.5). Nor does anyone even secretly appropriate plunder for himself; this is because the Romans maintain the good faith (πίστις) of oaths they have taken. Thus no one fears being cheated (16.6 and 8–9).

Like the Roman system that attempted to enforce courage on the battlefield, the system that attempted to enforce discipline in looting was not infallible—as the examples of Astapa and Phocaea show (see above, p. 180). Moreover, what made it work even as well as it did was the good behavior of the officers, who had sole control over the booty and the proceeds from its sale (which was then divided). But Polybius by Book 10 had already underlined strongly to his audience that Roman aristocrats truly felt bound by oaths they took (see 6.56.11–15); the same could not be said of the Greek elite (56.13).[35] And the oath that tended so strongly to keep Roman officers honest here (and the system working) was an oath that all soldiers swore,

35. On the focus of Polyb. 6.56.11–15 on the religious piety of Roman nobles—a fact often forgotten in modern discussions of 6.56, as if the focus of that famous passage is totally on how the Roman masses are manipulated by religion—see now M. G. Morgan, "Politics, Religion and the Games in Rome, 200–150 B.C.," *Philologus* 134 (1990) 14–15.

"to steal nothing from the camp" (see Polyb. 6.33.1–2).[36] Polybius wishes
that his Greek audience would imitate the Roman system (10.17.5)—and if
he thinks the system *can* by imitated by the Greeks, then he does not think
the Romans are necessarily extraordinary as human beings. But it was a
system that depended not only on carefulness and caution, but on good faith
and honesty.[37]

The question then becomes: where did that Roman aristocratic honesty—
that determination to hold to oaths once sworn—come from? This brings us
to the topic not of Polybius' view of the mass of the Roman soldiery, but of his
view of the Roman aristocracy. It should be clear by now that the historian
did not view the mass of the Roman people as much different from the Greek
plethos: in their "natural" state—and this is true whether in military or civilian
garb—they shared many of the same failings.[38] But one must also stress that
Polybius did not view even the Roman aristocracy as men in any way *naturally*
different from, or superior to, their Greek counterparts. On the contrary,
the *Histories* from first to last contain description after description of deeply
flawed Roman aristocrats: the cowardly Cn. Cornelius Scipio Asina (1.21.7),
the deceitful Ti. Sempronius Longus (3.75.1), the drunken M. Livius (8.27.1),
the tasteless and extravagant L. Anicius (30.22), the stupid L. Malleolus
(36.14), the wordy, untalented, and cowardly A. Postumius Albinus (39.1).[39]
Nevertheless, Polybius clearly also thought that Roman aristocrats, taken
as a group, did perform to quite high standards of honesty and valor (see
6.52.10–11, 55.4 and 56.11–13; 18.35.1–2). The reasons, however, lay mostly
with yet another Roman *system*—this time, the system of upbringing to which
these men were subjected.

36. For the connection between Polyb. 10.16 and the oaths described at 6.33.1–2, see
Walbank, *Commentary* II 217.

37. For Polybian attacks on the greed and corruption of the Greek elite, see—besides
6.56.13—18.34.7 and 36.17.5–10.

38. For the unsteadiness of the Roman populace in the face of bad news, see Polybius'
comments at 3.85.8–9, 112.7, cf. 118.7; 29.1.1–3. Indeed, it is Polybius' considered opinion
that if the *polloi* at Rome had been as powerful a force in decision-making during the
Hannibalic War as were the masses at Carthage, then Rome would not have survived
(6.51.5–8). The Greek *plethos* was no different: see, e.g., Polyb. 2.47.8 and 4.14.2 (Achaea);
2.64.6 (Argos); 20.6–7 (Boeotia). The Alexandrians were worse, however: see, e.g.,
Polyb. 15.25.24(17), 26(19), 36(27); 15.27.1 and 3, 38.8.33.5–9. On Polybian distrust of
the masses in general, see now F. W. Walbank, "Polybius's Perception of the One and the
Many," in I. Malkin and Z. W. Rubinsohn, eds., *Leaders and Masses in the Roman World:
Studies in Honor of Zvi Yavetz* (Leiden, 1995) 201–22.

39. Other examples: the unfair C. Sulpicius Galus, cos. 166 (Polyb. 31.6); the cowardly
M. Claudius Marcellus, cos. III, 152 (35.4.3); and Ti. Sempronius Gracchus, cos. II,
163—naive (30.27), incompetent (30.30.7–8), deceitful (31.1.1), stingy (31.27.16).

The historian's discussion of this aspect of Roman culture, like his discussion of the way the Roman army system tended to produce steady and courageous men on campaign and in the battle line, forms an important part of Book 6—the volume of the *Histories* explicitly devoted to Polybius' analysis of how the Romans not only recovered from the devastating defeat at Cannae, but went on to gain hegemony over the entire Mediterranean world. One aspect of his analysis covered in detail the legal structure of the Roman state—put crudely, a system of republican checks and balances between three co-equal branches of government (6.3–18). Polybius believed that it was the inherent stability of this system that enabled the Roman state, better than any other state, to survive and prevail against the inevitable shocks inflicted upon it from the lawless international environment (6.43–52).[40] As we have just seen, Polybius also put great stress in his analysis upon the systems within the Roman military that produced an efficient fighting force out of the raw material the Roman people provided (6.35–39). But equally relevant to our present topic is Polybius' analysis of the Roman system of upbringing which produced, out of its *aristocratic* raw material, the generations of honest and valiant men destined to command armies, decide policy, and ultimately win victory—first over Carthage, and then over the rest of the world (6.52–56).

Polybius devotes the final portion of Book 6 precisely to that upbringing, and the volume is structured so as to lead the audience up to the single example of Roman aristocratic decision-making which, for Polybius, exemplifies the moral and political success of that upbringing. As mentioned above (p. 180), Polybius did believe that the Romans started out with quite good human raw material. And at 6.52.10, the beginning of the final portion of

---

40. For Polybius' view of the international environment as a lawless jungle with no authority existing to impose justice, see esp. his comments at 5.67.11 (and cf. 5.106.5). Best modern commentary on this passage: C. Wunderer, *Polybios: Lebens- und Weltanschauung aus dem zweiten vorchristlichen Jahrhundert* (Leipzig, 1927) 46. On the absence of a true system of international law in antiquity, see esp. E. Badian, "Hegemony and Independence: Prolegomena to a Study of the Relations of Rome and the Hellenistic States in the Second Century B.C.," *Actes du VIIᵉ Congrès de la F.I.E.C.* (Budapest, 1983) 401–405 (who does not cite Polyb. 5.67.11). On the Roman republican constitution as a system of checks and balances according to Polybius, see esp. K. von Fritz, *The Theory of the Mixed Constitution in Antiquity: A Critical Analysis of Polybius's Political Ideas* (New York, 1954), esp. chs. 4 and 6; and F. W. Walbank, *Polybius* (Berkeley, 1972) 130–50. One should not mistake Polybius' tough-minded view of the nature of international relations for either approval or acceptance; on the contrary, as R. von Scala demonstrated long ago, the Achaean historian urged upon his audience here a wide variety of reforms and restraint on behavior: see *Die Studien des Polybios* I (Stuttgart, 1890) 299–324.

Book 6, that idea is stated explicitly: it is the historian's belief that *all* the Italic peoples are naturally (φύσει . . .) superior to Phoenicians and Africans, both in physical strength and in personal courage (τῇ τε σωματικῇ ῥώμῃ καὶ ταῖς ψυχαῖς τόλμαις). Here, at first sight, is a better passage for both Harris and Rawson to have used in their attempt to ascribe to Polybius a belief in "natural" Roman military superiority. But if in 6.52 Polybius mentions Phoenicians and Africans, he does not mention Greeks or Macedonians, and the reason is that in 6.52 he is merely offering his audience reasons why the Romans eventually won the war against Hannibal. Moreover, this single short statement on "natural" advantages over Phoenicians and Africans is then followed by Polybius' programmatic remark that he now intends to indicate the pains *consciously* taken by the Roman state to produce the kind of men it needed (52.11).[41] What follows is three full chapters (6.53–56) in which aspects of the conscious Roman program of upbringing for aristocratic men are detailed.

First comes an elaborate discussion of the moral-political spectacle of the Roman aristocratic funeral (6.53.1–54.2). There is no need here to describe this famous passage closely. But Polybius, in two very emphatic statements, makes clear what *his* point is in describing this custom carefully: the spectacle of the funeral-processions, and of the public display of the wax *imagines* of the ancestors carried in those processions, serves to inspire in young men the fierce desire to emulate the virtues of those ancestors (6.53.10 and 54.3).[42] The historian then offers proofs of the effects of this Roman custom: men who have not hesitated to engage in single combat in order to decide a battle, or who have sacrificed themselves for the good of the state, or who have even put their own sons to death—completely contrary to nature (φύσιν . . .)—for the good of the state (6.54.4–5).[43] Moreover, Polybius

41. It is likely that a similar idea found at Livy 42.59.2—praising the natural courage of Italic (not specifically Roman) cavalry—derives from Polybius as well (*ingenio impavida gens* . . .). The scene is the battle of Callinicus during the Third Macedonian War (for which Polybius is Livy's obvious source), and the emphasis on the usefulness of cavalry in battle (42.59.4–5) recalls Polybius' comments at 3.117.5. See, briefly, Nissen, *Kritische Untersuchungen* 254–55. Yet the Italic cavalry are in fact defeated here by the *truly* ferocious Thracian auxiliaries of Macedon (*ferae* . . . 59.2); and the useful cavalry in this battle are Greeks (Thessalians), not Italic (59.4). Note that at Callinicus the Macedonian phalanx—as usual—routs the Greek infantry (ibid.).

42. Polybius' insight on the impact of the *imagines* upon aristocratic young men is confirmed by Sall. *Jug.* 4.5: cf. Walbank, *Commentary* I 739–40. See now H. I. Flower, *Ancestor Masks and Aristocratic Power in Roman Culture* (Oxford, 1996).

43. In 6.54 these men go unnamed. But it is likely that Polybius was aware of the various Roman legends surrounding, e.g., L. Junius Brutus (see Livy 2.5), A. Postumius (see Livy 4.29), and/or T. Manlius Torquatus (see Livy 8.7). Cf. Walbank, *Commentary* I 740.

says that these deeds *themselves* in turn become stories that are told to the young for the purpose of inspiration (6.54.6). He then gives an example of the latter phenomenon in detailing the suicidal courage of Horatius at the bridge (55.1–3). To Polybius, this story shows "the ambition and thirst for glory which the Romans instill in their young men *through their customs*" (διὰ τῶν παρ' αὐτοῖς ἐθισμῶν: 55.4).[44] Finally, Polybius discusses the impact of Roman religious piety upon all Romans, the aristocrats as well as the masses (6.56). One result of Roman religious terror, he says approvingly, is that Roman public officials and commanders are scrupulously honest, especially concerning sworn oaths (56.12–15)—which was not something one could say about either Carthaginians or Greeks (56.1–2 and 13). It is another example of the superiority not of Roman *physis*, but—precisely—of Roman customs and institutions (ἔθη καὶ νόμιμα: 56.1).

Indeed, it is likely that Polybius had already made important and positive comments concerning the character of Roman upbringing much earlier in Book 6, so that his long and approving discussion in 6.53–56 came as no surprise to his readership. For scholars have long argued that it is in the context of the historian's explication of the virtues of the early Romans—what is sometimes called the *Archaeologia* of Book 6—that the Polybian fragment currently numbered 6.11a.11 ought to be placed. And that fragment reads: "It is necessary that every branch of virtue be practiced by those who aim at a good education; and the training should be immediately from childhood, with physical courage the most important subject."[45]

The impact of all this aristocratic training can be seen, Polybius says, in the extraordinary act of the Roman Senate with which he has decided to bring Book 6 to an end (6.58.1: explicit). Hannibal, after Cannae, offered to ransom the eight thousand Roman prisoners he had captured in the battle (58.2–5); it is very probable that both sides saw this as a possible peace-feeler.[46] But the *Patres* refused even to consider the arrangement, even though many had kinsmen among the prisoners (cf. 6.58.10); instead, they let

---

44. My italics. It is worth noting that only Polybius, of all our ancient authorities on the Horatius story, alleges that the Roman hero actually *died* defending the bridge: see Walbank, *Commentary* I 740–41. Polybius evidently found such an outcome morally satisfying in terms of inspiration to courageous behavior: for detailed discussion of his ideology here, see now Eckstein, *Moral Vision*, ch. 2. Other Polybian examples of praise for soldiers (and even generals) who died fighting in the battle-line: see 2.1.7–8 (Hamilcar Barca); 3.116.2–3 (L. Aemilius Paullus of Cannae); 16.9.1–4 (Theophiliscus of Rhodes).

45. For discussion of the *Archaeologia* as an important (though now mostly lost) part of Book 6, see esp. Walbank, *Polybius* 147–49. On the context of 6.11a.11, see Walbank, *Commentary* I 663–64, cf. 673.

46. Cf. Livy 22.48.7–9 (explicit), with the detailed comments of W. Hoffmann, "Hannibal und Rom," in K. Christ, ed., *Hannibal*, Wege der Forschung 371 (Darmstadt, 1974)

Hannibal sell them off into slavery—meanwhile sending a message to the remaining Roman armies that the only choice was victory or death (58.11). This they did, Polybius stresses, even though the Roman position seemed almost hopeless (58.7). And they even returned a captured Roman noble who had attempted to use the occasion of his presence on the embassy to escape from captivity—thereby violating an oath he had sworn to Hannibal (58.12). The upbringing which the Roman aristocracy received was not infallible, as the example of the noble captive showed; "nature" (here in the form of desire for personal survival) sometimes won out. But Polybius' discussion of the positive impact of Roman ἔθη καὶ νόμιμα had all along been leading up to the decision made by the *Patres* as a group to continue fighting even after Cannae (58.1). And so he now concludes that the senators of Rome

> neither yielded so far to catastrophe as to disregard the conduct proper to their own dignity (τοῦ πρέποντος αὐτοῖς), nor omitted anything required by the situation. . . . So Hannibal was struck with astonishment by the un-shaken firmness and the nobility of spirit (τὸ μεγαλόψυχον) they displayed (58.8, 13).

The point of the spectacular funeral-processions, of the wax *imagines* of the ancestors, of the telling of traditional stories about the great Roman heroes, was—Polybius insisted—to create a fierce desire in the new generation to emulate the virtues of their predecessors (6.53.10, 54.3, 55.4). In the Roman decision to continue the war against Hannibal and Carthage even after the disaster at Cannae—in the Roman determination never to do anything against τὸ πρέπον αὐτοῖς—Polybius wanted his audience to see the admirable fruit borne by that Roman system of practical education. Thus it was not *physis* but *nomos* that made the Romans great; and it is precisely because the Romans are but men to Polybius that he spends so much time in Book 6 analyzing the social *systems* that created Roman success.[47]

56–57. Polyb. 7.9.12 (the text of Hannibal's treaty with Philip V) also makes it clear that in Polybius, Hannibal was hoping to conclude peace with Rome after Cannae.

47. For other examples of Polybius' view that social systems, including education of various kinds (or the lack thereof), play a crucial role in the creation of human personalities, see 1.81.10 (where the often brutal and cruel behavior of mercenaries is ascribed to bad, uncivilized upbringing from childhood, combined with living amid ἔθη μοχθηρά), and 2.17.9–11 (where the barbarous conduct of the Celts of the Po Valley is ascribed to the primitive physical and barren intellectual circumstances in which they lived). Since social systems are so important to human development in Polybius, improvement in human behavior would seem—theoretically—quite possible. But Polybius in fact believes that such change for the better is, as a practical matter,

The other aspect of the problem for Polybius, though, was change—and decline. *Physis* was very resistant to change: the Macedonians of the 140s B.C. were just as ferocious in battle as their ancestors had been under Alexander the Great almost two hundred years before (cf. Polyb. 36.17.13–14).[48] But it was *nomos*, according to Polybius, that had produced the admirable Romans of the age of Hannibal—and *nomos* was more malleable, more fragile. The historian in fact perceived a sharp degeneration in Roman conduct (both personally and as a community) in the post-Hannibalic period, and he traced this degeneration to a transformation of crucial aspects of the Roman social system—changes in the Roman style of life and upbringing. Ironically, these changes for the worse (Polyb. 24.10.10 and 31.25.3, explicit: ἐπὶ τὸ χεῖρον) were caused by the very wealth and unchallenged power that had been won for Rome by the virtuous men of the previous generations.

In a certain mood, Polybius saw this degeneration already beginning with the arrival of the luxurious spoils of Syracuse in Rome in 211—just five years after the *akmé* in society described in Book 6 (9.10).[49] And the later way-stations of moral decline were, to him, clear enough: in the 190s B.C. most Romans (though not all) were still honest and upright (18.35.1); by 180 the Senate was becoming corrupted by Rome's unchallengeable power—and by servile flattery (24.8–12); in 172 a majority of the *Patres* consciously determined upon a policy of vicious deception toward Macedon, thereby departing from old-fashioned and virtuous ways (Livy [P] 42.39–43, followed especially by the bitter comment at Livy [P] 42.47–59).[50] Most importantly, in the 160s and 150s the younger generation of Roman aristocrats seemed to Polybius almost totally debauched by their new and luxurious style of life:

---

extremely difficult (see, e.g., 10.47.5–11), whereas change for the worse is all too easy (see immediately below). And these latter phenomena *are* the result of *physis*: i.e., human nature. On Polybius' pessimism here, see now Eckstein, *Moral Vision*, ch. 8.

48. Polybius apparently thought that given enough pressure from circumstances, even basic *physis* could change (his explanation for Hannibal's cruelty in Italy: 10.26). Something similar evidently had happened to the Macedonians over time, too—as a result of constant pressure from (and exposure to) barbarous neighbors (see above, p. 182 and n. 26). Still, such situations obviously occurred only very rarely.

49. See the comments of E. S. Gruen, *The Hellenistic World and the Coming of Rome* I (Berkeley, 1984) 348. In fact, "corruption" of the Roman populace was detected by Polybius as early as 232, with the land reform of C. Flaminius (see 2.21.7–9): i.e., its roots existed even before Rome's *akmé* was reached.

50. On the Polybian derivation of this famous Livian passage, with its reference to the emergence at Rome of *nova ac nimis callida sapientia*, see Nissen, *Kritische Untersuchungen* 250; J. Briscoe, "Q. Marcius Philippus and Nova Sapientia," *JRS* 54 (1964) 68 and n. 22; F. W. Walbank, "Polybius between Greece and Rome," *Entretiens Fond. Hardt* 20 (1974) 10–11 and 23.

devoted to partying with prostitutes of both sexes, to drinking and feasting and extravagance, "having in the period of the war with Perseus become quickly infected with the dissoluteness of the Greeks in these respects" (31.25.4). It was all the result of the influx of new wealth into Rome (cf. 25.5). Thus there were soon not many young men left who—like Scipio Aemilianus under the tutelage first of his father L. Aemilius Paullus and then of Polybius himself—devoted themselves to the old stern and frugal ways, or consciously trained themselves to be courageous (31.25–30). The social and moral consequences of this transformation of *nomos* among the aristocratic young (i.e., the breakdown of a crucial Roman social-cultural *system*) were underlined by Polybius four volumes later, in his bitter comments on the failure of the new generation of the Roman elite to volunteer for the wars that broke out in Spain in the late 150s. Instead, these young men made every desperate attempt to escape service: conduct so disgraceful, cowardly, and shameful (αἰσχρόν, ἀπρεπές, ἀναισχυντία), and on such a scale, as had never—Polybius said—been seen in Rome before (35.4.4–7).[51]

The excoriating criticism of the younger generation of Roman aristocrats that appears in Polybius 31.25 is supported in that passage by remarks quoted from M. Porcius Cato the Censor—remarks that Polybius acknowledges with warm approval (25.5a). And the historian's relationship with Cato the Elder repays careful examination. Momigliano commented in the essay cited at the beginning of this paper that within the Roman aristocracy, Polybius found people who in fact did not differ from educated Greeks in their interests, their ideas, their emotional reactions.[52] Now as it happens, Momigliano was not thinking here of Cato[53]—and a close link is not often made, perhaps because Cato is viewed as a moralist, while Polybius is (mis)perceived as a total pragmatist.[54] Nevertheless, I wish to bring the discussion here to

---

51. On the integral—and moralizing—connection between Polyb. 31.25 and Polyb. 35.4, see esp. Gruen, *Hellenistic World and the Coming of Rome* I 348. By contrast, Walbank, *Commentary* III 646, adopts the position that Polyb. 35.4 is merely a passage of political propaganda inserted into the *Histories* to emphasize the virtues of Scipio Aemilianus by exaggerating the faults of his contemporaries. But Polybius was a person deeply concerned with issues of personal bravery and seems to have found physical cowardice sincerely repulsive: see (e.g.) 3.116.13; 4.8.5–6; 29.17–18; 39.1.11–12; and now Eckstein, *Moral Vision*, ch. 2.

52. *Alien Wisdom* 23.

53. Momigliano's focus (pp. 23–24) is on Polybius' perception of Scipio Aemilianus.

54. This is a misperception I hope to correct somewhat in *Moral Vision*. Any significant connection between Polybius and Cato is denied especially by A. E. Astin, *Cato the Censor* (Oxford, 1978) 226 and n. 42.

an end by arguing that Cato and Polybius probably came into significant contact via the circle of L. Aemilius Paullus, and that when they did they will have found much in common in their outlook and concerns. This experience, too—not of Romans as ordinary men benefiting from a constellation of good social-cultural systems, but of an extraordinary Roman with an intellectual and moral kinship to Polybius himself—would then have been an additional factor in the Achaean historian's conclusion that Roman society was made up of recognizable human beings, not different in *physis* from (in this case) aristocratic intellectuals among the Greeks.

The overtly attested interactions between Polybius and the Censor are only two. When Polybius was striving in the late 150s to get the Roman Senate to allow the return home of the Achaean detainees in Italy (including himself), he worked first via Scipio Aemilianus, who in turn strongly influenced Cato; and in the end, it was Cato who spoke out decisively to the *Patres* on the Achaeans' behalf (Plut. *Cat. Mai.* 9.3).[55] Later, when Polybius wanted the Senate to grant additional political favors to the detainees, he went directly to Cato himself—but was warned off from his effort by Cato, with a reference to Odysseus deciding (having escaped once) to enter the cave of the Cyclops once again (Polyb. 35.6 = Plut. *Cat. Mai.* 9.40). The point in the latter passage is not any threat that Cato posed, but rather the danger constituted by the *Patres* as a group.[56] To this evidence may be added Polybius' approving reference to the Censor's bitter remarks about the younger generation at Rome (31.25.5a; see above); his approving reference to Cato's attack on the incapacity and low intellectual ability of the men sent by the Senate on the diplomatic embassy to Asia Minor in 150/149 (36.14; cf. Plut. *Cat. Mai.* 9.1); and his approving reference to Cato's biting criticism of the ex-consul A. Postumius Albinus (39.1 1–5; cf. Plut. *Cat. Mai.* 12.1). Our evidence may be slim, but it all points in one direction: a similarity in outlook between the Roman senator and the Greek intellectual on many issues, a similarity of which Polybius at least was perfectly conscious.

Moreover, it is very likely that Polybius gained a special connection to Cato because of their *mutual* personal connection to the house of the Aemilii Paulli. Polybius, of course, was a close friend of both of the surviving sons of L. Aemilius Paullus the victor of Pydna—namely, P. Cornelius Scipio Aemilianus and Q. Fabius Maximus Aemilianus (see Polyb. 31.24–30). As for Cato, at some point between 167 and 161 the son of the Censor married Aemilius Paullus' daughter Aemilia Tertia, i.e., the sister (or perhaps

---

55. The historicity of this speech is secured via *ORF*[3] frgs. 87–89.

56. See the comments of C. Nicolet, "Polybe et les institutions romaines," *Entretiens Fond. Hardt* 20 (1974) 246.

half-sister) of Scipio Aemilianus and Fabius Aemilianus.[57] One may note Cato's son secured this marriage because (we are told) Paullus was impressed with his virtuous and valorous character, as demonstrated during the fighting against Perseus;[58] this was exactly the type of Aemilian sentiment of which Polybius explicitly approved (see 31.29.5–7). Marriages of this sort naturally had political implications—which in turn implies steady contact between the principals. That would have been especially the case with the marriage of Aemilia and Cato's son, which lasted until the latter's death in 152, and which produced male offspring (the later consuls of 118 and 114) who must have been important to Cato.[59] Cato's cooperation with Aemilius Paullus is already visible in the *Contra Ser. Galbam ad milites*, his powerful defense of Paullus' right to a triumph in 167.[60] And later, we find the Censor heaping praise on the military courage of Paullus' son Aemilianus—a fact duly noted by Polybius (36.8.7), who had himself encouraged precisely this aspect of Aemilianus' education (see 31.29; cf. 6.11a.11, discussed above, p. 189). Meanwhile, relations between Cato's daughter-in-law Aemilia Tertia and Polybius' close friend Aemilianus were (we know from Polybius) very cordial (see 31.28.8). The family circle thus seems complete; and it does not seem much of a leap to conclude that Polybius and Cato—through their strong mutual ties to the Aemilii—probably came into some sort of significant contact in the years between 167 and 150.

In view of the above, the many parallels in thought between Polybius and Cato become very suggestive. Some of these parallels are well known. To take the most obvious, there is the mutual interest in historical studies, and the belief in their beneficial importance: Cato in the *Origines*, of course, was creating a whole new genre of Latin historiography just in the years when Polybius himself was writing the first 15 volumes of the *Histories*.[61] Other well known parallels include: praise of the "mixed" constitution of the Roman republic; the assertion that the special qualities of that mixed constitution

---

57. See the suggested stemma in A. E. Astin, *Scipio Aemilianus* (Oxford, 1967) 357. The ancient sources speak only of Aemilia Tertia as Aemilianus' sister, however: Plut. *Cat. Mai.* 20.12, 24.2; *Aem.* 5.6, 21.1; Cic. *Sen.* 15 and *Verr.* 2.4.22; Vell. 2.8.1.

58. See Plut. *Cat. Mai.* 20.10–12, cf. *Aem.* 21.1–2; Justin 33.1–2.

59. On the marriage and its success, see Astin, *Cato the Censor* 104–105 and n. 2; cf. the stemma in Astin, *Scipio Aemilianus* 357.

60. For discussion of the political situation in which Cato delivered this speech, see J.-L. Ferrary, *Philhellénisme et impérialisme: Aspects idéologiques de la conquête romaine du monde hellénistique* (Rome, 1988) 533 and n. 25.

61. Cato probably began work on the *Origines* ca. 174 (i.e., seven years before Polybius' arrival in Rome): see F. Della Corte, *Catone Censore*[2] (Florence, 1969) 153. But composition continued down to ca. 154: see Nicolet, "Polybe et les institutions romaines," 250.

derived from the fact that it had evolved over time, and was not the product of one heroic lawgiver; the assertion that Carthage, like Rome, had a "mixed" constitution (of three elements); the privileged place in his exposition of the Roman *politeia* given public finance by Polybius, a subject to which Cato was also continually drawn; the mutual attack on the rhetorical behavior of the Athenian embassy of 155 to Rome; the mutual distaste for dancing; even the emphasis on the role of light-armed infantry (*velites*) in the guarding of the Roman camp at night.[62]

But several other important parallels in thought, not much discussed by scholars, can be added to this list. Cato was the most prominent Roman orator of his day, and advocated a spare and factual style: *rem tene, verba sequentur* (Sen. *Controv.* 1 pr. 9). He was famous for his simplicity and *brevitas*[63]—which was itself a reflection of his restrained style of life (cf. esp. Plut. *Cat. Mai.* 4). And Polybius in fact advocated similar ideas, as can be seen from his depiction of his hero the Achaean statesman Philopoemen. Polybius stresses that Philopoemen's style of dress was always simple and his way of life restrained (10.22.5, 11.10.3); it was the result of good upbringing from youth (cf. Plut. *Phil.* 3.4).[64] And the simplicity of his way of dress and living was directly reflected, Polybius says, in Philopoemen's way of public speaking— which was honest, simple, and brief (11.10.3–5), yet so powerful in inspiring trust that it overcame the long-winded and flowery speeches of his many political opponents (10.6). "So true is it," the historian proclaims, "that a single word spoken at the right moment by a man of inherent trustworthiness not only deters his hearers from the worst, but incites them on to the best" (10.1)—especially when the speaker can reinforce his counsel by the example of his own life (10.2). We may therefore conclude that Polybius' views on the proper purpose and proper (simple) style of oratory in public affairs—which was an issue of great concern to ancient intellectuals—were in fact very close to those expressed by Cato. It is difficult to believe that Polybius did not know the views on this subject that were held by the most famous contemporary orator in Rome, or how closely those views agreed with his own.

Again, if Polybius was willing to trace the start of Roman moral decline to the importation of luxurious objects of art taken as the spoil of Syracuse in 211 (see esp. 9.10.12; cf. above, p. 191), it is striking that the same was true of Cato—who apparently proclaimed this in a famous speech (see Livy 34.4.4).

62. On all these parallels, see the convincing discussion of Nicolet, "Polybe et les institutions romaines," 245–50.

63. See Quint. *Inst. Or.* 8.3.33; Plut. *Cat. Mai.* 12.7; cf. Plin, *Ep.* 1.20.4.

64. For strong arguments that Plutarch's *Life of Philopoemen* is based very closely on Polybius' encomiastic biography, see esp. P. Pédech, "Polybe et l'éloge de Philopoemen," *REG* 64 (1951) 82–103.

And to judge from Plut. *Phil.* 3.4, Polybius firmly believed that the most honorable way of acquiring wealth (δικαιοτάτῳ ...) was through energetic work at traditional investment farming—and the same was true of Cato: it was wealth gained through that type of farming that was truly *honestum*.[65] Moreover, here we can be quite certain that the Greek historian knew what Cato's position was—because 31.25.5a, the passage where Polybius repeats and approves Cato's moral strictures against the extravagant style of life of the younger generation at Rome, contains an explicit comparison to the virtues of old-fashioned agricultural work.[66]

Yet another area of agreement between Cato's thought and that of Polybius may be added here. Cato in the *Origines* asserted that one of the roots of the Italic peoples was the migration of Arcadians to Italy under their legendary leader Evander; he even connected Evander indirectly with the founding of Rome itself.[67] Strikingly, in the *Histories* Polybius gave a similar outline of early Italic history: he also had Evander leading a migration from Arcadia, and being indirectly connected to the founding of Rome (see 6.11a.1). Moreover, Polybius was (of course) himself an Arcadian, and would thus have had a special interest in Evander.[68] It is hard to believe that Cato—who clearly had his own special interest in both Arcadia and Evander, and who emphasized their role in the origins of the Italic (and even Roman) peoples—would not have taken advantage of Polybius as a source of information (or simply confirmation) on these subjects.

Finally, I would note Cato's remark to Polybius in 35.6, comparing him to Odysseus. It is well known that in Book 12 of the *Histories*, Polybius in fact compared himself to Odysseus—specifically to Odysseus as the intelligent and experienced man of the world who had "wandered far and wide" and suffered enormous toil for the sake of higher goals (see 12.27.10–28.1, with three quotes from the *Odyssey* itself); "it seems to me that the dignity of history also requires such a man" (28.1).[69] Now, Cato's quip to Polybius

65. On Cato's attitude toward investment farming, see the discussion in Astin, *Cato* 255.

66. According to Polybius, Cato's position was the following: "No better proof could be had of the degeneration of the republic than that pretty-boys now fetch more than the cost of a farm, and jars of fancy salted fish cost more than ploughmen."

67. *HRR* frg. 15 = Lydus, *De Mag.* 1.5. Note that Cato also had one of Evander's officers as the founder of Tibur: *HRR* frg. 56 = Solinus 2.7. For discussion, see now E. S. Gruen, *Culture and National Identity in Republican Rome* (Ithaca, N.Y., 1992) 60 and n. 62.

68. This is shown by 6.11a.1. But note also that Polybius' hero Philopoemen met his final defeat at a place called "Evander's Hill," on the Arcadian-Messenian frontier (cf. Plut. *Phil.* 18.4–8).

69. For discussion of this important passage, see Walbank, *Polybius* 51–52, cf. 25.

about Odysseus daring to enter the Cyclops' cave a second time would carry far more point if the Censor personally *knew* in 150 that Polybius had taken to comparing himself to Odysseus. Walbank leans in this direction, but is very cautious—because it is not clear to him how Cato would have learned of Polybius' attitude.[70] Perhaps Cato had already read it in Book 12; or—we can now say—perhaps Cato had simply heard Polybius say this in private conversation within the Scipionic circle.[71]

Some of the connections between Cato and Polybius traced above must remain, admittedly, somewhat speculative. Nor has any attempt been made to determine whether Cato influenced Polybius' thought or Polybius influenced Cato's; this is because in the current fragmentary state of our evidence, the question is insoluble.[72] The goals of the above discussion have been much more limited. I have argued, first, that we have very good reasons to believe Polybius and Cato had significant contact with each other (especially via their mutual personal connections with the family of L. Aemilius Paullus), and second, that in M. Porcius Cato, Polybius would have perceived a man much like himself: motivated by similar intellectual interests, moved by similar moral concerns, reacting to the pressing problems of society with similar strong emotions.[73] The experience would thus have confirmed Polybius in his conclusion that Romans—both high and low—were men not different

70. Ibid., 52; cf. 25.

71. In general, Polybius appears to have written all the way down to Book 15 of the *Histories* before Cato died in 149 (see Walbank, *Polybius* 18–19, for definitive arguments). Moreover, Cato—a fellow historian—might well have been interested in Book 12, which was a discussion of historical method; and Cato's Greek would certainly have been up to reading it (see now Gruen, *Culture and National Identity* [above, n. 67] 56–58). Unfortunately, it is not clear whether the version of Book 12 we currently possess, with its reference to Odysseus, was actually in existence in 150 (see Walbank, *Polybius* 25 and 48). What *is* clear, however, is that in Polybius' conception, all of Odysseus' adventures in the West had occurred within the Pillars of Hercules (see 34.4.5–7), so that it was perfectly reasonable for the historian to have begun thinking of himself as an Odysseus-like figure, on the basis of his already extensive travels, by 150: i.e., he did not have to await his exploration of the outer ocean—after Cato's death—to see the parallel strongly (despite Walbank, *Polybius* 25). By 150, Polybius had already visited Gaul, Spain, and Africa; he had already crossed the Alps; he had already visited cities in southern Italy, crossed the straits of Messina, and visited Sicily: it was an Odyssean itinerary. It is also clear that once Polybius got the Odyssean ideal in his head, he did not restrict himself to asserting it just once (see Paus. 8.30.8, with the comments of Walbank, *Polybius* 52).

72. For contrasting views, see Nicolet, "Polybe et les institutions romains," 245–50, as opposed to (e.g.) Astin, *Cato* 226 and n. 42.

73. Cf. Momigliano, *Alien Wisdom* 23 (though he did not have Cato specifically in mind: see above, p. 192 and n. 53).

from Greeks. And if they were not different from Greeks, that would have confirmed Polybius, in turn, in his conclusion that it was the constellation of social-cultural *systems* in which the Romans lived, their *nomos*—and not a fundamental difference in their nature (*physis*)—that explained the Romans' extraordinary success.[74]

One last point. It was precisely because there was no dissimilarity in *physis* between Romans and Greeks that Polybius was led not only to assume that the political structures of the Roman state could be compared with profit to those of Greek states (see 6.43–50), but also—and just as importantly— to believe that his Greek audience could take some of the Roman lessons and customs to heart (see, e.g., 10.17.5). That is, Polybius thought that Greek society was (at least theoretically) penetrable by the healthy aspects of Roman culture. The problem that Polybius confronted in the last ten volumes of the *Histories*, however, was that rather than the Greeks coming to adopt healthy Roman practices, and so developing healthy Roman-like virtues, the reverse had proven to be true. It was the Romans who were turning out to be highly penetrable by *Greek* culture—and especially, it seemed to Polybius in sadness and anger, the most disreputable aspects of that culture (see 31.25.4, explicit). The Romans were human beings to him; human beings were flawed; and as their social-cultural systems, their *nomoi*, began to change, the flaws of the Romans were beginning now to come to—or return to—the surface.

---

74. Contrast the view of Kromayer-Veith, sharply differentiating between the "nature" of Romans and Greeks, referred to at the beginning of this essay ("Der Römer war an sich Soldat . . .") (p. 176 and n. 3).

TEN

The Court Society
of the Hellenistic Age

Gabriel Herman

—I—

Seen from the perspective of earlier Greek power structures rather than that
of subsequent monarchies, ancient or medieval, the Hellenistic kingdoms
appear imposing social formations. Indeed, if centre stage was held during
the Minoan and Mycenaean ages by the palace complex, in dark-age Greece
by the petty ruler's *oikos*, and during the Archaic and Classical ages by the
polis, then it might be said that in the Hellenistic age it was the territorial
kingdom which had moved from the wings to the centre. This was mainly
due to the predominance that these kingdoms achieved over other social
formations. Until they were gradually eclipsed by Rome, the Hellenistic
kingdoms seem never to have relinquished their hold on the fundamental
sources of power within the world created by Alexander's conquests: the
vast revenues wrung from subject populations in the form of booty and
taxes, and the (predominantly) mercenary armies which were deployed to
crush opponents within and without the territories under a king's sway. So
effective was this concentration of power, and so thoroughly did it pervade
all echelons of society, that the kingdoms' unrivalled superiority was felt,
in ways which have left their imprint upon the surviving documentation,
by widely disparate people and organizations: officials in the king's service,
cities (Greek and indigenous), temples, petty rulers, bandits, peasants, serfs.
The existence of one kingdom or another might be jeopardized by other
kingdoms, or by powers outside the Hellenistic sphere, and in the end the
entire Hellenistic world succumbed to Rome. Territorial monarchy as a

I am very grateful to Israel Shatzman, Frank Walbank and the editors for their helpful
comments and criticism.

199

system of rule remained rock-solid, however: the Hellenistic world itself produced no viable alternative to it.

Whenever one encounters this sort of paramount power structure in history, one is entitled to pose the following deceptively simple question: how did any individual (in this case a monarch), assisted only by a small coterie of hangers-on, manage to impose his will for so long upon such vast territories and upon subjects who so overwhelmingly outnumbered his own followers? This sweeping question can be broken down into a series of more modest ones. How were the highest echelons of the ruling circles structured? What was the position of the monarch therein? How did these ruling elites relate to their monarchs, on the one hand, and to the subject populations, on the other? Finally, were the Hellenistic kingdoms in any way unique in these respects, or did they merely follow a pattern typical of autocratic systems throughout history?

The pivotal element of the system was, in my view, the court. The court was, to be sure, only a small fraction of the king's domain, but its size was inversely related to its importance. In the first place, the court was the king's primary zone of influence, one which was all the more important because he had at his disposal no administrative apparatus outside it (one analogous, for example, to the senate and the magistrates in relation to the Roman emperor, or the estates and their assemblies in relation to the early modern European monarchs). Within the court were taken the decisions which shaped the destiny of the kingdom, and within it were found the most formidable groupings both of the king's supporters and of his opponents. It was therefore imperative that any king who wished to rule successfully should have a good understanding of the court's structure and of its unwritten rules, and that he should, even more importantly, keep an eye on the shifting power relations between its various sections. The court was the king's immediate social milieu, and exercised the strongest influence upon his personality and actions.

This brings us to the court's second function. The court was also an intermediary, so to speak, through which the king controlled his secondary and much wider zone of influence: his subjects. Its tentacles reached into every section of the kingdom, so that the king's power was manifested to his subjects through the members of his court.[1] As we shall see, however, the king was not infrequently far from happy with this state of affairs, often

---

1. A good example of the effective control of remote territories is supplied by R. S. Bagnall, *The Administration of the Ptolemaic Possessions Outside Egypt* (Leiden, 1976). In the third century B.C. the Ptolemaic kings controlled, through their courts, not only Egypt itself, but also parts of north Africa, Syria, Palestine, Asia Minor and the Aegean islands.

striving to establish channels of communication with his subjects that were free from any court interference.

Despite these considerations, modern research has paid little attention either to the Hellenistic court or to the society to which it gave rise. Berve's painstakingly detailed collection of the primary material relevant to Alexander's court is marred by the lack of any clearly elaborated theory of court society.[2] In this respect, Bickerman broke new ground, using (implicitly) the model of the pre-Revolutionary French court to give a three-dimensional picture of the Seleucid courts. Unfortunately, however, he did not extend his analysis to the remaining Hellenistic kingdoms.[3] Welles has collected by far the most useful corpus of non-literary material pertinent to the subject, but he entertains anachronistic ideas regarding the social milieu within which the documents were produced.[4] Habicht's strikingly original article "Herrschende Gesellschaft," though not touching directly on the courts, helps to identify the people who made up the royal administration and their Greek associates as the veritable "ruling class" of the Hellenistic age.[5] Finally, Walbank's remarks in his commentary on Polybius are invaluable to the understanding of what our one major contemporary literary source has to say on the subject.[6]

All this literature together does not give us much to go on, and the primary material on which it draws is not particularly extensive. I shall argue, nevertheless, that if placed in a more suitable analytical framework this material can yield up patterns which have long gone unnoticed, though they have been staring us in the face. My framework will be provided by a work which, though originally published in 1976, has only made its mark in recent years: Norbert Elias' *The Court Society*.[7]

Elias' main achievement in this book is the discovery of the court as a subject for investigation. Studies of courts have been published before, but they have all been marred by a tendency to concentrate on curiosities, on the "pomp and circumstance" of courtly life. Elias proposed that the court should be studied empirically as a system of power relations given its structure

2. H. Berve, *Das Alexanderreich auf prosopographischer Grundlage* (Munich, 1926, Arno reprint 1973), esp. chs. III and IV, "Die Hoforganisation" and "Die Hofgesellschaft."

3. E. J. Bickerman, *Institutions des Séleucides* (Paris, 1938).

4. C. B. Welles, *Royal Correspondence in the Hellenistic Period* (London, 1934, Ares reprint 1974).

5. Chr. Habicht, "Herrschende Gesellschaft in den hellenistischen Monarchien," *Vierteljahresschrift für Sozial- und Wirtschaftsgeschichte* 45 (1958) 1–16.

6. F. W. Walbank, *A Historical Commentary on Polybius*, 3 vols. (Oxford 1957–1979).

7. N. Elias, *Die höfische Gesellschaft* (1976), trans. E. Jephcott as *The Court Society* (Oxford, 1983).

by unwritten rules prescribing specific behaviour, both to the ruler wishing to master that system and to the courtier wishing to be part of it. Arguing that court societies "have no less importance than other elite formations such as parliaments and political parties which are paid a great deal of attention on account of their topicality,"[8] Elias suggested subjecting them to rigorous analysis.

It is not necessary to agree with every one of Elias' conclusions in order to accept his overall scheme. For instance, his idea that the court of Louis XIV served as an instrument for "domesticating" the nobility, thus paving the way for the absolute state, is not wholly convincing. Nor would historians of other periods readily subscribe to his contention that court societies grew out of the households of petty rulers. (The Hellenistic courts outside Macedon, for instance, evolved out of bands of Greek and Macedonian warriors which became infused with Oriental court traditions; the rulers' households became attached to these groups only at a later stage.) Elias' general framework, however, transcends these particulars, and can, in a manner which will soon become evident, promote understanding of court societies other than that of the *ancien régime*.

— II —

In order that the relevance of this framework to the Hellenistic monarchies may be established, it must be shown that we are indeed dealing with genuine court societies. This proposition, generally accepted in modern research, is not always formulated in a manner that is well suited to comparative purposes. Nor is the general category of "court society" without its difficulties. Even though court societies are marked by exceedingly clear attributes, they tend to elude more precise definition. For instance, if one accepts, with Elton, that "the only definition of the court which makes sense ... is that it comprised all those who at any given time were within 'his grace's house'; and all those with the right to be there were courtiers,"[9] then one must conclude firstly that a ruler always had the last say in establishing the composition of his court (which is historically false), and secondly that people closely attached to the ruler's person who did not become courtiers should be excluded from the group analytically defined as a "court society" (which is methodologically incorrect). Elias' definition has its own difficulties. If the French court was "nothing other than the vastly extended house and

---

8. Ibid. 29.

9. G. Elton, *Studies in Tudor and Stuart Politics and Government* III (Cambridge, 1983) 38–57, at 39.

household of the French kings and their dependents, with all the people belonging to them,"[10] then must any court society which did not begin as a household fail to qualify as such?

Court societies can, however, easily be identified even if clearly delineated boundaries are lacking. A lack of satisfactory definitions does not, in other words, preclude understanding. Nobody to my knowledge has yet managed satisfactorily to define "state," and yet scholars have been able to highlight the characteristic features of the state so as to differentiate it effectively from other social formations, including some that are deceptively similar to it.[11] If equal success is to be achieved in identifying court societies by this method, it must first be established whether or not the distinguishing features of the court societies of other historical periods also mark the Hellenistic kingdoms.

This task has been made easier by the publication of a collection of essays inspired by Elias' *Court Society*.[12] Dissatisfied with the definitions put forward by Elton and Elias, the authors have identified a number of features which reappeared systematically in early modern European courts at some distance from each other (for example, those of England, Burgundy, Germany, Spain, France, Austria, the Vatican and the Netherlands). It is of no negligible importance, for the purposes of this article, that three of the features regarded by these scholars as adequately characterizing a court society may easily be identified in the Hellenistic monarchies.

First of all, a court society differs markedly from the social formation out of which it grew, whether this be a royal household or a band of warriors gathered around a leader. What turns this sort of simple formation into a "court society" is the emergence of norms, rules of conduct (in particular those regulating access to the ruler) and ceremonial practices which affect, and to a certain extent regulate, the behaviour of the ruler and that of the individual members. We may refine this observation further. According to Asch, "the court was first of all a social milieu, with its own very specific rules regulating behaviour, and its own specific culture—culture meaning in this case not just 'arts and literature' but a whole way of life with its own values."[13]

10. Elias, *Court Society* 41. To be sure, Elias does not claim universal validity for this definition, but the claim is implicit in his writing.

11. Cf., e.g., W. G. Runciman, "Origins of states: The case of archaic Greece," *CSSH* 24 (1982) 351–77, and, less satisfactorily, M. Mann, "The autonomous power of the state: Its origins, mechanisms and results," *Archives européennes de sociologie* 25 (1984) 185–213.

12. R. G. Asch and A. M. Birke, eds., *Princes, Patronage and the Nobility: The Court at the Beginning of the Modern Age* (Oxford, 1991). It should be pointed out, however, that not all of the authors accept Elias' ideas wholesale.

13. Ibid. 9.

Some apparently trifling anecdotes concerning the Hellenistic rulers seem to point in precisely this direction. It is related, for instance, that the Antiochus surnamed Epiphanes acquired the nickname Epimanes ("mad") because he broke the rules of etiquette by fleeing from his court attendants and conversing with the common people of Antioch (Polyb. 26.1, Diod. 31.16). Antiochus IX, it is said, used to sneak out of his palace attended only by two or three slaves so that he might go hunting unencumbered by courtiers (Diod. 34.34). Polybius tells us that Antiochus III, while plotting against Hermeias, had to feign illness in order to dislodge his regular attendants from their usual duties (Polyb. 5.56.7). More examples of this sort will be encountered in what follows, but it can be established at this point that these incidents could not have taken place had the contemporaries of these three rulers not believed in certain norms, rules of conduct and patterns of interaction which were unique to the courts and absent from the social formations out of which the courts grew. For example, pre-Hellenistic sources recounting the adventures of bands of soldiers (for example, Greek myths, Homer, and, more importantly, Xenophon's *Anabasis*) are significantly free from any indication that these "societies" may have been regulated by similar rules of conduct (this should come as no surprise, since the "societies" existed so briefly). The norms, rules of conduct and patterns of interaction attested to by the Hellenistic sources constitute one of court society's characteristic features.[14]

Another feature which students of early modern Europe have thought necessary to the identification of a court society is the very concept of the court. The terms used in early modern Europe to designate "court" may have varied (sometimes terms which suggested the idea of "household," in the extended sense, were used, while elsewhere "court" was a specific term), but the idea of the court was always clearly present. This linguistic and conceptual usage is exactly paralleled in the sources relating to the Hellenistic kingdoms.

The courts of the Hellenistic rulers often centred on palaces (Greek αὐλή, τὸ βασίλειον or τὰ βασίλεια). The Seleucids' most important palace was at Antioch, and that of the Ptolemies at Alexandria; the Antigonids retained their ancestral palace at Pella, while the Attalids constructed a new and imposing one at Pergamum.[15] Apart from these central palaces, every kingdom seems to have had a series of minor palaces scattered all over

14. This is, of course, not to deny that courts and court societies also existed in Classical times, especially in the East.

15. For which see E. V. Hansen, *The Attalids of Pergamon*² (Ithaca and London, 1971) 234–84.

the king's dominions. The Seleucids, for instance, had palaces (or at least royal residences) at Sardes, Seleucia on the Tigris, Susa, Mopsuesta and Gabae, as Bickerman has shown.[16] The terms used to designate "palace" did not, however, just mean a building; they could convey the abstract idea of "court." Demetrius thus took refuge in the palace (αὐλή) at Antioch (1 Macc. 11.46), but what Apelles was denied access to was the court (αὐλή) of Philip V at Corinth, not his palace (Polyb. 5.26.9). It was this elevation of the physical entourage to the level of an abstraction which allowed the Hellenistic courts to become migratory,[17] assimilating them, in this respect, to the courts of medieval kings.

The third feature thought typical of court society by the historians of early modern courts was the appearance of the quintessential representative of that society, the courtier. Polybius displays great familiarity with both courts and courtiers. Commenting on the rise and fall of Apelles, he remarks: "So brief a space of time suffices to exalt and abase men all over the world and especially those in the courts of kings (ἐν τοῖς βασιλείοις), for those are in truth exactly like counters on a reckoning-board. For these at the will of the reckoner are now worth a copper and now worth a talent, and courtiers (οἵ τε περὶ τὰς αὐλάς) at the nod of the king are at one moment universally envied and at the next universally pitied" (Polyb. 5.26.13). Polybius maintains an extremely hostile attitude towards the specialist in court life who is his subject, and he could not thus have characterized Hermeias had he not expected his readership to share his views: "Having attained this position of authority he was jealous of all the holders of prominent posts at court (πᾶσι μὲν ἐφθόνει τοῖς ἐν ὑπεροχαῖς οὖσι τῶν περὶ τὴν αὐλήν), and as he was naturally of a savage disposition, he inflicted punishment on some for errors which he magnified into crimes, and trumping up false charges against others, showed himself a cruel and relentless judge" (Polyb. 5.41.3). This sort of full-blown idea of court society and the courtier turns up relatively late in the annals of Europe's early modern monarchies.

To the features so far examined, two further peculiarities of the circles centring on the Hellenistic rulers should perhaps be added—the specialization of courtly functions,[18] and lavish consumption as a means of display.[19]

---

16. For Alexander's royal residences during his campaigns, see Berve, *Alexanderreich*, vol. 1, 18.

17. For the "court" on the battlefield, see Polyb. 4.77.1 and 5.81.

18. For which see F. W. Walbank, "Monarchies and monarchic ideas," in F. W. Walbank et al., eds., *The Cambridge Ancient History*[2], vol. 7, Part 1 (Cambridge, 1984) 62–100, at 68, and below, pp. 211–13.

19. For which see Walbank, ibid. 84, and below, pp. 217–18.

All these features taken together may serve to establish that the circles in question fall neatly within the category of court societies, abstracted, for the purposes of analysis, from the concrete examples of early modern European courts. Since the possibility of one set emulating another can be more or less ruled out, the conclusion presents itself that the emergence of court societies has more to do with universal social configurations than with concrete historical circumstances: it is a sociological rather than a historical phenomenon. This inference is reinforced by considering monarchic rule in the ancient world generally.

Social formations such as court societies, in which power is concentrated in the hands of a ruler and his immediate entourage, differ markedly from formations in which power is dispersed within a wider group, its exercise being regulated by explicitly formulated rules (the Athenian democracy and the Roman republic may be viewed as the ancient prototypes of the latter arrangement). Monarchies, and, concomitantly, court societies, emerge "naturally": they tend to appear upon the scene spontaneously and unannounced, showing no signs of lengthy preparation. Formations of the type represented by the Athenian democracy and the Roman republic emerge, by contrast, "artificially": they make their appearance gradually, and their takeover is anticipated by a laborious period of evolution by means of trial and error. Proof of this is readily furnished by the political map of the ancient world. We do not need Herodotus' urging of the superiority of monarchy over oligarchy and democracy (Hdt. 3.80–83) to realize that whenever one of the ancient world's political systems began to grow unstable an irresistible drift began towards monarchic rule. It should therefore come as no great surprise that the only genuinely "political" units of the ancient world—the Athenian democracy and the Roman republic—were both outnumbered and outlasted by régimes of the monarchic type.[20] The social structures built around the *basileis* and *heroes* of the Homeric poems, the Greek tyrants, the

---

20. I am here following M. I. Finley, *Politics in the Ancient World* (Cambridge, 1983), according to which genuinely "political" units are those in which binding public decisions are taken by voters and participants extending well beyond the small circle of a ruler, his family and his intimates. Descriptions of social formations in antiquity which approximated to court societies include P. Cartledge, *Agesilaos and the Crisis of Sparta* (London, 1987) ch. 9; J. A. Crook, *Consilium Principis* (Cambridge, 1955); F. Millar, *The Emperor in the Roman World* (London, 1977, repr. 1992) ch. 3; R. P. Saller, *Personal Patronage Under the Early* [Roman] *Empire* (Cambridge, 1982); P. R. C. Weaver, *Familia Caesaris* (Cambridge, 1972). The interest of aristocrats in monarchic rule in the course of the 4th century B.C. is brilliantly analysed by W. Eder, "Monarchie und Demokratie im 4. Jahrhundert v.Chr.: Die Rolle des Fürstenspiegels in der athenischen Demokratie," in W. Eder, ed., *Die athenische Demokratie im 4. Jahrhundert v.Chr.* (Stuttgart, 1995) 153–74.

great kings of Persia and the petty rulers of Asia minor, the client kings of
Rome, and finally the Roman emperors themselves, may all be conceived
of as variations on the theme of monarchic rule; all must have carried within
them the potential to evolve into a court society, even if some of them never
realized this potential.

It follows from this that monarchic systems in general, and court societies
in particular, should be accorded no less (and perhaps even more) attention
than those political systems whose structure derives from explicitly formulated rules. I propose to make a modest start upon a potentially vast project
by examining the Hellenistic age. It is my intention to show in this article that
Elias' model can profitably be applied to the study of the societies centring
upon the Hellenistic rulers. I do not mean to urge the drawing of analogies
between the Hellenistic and the early modern court, and I would strongly
resist any attempt at extrapolating from one set to another. I am, however,
suggesting that both types of society may usefully be viewed with the same
set of concepts in mind, and, furthermore, that more and better information
can be extracted from the surviving documentation if these concepts are
understood.

These, then, are the principles which will be adhered to in analysing the
three most important Hellenistic courts of the period dealt with in Polybius'
Histories.

— III —

The three main Hellenistic courts will be treated as comparable entities.
This approach is justified by their identical origins (all three arose from
Alexander's court) and also by the fact, observed by Walbank,[21] that over
time the three kingdoms gradually came to resemble each other more and
more, adopting some remarkably similar structural features. As we shall see,
there are some grounds for believing that this continuing adjustment was
a response to factors which operated at an international rather than local
level. The court of the Antigonids was in some respects different from the
other two; it evolved, in all probability, from a royal household rather than
a band of warriors,[22] and ruled over Greek and Macedonian, rather than
non-Greek, subjects. These differences are, however, insufficient to warrant
putting it in a separate category of its own: the Antigonid court displayed
all the features of a court society that have been outlined above, and was,

21. Walbank, "Monarchies" 65.
22. Cf. N. G. L. Hammond, *A History of Macedonia*, vol. II (Oxford, 1979) (chs. v–xix
and xxi written by G. T. Griffith) 1–22.

moreover, mentioned by Polybius in the same breath with the courts of the Ptolemies and the Seleucids.

One feature common to all three monarchies was a court made up almost entirely of Greeks and Macedonians, the Macedonian element naturally being greater in the kingdom of the Antigonids than in those of the Seleucids and the Ptolemies. Persians and other non-Greeks did occasionally find their way into the courts, but certainly not in significant numbers. These observations do not, however, enable us accurately to predict the ethnic origins of new recruits to the court; when we consider these, we hit upon one of the most striking characteristics of Hellenistic court society. The new courtiers, rather than being recruited from within the ranks of the Macedonian nobility, came predominantly from Greek cities, more often than not cities a long way away from the recruiting courts.[23] The court was thus, so to speak, a cosmopolis.

In my book *Ritualised Friendship and the Greek City*, I suggested that many of the courtiers who were not inherited from a ruler's predecessor were recruited through the instrumentality of *xenia*, an ancient form of fictive kinship,[24] and pointed out that the way in which Cyrus the Younger raised a thirteen thousand-strong army foreshadowed this method of recruitment. Like Cyrus before them, the Hellenistic rulers (and, perhaps to an even greater extent, their closest associates) availed themselves of pre-existing *xenia* networks to draw new allies into their orbit. These networks account not only for the preponderance of Greeks among the newly recruited Hellenistic court members, but also for the increasing similarities between the three courts which had already become noticeable.

The Hellenistic court societies, then, did not operate *in vacuo*. Instead, they were part of a wider, interactive, international society of ritualised friends. This society had since time immemorial constituted a world of its own, binding together the social elites of the Greek world through upper-class ideals. Its tenets informed both the recruitment of manpower and the formation of coalitions that might successfully undertake anything from the overthrow of an individual city-state to the deposition of a ruler as powerful as the Great King of Persia.[25]

---

23. Cf. Habicht, "Herrschende Gesellschaft," and Walbank, "Monarchies" 68.

24. G. Herman, *Ritualised Friendship and the Greek City* (Cambridge, 1987) 154–55.

25. The *xenoi* whom Cyrus the Younger turned into generals were leading Greeks, expelled from their cities of origin, who were capable of raising armies even though they were scattered all over the Greek world. In return for their assistance, they expected to be nominated by Cyrus to important posts, should the attack on Artaxerxes be crowned with success. Short of that, they hoped to be helped to positions of power in their own cities.

As a first step towards understanding Hellenistic "court politics," we should therefore explore the relation between court societies and friendship networks. A few scattered examples will suffice to give a general picture: the random glimpses of life at court that they offer may be taken as typical. Take, for instance, what happens to Cleomenes, the "king" exiled from Sparta, when he is staying with Ptolemy Philopator in Alexandria. Cleomenes participates in a series of events whose course is laid down by the dictates of private alliances (networks of *xenia*), a formal political structure (the Spartan state), and a court society (that of the Ptolemies). At court, Cleomenes is betrayed by Nicagoras of Messene, whose *xenos*, Archidamos the Spartan, Cleomenes once put to death. This betrayal triggers off a chain of events culminating in a revolt by Cleomenes against Ptolemy. Various strings are pulled by Sosibius, then "head of affairs" (μάλιστα προεστάτει τῶν πραγμάτων) at Philopator's court, and it is reasonable to assume that the entire fiasco and the subsequent death of Cleomenes were likely to bring about a great improvement in the position of Sosibius (and his "friends") at court (Polyb. 5.35–39). Court societies and networks of *xenia* thus react upon one another.

Another example of this sort, rather complex but extremely instructive, involves the separatist general Achaeus, who proclaimed himself king in 220 B.C. In an effort to carve a dominion for himself out of the Seleucid territories in Asia Minor, Achaeus decided to help the people of Pednelissus fight off the besieging forces of Selge. Achaeus' general Garsyeris repelled the Selgians so successfully that he ended up besieging Selge itself. The people of Selge, dismayed at this reversal of fortune, sent out a man called Logbasis to conduct the ensuing negotiations. Logbasis, a Selgian citizen, had not only been a *synetes* and *xenos* of the late Antiochus Hierax, one of Achaeus' kinsmen, but had also acted as a foster-parent to Laodike, who later became Achaeus' wife.[26] Allowing his house to be used as a Trojan horse by Garsyeris' forces, he treacherously betrayed his city (Polyb. 5.76.11). The Selgians took revenge by massacring him and his sons, but had to give in to Achaeus, paying out some seven hundred talents and releasing their Pednelissian prisoners. Achaeus' triumph, however, was short-lived. In 215 (or 214) B.C., we find him being besieged by Antiochus in Sardis. At this point in the story the Ptolemaic court of Egypt puts in an appearance. In order to spite King Antiochus of Syria, Sosibius (Ptolemy's "head of affairs") contrived a plan to save Achaeus. He commissioned a Cretan by the name of Bolis, who had "long occupied a high position at the court of

26. Polyb. 5.74.6 : "he had brought up the young lady as his own daughter and treated her with special kindness."

Ptolemy,"[27] and who was moreover a relative and friend (*syngenes kai philos*) of Cambylos, the commander of the Cretans in Antiochus' army, to go and rescue him. Bolis, amply furnished with money, proceeded first to Nicomachus of Rhodes, "whose affection for Achaeus and fidelity towards him were regarded like those of a father to son," and next to Melancomas at Ephesos. These two had formerly "acted as Achaeus' agents in his negotiations with Ptolemy and all his foreign schemes" (Polyb. 8.15.10). In the end, however, prompted by an irresistible logic (why rescue Achaeus when they could deliver him to Antiochus, thus pocketing handsome rewards from two sources?), Bolis and Cambylos sold out. We need not go into the well-nigh incredible ruse which they masterminded to trap Achaeus and hand him over to Antiochus. My point is that the succession of events outlined above, which brought about Achaeus' downfall and significantly changed the political boundaries of the Hellenistic world, reveals extensive interplay between the court of the Hellenistic kings and an international network of "friends," some of whom were only loosely associated with the courts.

   That we have here a pattern rather than a selection of atypical incidents is further confirmed by the case of Theodotus, governor of Coele-Syria under Ptolemy Philopator. Deeply dissatisfied with the way in which Ptolemy discharged his royal duties, Theodotus conceived a plan to contact King Antiochus of Syria with a view to handing over to him the cities in his province. No explicit evidence for the existence of a bond of *xenia* between Theodotus and Antiochus (or one of the latter's subordinates) has survived, but Theodotus' actions imply that he was able somehow to contact the Seleucid king through a network of "friends"—or, perhaps, of "friends of friends" (Polyb. 5.40). This assumption gathers support from Polybius' description of the diplomatic encounters which subsequently took place between Ptolemy and Antiochus. During these negotiations, according to Polybius, "the controversy was conducted by the common friends (διὰ τῶν κοινῶν φίλων) of both monarchs" (Polyb. 5.67.11). Translated into our own analytical terms, this means that the diplomats in question were, in the capacity of negotiators, restricted to the spheres of individual monarchs; in the capacity of "friends," however, they shared membership in a wider system. Monarchs, generals and Greek citizens participated in both court politics and international "friendship" networks, and so closely were these systems interlocked that any move made in one might affect the overall performance of the other. It is to the analysis of the forces at work at court that we now turn.

---

27. χρόνον δὲ πολὺν ἐν τῇ βασιλείᾳ διατετριφὼς ἐν ἡγεμονικῇ προστασίᾳ, Polyb. 8.15.1.

— IV —

Polybius disliked everything that the royal courts and the royal courtiers stood for (though not, I hasten to add, the kings themselves). The Hellenistic courts were, in his view, vipers' nests of intrigue, scheming, manipulation, slander, dissemination of misinformation and rumour, and conspiracy. Calumny, malice, envy and trickery were, according to him, weapons peculiar to court society which courtiers wielded with extraordinary adroitness in an incessant effort to enhance their own positions and undermine those of others. "This is indeed a new kind of calumny," he wrote of the machinations of Apelles, "to damage the fortunes of one's neighbours not by blame but by praise, and this variety of malice, envy and trickery is especially and primarily the invention of courtiers (τῶν περὶ τὰς αὐλὰς διατριβόντων) to serve their mutual jealousies and ambitions" (Polyb. 4.87.4–5). His generalization is backed up by the events he describes. Having plotted the death of Epigenes (Polyb. 5.50.10–14), Hermeias schemes against the king and some of the king's friends, but falls victim to a counter-plot instigated by the king's physician, Apollophanes (Polyb. 5.56.12). Nicagoras enters into a plot with Sosibius to bring about the downfall of Ptolemy's guest Cleomenes (Polyb. 5.39). Sosibius plots to murder Magas and Berenice (Polyb. 5.39). Apelles first attempts to damage the credit of Aratus (Polyb. 4.82.3), then forms a conspiracy with Leontius and Megaleas against Philip (Polyb. 5.2.7).

A superficial reading of Polybius could easily convey the impression that he is describing chaos, or unmitigated anarchy: the rules of the game are constantly being broken, honest players lose to dishonest ones, and the more unscrupulous one is, the more likely one is to succeed. A closer reading of the passages relating to court intrigues reveals, however, that this is not the case. Though supernatural paraphernalia do occasionally creep into the *Histories*,[28] Polybius remains at bottom a good rationalist, subscribing to the theory that human events are rooted in human motivations.[29] When we look at the motivations he assigns to the various actors, some surprising regularities emerge, revealing Polybius as a keen observer of the interplay between human aspirations and the constraints imposed by the larger social systems.

28. Cf. F. W. Walbank, "Supernatural paraphernalia in Polybius' *Histories*," in I. Worthington, ed., *Ventures into Greek History* (Oxford, 1994) 28–42.

29. Cf. Polyb. 2.38.5: "[to say that something] is a result of chance ... is a poor explanation. We must rather seek for a cause, for every event whether probable or improbable must have some cause," with Walbank's comments: "while the supernatural control operates in a general way, the ordinary laws governing political and military action and its likely results still hold good," "Supernatural paraphernalia" 32.

Consider, first of all, the position of the king. Most Western political thinkers are obsessed with the idea of the absolute monarch, one who, in Beloff's words, "by formal definition ... has limitless means of action and is subject to no control."[30] Elias, however, demurred: "the power of the individual ruler was by no means so unrestricted or absolute, even in the age of so-called 'absolutism,' as this term suggests. Even Louis XIV, the *Roi Soleil*, who is often taken as the supreme example of the omnipotent absolute monarch, proves on closer scrutiny to be an individual who was enmeshed through his position as king in a specific network of interdependencies. He could preserve his power only by a carefully calculated strategy which was governed by the peculiar structure of court society in the narrow sense, and more broadly by society at large."[31] Musti, writing on the Seleucid monarchy, assumes that the king's power was absolute,[32] but Polybius' portrait of the Hellenistic monarch in fact confirms Elias' view. Antiochus, for instance, was subservient to forces operating at court even to the extent of not being "his own master" (Polyb. 5.50.5, cf. 5.45.7). Ptolemy Philopator, by failing to attend to the business of state and rendering himself inaccessible to his courtiers, brought about a whole series of conspiracies against himself (Polyb. 5.34.10). Apelles, the chief courtier of the young king Philip, "assumed more authority than his position warranted, giving out that the king was still young and was ruled by him in most matters" (Polyb. 5.26.4). Attalus II prudently decided to give in when he encountered the joint opposition of his "friends" to his own scheme of action (Welles, *RC* 61). If one shortsightedly regards the Hellenistic king's position as entirely defined by his formal rights, he indeed appears absolute: possessed of limitless means of action, he was subject to no control, and his decision could not be appealed against to any other person or body. There was, however, a striking contrast between this legal definition of his position and his standing within his immediate milieu. In his social existence, his freedom of action was curtailed in more than one respect. He was enmeshed in a network of interdependencies centred on the court, and could preserve his position only by skilfully outmanoeuvring the factions and coalitions that were constantly coalescing with the intention of bringing him down. To succeed in this, he was constrained to resort to a certain series of long-term strategies and to some improvised, short-term ones.

30. Max Beloff, *The Age of Absolutism 1660–1815* (London, 1954) 51.

31. N. Elias, *Court Society* (above, n. 7) 3.

32. In F. W. Walbank et al., eds., *The Cambridge Ancient History*[2], vol. 7, Part 1 (Cambridge, 1984) 179. See S. Sherwin-White and A. Kuhrt, *From Samarkhand to Sardis* (London, 1993) 118–19 for a discussion of the allegedly "personal," "national," "despotic" and "absolutist" character of the Seleucid monarchy.

The examples adduced in the sections to come reveal three strategies in particular which the Hellenistic rulers seem consistently to have used to tip the balance of power relations at court in their favour. One of these was suppressing anyone possessed of an independent power base and, conversely, promoting anyone who owed everything to the ruler and was nothing without him. Another was forming close emotional ties of friendship with eminent people outside the court circle, thereby bypassing that circle and to some extent counterbalancing any hostile groups within it. The third strategy was playing the various courtiers off against each other. The logic in accordance with which all this worked will emerge from what follows.

— V —

The courtiers, to whom Polybius usually referred using the circumlocution "those belonging to the court" (οἱ περὶ τὴν αὐλήν),[33] were a bizarre mélange of people. First came the king's family, both nuclear and extended, presumably including concubines and illegitimate offspring. Then there were his bodyguards (*somatophylakes*), most of whom were recruited from among the royal pages (*basilikoi paides*).[34] The highest-ranking group of courtiers was designated by the name of "friends" (*philoi*), and in what follows I shall dwell at some length upon the informal subdivisions that formed within that prestigious group.[35] Another group contained people who were staying at the court for various lengths of time; attached to it only loosely, they were nonetheless capable of carrying out important missions on its behalf. These men might be intellectuals, politicians from Greek cities, or exiles.[36] Finally, there was a whole body of specialist assistants catering to the needs of the higher functionaries. This group included physicians, secretaries, scribes, cooks, bakers, attendants, and a whole spectrum of specialist and

33. Cf. also Polyb. 5.41.3, 5.50.14; App. *Syr.* 45; Josephus *AJ* 12.215. See also G. Corradi, *Studi ellenistici* (Torino, 1929) 260; Bickerman, *Séleucides* 36.

34. See Herman, *Ritualised Friendship* 126, n. 34; Corradi, *Studi* 290–317; and now N. G. L. Hammond, "Royal pages, personal pages, and boys trained in the Macedonian manner during the period of the Temenid monarchy," *Historia* 39 (1990) 261–90.

35. I shall not, however, dwell on the formal hierarchical subdivisions which appeared within the court of the Ptolemies at the end of the 2nd century B.C., for which see L. Mooren, *La hiérarchie de cour Ptolémaïque* (Louvain, 1977).

36. Cf. Bickerman, *Séleucides* 39. For the epigraphical representation of the people "staying with the king," see G. Herman, "The friends of the early Hellenistic rulers," *Talanta* 12–13 (1980–1981) 103–49.

non-specialist slaves.[37]   Most of these people, at least the more powerful among them, were surrounded by their families[38] and, even more importantly, by clusters of individual followers, presumably supported out of their private resources. I know of no source which might indicate where all these people lived, but it would be reasonable to assume that at least some of them had lodgings in the king's quarters. Others may have lived in nearby cities or on private estates.

The *philoi* circle was at the heart of the Hellenistic kingdom's concentric power structure. It was constantly plagued by divisions. There were, to begin with, rivalries between the "friends" attached closely to the monarch's person and those sent away temporarily to discharge official functions at the periphery of his realm. In speaking of Egypt, for instance, Polybius contrasts the courtiers proper (οἱ περὶ τὴν αὐλήν) and the officials who administered the country (οἱ τὰ κατὰ τὴν Αἴγυπτον χειρίζοντες) with the agents charged with the conduct of affairs outside Egypt (οἱ ἐπὶ τῶν ἔξω πραγμάτων διατεταγμένοι). The negligent and indifferent behaviour of Ptolemy Philopator towards these last was, it appears, in striking contrast to that of the kings who had gone before him, who paid even more attention to these agents than they did to the government of Egypt itself (Polyb. 5.34). Later on Polybius explains Theodotos' conspiracy against Ptolemy Philopator in terms of Theodotos' mistrust of the courtiers (οἱ περὶ τὴν αὐλήν) who have not only robbed him of the glory of an important victory, but also plotted to kill him (Polyb. 5.40.2–3). Molon and Alexander of the Seleucid empire are said to have staged a revolt because of, among other things, their fear of Hermeias, who had become all-powerful in Antiochus' service (Polyb. 5.41.1).

An almost identical, and perhaps even deeper, rift divided those whose position derived from power built up within the court from those who drew their support from the armies—one of three pillars of power in the Hellenistic world, along with "kings" and "friends" (cf. *OGIS* 219). One of the reasons Polybius gives for Sosibius' plot to destroy Cleomenes is the latter's popularity with the soldiers. "Don't you see," bragged Cleomenes in front of Sosibius, "that nearly three thousand of them are from the Peloponnese and about a thousand are Cretans, and I need but make a sign to these men and they will all put themselves joyfully at your service?" (Polyb. 5.36.4). Hermeias, who

---

37. The picture of the Ptolemaic administration offered by the papyri is, of course, far more refined and sophisticated than that which emerges from Polybius' *Histories*; see W. Peremans and E. van't Dack, *Prosopographia Ptolemaica* (Louvain, 1950), esp. vol. I.

38. E.g., Polyb. 5.56.15: "The women in Apamea ... stoned the wife of Hermeias to death and the boys did the like to his sons."

owed his power in the Seleucid court to his nomination by Antiochus' brother Seleucus, was particularly envious of Epigenes, a capable speaker and man of action "who enjoyed great popularity with the soldiers" (Polyb. 5.41.3–5). Apelles, of Philip's court, was envious of Alexander, the captain of Philip's bodyguard; he intended to replace him, as well as another commander, Taurion, "and direct these and all other matters through himself and his friends" (Polyb. 4.87.5 and 9).

These, then, were the subdivisions within the *philoi* circle which (apart, of course, from pretenders belonging to the royal family) posed the most formidable threat to the king. It is plain that any king with a good grasp of the facts would have encouraged the rivalries between these factions in order to be able to combat each in isolation, lest they all join forces to depose him. That the "friends," "kinsmen" and "bodyguards" never managed, throughout the Hellenistic age, to coalesce into a hereditary nobility may be regarded as some measure of this tactic's success.

— VI —

Such people as Hermeias, Sosibius and Apelles are in a sense enigmatic. Polybius is in most cases reluctant to pursue the manner in which they fought their way to the top, satisfying himself with a few lapidary statements concerning their positions at critical moments. Hermeias, as we have seen, was in a position of authority because he had been nominated by Antiochus' brother Seleucus (Polyb. 5.41.2). In no time at all he is presented as capable of subjecting to his will both the councillors (whom he rules by fear) and the troops (to whom he renders a service: Polyb. 5.41.2). Sosibius' origins are obscure; when we catch our first glimpse of him he is already "the head of affairs" (μάλιστα ... προεστάτει τῶν πραγμάτων, Polyb. 5.35.7). Apelles, one of the guardians of the young king Philip nominated by Antigonus Doson, "had at this time very great influence with the king" (Polyb. 4.76.1). Polybius does, however, give some clues as to the power sources that these people could tap in order to enhance their positions, and these may allow us to grasp the essentials of Hellenistic courtly politics.

To start with, these powerful courtiers had one thing in common: they all seem to have been lacking in military expertise. This suggests that they had been promoted by their kings because, being incapable of leading an army, they could never become serious rivals for the throne. In other words, if the kings wanted to keep their thrones they must enhance the power of the managerial sectors of their courts at the expense of the military, carefully keeping alive (and preferably exploiting) the rivalries and tensions between the two. Above all, they must beware of anyone who united in his person both skills. In this respect, Cleomenes the Spartan was dangerous: not only was he endowed with the qualities of a commander and a king (ἡγεμονικὸς καὶ βασιλικὸς τῇ φύσει), but he had furthermore a great aptitude for the conduct of affairs (πρὸς πραγμάτων οἰκονομίαν εὐφυής, Polyb. 5.39.6). It was the spectre of his giving free rein to these skills that finally persuaded Ptolemy Philopator to do away with him.

Court politics was a dangerous game, and it was Sosibius who profited most from this entire incident. An increase in power such as this would translate itself into enhanced influence upon the king, and this was probably the most precious asset that a Hellenistic courtier could acquire. When Apelles sensed a reduction in royal favour, he resorted in desperation to plotting against the king (Polyb. 5.2.7). Hermeias was greatly elated when he had the young Antiochus wholly under his influence (Polyb. 5.45.7), but when he realized that he had displeased him by disparaging Epigenes in council he performed a *volte-face*, pretending that he had suddenly come round to Epigenes' point of view (Polyb. 5.49.7). Staying close to the king and having unrestricted access to his person was the pinnacle of the courtier's aspirations. Apelles flattered Taurion by saying that "he was the most proper person to be attached to the king's person in the camp"; he simultaneously traduced Alexander, the captain of the bodyguard, "wishing to be himself charged with the protection of the king's person" (Polyb. 4.87.2,5). Apelles' craving to be accepted at court was finally frustrated when his way to the royal quarters was barred, on the pretext that the king was engaged. Deeply disconcerted at this unexpected sign of disfavour, Apelles remained "for some time in a state of bewilderment," and then "withdrew much abashed" (Polyb. 5.26.9–10).

The according or withholding of royal favour could directly affect the potency of the second source of power at a courtier's disposal: his entourage. The upshot of the incident just related was that Apelles' followers "at once began to drop away quite openly, so that finally he reached his lodging accompanied only by his own servants" (Polyb. 5.26.11). The size of the following one was able to gather around one's person must have been viewed as an index of one's importance. Every powerful courtier had a substantial following,[39] and if he wished to preserve or augment it, he was well advised to treat his followers with respect and shower benefits upon them. Sosibius, for instance, before embarking on his plot against Cleomenes, duly convened his "friends" for a council of war (οἱ δὲ περὶ τὸν Σωσίβιον ... συνεδρεύσαντες; Polyb. 5.35.7). The protection that a strong following could give was considerable: after Philip had fined Megaleas and Crinon and ordered their imprisonment, Leontius, their accomplice, nonetheless felt able to brave coming to the royal tent "accompanied by peltasts" (Polyb.

---

39. On personal followers in general, see Herman, *Ritualised Friendship* 151.

5.16.2). It may also have been the fear that they might belong to Hermeias' circle of "friends" that dictated the dismissal of Antiochus' usual attendants (θεραπεία) prior to the assassination of Hermeias (Polyb. 5.56.7). Failure to satisfy the aspirations of one's followers could, on the other hand, lead to one's downfall. It was not long after Xenoetas had begun to treat his "friends" disdainfully that he fell into the trap set for him by Molon and perished (Polyb. 5.46.6, 48.2). Not even a king could neglect his "friends" and go unpunished. One of the major flaws which Polybius diagnosed in Ptolemy Philopator's character was his habit of becoming inattentive (ἀνεπίστατος) and inaccessible (δυσέντευκτος) to his courtiers (οἱ περὶ τὴν αὐλήν, Polyb. 5.34.4). This negligence sparked off a whole series of conspiracies against him (Polyb. 5.34.10). The moral which Polybius wishes his readers to draw from this incident is underlined by the counter-example of Cleomenes the Spartan, that paragon of military leadership, whose friends joined him in his doomed dash for freedom and finally committed suicide along with him (Polyb. 5.39.2–5).[40]

Royal favour was also a necessary precondition if the courtier was to draw upon a third source of power, namely wealth. The kings showered money, gifts and offices upon their favourites at such a rate that contemporary sources considered their "friends" to be among the richest men of the Hellenistic world. Here I suspect that the kings again distinguished between their military and their administrative courtiers: a soldier would be given estates, out of whose proceeds he would be expected to finance his activities,[41] whereas an administrator would probably be given gifts of money and valuables.[42] However this may be, three outstanding features of these remarkable transactions may here be noted. Firstly, the benefits in question were bestowed not as a *quid pro quo* for specific services, but with a view to good long-term performances, in the expectation of abiding loyalty. Secondly, they were bestowed in an excessively liberal spirit, in conformity with the obligation to spend on a scale befitting a king. Paradigmatic expressions of this concept may be found in certain sayings and anecdotes. When a "friend" asked Alexander to provide dowries for his daughters, Alexander offered fifty

40. The saying, attributed to Lysimachus, that it is not honourable to preserve one's own safety by abandoning one's army and one's friends, is very relevant to this (Diod. 21.12, with Walbank, "Monarchies" 70).

41. Cf. M. Rostovtzeff, *A Large Estate in Egypt in the Third Century BC* (Madison, 1922, Arno Repr., 1979), esp. ch. 5, and H. Kreissig, *Wirtschaft und Gesellschaft im Seleukidenreich* (Berlin, 1978), esp. 40–46, and the original article by M. M. Austin, "Hellenistic Kings, War, and the Economy," *CQ* 36 (1986) 450–66.

42. It is around this stereotype that some of the jokes ridiculing the "friends" are constructed; cf. Herman, "The 'friends' of the early Hellenistic rulers."

talents. When the "friend" said that ten talents would be enough, Alexander is said to have retorted, "Enough for you to accept, but not enough for me to give" (Plutarch, *Moralia* 127B, 1099C, and *Alexander* 677B). According to an aphorism attributed to Diotogenes, "The king should possess riches, but only to the extent to which they are essential to benefit his friends" (Stob. *Ecl.* 4.7.62).[43] Thirdly, all of these handouts might be taken away again, or simply cease to flow, at the king's pleasure. Only seldom does Polybius refer to the state of a courtier's finances, but maintaining a favourable balance should presumably be considered an important motive for the actions of any courtier in court society.

The monarch whose struggle for control of his court has been most extensively documented is Philip V of Macedon, and it is my suggestion that the story of his rivalry with Apelles and his group may be considered a paradigm of the aulic relationships in all the Hellenistic kingdoms.

— VII —

Philip inherited Apelles from his father as one of his guardians, and as we have seen, Polybius introduces Apelles at a moment at which he was "highly influential with the king" (Polyb. 4.76.1). Very soon, however, Polybius makes it clear to us that the relationship between the two was strained to the utmost. Philip and Apelles simply pulled in opposite directions. To such an extent did their policies diverge, Polybius' account suggests, that the conduct of foreign affairs was dictated not by any careful consideration of Macedon's interests, but rather by Apelles' desire to thwart Philip's plans. To please his Macedonian followers, Apelles designed a policy towards the Achaeans which was at variance with that of his royal master (Polyb. 4.76). He then blatantly ignored Philip's instruction "to issue no orders to the Achaeans without consulting their strategos." Jealous of both the elder and the younger Aratus of Sicyon on account of their exceptionally close friendship with Philip, he did his best to undermine their position in the Achaean League and to damage their reputation. When Philip's scheme to detach the Eleans from the Aetolians and bring them over to his side failed, Apelles laid the blame on Aratus, insinuating that he had used his influence over the Elean strategos to frustrate Philip's plans. Only after the hollowness of his accusations had been exposed did Philip start to entertain some suspicions of Apelles.

Apelles carried on with his machinations relentlessly. He first devised a stratagem to remove from power Philip's chamberlain and the commissioner

---

43. See Walbank, "Monarchies" 84 for further examples.

of the Peloponnese (Polyb. 4.87.9). He then proceeded to sabotage Philip's plans to prosecute the war against the Aetolians, Lacedaemonians and Eleans. He arranged for Philip's supplies to be cut off, and managed to leave Philip in such need of money that he "was compelled to pawn some of the plate in use at his table and subsist on the proceeds" (Polyb. 5.2.11). Leontius, one of Philip's generals who was Apelles' accomplice, manipulated the course of a siege so as to turn an almost certain victory into a defeat. Later on, Leontius recommended a course of action which, had it been adopted, would have been a serious setback for Philip's war effort. Even during the march on Thermum he tried to delay Philip's advance, and it was only at Aratus' instigation that Philip ignored Leontius' advice (Polyb. 5.7.2–4).

Matters came to a showdown at a banquet thrown by Philip to celebrate the victory which he had won despite all these obstacles. It is at this point that we glimpse a factor of paramount importance in the struggle for supremacy over the Hellenistic court: etiquette.

Polybius is at his best in recounting the psychology and body-language of the protagonists at this juncture. During the course of the banquet, Megaleas and Leontius "aroused the suspicions of the king and his guests, as they did not show the same joy as the rest at the recent events" (Polyb. 5.15.1–2). Later on they got drunk, and, meeting Aratus on his way home, abused him and pelted him with stones. Philip then sent for Megaleas and Crinon—Leontius had somehow slipped away—and reprimanded them severely. Upon this, they not only failed to express any regret, but "aggravated their offence, saying that they would not desist from their purposes until they had paid out Aratus. The king was highly indignant at their language and at once inflicted on them a fine of twenty talents, and ordered them to be imprisoned until they paid it" (Polyb. 5.15.8–9). The next day, Leontius came to the royal tent accompanied by peltasts, hoping to intimidate the boy-king. "Coming into his presence he asked who had dared to lay hands on Megaleas and who had taken him to prison. But when the king confidently replied that he himself had given the order, Leontius was dismayed and with a muttered protest departed in a huff" (Polyb. 5.16.2–4).

Rather surprisingly, Apelles' followers were arrested not for plotting against the king, but for insubordination and for breaking the unwritten rules of proper courtly behaviour (a point which should be remembered in what follows). What is more, even though they had been tried and found guilty by a council of Philip's "friends," Megaleas was freed on Leontius' surety, and all but one of the conspirators resumed their commands. The impression that the king was not in full control of the situation is confirmed by the next move of Apelles' followers, which was to stir up sedition within the army. Only Philip's direct appeal to the troops prevented the trouble from degenerating into an outright mutiny. At this juncture, Leontius recalled Apelles.

Apelles had in the meantime developed an impressive power base in Thessaly and Macedonia. Such was the extent of his authority that he could even afford to usurp some of the royal functions. However, in a classical manifestation of *hubris* he somehow missed the message that Philip was displeased. His misguided self-confidence may have been abetted by a magnificent reception in Corinth thrown in his honour by none other than Leontius and Megaleas. Trusting that all that was needed to recover the king's favour was a personal meeting with him (Polyb. 4.87.5, 5.2.7), Apelles proceeded to the royal quarters. As we have seen, however, his way was unexpectedly blocked by one of the ushers (Polyb. 5.26.10–11), and this additional mark of royal displeasure was the straw which broke Apelles' back.

— VIII —

It is unnecessary, for our purposes, to dwell on the sequel—the execution of most of the conspirators, the change for the worse in Philip's character, and the subsequent end of the friendship between Philip and Aratus. It is, however, of some importance to review Polybius' attitude to the Apelles affair critically. There can be no doubt that his account is extremely one-sided. Philip, Aratus and the Achaeans are presented in a positive light, while Apelles and the Aetolians appear in an exceedingly negative one. To explain this partisan view, Errington has suggested that Polybius had uncritically accepted the only surviving version of the purge, the version that Philip constructed to justify his violence after the event.[44] This explanation is not, in my view, unlikely; it is, however, inadequate. Polybius was too good a historian slavishly to accept an account just because there were no others. He must have been predisposed to accept Philip's version of the affair, and I believe that it is possible to show why.

As I have already indicated, Polybius passionately disliked everything that royal courts and courtiers stood for. In his history he lashes not only Apelles, but also other courtiers, with his savage comments. We have already heard him slander Hermeias (Polyb. 5.41.3). An even clearer indication is his astonishingly unfair reaction to Hermeias' assassination. Antiochus, it may be recalled, played a dirty trick on Hermeias, luring him into a deadly trap. Polybius' comment on this was, "So perished Hermeias, meeting with a punishment by no means adequate to his crimes" (Polyb. 5.56.13). Achaeus,

44. R. M. Errington, "Philip, Aratus, and the 'conspiracy of Apelles,'" *Historia* 16 (1967) 19–36.

of course, was no courtier, but an able military commander, and even the fact that he staged a rebellion against a legitimate monarch, being executed as a traitor on that account, did not prompt Polybius to pass equally severe judgement upon him. Quite to the contrary, his last words on the subject imply a modicum of admiration for Achaeus: "Thus did Achaeus perish, after taking every reasonable precaution and defeated only by the perfidy of those whom he had trusted . . ." (Polyb. 8.21.10).

It is not difficult to diagnose the reason for Polybius' bias. Polybius judged courtiers according to the standards of the Greek citizen, whose position in society was determined by his performance in the service of the state and whose achievements were assessed against criteria communally agreed upon. Judged by such criteria, courtiers fared badly. Prestige in court society was a function of intrigue designed to undermine the positions of one's peers, and of flattery intended to ingratiate one with one's superiors. Consequently, the court was a mass of conflicts, short-term alliances, liaisons and manipulations. The courtiers manipulated each other and were in turn manipulated by the king. All this was a veritable struggle for survival, since the court, unlike the city-state, offered no security: as Polybius observed, "courtiers at the nod of a king are at one moment universally envied and at the next universally pitied" (Polyb. 5.26.13). The outcome was that the courtiers developed extreme sensitivity to the outward paraphernalia of power, importance and status. It is this preoccupation with manners, appearance and bearing that seems to have become the distinguishing feature of the new kind of culture that radiated from the Hellenistic courts.

There may have been more peaceful times at court, when the various pressures and counter-pressures, blows and counter-blows cancelled each other out sufficiently to give some degree of stability, with the ever-present tensions kept below the surface. By the first century B.C., moreover, the situation may have changed entirely, as the penetration of Roman power into the Hellenistic world upset the delicate balance of power relations between the rulers and their courts. The relentless rivalry at court during the third century and part of the second century B.C. that Polybius recounts, however, is nothing exceptional, and he has not misread the situation. This sort of rivalry was endemic in court society: the running of the Hellenistic kingdoms was inseparable from the struggle for supremacy.

The incessant struggle for prestige and royal favour created a tense, unpleasant atmosphere, one which not only Polybius, but even the kings, found difficult to put up with at times. I believe that the clue to unravelling the hidden mechanisms of Hellenistic court politics must be sought in these power relations, in this atmosphere of latent but relentless rivalry between the king and the courtiers, and among the courtiers themselves. This is by no means an unreasonable suggestion. It might be objected that unwritten rules, etiquette and ceremony operate in all social formations, as indeed they do. However, they take on added importance in societies whose structures are not determined by explicit, independently established rules of conduct. In such societies they cannot be dispensed with, even though they are borne unwillingly by all, because they have definite functions to fulfil. They allow the king to assert his power by distributing distinctions and favours, and also to send out messages of pleasure or displeasure by means of gesture, body-language and private actions; they enable the courtiers to find out their exact ratings in the court hierarchy at any given moment. In other words, such unwritten rules of behaviour approximate closely to the clearly graded scales of prestige found in societies deriving their structure from formal rules. In order to observe the operation of these principles within the Hellenistic courts, we shall return to Apelles' mutiny.

As we have seen, Megaleas and Crinon, in spite of all their plots, were initially accused only of insubordination and breaking the unwritten rules of courtly behaviour. The king imposed a fine on them and ordered their imprisonment. When he convened a council of his "friends," however, these "friends" rather unexpectedly proceeded to try the rebels not for their dissolute behaviour, but for a long list of subversive activities: obstruction, insubordination and plotting. How are we to account for this inconsistency?

The explanation must be that Philip was at first reluctant to accuse the rebels of subversion. He must have feared that his other courtiers, who were not as yet (he hoped) involved in the conspiracy, might take the rebels' side.[45] In order to make absolutely certain that any undecided courtiers took his side rather than that of Apelles, he had to mobilize public opinion in his own favour. In a stroke of genius, Philip resorted to etiquette, in the maintenance of which, as he knew all too well, all courtiers had a vested interest. He won over the support of the silent majority by offering clear proof that the rebels had disregarded etiquette. So substantially did he augment his power as a result of this master-stroke that he could at last afford to signal Apelles' destruction, which he did, still in accordance with the practices of etiquette, by means of a trivial, albeit heavily loaded, gesture.

— IX —

I cannot claim to have touched in this paper upon all, or even most, of the many facets of life at the Hellenistic courts. More work must be done, and more sources than Polybius must be consulted, if we are to obtain a plausible picture of, say, the role of women, or that of the so-called intellectuals, in

---

45. See Polyb. 5.36.1 for an example of the court's ability to take joint action.

courtly politics. For the moment, I have deliberately restricted my analysis to Polybius, and to the horizons which bound his histories. I have done so partly because Polybius displays great familiarity with the Hellenistic courts, his insights—unlike those of the later, secondary sources—being those of a participant observer.[46] The chief reason for limiting myself to Polybius, however, is the unique moral point of view from which he sees the Hellenistic courts. The fact that he makes explicit the scale of values according to which he judges actors and actions makes his history the first major literary piece of the Western world to present a three-dimensional picture of any court society at all.

Polybius' observations, furthermore, allow us to view in outline certain features of the Hellenistic courts which have only rarely been encountered within comparable autocratic systems in Western history. One is the intensive cooperation that took place between courtiers and eminent people possessed of independent power bases all over the Greek world. Another is the absence from these kingdoms (outside the court) of any agency analogous to popular assemblies, or to councils of elders or noblemen, which could be used to further the king's ends, or conversely serve as a centre for opposition to them. A third peculiarity visible from this perspective is that no local, indigenous noblemen appear to have taken part in the courtly power game in the Hellenistic monarchies outside Macedon. Egyptian, Phoenician and Jewish noblemen may not, in reality, have been stamped out entirely by the Greco-Macedonian conquerors, but during the period we are considering they seem to have been weakened to the point of being considered unworthy of inclusion in Polybius' conspectus.

The last point concerns courtly etiquette. In contrast to the frozen formalism that emerges from the first-century sources, Polybius represents life at the Hellenistic courts as notably free from excesses of traditional ceremony and protocol.[47] As we have seen, however, this does not mean that etiquette at court was negligible or unimportant. I suggest, therefore, that we should draw a distinction between the excessively rigid, formalized and

46. Cf. Walbank, "Supernatural paraphernalia" for a possible bond of *xenia* between Lycortas' family and the Ptolemaic royal house, which could explain the familiarity of Polybius with at least one royal court.

47. Cf. M. Cary, *A History of the Greek World from 323 to 146 BC*[2] (London, 1951) 249: "Hellenistic kings had one striking feature in common with the Roman Caesars, in that they combined autocratic power with a comparative simplicity of outward style. Just as the establishment of the Caesars reflected their republican origin, so the courts of the Hellenistic rulers were modelled on that of the old Argead dynasty of Macedon, to whose pattern Alexander's successors reverted by a deliberate reaction from the orientalizing habits of their chief."

pompous kind of etiquette and ceremony of which the court of Philip II of Spain has become a symbol, and the infinitely more flexible, almost informal kind of etiquette that we have encountered in the Hellenistic courts. Even if the latter type amounts only to spontaneous body language and non-verbal communication, it is perhaps a no less formidable instrument of rule and of the distribution of power.

ELEVEN

Decolonizing Ptolemaic Egypt

Roger S. Bagnall

A decade ago, Edouard Will contributed to the volume of essays in honor of Chester Starr an important paper called "Pour une 'anthropologie coloniale' du monde hellénistique."[1] In this article Will urged historians of the Hellenistic world to adopt consciously the anthropological and sociological approaches to the modern colonial world that have developed particularly in the postwar era of decolonization. This idea was of course not wholly new, as Will himself pointed out. It can, for example, be seen in Jean Bingen's paper at the 1968 Congress of Papyrology in Ann Arbor, which I shall consider later; and it is clear that the relevance of the modern colonial experience to the Hellenistic world had struck Claire Préaux long before she wrote the striking passage quoted by Will from her magisterial work of synthesis published in 1978, *Le monde hellénistique*; speaking of scholarly generalizations about Greek economic rationalism versus Egyptian traditionalism, she noted that "There is, perhaps, in this generalization and in the pleasure of underlining the penetration of a superior technique into an indigenous milieu, an unconscious projection of the colonialism of the first half of our century."[2] Will's teaching, too, had already affected the late Claude Orrieux, who made use of colonial paradigms in his two books (to one of which, published in 1983, Will wrote the foreword) on Zenon, the estate manager

A version of the present paper was given to the Program on the Ancient World at Princeton University in December 1994; I owe thanks to William A. P. Childs for the invitation to speak and to those present for many useful comments. I am also grateful to James G. Keenan and Dorothy J. Thompson for comments on various drafts.

1. In John W. Eadie and Josiah Ober, eds., *The Craft of the Ancient Historian* (Lanham, Md., 1985) 273–301.

2. *Le monde hellénistique* (Paris, 1978) I 380, cited by Will (above, n. 1) 281.

in the Fayum who assembled the largest archival body of papyri to survive to the present.[3]

In reality, the act of modeling our approach to the Hellenistic world after the modern imperial and colonial experience is by itself in no way a novelty. Will was quite well aware of this fact. Much of the first half of his article is devoted to a description of what he sees as the intellectual limits of the classic works on the Hellenistic world by earlier historians, culminating in the pre-war work of Michael Rostovtzeff and Claire Préaux.[4] Will views these works as lacking in a clear approach to the sociological problems posed by the relations between colonizing and colonized. For this reason, he believes, the authors of these accounts were insufficiently interested in the agrarian world, too much interested in the state and its role, and too much devoted to the point of view of the dominating power, the Greek settlers and Macedonian rulers. This last defect was reinforced by the lack of any critical self-consciousness about European colonization and imperialism. Problems were framed in terms of hellenization, that is, of what might now be called the imposition of the culture of the rulers upon the ruled. In short, the problem Will describes was not so much one of ignorance of the colonial experience as an unthinking but positive outlook on the whole business from the point of view of a citizen of a colonizing power.

Will's point, therefore, is in part political: an appeal to change the point of view from which colonialism is seen. In the postwar world of decolonization, western scholars have no longer been able to look at a colonial world with the same "good conscience" they once had, confident that European domination was good for the ruled as well as for the rulers. Will argues that the new vistas opened up by this change of outlook, when coupled with a Marxist-influenced interest in the relations of production, make possible an entirely new approach to the society of the Hellenistic world. In this view, the analysis of states becomes of secondary interest, the relations of Greeks and non-Greeks of central importance. He thus asserts the necessity for a self-conscious, rather than unthinking, use of perspectives offered by the

3. *Les papyrus de Zénon: L'horizon d'un grec en Egypte au IIIe siècle avant J.C.* (Paris, 1983); *Zénon de Caunos, parépidémos, et le destin grec* (Paris, 1985). Orrieux's work is based in significant part on a confident distinction between papers concerning Zenon's employer Apollonios and those concerning Zenon's private affairs; this distinction has been demolished by G. F. Franko, *BASP* 25 (1988) 13–98. But much of what Orrieux discerns as a Greek colonial mentality remains intact. Although I shall not discuss these works in any detail in this paper, they have much to offer as examples of the value of Will's approach.

4. Particularly Rostovtzeff's *Social and Economic History of the Hellenistic World* (Oxford, 1941) and Préaux's *L'économie royale des Lagides* (Brussels, 1939).

historian's contemporary world, and argues that the different approaches to the colonial world that have developed in an era of decolonization offer just the useful contemporary perspective needed. Now that Asia and Africa have been decolonized, in other words, it is time to decolonize Ptolemaic Egypt and its neighbors.

This raises the question whether a consciously anticolonialist or anti-imperialist political commitment is a prerequisite for pursuit of an inquiry of this sort. The fact that the discussion to date is almost exclusively fran-cophone, specifically French and Belgian, and consciously leftward-leaning, might suggest an affirmative answer. Positive views about colonialism—nostalgia, even, as Edward Said would call it—are perhaps more vigorously alive in the Anglo-Saxon world than on the continent, although the descent of Algeria into chaos may well be changing this and reawakening French sentiment that letting that land go was a mistake.[5] But in a broader sense it would be as much an error to try to confine critical discussion of ancient colo-nialism to vehement critics of modern as to engage in any other essentialist exclusivism. I shall therefore proceed on the view that despite the politi-cal commitments underlying much of the modern scholarship that offers us models for exploration, those who do not fully share those commitments may still have an interest in testing the models to see if they are useful.

The avenue that Will describes for pursuing his goals is by definition an explicitly comparative one. If we define the Hellenistic world as colonial, then a wide range of colonial and post-colonial zones (in the latter Will includes South America) offer a range of "living societies accessible to more penetrating methods of investigation than the methods proper to the ancient world." Although Will recognizes that important differences must be taken account of, both among modern colonial worlds and ancient societies, he asserts that accepting the "colonial hypothesis" opens up such a large range of useful modern literature that we can renovate our entire approach to Hellenistic society.

On this basis, Will proceeds to offer three sets of observations. The first is a four-part typology of relations of colonized to colonizers. The second is a pair of important differences between antiquity and the recent past. The third is a pair of illustrative examples in which he believes that the use of comparative material helps to illuminate the situation in antiquity, in particular in Ptolemaic Egypt. I shall follow this outline, arguing first that the typology is inadequate and not very useful; that many more important

---

5. Part of Edward Said's *Culture and Imperialism* (New York, 1993) is devoted to criticism of various contemporary strands of thought less inclined to blame everything on the colonizing powers. Cf. esp. p. 21 on Salman Rushdie's criticism of nostalgia for the Raj.

differences need to be registered and absorbed; and that Will's two examples may teach a different lesson from the one he intended. I shall then proceed to suggest different ways of using the history and literature of colonialism to illuminate Ptolemaic Egypt and, potentially, other Hellenistic states. All of this is very tentative, partly because of the limited and unsystematic character of my own reading in this literature, but still more because of my sense that an approach through colonialism grasps only a fragment of the power relationships in question.[6]

I. MODELS OF INTERACTION

The typology offered by Will, borrowed from an anthropologist of Africa, sees four main types of indigenous reaction to external domination: (1) active acceptance, most typical among notables intent on retaining power and among those looking to gain power, typically entailing a considerable measure of assimilation; (2) passive acceptance, usually by far the majority stance, natural among those already in a state of dependence and witnessing no major change in their status; (3) passive opposition, generated in many cases by a high level of anxiety over social and economic change, manifesting itself especially in withdrawal, strikes, and disappearance; and (4) active opposition, manifesting itself ultimately in revolt, whether spurred by political, economic, or cultural factors. Will notes that these stages are not necessarily a logical or chronological progression, that they are a theoretical typology that may well vary from time to time and place to place, and that each group can develop internal fissures under various pressures; he cites particularly the tendency of victorious revolutions to fissure between those more ready to adopt the techniques of the foreign dominators and those intent on purifying their culture from such foreign attributes.

Ancient historians cannot simply borrow anthropological theory and schemes without criticism. Anthropology is no more monolithic than any other discipline in its analytic frameworks and broad views. The four-part scheme deployed by Will seems to me even more inadequate than he would admit, not simply because it is not complex enough, but because its underlying binary opposition between acceptance and rejection is not very helpful, tending to frame reaction to foreign domination in the outsider's terms. From the point of view of the indigenous population, acceptance and rejection may not be the real choices; even some types of rejection may be types of acceptance. Within resistance and even rebellion, there may

6. For a more developed version of this discussion see my *Reading Papyri, Writing Ancient History* (London, 1995).

be many modes of dealing with the imprint of the colonizing culture on the colonized.[7] To quote John and Jean Comaroff, "When the colonized respond in the genre of rational debate—at least as defined in European terms—the hegemony of the colonizing culture may be well on the way to instilling itself in its new subjects; that is why truly counter-hegemonic reactions so frequently seek out alternative modes of expression."[8]

Equally, what Will's model would term passive acceptance may often disguise subtler forms of passive rejection.[9] That these may not be understood as resistance by the colonizer and are often characterized as "laziness,"[10] flight, theft, sabotage and the like only underscores their value. Nor are they distinctive to colonial settings. In sum, the twin polarities of this model, although not without value as a starting point, appear to me eventually only to impose an artificial spatial organization on the range of indigenous responses. It may not even be excessive to describe the model as being itself a typical product of European attempts to exercise intellectual control over the colonial situation.

II. CRITICAL DIFFERENCES

The first of the two key differences Will sees is that the conquest of the East by Alexander and his successors was essentially military and political in character and origin, whereas modern colonization was heavily driven by economic interest, that is, by either access to resources or the development of trading networks. This distinction is broadly characteristic of the difference between ancient Greek culture and modern capitalist civilization, in Will's view. It might be more realistic to describe the economic aims and results of Alexander and his companions as being the transfer of accumulated wealth by the distribution of war booty,[11] that of the European powers as modern capitalism. Alexander's successors, however, the early Hellenistic kings,

7. Cf. E. Said, *Culture and Imperialism* 214.

8. J. and J. Comaroff, *Ethnography and the Historical Imagination* (Boulder, Colorado, 1992) 257.

9. See the discussion of peasant reactions in James C. Scott, *Weapons of the Weak: Everyday Forms of Peasant Resistance* (New Haven, 1985), from which it is clear that much of what is classified by the typology Will invokes as "passive acceptance" is actually a form of resistance. That these are described by Scott as specimens of "class struggle" (xvi, 289–303) rather than of resistance to colonialism is immaterial here, but it raises other issues discussed later in this paper.

10. Cf. E. Said 203, with references.

11. On which one may see the memorable pages of Cl. Préaux, *Monde hellénistique* I 295–98.

sought through systematic economic exploitation of their holdings to provide the resources for their political aspirations, and it is not obvious that in the end this came down to as profound a difference between ancient and modern as Will would hold.

The second distinction is that almost all modern colonialism was accompanied by, and sometimes largely executed by, a religious missionary movement, propagating a universalizing monotheistic religion; by contrast, both conquerors and conquered in the Hellenistic world were polytheists, open to the cults of others and not particularly intent on imposing their own on anyone.

This list needs expansion, and I believe that the two additions I shall offer—and to which more could certainly be added—are no less fundamental than the two points Will makes. First, modern imperialism and colonialism have been characterized by systematic racism. The indigenous populations of the colonized countries were generally viewed not only as inferior and backward—and therefore proper receptacles for the bounty of the western civilizing mission—but as ineradicably inferior, incapable ever of rising to the level of the colonizers.[12] Certainly the Greeks—like other ancient peoples— habitually regarded themselves as superior to others, and even described them at times as slaves by nature.[13] But even so they lacked systematic racism, particularly one based on skin color, and their attitudes toward "barbarians" were by no means entirely negative.[14] Indeed, the ancient experience of the continuity of the color spectrum in the Mediterranean and the proximity of a wide variety of hues bears no resemblance to the modern encounter of northern Europeans with distant peoples of radically different color. The Greeks also had a high regard for some of the ancient civilizations of the Near East, especially that of Egypt, and their relationship to that country was thus naturally schizophrenic. Moreover, it was routinely possible for an Egyptian in Ptolemaic Egypt, by education, employment and status, to become an official "Hellene," a development largely (although not wholly) alien to modern colonial practice and ideology.[15]

---

12. Cf., e.g., Said 101–102; 228 ("Irish people can never be English any more than Cambodians or Algerians can be French").

13. See, e.g., Yvon Garlan, *Slavery in Ancient Greece* (Ithaca, 1988) 120–26, who describes the development of this ideology along with contrary views.

14. On the lack of racial prejudice based on color, see F. M. Snowden, *Before Color Prejudice* (Cambridge, Mass., 1983) 63–108. For an example of the complex range of views, some admiring, displayed by the Greeks toward barbarians, see S. W. Hirsch, *The Friendship of the Barbarians: Xenophon and the Persian Empire* (Hanover, 1985).

15. Such official hellenization was, I think, much farther-reaching than for example acquisition of non-native status in Dutch Indonesia. For the process by which individuals

Secondly, modern colonialism is virtually defined by the existence of a metropolitan center outside the colonized land, to which the wealth extracted from the colony flows and where ultimate power resides.[16] For the Hellenistic kingdoms, there was no such metropolitan center. One may legitimately think of the assemblage of kingdoms as a kind of continuing Macedonian empire, but that is true only in the sense that the United States continued after 1783 to be a kind of continuing British empire. Nor can one clude this difficulty by claiming that Alexandria was such a metropolitan center. In reality, Egypt's metropolis was tightly woven into the economic and political fabric of the country on whose ground it stood. It cannot be taken for an equivalent to Paris, London, or Brussels. Particularly in the conditions of travel and communication prevalent until the late nineteenth century, distance is not a negligible aspect. Anyone who doubts its impact would be well advised to ponder the alienating and terrifying impact of the distance between Indonesia and the Netherlands with its court system that dominates the concluding sections of Pramoedya Ananta Toer's *This Earth of Mankind*, a book to which I shall return later. I do not mean to minimize the extractive force of the Ptolemaic government with respect to Egypt and its other possessions. But it is impossible to imagine a Ptolemaic official describing Egypt in the terms John Stuart Mill uses: "Our West Indian colonies, for example, cannot be regarded as countries with a productive capital of their own ... [but are rather] the place where England finds it convenient to carry on the production of sugar, coffee, and a few other tropical commodities."[17] It was Rome, not the Ptolemies, that to some extent treated Egypt in this manner.

A still broader concern about colonialism needs to be raised at this point. This is, simply, that categorization, however useful, has sharp limits. This is true of the modern comparanda; "colonial" is, though a useful category, one that covers a wide variety of circumstances. Like the Greek-centered approaches that Will deplores, it is itself a categorization constructed from the point of view of the colonizer. It tends to obfuscate the enormous differences in social, political, and economic organization of the societies

---

came to hold status and names dependent on their official posts, see Willy Clarysse, "Greeks and Egyptians in the Ptolemaic Army and Administration," *Aegyptus* 65 (1985) 57–66 and "Some Greeks in Egypt," in J. H. Johnson, ed., *Life in a Multi-Cultural Society: Egypt from Cambyses to Constantine and Beyond* (*SAOC* 51, Chicago, 1992) 51–56.

16. It is true that Said (63) tries to use colonialism as a description of the treatment of the indigenous population of North America by the European settlers as they expanded across the continent even after American independence, but this seems to me to be stretching a concept for the sake of a political point.

17. *Principles of Political Economy* III (Toronto, 1965) 693, quoted by Said 59.

visited with outside domination. This problem has long been recognized and discussed, but with no agreed-upon results. Moses Finley proposed three essential requirements for the use of the term "colony": significant emigration, continuing dependency on the colonizing country, and expropriation and settlement of land.[18] He excluded the Hellenistic kingdoms from his definition, above all because they failed to meet the second of these conditions, as we have already noted.

The straightforward description of Ptolemaic Egypt as a colony thus encounters some significant structural difficulties. But this does not justify our discarding colonialism altogether as an approach to the Hellenistic world or to antiquity in general. One finds just such a rejection in a recent work of Edward Said:[19] "But modern European imperialism was a constitutively, radically different type of overseas domination from all earlier forms. Scale and scope were only part of the difference, though certainly not Byzantium, or Rome, or Athens, or Baghdad, or Spain and Portugal during the fifteenth and sixteenth centuries controlled anything like the size of the territories controlled by Britain and France in the nineteenth century. The more important differences are first the sustained longevity of the disparity in power, and second, the massive organization of the power, which affected the details and not just the large outlines of life." The logical conclusion of this statement might well be that using "colonial" as a category is a blunder caused by failure to appreciate the great differences between ancient and modern imperialisms.[20]

This argument will not do. For one thing, Said's claims about scale are both wrong and irrelevant. The Persian empire, for example, was at least as large as any modern colonial empire except perhaps the British, and in any case Said's own argument implicates the Belgians and Dutch just as much as the British and French. So scale is a red herring. Said is equally wrong about longevity; the Ptolemaic kingdom lasted as long as the British empire or the Dutch, and the Roman empire—and, even more strikingly, the Byzantine—lasted still longer. The main period of European colonialism, when it reached such a large scale, was actually just a little over a century in duration, from the mid-nineteenth century to the mid-twentieth.

18. "Colonies—An Attempt at a Typology," *TransRoyHistSoc* 5 ser. 26 (1976) 167–88; I owe the reference to the editors of this volume.

19. *Culture and Imperialism* 221.

20. There is another categorical problem that I cannot discuss here, the tendency to blur imperialism and colonialism, or even (in Said's case) to confound imperialism and all projections of national power. For present purposes, I take colonialism to be distinguished from imperialism above all by the settlement of significant numbers of members of the imperial power in the conquered territory.

Said's argument thus reduces itself to the question of the "massive organization of power." I am inclined to think that many "details" of life in Egypt were affected by foreign domination and settlement, and that this was true in other Hellenistic kingdoms as well, where the planting of Greek cities on the landscape certainly reorganized the control of land and other productive resources as much as the Ptolemaic management of Egypt. In any event, such questions need examination on a scale appropriate to the level of detail meant, and any *a priori* exclusion of the colonial model from discussion of the ancient world will only prevent such examination. But all of the reservations offered here suggest at least that focusing on colonialism per se may be less rewarding than thinking about colonialism in conjunction with the larger phenomenon of imperialism and hierarchical systems in general.

III. TWO CASE STUDIES

We come now to Will's two case studies. The first is the use of petitions addressed to the king in Ptolemaic Egypt. Will wonders if they ever reached their destination and had any outcome. He brings to bear, by way of comparison, the operation of a Peruvian system of petitions to high officials, in which the petitions generally went nowhere, being perpetually described by bureaucrats as in the course of transmission. During these long silences the petitioners became effective dependents of the bureaucratic office, but acquired in this way the ability to say to others that their case was under official scrutiny. Did the Ptolemaic system work this way, he wonders?

The second is the impact of the introduction of coinage in a society not accustomed to it, and particularly its use as a medium for payment of obligations to the government. He points out that Peruvians were driven to accept wage labor, especially in mines, in order to earn enough currency to pay the money taxes imposed by the government.[21] Moreover, the actions of the foreign government and settlers tended to turn money into the single standard of wealth, in contrast to traditional local ways of measuring it; this process was ultimately destructive to the local economy.[22] Did the same thing happen in Egypt?

It is by no means clear that either of these questions would, if pursued in detail, lead to the conclusion that Ptolemaic Egypt did, in fact, show the

21. A striking parallel exists in the development of wage labor in South Africa, also to meet tax burdens: see J. and J. Comaroff, *Ethnography and the Historical Imagination*, 162–63 etc.

22. Again well paralleled in South Africa, cf. J. and J. Comaroff, *Ethnography and the Historical Imagination*, 128 etc.

same phenomena as colonial or post-colonial Peru (or South Africa, for that matter). Ptolemaic petitions normally do not have a date of submission, but the surviving ones very commonly have an official subscription giving instructions for the handling of the case—which does have a date. We cannot, therefore, measure the time elapsed between complaint and action.[23] We do, on the other hand, know that at least some petitions received official response, although it is likely enough that the surviving petitions come mainly from recycled official archives composed precisely of petitions that had been dealt with. It would not do for us to assume that the Ptolemaic administration was entirely honest and efficient, but neither do the actual documents give any warrant for a precise comparison to the Peruvian situation Will invokes.[24]

As to money, the Egyptians were very well acquainted with silver, even if largely uncoined, as a standard of value before the Ptolemies. And Ptolemaic taxation in money was relatively light, achieving a symbolic value as much as anything; the bulk of the taxes continued to be collected in kind. It is therefore by no means clear that the Ptolemies created the kind of pressures for their subjects supposed by Will's parallels. It may be argued, indeed, that the Egyptian economy before Alexander's conquest was less isolated and "primitive" than has often been supposed.[25] This is not to deny all impact, only to argue that the parallelism between the Egyptian economy before the Macedonians and the Peruvian before the Spaniards may not be very strong.

Even this brief analysis is sufficient to show that the parallels may actually produce very misleading views. One may reply, as I think Will certainly would, that the value of the parallels is in formulating questions, not in providing their answers. That is part of the truth. But there is another answer, which seems to me more interesting and more characteristic of comparative studies generally. We agree that the parallels allow the formulation of hypotheses about how certain aspects of Egyptian society in the Hellenistic period might have functioned. Let us suppose that these hypotheses can be not merely called into doubt (as I have tried to do briefly above) but definitely refuted. The value of the negative results is not only that we learn some particular (negative) characteristic of ancient society; it is also that the

23. Some evidence from the Roman period seems to me to indicate reasonably quick turnaround time, much faster than modern courts offer; cf. R. Bagnall, *Egypt in Late Antiquity* (Princeton, 1993) 169–70.

24. That is not to say that some elements may not have been comparable: the basic psychological importance of submitting appeals against perceived injustice regardless of the likelihood of direct redress, say.

25. This argument was made in a paper on "Money and Coinage in Ptolemaic Egypt" by Sitta von Reden at the XXIst International Congress of Papyrologists, Berlin, August 1995.

reasoning leading to the hypothesis can now be unpacked and examined. What fundamental or contingent characteristics of the ancient world, and of the particular society in it that we are studying, underlie and produce this interesting difference between Egypt and Peru?[26]

IV. APPLYING WILL'S APPROACH

The most extensive and explicit response to Will's article known to me is a trio of long articles—together, a small book—by Barbara Anagnostou-Canas, who acknowledges assistance from Orrieux. The first article is on the military apparatus used by the Ptolemies to control Egypt, the second on the native rebellions against Ptolemaic rule, and the third on the control of land.[27] With specific reference to the article in the Starr Festschrift, Canas accepts the hypothesis of Ptolemaic Egypt as a colonial society and proceeds to apply this view to these two aspects. These are careful, detailed studies, with exhaustive references to the literary and documentary sources and modern bibliography. Their method, however, is essentially that of all preceding studies on the same subjects: the sources are collected and analyzed, then conclusions are given. The conclusions are framed in the language of colonialism, both with a few comparative remarks and with judgmental tones, already visible in the programmatic statement at the outset of the military article: "It is a matter of studying the negative part of the occupation of Egypt by the Greeks for three centuries."[28] What Canas does not do is what Will is actually suggesting, to create a model from the comparative evidence and test the Ptolemaic material against it. To my mind, therefore, these articles are, despite their claims, only a partial attempt to put Will's precepts into practice.

It is perhaps then unsurprising that the results of these articles are not particularly novel. The Ptolemies controlled Egypt in the first place by their military presence, consisting of military settlers on the land, garrisons in key places, and requisitioning of housing from the indigenous population for the

---

26. It is, to be sure, true that such differences themselves are interesting in large part because they coexist with important similarities, as Josiah Ober points out to me.

27. "Rapports de dépendance coloniale dans l'Égypte ptolémaïque I: L'appareil militaire," *BIDR* 3 ser. 31–32 (1989/90) 151–236; "Rapports de dépendance coloniale dans l'Égypte ptolémaïque II: Les rebelles de la chôra," *Proceedings of the XIXth International Congress of Papyrology* (Cairo, 1992) II 323–72; "La colonisation du sol dans l'Égypte ptolémaïque," *Grund und Boden in Altägypten (Rechtliche und sozio-ökonomische Verhältnisse). Akten des internationalen Symposions Tübingen 18–20 Juni 1990*, S. Allam, ed. (Tübingen, 1994) 355–74. These are cited below as "Canas I," "Canas II" and "Canas III."

28. Canas I, 156.

troops. Greeks took over much of the better land. There was for a long time no actual use of force, merely its presence and threat, and the Ptolemaic regime can be described as *douce* rather than *dure*.[29] But it was all the same a regime in which force was the ultimate guarantor of foreign domination, and actual force had to be used to repress various rebellions. A key element in military control of Egypt after the late third century was the use of Egyptians enrolled in the army to keep their own fellow-countrymen in subjection. The rebellions, in Canas' view, were essentially nationalist uprisings produced by the intense economic pressure put on the population by the Ptolemaic extractive system. They ultimately failed in part precisely because of the collaboration of many Egyptians with the foreign regime, involving both the official support of the priesthoods and the presence of Egyptian troops in the royal armies.[30] Most of the more controversial elements of this description have been the key objects of scholarly argument for more than a half century between those who have seen the revolutions as nationalistic—thus primarily directed against colonial rule—and those who have viewed them primarily as fueled by economic considerations and local separatism.[31] Canas does not demonstrate a link between the supposed economic oppression (itself not demonstrated, for that matter) and the revolts, but simply asserts it.[32] She may be right or wrong in her views, but I would set out to support or counter them with much the same traditional tools she uses.[33] The references to colonialism serve mainly as decoration and flavoring, rather than occupying any structural role in the argument. I do not think they are inappropriate or even wrong, and in some cases the point seems well made that indeed Ptolemaic Egypt had some clear resemblances to later colonial societies.[34] But that is something different from using a colonial anthropology to generate fertile hypotheses about the Hellenistic world.

29. In particular, Canas (I 165 etc.) is clear about the absence of juridical discrimination; she seems unaware, however, that the Greeks were exempted from some taxes the Egyptians paid (I 166).

30. Canas II 371.

31. Canas II, 323–25 gives a good summary with bibliography.

32. See, e.g., Canas II 334, 361.

33. Most particularly, Canas tends to take all statements, whether in documents or in polemical literature, at face value, without any attempt to look at propagandistic motives. And (Canas II 340) she shows no awareness of the persistence of local separatism in Egyptian politics through more than two millennia of pre-Ptolemaic history.

34. Canas III seems to me the weakest of the group in this regard, for what it shows is the close resemblance of the Ptolemaic land regime to the situation in Pharaonic times, with little more than a change of favored elites. It seems stretching the definition of colonialism to see it in such arrangements.

V. LOOKING FOR VALUE

If Will's two cases give us only negative results, and Canas' application does not show much added value, we may naturally ask if other approaches and cases can give more positive outcomes. To this question I believe the answer is yes. At the papyrological congress of 1968, as I have already mentioned, Jean Bingen presented some reflections on a complex and difficult document from the Zenon archive.[35] Zenon, the estate agent in the Fayum for the finance minister Apollonios, had rented out a substantial parcel of grainland to a group of Egyptian farmers, who were to pay their landlord one third of the eventual crop. The practice of sharecropping was well known in Egypt and readily understood by the farmers. While the wheat crop was still standing, orders came from Apollonios that the amount of the farmers' payment to him should be established on the basis of an estimation in advance, rather than after the harvest. The precise meaning of this step within this particular context is unclear, but at a minimum it would be analogous to other Ptolemaic measures to provide the government (in this case, of course, the private landlord) with stable and predictable revenues, thus placing potential risks and rewards of fluctuation in crop size (and perhaps value) on others. Such techniques, including estimation of standing crops, were well-known parts of Greek economic management, but entirely foreign to the Egyptians.

The result of the attempt by Panakestor to put Apollonios' order into effect was that the farmers first replied that they would think about it and answer later. That answer, given a few days later, was to retreat into a temple and refuse to take part in the exercise, preferring to abandon the entire arrangement rather than be party to the process of estimation. Bingen points out that "flight is a characteristic reaction of an archaic group, in the ethnographic sense of that word, in the face of the intrusion of a more evolved group, and particularly before the intrusion of a group which, being aware of the innovative efficacy of human intervention, disturbs the existing interdependent order." Third-century Egypt, of course, is not a prehistoric peasant culture, nor was the third-century Greek world a modern capitalistic society. But the mechanism of behavior is essentially the same, the simple refusal even to discuss matters, the refusal to play the outsiders' game. Bingen points out that the fact that the peasants flee to the temple rather than simply taking to flight is a measure of the difference between the institutionally well-developed character of Egyptian society and the

35. J. Bingen, "Grecs et Égyptiens d'après PSI 502," *Proceedings of the XIIth International Congress of Papyrology* (Toronto, 1970) 35–40.

less institutionalized societies involved in many colonial confrontations of this sort.

The farmers' behavior could be seen as a type of Will's "passive rejection" reaction, the use of withdrawal and strikes; but actually the situation is more complicated. The farmers are very willing to enter into contractual relationships with the outsiders, to help them in the enterprise of agricultural development of new land. But they are willing to do it only in their own way, not with the outsiders' new management techniques. It is certainly possible that Apollonios' attempt to impose advance estimation at this late stage in the agricultural cycle was not a neutral and innocent act, any more than the forced imposition of fixed cash rents payable in advance has been a neutral act in the Green Revolution that transformed agriculture in Malaysia and elsewhere in the third world;[36] the farmers may have been right to see it as a trap they had to avoid. In any case, these farmers are neither simply accepting nor simply rejecting foreign domination; these just are not the categories that appear as choices in their particular situation.

In this case, then, not only the similarities of the Egyptian situation to that seen elsewhere but also its differences are illuminated by the comparison. Bingen's paper was written for oral presentation (within a time limit) and is interpretive rather than heavily documented. The ethnographic parallels are barely supported by bibliographic citation, let alone explored in detail; in fact, his reference was to a generalizing description in a theoretical work, not to a specific instance in a particular society. Nor are we dealing with hypotheses from anthropology, sociology, or modern history tested against the papyri. But this case shows that progress in interpreting the documents can come from an imagination informed by knowledge of the colonial world.

It seems to me that it is precisely the informing of the imagination that is at the heart of the gains realizable from this sort of comparative study. The surviving documents, after all, record only some aspects of life, leaving others either barely mentioned, at least in any explicit fashion, or entirely absent. If we know what we are looking for, we can sometimes find indirect traces of it in documentation created for some entirely different purpose, and to know what we are looking for we are dependent on the enrichment of our imagination about human experience. The imaginative literature growing out of the colonial experience thus seems to me at least as likely as works of social science about that experience to help us grasp elements of life that we otherwise would miss, and I shall offer one example. This is

36. See J. Scott, *Weapons of the Weak* (above, n. 9) 72–74.

the group of four novels by Pramoedya Ananta Toer, beginning with *This Earth of Mankind*, which I mentioned earlier.[37]

The narrator of the quartet is a Native Javanese student—the only student of his race, in fact—at the Dutch High School in the Javan port of Surabaya. Eighteen years old when the story begins, in 1898, he is the son of a provincial official in Dutch service and a descendant of Java's old nobility. There are many elements of the society he moves in and depicts that are grossly dissimilar to that of Ptolemaic Egypt, among them the great importance of race and caste in official stratification, the Dutch attempt to restrict Javanese learning of Dutch, and the dominance of economic activities aimed at producing a large economic surplus for the home country, which did indeed become very rich over the centuries in large part as a result of this colonial empire. And Java was only one island in what is now Indonesia, and Javanese (itself a complex language with multiple registers of speech) was only one of the native languages of the region.

All the same, there are elements of the situation that bear marked resemblances to what we know of Ptolemaic society. The impingement of foreign ideas about economic development and entrepreneurship onto the traditional economy of the island plays a large role, and the intertwining of colonizers seeking riches with the native population that lived with them and actually did the work is a central theme. The complicity of native elites[38] in the colonial management of the country is depicted in varied detail, including the natives' tendency to view the oppressors' culture as superior to their own, but at the same time their ability to use the colonizers' language as a tool for resistance. Intra-family disputes over acculturation to foreign ways are very noticeable. Patterns of language use are complex and reflect both power relationships and ethnic diversity; Java was even more linguistically diverse than Egypt, where Aramaic must have been commonly spoken in some centers alongside Egyptian and Greek.

What I find most striking here is not the structural similarities, however, but Toer's ability to give voice to the way in which these were *experienced* by the people affected, above all by liminal figures like the narrator, whose Netherlandization in culture is much resented by his family, even though

37. 1975; trans. Max Lane, New York, 1990. The second novel is *Child of All Nations* (1980; trans. Max Lane, New York, 1991), the third *Footsteps* (1985; trans. Max Lane, New York, 1994), the fourth *House of Glass* (1988; trans. Max Lane, New York, 1996). *Child of All Nations* has a striking instance in its final chapter of language as a mode of resistance to colonial exploitation.

38. It may be significant that these Javanese elites descended from a local ruling class with a history of local imperialism of their own, rather like the Egyptians. (I owe this point to a member of my audience at Princeton.)

they have pushed him into the educational track that has produced it, and who suffers monstrous and crushing blows from the injustices perpetrated by the Dutch legal system, operating across thousands of miles of ocean and in callous disregard of the realities of Javanese life. One does not need to suppose that the Ptolemaic system was as brutal as the Dutch—I do not think it was, in fact—to recognize the narrator's usefulness to us as a reminder of the subjective and internal side of what we see in the documents only from the outside.

One example will have to suffice; it comes from the second novel, *Child of All Nations*, and I have chosen it for its point of contact with Bingen's article. The narrator, Minke, visits a rural village dominated by a sugar factory. The factory has put heavy pressure on local small landowners to rent out to it, for cash, a large portion of their fields, which are to be planted in cane rather than in the rice a farmer would plant for himself. From a European point of view, tracts of land traditionally used for subsistence farming are being converted to the more profitable production of a cash crop for an international market. Zenon would surely feel at home, and no doubt the correspondence of the mill would, like his records, show an essentially orderly process with only minor difficulties. The farmer interviewed by Minke, however, puts it this way: "I don't want to rent out my land but every day I'm threatened, taunted, insulted. Now they threaten that the lane to my house will be closed off. If you want to get to your house and land, they say, you'll have to fly. They have already closed the channels bringing water to my paddy fields. I couldn't farm the paddy, so I had to rent it out."[39] It is clear that it is not only the inadequacy of the payment, or the fact that only about two-thirds of what is contracted for is really paid, that creates the peasant's resistance (for in this case it does turn into armed resistance). Rather, it is the disrespectful treatment and the informal use of coercion, such as cutting off the water supply, both by the Europeans and by the natives in the employ of the Europeans. Egypt, especially the Fayum, would have offered excellent opportunities for precisely such behavior. I am persuaded that an attentive rereading of the papyri with an imagination sensitized by works such as Toer's has a great potential to alert scholars to disguised realities of this colonial society, even where those may turn out to be very different from the systematic brutality of European imperialism a century ago.

This approach, finally, has the additional value of avoiding a sterile confrontation between the merits of drawing models from the colonial experience and those of looking to other types of power relationships and social structures to inform us. Many of the phenomena described in studies

39. *Child of All Nations* 165.

of colonialism are not unique to the colonial milieu, but may legitimately be seen as products of hierarchy and unequal power, both economic and political. They are thus found in societies that cannot reasonably be called colonial and in those whose colonial phase is in the past. The description of peasant everyday resistance tactics to which I alluded earlier comes from a book by James Scott about a Malaysian village experiencing the Green Revolution. This setting is in no way specifically colonial; indeed it concerns the internal workings of a purely Malay society in the 1970s. The author analyzes his findings entirely in terms of class conflict, in a Marxist sense. Now this book is rich in material that I find highly suggestive for the analysis of Ptolemaic and Roman Egypt. It would not be difficult to offer parallels to many aspects of it from colonial regimes. In part this is the result of documentation. Many of the traditional and hierarchical societies for which we have the most information are the colonial states of the nineteenth and early twentieth century, because Europeans used the technology of writing to record their dealings with their subjects in enormous detail—just as did the Ptolemies.

It follows, then, that those power relationships that are distinctive to colonialism are only a subset of those that can help us understand the societies of the Hellenistic world. Much can be learned elsewhere as well, and we need not assert that the specifically colonial elements of the situation are more or less important to our understanding than those aspects of power relations that are not distinctive to the colonial setting. Both can inform our imaginations, and both deserve the most rigorous testing against the uneven but abundant documentation left us by the people of Ptolemaic Egypt, sifted through the mesh of destruction by climate, insects, and humans.

TWELVE

The Infrastructure of Splendour: Census and Taxes in Ptolemaic Egypt

Dorothy J. Thompson

In 279/8 B.C. Ptolemy II Philadelphus held a festival in Alexandria in honour of his parents, Ptolemy Soter and Berenice, the founders of the Ptolemaic dynasty.[1] It was a gala occasion, marked by lavish hospitality, special constructions, a military march-past and a great procession to entertain the visitors. Ptolemaic wealth and power were on display not only for the inhabitants of Egypt, old and new, but also for the envoys invited from all over the Aegean world. If not the full order, nevertheless some sense of the magnificence of the procession comes through Athenaeus' account. There was gold and silver in profusion, statues and precious objects, entertainment for all, a display of exotic animals, a march-past of military power. "What kingdom, my fellow-banqueters, was ever so rich in gold?" concludes the narrator.[2]

Of the several sources of Ptolemaic wealth, income from taxation formed one of the most important. The aim here is to present new papyrological evidence for the Ptolemaic census and the system of taxation that depended upon it.[3] The various tax registers to be discussed form a bilingual corpus of texts (in Greek and demotic) from the third and second centuries B.C. These are documents extracted from cartonnage (recycled

---

1. For the date, see F. W. Walbank, *LCM* 9 (1984) 52–54, reviewing E. E. Rice, *The Grand Procession of Ptolemy Philadelphus* (Oxford, 1983); in "Two Hellenistic Processions: A Matter of Self-definition," *SCI* 15 (1996) 121 n. 16, Walbank discusses (and rejects) the date of 279/8 proposed by V. Foertmeyer, "The Dating of the Pompe of Ptolemy Philadelphus," *Historia* 37 (1988) 90–104.

2. Athenaeus, *Deipn.* 5.203b; cf. 196a-203b, excerpting Callixenus of Rhodes.

3. This corpus of papyri will be edited by W. Clarysse and myself, as *Counting the People.*

papyri used as mummy casing) which, when separated out, despite the traces of plaster and paint that mark them, still retain the texts of the documents that were discarded. Indeed, were it not for this practice of reusing waste paper our knowledge of Ptolemaic Egypt would be much the poorer. Most of this material comes from cemeteries of the Fayum, the basin lying some eighty kilometres southwest of Cairo which, in the third century B.C., was renamed the Arsinoite nome in honour of Arsinoe Philadelphus, the queen of Ptolemy II; a few of the texts came from elsewhere. Some of these registers were the subject of early editions; about half of them are previously unpublished. Here, as is frequently the case in papyrological studies, it is only when new documents are found that the significance of older texts becomes clear. It is with the levy of taxes that these texts are mainly concerned, but they also shed light on the census that preceded. These are the twin operations for discussion here, commencing with the census.

To record the people was nothing new in Egypt. A census, at least on a limited basis, first appears in the late Middle Kingdom,[4] and from the New Kingdom a broader census is known, not only of all the people but livestock and poultry too.[5] By counting his people, the pharaoh could know how great was the workforce available for work on the dykes or royal building projects. In pharaonic Egypt this seems to have been the principal aim of the census—to discover the availability of labour, not of soldiers or those to pay taxes. So, when the sixth-century B.C. pharaoh Amasis required every Egyptian to declare annually to the nomarch "whence he gained his living," his prime interest was to identify those whose occupation would prevent their involvement in *corvée* labour.[6] This emphasis differs from the primarily fiscal interest of the Ptolemies.

The relationship of the Ptolemaic census to earlier operations in the country cannot be established exactly. Nor on present evidence is it known whether the Ptolemaic census started under Ptolemy I or II,[7] though the new fiscal measures of Ptolemy II assume such an operation in action. As a state operation concerned with collecting the information needed

---

4. D. Valbelle, "Les recensements dans l'Égypte pharaonique des troisième et deuxième millénaires," *CRIPEL* 9 (1987) 33–49.

5. Valbelle (1987) 41.

6. Herodotus 2.177.2. D. W. Rathbone, "Egypt, Augustus and Roman taxation," *Revue d'histoire ancienne* 4 (1993) 92, emphasises the symbolic aspect of this requirement as a quantification of royal power.

7. The influence of Demetrius of Phaleron has been suggested, most recently by S. B. Pomeroy, "Family history in Ptolemaic Egypt," *Proceedings of the XXth International Congress of Papyrologists* (Copenhagen, 1994) 594.

for effective government, the census joined other operations of central control, and especially the survey of land.[8] For whereas some states concentrate on taxing the land and others on taxing the people, in Ptolemaic (as in Roman) Egypt both were taxed. In Republican Rome, the census served both to record the military strength of the state and to define Roman citizen status; in the monarchy of Hellenistic Egypt the fiscal aim of the census, as of the related land survey and crop reports, was clearly prime.

How was the Ptolemaic census conducted? Two methods may be envisaged: either through personal declaration or through external registration by responsible officials. A combination is also possible, and even likely.[9] For some, household declaration appears to have been the practice; for others, personal details may have been collected by royal officials, the village and royal scribes who appear in some of the records.[10]

The handful of personal declarations that survive display as many discrepancies as features in common. To date only five are known. Of these, two, and possibly four, are from the same census under Ptolemy III (241–240 B.C.); these four also all derive from an army context.[11] The fifth declaration, from a somewhat later date, records a household where the household head is a woman resident in Krokodilopolis, the capital of the Arsinoite nome.[12] The inclusion in some of these declarations of children under taxable age suggests an operation which was still developing.[13] Specific reference to the salt-tax is made in two of these examples,[14] and the fiscal connection of the census

---

8. Cf. the royal order for a comprehensive land survey in 258 B.C. in S. M. Burstein, *The Hellenistic Age from the Battle of Ipsos to the Death of Kleopatra VII* (Cambridge, 1985) 122–23, no. 97.

9. As for the contemporary *apomoira*-tax, *P.Rev.* 36 (259 B.C.). For papyrological references, see J. F. Oates, R. S. Bagnall, W. H. Willis and K. A. Worp, *Checklist of Editions of Greek and Latin Papyri, Ostraca and Tablets*, 4th ed., *BASP Supplement* 7 (Atlanta, GA, 1992). For demotic editions, see *Lexikon der Ägyptologie* IV (Wiesbaden, 1982) s.v. "Papyri, Demotische."

10. *P.Petrie* III 93 (= *P.Gurob* 27, introduction).

11. *P.Frankf.* 5 (241–240 B.C.), household of 8 family members, together with a declaration of livestock; *W.Chrest.* 198 (23 January 240 B.C.), household of 15 including children and hired hands; *P.Lille* I 27 = *W.Chrest.* 199 = Scholl, *Corpus* 87 (253–231 B.C.), family of 7 (5 children) with 13 slaves in one location and 3+ elsewhere; *P.Alex.* 553 = *W.Ost.* I pp. 823–24 (third cent. B.C.), household of 4.

12. *P.Tebt.* III 814.45–58 (227 B.C.?), a household of 2 families, one of 2 females and one of 4 males.

13. Ages recorded in *W.Chrest.* 198 (240 B.C.) and *P.Alex.* 553 (third cent. B.C.).

14. *P.Frankf.* 5 (Year 7, 241–240 B.C.), *eis ta halika*; *P.Tebt.* III 814.45–58 (227 B.C.?), *apographe halikon*.

operation is clear.[15]   There is no standard form of declaration, though all are in Greek; nor is it clear whether such declarations as do survive were made only to tax officials or whether, as later in Roman Egypt, they might be directed simultaneously to other officials within the bureaucracy.[16] The lack of a standard form, combined with the limited number of surviving texts, does not allow the sort of demographic analysis possible from the Roman census returns.[17] Nor is a regular, periodic census known from Ptolemaic Egypt.[18] Those census declarations that do survive are from a limited section of the population—from reasonably well-off families, those with slaves or other workers attached, with livestock and agricultural produce. These were army families, and those from the urban centres; all of these families could function in Greek. Egyptian village families, in contrast, were smaller;[19] these, perhaps, were simply registered by royal officials. The discovery of further documentation may help to clarify this picture.

It is the fiscal application of this census that is illuminated by our new evidence—registers produced for the calculation of dues and for the collection of taxes: the salt-tax, obol-tax, trade and animal-taxes. For it was by a multiplicity of low-level taxes that the rulers exploited the wealth of Egypt and the people who lived in their land.[20] When put together with both Greek and demotic ostraka from Upper Egypt recording the payment of taxes and with the records of tax collectors that have recently been published,[21] these registers provide a coherent picture of the levy of personal taxes as this developed and changed through the second half of the third century B.C. into the second century.

From 263 B.C. it was the salt-tax that formed the most important of the various Ptolemaic taxes.[22] The relation of the salt-tax to the supply of salt

15. The added details for livestock (*P.Frankf.* 5) or agricultural produce (*W.Chrest.* 198 and *P.Alex.* 553) suggest an ever wider fiscal application.

16. Cf. R. S. Bagnall and B. W. Frier, *The Demography of Roman Egypt* (Cambridge, 1994) 21.

17. See Bagnall and Frier, *Demography* (1994).

18. The view of S. L. Wallace, "Census and poll-tax in Ptolemaic Egypt," *AJP* 59 (1938) 437, that a 14-year census period was instituted under Ptolemy IV, remains entirely without support; cf. V. Tcherikover, "*Syntaxis* and *laographia*," *JJP* 4 (1950) 190–91.

19. *P.Sorb.inv.* 212 recto col. ii (229 B.C.).

20. Cf. C. Préaux, *L'économie royale des Lagides* (Bruxelles, 1939) 379–405.

21. *CPR* XIII, in Greek, and *P.Lille dem.* III 101, in demotic, are contemporary and comparable (253–231 B.C.).

22. M. Rostovtzeff, *The Social and Economic History of the Hellenistic World* (Oxford, 1941) 470, suggested a Persian origin for the salt-tax, which also occurs in Seleucid Asia. Since the tax is unrecorded in Egypt before 263 B.C., a Macedonian origin seems more likely.

remains a mystery;[23] but the salt-tax (or *halike*) in Egypt fulfilled the function of a poll-tax, a capitation charge on the adult population of the country—both male and female—with very few exceptions.[24] The age range of those liable to the tax is not known; under the Romans all between the ages of fourteen and sixty-two were liable to the poll-tax. The rates of the Ptolemaic salt-tax have often been studied.[25] A reconsideration, however, of all known receipts results in the following tabulation of (Greek) rates for this tax (Table 1).[26]

TABLE 1.   Salt-tax rates

	Rate A	*Rate B*	*Rate C*
	263–254 B.C.	254/3–231 B.C.	from 243 B.C.[27]
males	1 dr. 3 ob.	1 dr	4 ob.
females	1 dr	0 dr. 3 ob.	1.5 ob.

Some developments are clear. A progressive lowering in the tax rate was accompanied by an extension of those exempted from it. Under the earlier rates instalment payments were regular; with the advent of rate C these disappear. Also coinciding with rate C is the disappearance of the obol-tax (one obol a year charged only on adult males); the obol-tax, it seems, was now subsumed within a salt-tax that otherwise stood at half its previous rate. The overlap of rates B and C in the period 243–231 B.C. remains a mystery. Who was subject to each is unclear; a category distinction appears most likely. With one obol as the standard daily wage during the third century B.C., the annual tax for males at rate C would equal just four days' wages. Since, however, most in Egypt did not work for wages and women too were liable to the salt-tax (although at a lower rate), we should not underestimate the hardship this tax was claimed to cause.[28]

23. Salt was sold by licensed purveyors and its sale was separately taxed: H. Cadell, "Problèmes relatifs au sel dans le documentation papyrologique," *Atti dell' XI congresso internazionale di papirologia* (Milan, 1966) 272–85; *TCDPap.gr.inv.* 273 (second cent. B.C.), reporting a salt-tax official involved in the arrest of a man caught breaking up salt, suggests a connection between the tax and the commodity.

24. Later, in Roman Egypt, a salt-tax and poll-tax (*laographia*) functioned together.

25. Clarysse and Thompson, "The salt-tax rate once again," *Chronique d'Égypte* 70 (1995) 223–29, with references to earlier studies by Uebel, Bagnall, Shelton and Vleeming.

26. Clarysse's new readings for many of these ostraka will be published separately from *Counting the People*; the database is also his.

27. The latest actual receipt is from 219–218 B.C., *O.Varia* 25; for continued levy, see *P.Berl.Eleph.dem.* 13537 verso 6–7 (21 July 217 B.C.); *P.Tebt.* III 880.3 (181–180 or 157/156 B.C.)

28. *P.Cair. Zen.* I 59130.19–20 (256 B.C.).

Exemptions from the salt-tax are recorded in this material. The categories so privileged and their progressive extension reflect governmental concerns. A ruling of Ptolemy II Philadelphus exempted schoolteachers, athletic coaches, (most probably) artists of Dionysus, and victors in the games of the various Alexandrian festivals.[29] The accounts of tax collectors show how the exemptions were put into effect, with those in the special categories subtracted from the total adult numbers before the calculation of the salt-tax dues.[30] Some indication is also provided of the numbers involved. These differed from village to village, depending in part on the number of immigrants, but overall for the Arsinoite nome teachers formed some 0.5 percent of the adult population, the same percentage as athletic coaches.[31] This encouragement of literacy, sport and culture throughout the Ptolemaic countryside tallies well with the record of Ptolemy II, who in Alexandria built up the Library and the Museum. The growing use of Greek in official records, in place of Egyptian demotic, is perhaps a product of this initiative.[32]

In the earlier period, when the obol-tax still functioned, two further groups—Hellenes and Persians—were exempted from that tax, though liable for the salt-tax. Hellenes overall accounted for sixteen percent of civilian adults in the Arsinoite nome, and Persians considerably fewer (not more than one percent). The identity of those included in these two privileged groups remains uncertain, though of the Hellenes some at least can be identified. Some of these tax-Hellenes were certainly ethnic Greeks, but the category also included those from Egyptian families who worked within the administration and came to form part of the privileged group.[33] Greek origins were clearly not necessary for the acquisition of an Hellenic designation; Jews too might count as Hellenes.[34] "Greeks" were no longer Greeks, nor probably

29. *P.Hal.* 1.260–64.

30. *CPR* XIII 1–3 (253–231 B.C.).

31. These and following percentages are based on *P.Lille* I 10 (with new fragment), *P.Lille dem.* III 99, *P.Sorb.inv.* 211 + 212, *P.UB Trier inv.* S109A/13 and *CPR* XIII 1 and 2. In Trikomia, with 42% Hellenes, teachers made up 0.9% of the adult population, *CPR* XIII 1; 2.12–29 (253–231 B.C.).

32. See D. J. Thompson, "Literacy and Power in Ptolemaic Egypt," in A. K. Bowman and G. Woolf (eds.), *Literacy and Power in the Ancient World* (Cambridge, 1994) 76–78.

33. So Thompson, in J. H. Johnson (ed.), *Life in a Multi-Cultural Society: Egypt from Cambyses to Constantine and Beyond*, Studies in Ancient Oriental Civilization 51 (Chicago, 1992) 326; Clarysse, "Some Greeks in Egypt," in ibidem, 52; cf. further *P.Lille dem.* III 101 ii.12 (253–231 B.C.), Petechonsis son of Imouthes, scribe, a Hellene according to his dues.

34. For Jews as Hellenes, see *CPR* XIII 4.109–201, with Clarysse, "Jews in Trikomia," *Congress* XX (1994) 193–203.

"Persians" Persians (though their identity is even more mysterious).[35] Here, it seems, is a new class in the making. As some thousand years later the Arabs were to use the taxation system as an encouragement to conversion, so, it now appears, the Ptolemies were granting dispensation to those prepared to "go Greek," to change their name and *patris*, join the gymnasium and play their part in the new, Greek-language sphere of Ptolemaic Egypt.

The case of the police in these registers is somewhat different. Recorded together with other special categories, the police were not, as far as we know, actually tax exempt; they were not however required to pay the salt and obol-taxes. In a complex banking transaction, in which no money changed hands, their tax formed part of their wages.[36] As regular policemen, or desert-guards, as guards of the granaries or guards of the village, and in yet other more specialised functions, the different police of Ptolemaic Egypt formed a sizeable and socially significant group. Overall they accounted for some two to three percent of the adult population, and they came from among the same Egyptian families as did some of the "Hellenes."[37] For the royal administration their cooperation was crucial, above all in the levy of taxes. The special treatment they received is not hard to understand.

Once the obol-tax was subsumed within the salt-tax, special categories for that tax appear to widen still further: doctors, fullers, brewers, priests and priestesses, and maybe even others, joined the teachers and coaches, the Hellenes and Persians as apparently privileged groups. Whether these represent real exemptions or, perhaps more likely, further book transactions is unclear. Just as a guard-tax (*phylakitikon*), levied on the population at large, was considered as used in part to support the police through a salt-tax remission, so too, the medical tax (*hiatrikon*) might be applied in a similar way. Other special groups were the object of state allowances or *syntaxeis* which perhaps were used in this way. All in all, the picture is one of progressive retreat from earlier levels of taxation. This extension of privilege and the diminution of rate were probably realistic moves on the part of the administration in response to pressure. What we do not know is whether the lowering of dues was accompanied by an improved rate of collection.

35. Known as Medes in demotic (*P.Lille dem.* III 99 verso v.1–7 [229 B.C.]), Persians might perhaps represent Greeks already in residence under the Persians before Alexander's conquest.

36. *P.Petrie* III 93 vii.21–27 (243–210 B.C.), correctly interpreted by Smyly. For the period of the B-rate all in this category were exempted, under the C-rate only males.

37. *P.Lille dem.* III 101 (253–231 B.C.); see further, Thompson, "Policing the Ptolemaic countryside," *Proceedings of the XXI international papyrological congress, Berlin, August* 1995 (forthcoming).

Before turning to look at the tax registers themselves and the administrative structure to which they belong, one aspect of the salt-tax is worth further comment—its definition in cash. Under the Ptolemies most land dues were still defined in kind.[38] The salt-tax, in contrast, was a money tax, and progressive monetarisation of the countryside is a feature of the Egyptian economy that followed Alexander's conquest. Through a system of low-level taxes, to which all were liable, the use of cash joined that of kind throughout the country.

Tax registers came in two main forms, in addition to summary records. There were household listings (A below, Table 2), in which the names of family members followed that of the household head, and there were occupational records, with details of family groups subordinated to the occupation of the household head (B below, Table 3). The following two extracts (Tables 2 and 3) from much longer registers, one in demotic and one in Greek, illustrate the two types:

TABLE 2.   A. Demotic Household List

P.Ash.dem. 1984.93 (4) (after 251/0 B.C.)

1		**The shrine of Anoubis**
2	<	Hetpanoubis son of Teos, the man of Anoubis, 41 (years)
3	<	Ta(?). . . his wife, 46
4		Tamounis, his daughter, 20 (years), **total** 3, of whom 1 (male).
5		**The house of Andromachos**, the 25-aroura man
6		Taues, his wife, (**total**) 2, (of whom) 1 (male).
7		**The house of Ptolemaios**, 100-aroura man
8		Mys, the one without (?) fields
9		Tasis, his wife, 3[. (years)]
10		Dorion, his son
11	<	Tasis, his wife, **total** 4, of whom 2 (male).
12		**The house of Philippos**, the one without (?) fields
13		Kallo (?), his wife
14		Dionysodotos, his son, **total** 3, of whom 2 (male).
15	<	**The house of Imouthes**, son of Marres, the man of the army, 36 (years)
16	<	Senyris, his wife, 31 (years), **total** 2, of whom 1 (male).
17	<	Tryphon (?), the veteran soldier, Year 35 (251/0 B.C.)

38. The *apomoira* on vineyards and orchards is a noteworthy exception, cf. note 9 above.

TABLE 2 (*continued*)

18	<	Philotera, his daughter
19		Demetrios, his son ... [**total** 3, of whom 2 (male)].
20		**The house of Teos**, son of Imouthes, the man of the army, 41 (years)
21		Esoeris, his wife, 29 (years), **total** 2, of whom 1 (male).

TABLE 3. B. Greek occupational register
P.Sorb.inv. 331, frag. 2 (ca. 232 B.C.)

284		**Dog-burier**:
285		Petosiris, son of Herieus
		Nempnophris, his wife, **total** 2, of whom 1 (male).
	X	**Brewers**: Pasis
	X	Terous, his nurse
	/	Petosiris, son of Pasis
290	/	Tetosiris, his wife, **total 4**, of whom 2 (male).
		Fullers: Petosiris
	⟦X⟧	Thethosiris, his daughter, **total** 2, of whom 1 (male).
	⟦X⟧	Psintaes, son of Kollouthes
		Tanaibis, his wife, **total** 2, of whom 1 (male).
295		Stototis, son of Teos
		Senyris, his wife, **total** 2, of whom 1 (male).
		Harpsalis, son of Petosiris
		Thasis, his wife
		Onnophris, **total** 3, of whom 2 (male).
300		Amenneus, son of Petosiris
		Thaubastis, his wife, **total** 2, of whom 1 (male).
		Petenoupis son of Chaiyris
		Anyris, his wife
		Tanithis, his mother, **total** 3, of whom 1 (male).
305		**Total** 14, of whom 7 (male).
		Bath manager: Pasys
		Tekous, his mother
		Orsenouphis, his son, **total** 3, of whom 2 (male).
		Olive-oil merchants: Sochotes
310		Thasis, his wife
		His father, **total** 3, of whom 2 (male).
		Carpenters:
		Thamous, son of Belles
		Thelois, his ⟦wife⟧ sister

	TABLE 3 *(continued)*	

315	Petesouchos, his son	
	Portis, son of Nobonychos	
⟦X⟧	Orsenouphis, his brother	
⟦X⟧	Omosis, his wife, **total** 6, of whom 4 (male).	

Registers of type A would provide the information needed for the tax farmers (*telonai*) to make their assessment and for the tax collectors (*logeutai*) to collect their dues. House by house, these registers record the names, family relationships (wife, daughter, mother, son, brother, sister) or other family attachment (both male and female slaves, nurse, or even groom) with occupations sometimes added for the household head, as here. Local differences, as with census returns, are a feature of the system; the example above (A) is one of the most detailed of all the house-by-house registers to survive. This, for instance, is the only surviving register where ages are noted. Copied perhaps from a census declaration or collected by a meticulous scribe, such information, regularly updated, would help in the deletion from the registers of those above taxable age. The practice, however, was not a general one; some offices were just more energetic than others in what they chose to record. In terms of nomenclature, this is a mixed community, with army-men with Greek names living among the local Egyptians of this Arsinoite village (identity unknown). Hetpanoubis (l.2), whose home is within the shrine of Anoubis, the jackal-god, reflects his allegiance in his theophoric name—a regular practice in Egypt. Not all householders lived in the houses they owned. In the case of Ptolemaios (l.7), the house is his, but another family lived there—Mys, his wife, son and daughter-in-law, four in all. The totalling at the end of each entry comes standardly in the form of "total x, of whom y," with only the number of males specified. Females in these lists are generally recorded by default, their numbers to be obtained by subtracting the males from the total.[39]

Registers of type B are organised according to occupation. On the basis of these lists the different trade taxes could be raised. So, together with the salt-tax records, details are found for the taxes the weavers paid on their lengths of cloth, the beekeepers on their hives or the gooseherds on their geese.[40] Much is the same as in household records; the occupational or status category heading was followed by household listings of those where

39. There are a few exceptions: *P.Sorb. inv.* 331, frag. 17 (ca. 232 B.C.) records *theluka*; 553–55 (second cent. B.C.), *gynaikeia*.

40. *P.Lille dem.* III 99 recto ii.1–8 (229 B.C.); *BGU* VI 1236.6–7 (243–210 B.C.).

the household head belonged to that category. So, in B above there are listed brewers, fullers, a bath manager, olive-oil merchants and carpenters, just a few of the thirty-five or so different occupations of this particular (incomplete) village record. As well as individual household totals, category totals are given (l. 305); all of those in households listed in this way were included under a category, which in practice may have been relevant to the household head alone. Thus, not all listed as brewers, for instance, were necessarily in that business; of the four here (ll. 287–90), it was maybe only Pasis who practised this trade. It is, of course, within the special categories— the teachers, coaches, etc.—that this form of record benefited the wider family group, since all enjoyed the special tax status of the household head. In the case of those with multiple roles, which role to record may well have been disputed. There were different interests at stake; the category adopted need not always reflect an individual's main occupation, especially for those with any chance of entering a privileged category. To this degree, such categorised figures are suspect. The significance of the different check marks in the left margin of these lists cannot be retrieved (see A and B above). In tax registers from Roman Philadelphia some markings represented the payment of taxes.[41] This may be the case here also, or they may reflect some form of cross-check between different forms of register. For through double registration—by both household and occupation—a check could be made on the accuracy of the records.[42]

Surviving registers not only shed light on who the taxpayers were and the taxes they paid. They also make possible a reconstruction of the system with its different levels of record and onward report. For the Arsinoite nome at least there emerges an outline picture of its administrative geography, combined with unusually detailed information for the adult population and units of habitation. It was at the village level that preliminary records were drawn up for later use. Some villages numbered over a thousand adults; some were no more than hamlets. In the second half of the third century B.C. the average Arsinoite settlement, on the basis of thirty-nine units, had a civilian adult population of 321, with a sex ratio of 104 males to 100 females. Administratively, starting from bottom up, villages were then grouped into those tax districts that constituted a tax collector's rounds. Containing around two thousand adults, these districts contained a varying number of villages, depending on their size. Districts with seven villages and hamlets

---

41. A. E. Hanson, "Ancient Illiteracy," *JRA Supplementary Series* 3 (1991) 189.

42. Such an aim was explicit in a similarly dual system of information gathering for the census of nineteenth-century Banaras: B. S. Cohn, *An Anthropologist among the Historians and Other Essays* (Delhi, Oxford, New York, 1987) 233–34.

are known, as are those with only two. What these tax districts were called is nowhere reported; perhaps they were simply the *topoi*, "places," referred to in various contexts.[43] Districts, in turn, were grouped into larger tax areas of around ten thousand adults; these were probably toparchies, though the actual term is absent. In the Arsinoite nome toparchies numbered some two to a meris, and there were three merides in the nome—Herakleides, Themistos and Polemon, named after their first administrators.[44] Elsewhere there was no meris level and a differing number of toparchies made up a nome.[45] The various units, therefore, forming the administrative structure for the salt-tax in the Arsinoite nome were village (or hamlet), district, tax area or toparchy, meris and, finally, nome. Above the level of toparchy figures only—no names—survive.[46] And since, as we have seen, all within a household came under the occupation of household head, at this stage it becomes impossible to separate out the brewer from his sons and sons-in-law, or to know the teachers who actually taught. To nome level, therefore, reports came in from the different toparchies or merides, and from the nome capital figures were presumably sent on to Alexandria, where documentation for all the nomes of Egypt was stored. But no papyri from Alexandria have survived the damp of the coastal region.

A closer consideration of one long toparchy record from the Themistos meris, written in a mixture of demotic and Greek, may serve to introduce some more of the problems and possibilities this material offers. There were five districts to this tax area; the detailed record in Greek for the second district (district B) starts as follows (Table 4).[47]

TABLE 4

1	Situation as of Year 18:	1387 107 11 75 271	
2	605 62	total 2518 (persons),	
3		of whom	
4	male	692 55 6 39 131 332 34	total 1289
5	female	695 52 5 36 140 273 28	total 1229

43. E.g., *P.Gurob* 27.11 (243–210 B.C.), total of *ton topon somata*.

44. *P.Gurob* 27 verso (243–210 B.C.) preserves figures for nine districts, probably two toparchies, of the Themistos meris. For a total adult population for the Arsinoite nome of at least 58,709 adults, see *P.Lille* I 10 (253–231 B.C.), to be reedited with added fragment; some military groups are missing here.

45. For some twelve toparchies in the Herakleopolite nome, see *BGU* XIV index IV D.

46. Cf. *P.Lille* I 10, a central record from the nome capital with numbers only.

47. *P.Sorb. inv.* 212.1–11 (229 B.C.).

TABLE 4 *(continued)*

6	For Year 19:	915 [62] 3 46 217 [396 50]	
7			total 1689
8	male	464 36 1 26 100 [206] 27	total 860
9	female	451 26 2 20 117 190 23	total 829
10	Hellenes	138 2 14 3[6] 2	total 192
11	male	72 1 7 23 1	total 104

Some of the accounting methods are illustrated here. Adult figures from the previous year (Year 18) are followed by current figures (those for Year 19, line 6), which in turn are then broken down in an occupational listing (line 10ff.). As invariably in the third century B.C., Hellenes come first in this breakdown. Immediately a problem arises. Hellenes occur in only five of the seven villages and hamlets of this district, but which five these may have been is unspecified. The lack of a symbol for nought in Greek is a major disadvantage in the compilation of records. Checking back becomes almost impossible. Here, detailed village listing by name was still available in the demotic part of this register, but at the next level, when names were discarded in favour of numbers, the use of these records became confined to the calculation of total taxes due. The possibility of audit was excluded in this system. Similarly, within the lists of names, the lack of alphabetisation may have contributed further to the difficulty of using these registers. For, although developed in Alexandria in the third century B.C., alphabetisation was slow to enter administrative practice.[48] Much, therefore, must have depended on those members of the bureaucracy involved, on the local officials and others who ran the system. For the transfer of information from village to district, to toparchy and meris, and on to nome level implies a permanent administrative structure capable of processing facts and figures on a regular basis. It is, however, not hard to imagine the potential for abuse when checking back and audit were so difficult.

The process of the bureaucracy at work is also illustrated. At all levels, revised and updated totals were recorded on an annual basis. Sometimes there was little change between years but sometimes there was significant change. A comparison of figures for two districts in the same Themistos record already met above illustrates this well (Table 5).[49]

48. L. W. Daly, *Contributions to a History of Alphabetization in Antiquity and the Middle Ages* (Brussels, 1967) 27–28, 45. For early administrative alphabetisation, see *P.Tebt.* IV 1107.36–193, 280–341 (113–112 B.C.); *SB* X 10209 (second to first cent. B.C.). *P.Saq.dem.* I 27 may represent an earlier demotic example.

49. *P.Sorb. inv.* 212 + 211 + 214 (229 B.C.).

TABLE 5.   Village population changes in two Themistos tax districts

District B
Year 18: 230 B.C.

Village	1	%	2	%	3	%	4	%	5	%	6	%	7	%	All	%
Males	692	50	55	51	6	55	39	52	131	48	332	55	34	55	1,289	51
Females	695	50	52	49	5	45	36	48	140	52	273	45	28	45	1,229	49
Total	1,387		107		11		75		271		605		62		2,518	

Year 19: 229 B.C.

Village	1	%	2	%	3	%	4	%	5	%	6	%	7	%	All	%
Males	464	51	36	58	1	33	26	57	100	46	206	52	27	54	860	51
Females	451	49	26	42	2	67	20	43	117	54	190	48	23	46	829	49
Total	915		62		3		46		217		396		50		1,689	

District C
Year 18: 230 B.C.

Village	1	%	2	%	3	%	4	%	5	%	6	%	7	%	All	%
Males	240	45	35	49	88	47	75	49	4	44	163	51	135	44	740	47
Females	289	55	37	51	98	53	77	51	5	56	159	49	173	56	838	53
Total	529		72		186		152		9		322		308		1,578	

Year 19: 229 B.C.

Village	1	%	2	%	3	%	4	%	5	%	6	%	7	%	All	%
Males	238	45	34	49	90	47	73	48	4	57	163	51	125	40	727	46
Females	289	55	36	51	101	53	79	52	3	43	159	49	185	60	852	54
Total	527		70		191		152		7		322		310		1,579	

For district B the thirty-three percent decrease in adult taxpayers (from 2,518 to 1,689) is remarkable; it is visible in every village. Further, although fluctuations may be observed between the various villages, overall the sex ratio of 105 (i.e. 105 males to 100 females) remains the same. By itself this decrease might be thought to indicate some natural catastrophe or large-scale emigration from the area. It appears even more remarkable when compared with figures for district C. For this district little change is recorded between the two years. In village 6 no change at all is recorded, though the figures may of course consist of different individuals; in village 4 the total remains the same but with a somewhat different makeup, and in village 1 the males have decreased by only 2, with no change at all recorded for the number of females. The difference in pattern between these two districts is not easily explained. Since it is inconceivable, however, that epidemic, natural catastrophe or change on the national scene affecting the population at large would respect the borders of tax districts, the efficiency (or lack of efficiency) of different tax collectors seems a more likely explanation.

In evaluating these census and tax operations, which develop within the first hundred years of the new regime and which, in terms of monetary taxes, form a new departure for Egypt, we are unable to compare them with what came before. Whether this is because earlier operations did not employ written records to the same extent, or whether it is simply the chance survival of Fayum mummy cartonnage made up of recycled documents which slants our picture, we can only guess. What is clear, however, is that there were intrinsic limits to the efficiency of these complex records in their third-century B.C. form. Within these limits, a careful check of the figures and information has revealed very few internal inconsistencies or arithmetical mistakes. The care with which these records were copied and passed on down the line suggests the scribes and officials involved were carefully controlled. What was declared and recorded was carefully checked, giving an impression of efficiency and reliability. That impression is not to be trusted.

Commenting on Chinese census figures Braudel notes that they are figures with a fiscal application and "qui dit fisc dit fraude, ou illusion, ou les deux à la fois."[50] Experience elsewhere suggests that ways would be found, even within small rural communities, of evading the enquiries of census and tax officials. The Roman census material shows a shortfall of young adult males;[51] the same group was underrepresented in the 1991 census in the United Kingdom. Just what the Ptolemaic shortfall may have been is a matter for speculation, but we may imagine that ways were found to ensure registration, if at all, in categories liable to the lowest rates of tax. It is, for instance, notable that in district C above, where the farmers are recorded overall these form only forty-seven percent of the total district population (though fifty percent of the men). That surely is an underestimate of the proportion of farmers in

---

50. F. Braudel, *Les structures du quotidien: Le possible et l'impossible* (Paris, 1980) 23.
51. See Bagnall and Frier, *Demography*, 97–98.

these agricultural communities. It may well be the case that some escaped registration—it is striking how few Egyptian households in the same record have sons or daughters registered at home—or it may be that through part-time temple service some farmers entered the lists as shrine bearers, ibis breeders or other lesser priests.[52] Some of the farmers may be hiding in other roles. The unusual menage of a single, male, athletic coach along with nine females in his household probably reflects a similar tendency; with his tax-free status he attracted otherwise unattached female relatives to his home to share the benefit.[53] The point to be noted again is that tax registers have their own inexorable tendency for inexactitude.

There are many aspects of further interest in these lists. Elsewhere I have considered the bilingualism of the material and how changes in the administration are reflected here.[54] The implications of nomenclature within the mixed population of Egypt, the makeup of individual households, the occupational profile of the population at large may all be studied further. Yet the actual operations of the census and salt-tax collection reveal the nature and efficiency of the Ptolemaic administration, as the Macedonian rulers of the third century B.C. developed their control over the population at large. Like the Romans later, the Ptolemaic rulers of Egypt were concerned for the revenues they could raise from men and women alike, from people as well as from land. New land was brought under cultivation, new crops introduced and new settlements established in rural areas. The existing scribal classes were encouraged to retool in Greek, and through census, survey and fiscal measures a new bureaucracy was developed in a country long familiar with such operations. The early success of this system is to be seen on the military front in the Syrian wars, as well as in the quality of entertainment provided at Philadelphus' great festival in Alexandria, when Ptolemaic wealth and power were on international view.

52. *P.Petrie* III 59b, for tax-exempt sacred categories.

53. *P.Sorb. inv.* 212 verso ii.9–10 (229 B.C.), district B; a massage parlour on the side might be an alternative explanation.

54. In Bowman and Woolf (eds.), *Literacy and Power* (1994) 67–83.

PUBLICATIONS OF F. W. WALBANK

1933

Aratos of Sicyon (Thirlwall Prize Essay, 1933). Cambridge: University Press, 1933

1936

"Aratos' attack on Cynaetha." *JHS* 56 (1936) 64–71

"The accession of Ptolemy Epiphanes." *JEA* 22 (1936) 20–34

Review of G. L. Barber, *The historian Ephorus* (Cambridge: University Press, 1935). *JHS* 56 (1936) 103–104

Review of W. W. Tarn, *Alexander the Great and the unity of mankind* (London: Milford, 1933). *JEA* 22 (1936) 109

1937

"The origins of the Second Macedonian War." *JRS* 27 (1937) 180–207 (joint with A. H. McDonald)

Review of E. Kornemann, *Die Alexandergeschichte des Königs Ptolemaios I. von Aegypten: Versuch einer Rekonstruktion* (Leipzig and Berlin: Teubner, 1935). *JHS* 57 (1937) 98–99

Review of G. Daux, *Delphes au IIe et au Ier siècle depuis l'abaissement de l'Étolie jusqu'à la paix romaine* (Paris: de Boccard, 1936). *JHS* 57 (1937) 99–100

Review of W. P. Theunissen, *Ploutarchos' Leven van Aratos met historisch-topographisch commentaar* (Nijmegen: Berkhout, 1935). *JHS* 57 (1937) 100–101

Review of R. Flacelière, *Les Aitoliens à Delphes: Contribution à l'histoire de la Grèce centrale au III siècle av. J.-C.* (Paris: de Boccard, 1937). *JHS* 57 (1937) 271–72

Review of W. H. Porter, *Plutarch's Life of Aratus with introduction, notes and appendix* (Cork and Dublin: Cork University Press, 1937), and A. J. Koster, *Plutarchi vita Arati* (Leiden: Brill, 1937). *CR* 51 (1937) 223–25

1938

"Φίλιππος τραγῳδούμενος: a Polybian experiment." *JHS* 58 (1938) 55–68
Review of R. J. Bonner and Gertrude Smith, *The administration of justice from Homer to Aristotle* (Chicago: University Press, 1938). *GaR* 8 (1938/1939) 61
Review of J. G. C. Anderson, *Cornelii Taciti de origine et situ Germanorum* (Oxford: Clarendon Press, 1938). *GaR* 8 (1938/1939) 126

1939

Review of *The Cambridge ancient history* 12, ed. S. A. Cook and others (Cambridge: University Press, 1939). *GaR* 9 (1939/1940) 54–55
Review of A. Aymard, *Les assemblées de la confédération achaïenne: étude critique d'institutions et d'histoire* (Bordeaux: Feret et fils, 1938) and *Les premiers rapports de Rome et de la confédération achaïenne (198–189 av. J.-C.)* (Bordeaux: Feret et fils, 1938). *CR* 53 (1939) 139–40

1940

Philip V of Macedon (Hare Prize Essay, 1939). Cambridge: University Press, 1940
"Licia telae addere (Virgil, *Georg.* 1.284–6)." *CQ* 34 (1940) 93–104

1941

"A note on the embassy of Q. Marcius Philippus, 172 B.C." *JRS* 31 (1941) 82–93

1942

"Olympichus of Alinda and the Carian expedition of Antigonus Doson." *JHS* 62 (1942) 8–13
"Alcaeus of Messene, Philip V and Rome, Part I." *CQ* 36 (1942) 134–45
Review of Carl A. Roebuck, *A history of Messenia from 369 to 146 B.C.* (Chicago: University Libraries, 1941). *CR* 56 (1942) 39–40
Review of Karl Barwick, *Caesar's Commentarii und das Corpus Caesarianum (Philologus* Suppl.-Band 31 no. 2) (Leipzig: Dieterich, 1938). *CR* 56 (1942) 80–81
Review of M. Rostovtzeff, *The social and economic history of the Hellenistic world* (3 vols., Oxford: Clarendon Press, 1941). *CR* 56 (1942) 81–84
Review of J. Göhler, *Rom und Italien: die römische Bundesgenossenpolitik von den Anfängen bis zum Bundesgenossenkrieg* (Breslauer historische Forschungen 13) (Breslau: Priebatsch, 1939). *CR* 56 (1942) 86–88
Review of Coleman H. Benedict, *A history of Narbo* (Princeton, N.J.: privately printed, 1941). *CR* 56 (1942) 88–89

1943

"Alcaeus of Messene, Philip V and Rome, Part II." *CQ* 37 (1943) 1–13

"Polybius on the Roman constitution." *CQ* 37 (1943) 73–89

Review of John Day, *An economic history of Athens under Roman domination* (New York: Columbia University Press, 1942). *GaR* 12 (1943) 91–92

1944

"Alcaeus of Messene, Philip V and Rome: a footnote." *CQ* 38 (1944) 87–88

"The causes of Greek decline." *JHS* 64 (1944) 10–20. Résumé in *PCA* 41 (1944) 11–12

Review of R. S. Rogers, *Studies in the reign of Tiberius: some imperial virtues of Tiberius and Drusus Julius Caesar* (Baltimore: Johns Hopkins, 1943). *GaR* 13 (1944) 29–30

Review of F. E. Adcock, *The Roman art of war* (Martin Classical Lectures 8) (Cambridge, Mass.: Harvard University Press, 1940). *GaR* 13 (1944) 30–31

1945

"Polybius, Philinus and the First Punic War." *CQ* 39 (1945) 1–18

"Men and donkeys." *CQ* 39 (1945) 122

"Phalaris' bull in Timaeus (Diod. Sic. xiii.90.4–7)." *CR* 59 (1945) 39–42

Review of G. M. Calhoun, *Introduction to Greek legal science* (Oxford: Clarendon Press, 1944). *GaR* 14 (1945) 30

Review of R. Taubenschlag, *The law of Greco-Roman Egypt in the light of papyri, 332 B.C.– 640 A.D.* (New York: Herald Square Press, 1944). *GaR* 14 (1945) 93

1946

The decline of the Roman Empire in the West. London: Cobbett Press, 1946

"Classical studies in Great Britain during the war," with an appendix on publications 1940–1945. *BAGB* n.s. 1 (1946) 73–105 (joint with I. F. Brash)

"Polybius and the growth of Rome." Résumé in *PCA* 43 (1946) 11–12

Review of J. L. Myres, *Mediterranean culture* (Frazer Lecture, 1943) (Cambridge: University Press, 1943). *GaR* 15 (1946) 31

Review of M. Feyel, *Polybe et l'histoire de Béotie au IIIe siècle avant notre ère* (Paris: de Boccard, 1942). *CR* 60 (1946) 41–42

1947

Review of J. Vallejo, *Tito Livio, libro xxi: edición, estudio preliminar y comentario* (Madrid: Instituto "Antonio de Nebrija," 1946). *CR* 61 (1947) 107–109

Review of S. Accame, *Il dominio romano in Grecia dalla guerra acaica ad Augusto* (Rome: Signorelli, 1946). *JRS* 37 (1947) 205–207

Review of J. H. Thiel, *Studies on the history of Roman sea-power in Republican times* (Amsterdam: North Holland Publishing Co., 1946). *Erasmus* 1 (1947) 655–58

1948

"The geography of Polybius." *C et M* 9 (1948) 155–82

Review of W. Kendrick Pritchett, *The five Attic tribes after Kleisthenes* (Baltimore: privately printed, 1943). *Liverpool Annals of Archaeology* 28 (1948) 88–89

Review of K. Hanell, *Das altrömische eponyme Amt* (Lund: Gleerup, 1946). *CR* 62 (1948) 83–84

Review of Esther V. Hansen, *The Attalids of Pergamon* (Cornell studies in classical philology 29) (Ithaca, N.Y.: Cornell University Press, 1947). *CR* 62 (1948) 149–50

Review of A. R. Burn, *Alexander the Great and the Hellenistic empire* (London: Hodder and Stoughton, 1947). *JHS* 68 (1948) 159–60

Review of H. E. Stier, *Grundlagen und Sinn der griechischen Geschichte* (Stuttgart: Cotta, 1945). *JHS* 68 (1948) 160–61

1949

Oxford classical dictionary, ed. M. Cary and others (Oxford: Clarendon Press, 1949). Articles on: Agis IV, Alexander son of Craterus, Alexander Polyhistor, Antigonus II, Antigonus III, Antigonus of Carystus, Aratus of Sicyon, Areus, Biography (Greek), Chamaeleon, Chremonides, Cleomenes III, Cleonymus, Craterus governor of Corinth, Demetrius of Phalerum, Demetrius II, Demetrius of Pharos, Demiourgoi, Demochares, Demophanes and Ecdelus, Duris, Hermippus of Smyrna, Idomeneus of Lampsacus, Lachares, Lydiades, Marcellinus, Olympiodorus, Philip V, Plutarch, Satyrus, Sosicrates, Stesimbrotus, Stratocles

"Roman declaration of war in the third and second centuries." *CP* 44 (1949) 15–19

Review of G. B. Cardona, *Polibio di Megalopoli: Storie interpretate in lingua italiana* 1: *Libri 1 e 2* (Naples: Edizioni scientifiche italiane, 1948). *CR* 63 (1949) 139

Review of J. O. Thomson, *History of ancient geography* (Cambridge: University Press, 1948). *EHR* 64 (1949) 360–61

Review of M. Cary, *The geographic background of Greek and Roman history* (Oxford: Clarendon Press, 1949). *JHS* 69 (1949) 101

1950

Chambers's encyclopaedia (Oxford: Pergamum Press, 1950). Articles on: Achaea (history), Aetolia, Alexander, Arcadia, Byzantium, Macedonia (ancient history), Thrace (history)

"Naval *triarii* (Polyb. 1.26.6)." *CR* 64 (1950) 10–11

"Greek history, 1945–1947." *YWCS* 34 (1950) 43–59

"The classics in England: some problems of the last decade." In *Atti del congresso della Sodalitas Erasmiana* 1 (Naples: Pironti, 1950) 112–17

"Social problems of antiquity." In *IXe congrès international des sciences historiques* 1: *Rapports* (Paris: Armand Colin, 1950) 261–79

Review of E. Mioni, *Polibio* (Problemi d'oggi, serie letteraria 3) (Padua: Cedam, 1949). *Erasmus* 3 (1950) 273–76

Review of A. J. B. Wace, *Mycenae, an archaeological history and guide* (Princeton, N.J.: University Press, 1949). *Erasmus* 3 (1950) 490–92

Review of H. Goldman and others, *Excavations of Gözlü Kule, Tarsus* 1: *The Hellenistic and Roman periods* (Princeton, N.J.: University Press, 1950). *Erasmus* 3 (1950) 759–62

Review of H. Bengtson, *Einführung in die alte Geschichte* (Munich: Biederstein, 1949). *JHS* 70 (1950) 79

Review of H. U. Instinsky, *Alexander der Grosse am Hellespont* (Godesberg: Küpper, 1949). *JHS* 70 (1950) 79–81

Review of R. Paribeni, *La Macedonia sino ad Alessandro Magno* (Milan: Vita e Pensiero, 1947). *JHS* 70 (1950) 81

Review of E. Kornemann, *Weltgeschichte des Mittelmeerraumes von Philipp II. von Makedonien bis Muhammed* (2 vols., Munich: Biederstein, 1948–1949). *JRS* 40 (1950) 129–32

Review of F. Schachermeyr, *Alexander der Grosse: Ingenium und Macht* (Graz, Salzburg and Vienna: Anton Pustel, 1949). *Gnomon* 22 (1950) 188

1951

"Polybius on the Pontus and the Bosphorus (iv.39–42)." In *Studies presented to D. M. Robinson on his seventieth birthday* 1, ed. G. E. Mylonas (St Louis, Mo.: Washington University, 1951) 469–79

"The problem of Greek nationality." *Phoenix* 5 (1951) 41–60; résumé in *PCA* 48 (1951) 23–24

Review of M. Cary, *The geographic background of Greek and Roman history* (Oxford: Clarendon Press, 1949). *History* 36 (1951) 250

Review of T. Sinko, *De Lycophronis tragici carmine Sibyllino* (extract from *Eos* 43 [1948/1949] 3–39). *CP* 46 (1951) 124–26

Review of K. M. T. Chrimes, *Ancient Sparta, a re-examination of the evidence* (Manchester: University Press, 1949). *CR* n.s. 1 (1951) 98–100

Review of R. Del Re, *Plutarco, Vita di Bruto, revisione del testo, introduzione e note*[2] (Florence: Le Monnier, 1948). *CR* n.s. 1 (1951) 115

Review of H. H. Scullard, *Roman politics, 220–150 B.C.* (Oxford: Clarendon Press, 1951). *EHR* 66 (1951) 566–68

1952

"Trade and industry under the later Roman Empire in the West." In *Cambridge economic history of Europe* 2, ed. M. M. Postan and E. E. Rich (Cambridge: University Press, 1952) 33–85

Review of H. L. Lorimer, *Homer and the monuments* (London: Macmillan, 1950). *Journal of Aesthetics and Art Criticism* 10 (1951/1952) 183–84

Review of E. Demougeot, *De l'unité à la division de l'empire romain: essai sur le gouvernement impérial* (Paris: Adrien-Maisonneuve, 1951). *CR* n.s. 2 (1952) 212–14

1953

The decline of the Roman Empire in the West. New York: Henry Schumann, 1953 (cf. 1946)

"The Roman occupation." In *A scientific survey of Merseyside*, ed. W. Smith (British Association Handbook) (Liverpool: University Press, 1953) 214–20

Review of E. Mireaux, *La reine Bérénice* (Paris: Albin Michel, 1951). *CR* n.s. 3 (1953) 12

Review of W. Hartke, *Römische Kinderkaiser: eine Strukturanalyse römischen Denkens und Daseins* (Berlin: Akademie-Verlag, 1951). *CR* n.s. 3 (1953) 47–49

Review of T. R. S. Broughton, *The magistrates of the Roman Republic* 1: *509–100 B.C.* (New York: American Philological Association, 1951). *CR* n.s. 3 (1953) 111–13

Review of G. Lopuszanski, *La date de la capture de Valérien et la chronologie des empereurs gaulois* (Cahiers de l'Institut d'études polonaises en Belgique 9) (Brussels: Institut d'études polonaises, 1951). *CR* n.s. 3 (1953) 126–27

Review of S. Davis, *Race-relations in ancient Egypt: Greek, Egyptian, Hebrew, Roman* (London: Methuen, 1951). *JHS* 73 (1953) 174

Review of J. L. Myres, *Geographical history in Greek lands* (Oxford: Clarendon Press, 1953). *EHR* 68 (1953) 629–30

Review of V. Ehrenberg, *The people of Aristophanes: a sociology of old Attic comedy* [2] (Oxford: Blackwell, 1951). *Journal of Aesthetics and Art Criticism* 11 (1952/1953) 85–86

1954

"The construction of the sixth book of Polybius." *CQ* n.s. 4 (1954) 97–122 (joint with C. O. Brink)

Review of W. H. Porter, *Plutarch's Life of Dion, with introduction and notes* (Dublin: Hodges, Figgis, 1952). *CR* n.s. 4 (1954) 18–20

Review of T. R. S. Broughton, *The magistrates of the Roman Republic* 2: *99–31 B.C.* (New York: American Philological Association, 1952). *CR* n.s. 4 (1954) 282–83

Review of S. Gerevini, *Plutarco, Vita di Flaminino: introduzione, testo, traduzione e commento* (Milan: Marzorati, 1952). *CR* n.s. 4 (1954) 298

Review of Paul-Marie Duval, *La vie quotidienne en Gaule pendant la paix romaine (Ier-IIIe siècles après J.-C.)* (Paris: Hachette, 1952). *Erasmus* 7 (1954) 49–51

Review of Maurice Holleaux, *Études d'épigraphie et d'histoire grecques* 4: *Rome, la Macédoine et l'orient grec, première partie*, ed. L. Robert (Paris: Adrien-Maisonneuve, 1952). *Erasmus* 7 (1954) 51–54

Review of J. Béranger, *Recherches sur l'aspect idéologique du principat* (Schweizerische Beiträge zur Altertumswissenschaft 6) (Basel: Friedrich Reinhardt, 1953). *Erasmus* 7 (1954) 624–27

Review of M. Grant, *Ancient history* (London: Methuen, 1952). *History* 39 (1954) 102

Review of P. Grimal, *La vie à Rome dans l'antiquité* (Que sais-je?) (Paris: Presses universitaires de France, 1953). *History* 39 (1954) 293

Review of Pauly's *Realencyclopädie der classischen Altertumswissenschaft* 21.2 (Polemon-Pontanene), ed. K. Ziegler (Stuttgart: Druckenmüller, 1952). *JHS* 74 (1954) 185–86

Review of H. H. Scullard, *A history of the Roman world, 753 to 146 B.C.* [2] (London: Methuen, 1951). *JRS* 44 (1954) 122–23

1955

"Tragic history: a reconsideration." *BICS* 2 (1955) 4–14

Review-discussion of K. von Fritz, *The theory of the mixed constitution in antiquity: a critical analysis of Polybius' political ideas* (New York: Columbia University Press, 1954). *JRS* 45 (1955) 150–55

Review of Piero Meloni, *Perseo e la fine della monarchia macedone* (Rome: "L'Erma" di Bretschneider, 1953). *JHS* 75 (1955) 194–95

Review of A. Aymard and J. Auboyer, *L'orient et la Grèce* (Histoire générale des civilisations 1) (Paris: Presses universitaires de France, 1953). *History* 40 (1955) 116–17

Review of A. Aymard and J. Auboyer, *Rome et son empire* (Histoire générale des civilisations 2) (Paris: Presses universitaires de France, 1954). *History* 40 (1955) 326–27

Review of Maria Teresa Piraino, *Antigono Dosone re di Macedonia* (Estratto dagli Atti dell'Accademia di Scienze Lettere e Arti di Palermo, serie 4, vol. 13, 1952–1953) (Palermo: Accademia, 1954). *Gnomon* 27 (1955) 300

Review of Maurice Holleaux, *Études d'épigraphie et d'histoire grecques* 4: *Rome, la Macédoine et l'orient grec, premiere partie*, ed. L. Robert (Paris: Adrien-Maisonneuve, 1952). *CR* n.s. 5 (1955) 220

Review of S. I. Oost, *Roman policy in Epirus and Acarnania in the age of the Roman conquest of Greece* (Arnold Foundation Studies n.s. 4) (Dallas: Southern Methodist University Press, 1954). *CR* n.s. 5 (1955) 303–304

1956

"Some reflections on Hannibal's pass." *JRS* 46 (1956) 37–45

Review of H. Hubert, *Les Germains* (Évolution de l'humanité) (Paris: Albin Michel, 1952). *Erasmus* 9 (1956) 484–87

Review of Denis van Berchem, *L'armée de Dioclétien et la réforme constantinienne* (Institut français d'archéologie de Beyrouth, Bibliothèque archéologique et historique 56) (Paris: Geuthner, 1952). *Erasmus* 9 (1956) 601–605

Review of S. Katz, *The decline of Rome and the rise of mediaeval Europe* (Ithaca, N.Y.: Cornell University Press, 1955). *CR* n.s. 6 (1956) 291–93

Review of J. A. O. Larsen, *Representative government in Greek and Roman history* (Sather Classical Lectures 28) (Berkeley: University of California Press, 1965). *Gnomon* 28 (1956) 383–85

Review of F. J. Wiseman, *Roman Spain* (London: Bell, 1956). *Bulletin of Hispanic Studies* 33 (1956) 234

1957

A historical commentary on Polybius 1: *Books 1–6*. Oxford: Clarendon Press, 1957

Review of P. R. Franke, *Alt-Epirus und das Königtum der Molosser* (Kallmünz-Opf.: Lassleben, 1955). *CR* n.s. 7 (1957) 59–60

Review of Piero Meloni, *Il valore storico e le fonti del libro macedonico di Appiano* (Annali delle Facoltà di Lettere, Filosofia e Magistero dell'Università di Cagliari 23) (Rome: "L'Erma" di Bretschneider, 1955). *CR* n.s. 7 (1957) 70–72

Review of G. Avenarius, *Lukians Schrift zur Geschichtsschreibung* (Diss. Frankfurt a/M, 1954) (Meisenheim am Glan: Anton Hain, 1956). *Gnomon* 29 (1957) 416–19

1958

Review of A. K. Narain, *The Indo-Greeks* (Oxford: Clarendon Press, 1957). *History* 43 (1958) 125–26

Review of Paul Cloché, *Un fondateur d'empire: Philippe II, roi de Macédoine (383/2–336/5)* (St Etienne: Dumas, 1955). *CR* n.s. 8 (1958) 156–58

Review of H. Berve, *Dion* (Akademie der Wissenschaften und der Literatur in Mainz: Abhandlungen der geistes- und sozialwissenschaftlichen Klasse, 1956 no.10) (Wiesbaden: Steiner, 1957). *CR* n.s. 8 (1958) 269–71

Review of M. Grant, *Roman history from coins* (Cambridge: University Press, 1958), and K. D. White, *Historical Roman coins illustrating the period 44 B.C. to A.D. 55* (Grahamstown: Rhodes University, 1958). *JRS* 48 (1958) 228–29

1959

Review of P. Lévêque, *Pyrrhos* (Bibliothèque des écoles françaises d'Athènes et de Rome 185) (Paris: de Boccard, 1957). *EHR* 74 (1959) 93–94

Review of T. S. Brown, *Timaeus of Tauromenium* (University of California Studies in History 55) (Berkeley: University of California Press, 1958). *EHR* 74 (1959) 333–34

Review of K. Latte and others, *Histoire et historiens dans l'antiquité* (Entretiens sur l'antiquité classique 4) (Vandoeuvres-Geneva: Fondation Hardt, 1958). *JRS* 49 (1959) 194–96

Review of R. Syme, *Colonial élites: Rome, Spain and the Americas* (The Whidden Lectures, 1954) (Oxford: University Press, 1958). *JRS* 49 (1959) 217

Review of *Acta congressus Madvigiani: Proceedings of the second international congress of classical studies, Copenhagen, 1954*, ed. C. Høeg and others (5 vols., Copenhagen: Munksgaard (1–4), Nordisk Sprag- og Kulturforlag (5), 1957–1958). *JRS* 49 (1959) 218

Review of A. J. Toynbee, *Hellenism: the history of a civilisation* (Home University Library) (London: Oxford University Press, 1959). *History* 44 (1959) 244–45

1960

"History and tragedy." *Historia* 9 (1960) 216–34

Review of N. G. L. Hammond, *A history of Greece to 322 B.C.* (Oxford: Clarendon Press, 1959). *History* 45 (1960) 131–33

1961

Review of T. R. S. Broughton, *The magistrates of the Roman Republic: Supplement* (New York: American Philological Asociation, 1960). *CR* n.s. 11 (1961) 168–69

Review of J. Carcopino, *Les étapes de l'impérialisme romain* (Paris: Hachette, 1961). *JRS* 51 (1961) 228–29

Review of G. Susini, *Ricerche sulla battaglia del Trasimeno* (Estratto dall'Annuario dell'Accademia etrusca di Cortona 11, 1956–1960) (Cortona: Accademia etrusca, 1960). *JRS* 51 (1961) 232–34

Review of M. I. Finley (ed.), *Slavery in classical antiquity: views and controversies* (Cambridge: Heffer, 1960), and Dev Raj Chanana, *Slavery in ancient India* (New Delhi: People's Publishing House, 1960). *Economic History Review* 14 (1961) 384–85

1962

Introduction to reprint of E. S. Shuckburgh, *The histories of Polybius* (Bloomington, Ind.: Indiana University Press, 1962), vii–xxv

"Polemic in Polybius." *JRS* 52 (1962) 1–12

"Surety in Alexander's letter to the Chians." *Phoenix* 16 (1962) 178–80

Review of E. Manni, *Fasti ellenistici e romani (323–31 a.C.)* (Supplementi a *Kokalos* 1) (Palermo: Banca di Sicilia, 1961). *CR* n.s. 12 (1952) 272–73

Review of B. Ferro, *Le origini della II guerra macedonica* (Estratto dagli Atti dell'Accademia di Scienze, Lettere e Arti di Palermo, serie 4, vol. 19, 1958–1959). *CR* n.s. 12 (1962) 273–74

Review of T. W. Africa, *Phylarchus and the Spartan revolution* (University of California Publications in History 68) (Berkeley: University of California Press, 1961). *CR* n.s. 12 (1962) 315–16

1963

The decline of the Roman Empire in the West. Revised edition in Japanese, trans. T. Yoshimura. Tokyo: Iwanami Shoten, 1963 (cf. 1946)

"Le istituzioni politiche." In *Tutto su Roma antica*, ed. G. Giannelli and U. E. Paoli (Florence: Bemporad-Marzocco, 1963) 193–211

"Polybius and Rome's eastern policy." *JRS* 53 (1963) 1–13

"Three notes on Polybius xii." In *Miscellanea di studi alessandrini in memoria di Augusto Rostagni* (Turin: Bottega d'Erasmo, 1963) 203–13

Review of W. Hoffmann, *Hannibal* (Göttingen: Vandenhoeck and Ruprecht, 1962). *JRS* 53 (1963) 249–50

Review of of P. Pédech, *Polybe, Histoires, Livre xii, texte établi traduit et commenté* (Collection Budé) (Paris: Les Belles Lettres, 1961). *CR* n.s. 13 (1963) 58–60

Review of Claude Mossé, *La fin de la démocratie athénienne* (Paris: Presses universitaires de France, 1962). *CR* n.s. 13 (1963) 317–19

1964

"Polybius and the Roman state." *GRBS* 5 (1964) 239–60

Review of F. E. Adcock, *Thucydides and his History* (Cambridge: University Press, 1963). *History* 49 (1964) 48

Review of C. Hignett, *Xerxes' invasion of Greece* (Oxford: Clarendon Press, 1963). *History* 49 (1964) 48–49

Review of A. W. Gomme, *More essays in Greek history and literature*, ed. D. A. Campbell (Oxford: Blackwell, 1962). *JHS* 84 (1964) 201–202

Review of E. J. Bickerman, *La cronologia nel mondo antico* (Florence: La Nuova Italia, 1963). *CR* n.s. 14 (1964) 186–87

Review of L. Moretti, *Ricerche sulle leghe greche (Peloponnesiaca-Beotica-Licia)* (Problemi e ricerche di storia antica 2) (Rome: "L'Erma" di Bretschneider, 1962). *Erasmus* 16 (1964) 482–83

1965

"Political morality and the friends of Scipio." *JRS* 55 (1965) 1–16

Speeches in Greek historians (Third Myres Memorial Lecture, 1965). Oxford: Blackwell, 1965

Review of R. Syme, *Sallust* (Sather Classical Lectures 33) (Berkeley: University of California Press; Cambridge: University Press, 1964). *History* 50 (1965) 341–42

Review of H. H. Schmitt, *Untersuchungen zur Geschichte Antiochos' des Grossen und seiner Zeit* (*Historia* Einzelschriften 6) (Wiesbaden: Steiner, 1964). *JRS* 55 (1965) 262–64

Review of *Studi annibalici: Atti del convegno svoltosi a Cortona—Tuoro sul Trasimeno—Perugia, ottobre 1961* (Estratto dall'Annuario dell'Accademia etrusca di Cortona 12, 1961–1964) (Cortona: Accademia etrusca, 1964). *JRS* 55 (1965) 309

1966

"The Spartan ancestral constitution in Polybius." In *Ancient society and institutions: studies presented to Victor Ehrenberg*, ed. E. Badian (Oxford: Blackwell, 1966) 303–12

Review of P. Pédech, *La méthode historique de Polybe* (Paris: Les Belles Lettres, 1964). *CR* n.s. 16 (1966) 37–40

Review of M. Fortina, *Cassandro, re di Macedonia* (Turin, etc.: Società editrice internazionale, 1965). *CR* n.s. 16 (1966) 243–44

Review of A. J. Toynbee, *Hannibal's legacy: the Hannibalic War's effects on Roman life* (2 vols., London: Oxford University Press, 1965). *CR* n.s. 16 (1966) 384–88

Review of L. Pareti and others (ed.), *The ancient world, 1200 B.C. to A.D. 500,* parts 1 and 2 (History of Mankind: cultural and scientific development 2) (London: Allen and Unwin, 1965). *History* 51 (1966) 197–98

1967

A historical commentary on Polybius 2: Books 7–18. Oxford: Clarendon Press, 1967

Philip V of Macedon, reprint with corrections. Hamden, Conn.: Archon Books, 1967 (cf. 1940)

"The Scipionic legend." *PCPS* 13 (1967) 54–69

"Political institutions." In *The world of Ancient Rome*, ed. G. Giannelli and U. E. Paoli (London: Macdonald, 1967) 193–211 (cf. 1963)

Review of K. F. Eisen, *Polybiosinterpretationen: Beobachtungen zu Prinzipien griechischer und römischer Historiographie bei Polybios* (Heidelberg: Winter, Universitätsverlag, 1966). *CR* n.s. 17 (1967) 35–36

Review of J. M. Moore, *The manuscript tradition of Polybius* (Cambridge Classical Studies) (Cambridge: University Press, 1965). *CR* n.s. 17 (1967) 151–53

Review of A. H. McDonald, *Republican Rome* (Ancient peoples and places 50) (London: Thames and Hudson, 1966). *CR* n.s. 17 (1967) 190–92

Review of P. Lambrechts, *De geestelijke weerstand van de westelijke provincies tegen Rome* (Med. van de k.Vlaamse Acad. van Belgie, klasse der letteren, 28.1) (Brussels: k.Vlaamse Academie, 1966). *JRS* 57 (1967) 251–52

Review of R. H. Barrow, *Plutarch and his times* (London: Chatto and Windus, 1967). *The Listener* (1967) 692–93

Review of H. Homeyer, *Lukian, Wie man Geschichte schreiben soll, herausgegeben, übersetzt und erläutert* (Munich: Fink, 1965). *Gnomon* 39 (1967) 833–35

1968

Review of V. La Bua, *Filino-Polibio Sileno-Diodoro: il problema delle fonti dalla morte di Agatocle alla guerra mercenaria in Africa* (Σικελικά 3) (Palermo: Flaccovio, 1966). *CR* n.s. 18 (1968) 299–302

Review of J. A. O. Larsen, *Greek federal states, their institutions and history* (Oxford: Clarendon Press, 1968). *CR* n.s. 18 (1968) 190–92

Review of D. Earl, *The moral and political tradition of Rome* (Aspects of Greek and Roman life) (London: Thames and Hudson, 1967). *CR* n.s. 18 (1968) 332–34

Review of E. J. Bickerman, *Chronology of the ancient world* (Aspects of Greek and Roman life) (London: Thames and Hudson, 1968). *JRS* 58 (1968) 251

Review of G. A. Lehmann, *Untersuchungen zur historischen Glaubwürdigkeit des Polybios* (Fontes et commentationes 5) (Münster: Aschendorff, 1967). *JRS* 58 (1968) 253–55

1969

The awful revolution: the decline of the Roman Empire in the West. Liverpool: University Press and Toronto: University Press, 1969

"The historians of Greek Sicily." *Kokalos* 14–15 (1968–1969) 476–98

"The treaty of Apamea (188 B.C.): the naval clauses." *JRS* 59 (1969) 30–39 (joint with A. H. McDonald)

"M. Gelzer's Theorie über die Ursprünge der römischen Historiographie." In *Römische Geschichtsschreibung*, ed. V. Pöschl (Darmstadt: Wissenschaftliche Buchgesellschaft, 1969) 272–79

Review of G. J. D. Aalders, *Die Theorie der gemischten Verfassung im Altertum* (Amsterdam: Hakkert, 1968). *CR* n.s. 19 (1969) 314–17

Review of P. Grimal and others, *Hellenism and the rise of Rome* (London: Weidenfeld and Nicholson, 1968). *CR* n.s. 19 (1969) 317–19

Review of Ioannes A. Vartsos, ʽΟ Πύρρος ἐν ʼΙταλίᾳ, Σκόποι καὶ Δράσις αὐτοῦ (Athens: Pechlivanides, 1967). *CR* n.s. 19 (1969) 332–34

Review of J. Touloumakos, *Der Einfluss Roms auf die Staatsform der griechischen Stadtstaaten des Festlandes und der Inseln im ersten und zweiten Jhdt. v.Chr.* (Göttingen: privately printed, 1967). *JHS* 89 (1969) 179–80

1970

A historical commentary on Polybius 1: *Books 1–6*, corrected reprint. Oxford: Clarendon Press, 1970

Oxford classical dictionary[2], ed. N. G. L. Hammond and H. H. Scullard (Oxford: Clarendon Press, 1970). Additional articles on: Anticleides, Polybius, Silenus

"Pyrrhus." In *Hommes d'état célèbres* 1, ed. J. Pirenne (Paris: Éditions d'art Lucien Mazenod, 1970) 284–87

"Polybius and Macedonia." In *Ancient Macedonia: First International Symposium*, ed. B. Laourdas and Ch. Makaronas (Thessalonica: Institute for Balkan Studies, 1970) 291–307

"The Achaean assemblies again." *MH* 27 (1970) 129–43

"An experiment in Greek union" (Classical Association Presidential Address, 1970). *PCA* 67 (1970) 13–27

Encyclopaedia Britannica (Chicago: Encyclopaedia Britannica, 1970). Articles on: Achaean League, Aetolia, Aetolian League, Alexander III (the Great), Aratus of Sicyon, Archelaus king of Macedon, Demetrius II, Epirus, kingdom of Macedonia, Paeonia, Perseus, Philip II, Philip V, Philopoemen, Plutarch, Polybius, Pyrrhus, Timaeus

Review of K.-E. Petzold, *Studien zur Methode des Polybios und zu ihrer historischen Auswertung* (Vestigia, Beiträge zur alten Geschichte 9) (Munich: Beck, 1969). *JRS* 60 (1970) 252–54

1971

"Livy's fourth and fifth decades." In *Livy*, ed. T. A. Dorey (London: Routledge and Kegan Paul; Toronto: University Press, 1971) 47–72

Review of H. H. Schmitt, *Die Staatsverträge des Altertums* 3: *Die Verträge der griechisch-römischen Welt von 338 bis 200 v.Chr.* (Munich: Beck, 1969). *JHS* 91 (1971) 195

Review of P. Pédech, *Polybe, Histoires, Livre I, texte établi et traduit* (Collection Budé) (Paris: Les Belles Lettres, 1969). *CR* n.s. 21 (1971) 186–88

1972

Polybius (Sather Classical Lectures 42). Berkeley: University of California Press, 1972

"Nationality as a factor in Roman history." *HSPh* 76 (1972) 145–68

Grote Nederlandse Larousse Encyclopedie (Hasselt, Belgium: Heideland-Orbis, 1972). Article on: the treaty of Apamea

Review of T. A. Dorey and D. R. Dudley, *Rome against Carthage* (London: Secker and Warburg, 1971). *JRS* 62 (1972) 181–82

Review of J.-A. de Foucault, *Polybe, Histoires, Livre III, texte établi et traduit* (Collection Budé) (Paris: Les Belles Lettres, 1971). *JHS* 92 (1972) 205–206

1973

Det västromerska rikets fall: ekonomiska, politiska och sociala orsaker. Stockholm: Wahlström and Widstrand, 1973 (cf. 1969)

"Iliria e jugut ne shekujt e trete dhe te dyte para eres se re." *Studime historike* (Tirana) 27 (1973) 137–47

"Symploke: son rôle dans les *Histoires* de Polybe." In *Association Guillaume Budé: Actes du IXe congrès, Rome, 13–18 avril 1973* (Paris: Les Belles Lettres, 1973) 1.28–38

Review of P. Pédech, *Polybe, Histoires, Livre II, texte établi et traduit* (Collection Budé) (Paris: Les Belles Lettres, 1970). *CR* n.s. 23 (1973) 30–32

Review-discussion of Arnaldo Momigliano, *The development of Greek biography* (Cambridge, Mass.: Harvard University Press, 1971). *History and Theory* 12 (1973) 230–40

1974

"Synchronisms in Polybius, Books 4 and 5." In *Polis and imperium: studies in honour of Edward Togo Salmon*, ed. J. A. S. Evans (Toronto: Hakkert, 1974) 59–80

"Polybius between Greece and Rome." In *Polybe*, ed. E. Gabba (Entretiens sur l'antiquité classique 20) (Vandoeuvres-Geneva: Fondation Hardt, 1974) 1–31

"Polybius and the Sicilian straits." *Kokalos* 20 (1974) 5–17

Encyclopaedia Britannica[15] (Chicago: Encyclopaedia Britannica, 1974). Articles in the "Macropaedia" on: Alexander the Great (1.468–73), The Hellenistic age (8.376–92), Plutarch (14.578–80), Polybius (14.762–64)

Review of W. V. Harris, *Rome in Etruria and Umbria* (Oxford: Clarendon Press, 1971). *CR* 24 (1974) 92–95

Review of G. E. M. de Ste. Croix, *The origins of the Peloponnesian War* (London: Duckworth, 1972). *History* 59 (1974) 446

1975

"*Symploke*: its role in Polybius' *Histories*." *YCS* 24 (1975) 197–212 (cf. 1973)

Review of J.-A. de Foucault, *Recherches sur la langue et le style de Polybe* (Paris: Les Belles Lettres, 1972). *CR* n.s. 25 (1975) 28–30

Review of F. P. Rizzo, *La Sicilia e le potenze ellenistiche al tempo delle guerre puniche: i rapporti con Cos, l'Egitto e l'Etolia* (Supplementi a *Kokalos* 3) (Palermo: Banca di Sicilia, 1973). *CR* n.s. 25 (1975) 268–69

Review of W. den Boer, *Some minor Roman historians* (Leiden: Brill, 1972). *CR* n.s. 25 (1975) 275–76

1976

"Southern Illyria in the third and second centuries B.C." *Iliria* 4.1 (1976) 265–72 (cf. 1973)

Foreword to *Illustrated encyclopaedia of the classical world*, ed. M. Avi-Yonah and I. Shatzman (Maidenhead: Sampson Low, 1976) 6–7

Review of Pierre Briant, *Antigone le Borgne: les débuts de sa carrière et les problèmes de l'assemblée macédonienne* (Centre de recherches d'histoire ancienne de l'Université de Besançon 10) (Paris: Les Belles Lettres, 1973). *CR* n.s. 26 (1976) 93–95

Review of B. Shimron, *Late Sparta: the Spartan revolution 243–146 B.C.* (*Arethusa* Monographs 3) (Buffalo, N.Y.: Dept. of Classics, State University of New York at Buffalo, 1972). *CR* n.s. 26 (1976) 140–41

Review of T. Schwertfeger, *Der achaïsche Bund von 146 bis 27 v.Chr.* (Vestigia, Beiträge zur alten Geschichte 19) (Munich: Beck, 1974). *CR* n.s. 26 (1976) 238–39

1977

"Were there Greek federal states?" *SCI* 3 (1976/1977) 27–51

"Polybius' last ten books." In *Historiographia antiqua: commentationes Lovanienses in honorem W. Peremans septuagenarii editae* (Leuven: University Press, 1977) 139–62

"The original extent of the via Egnatia." *LCM* 2 (1977) 73–74

"The causes of the Third Macedonian War: recent views." *Ancient Macedonia* 2: Papers read at the Second International Symposium held in Thessaloniki, 19–24 August 1973 (Thessalonica: Institute for Balkan Studies, 1977) 81–94

Review of H. J. Mason, *Greek terms for Roman institutions: a lexicon and analysis* (American Studies in Papyrology 13) (Toronto: Hakkert, 1974). *CR* n.s. 27 (1977) 136

Review of R. J. A. Talbert, *Timoleon and the revival of Greek Sicily 344–317 B.C.* (Cambridge Classical Studies) (Cambridge: University Press, 1974). *CR* n.s. 27 (1977) 217–18

Review of Klaus Meister, *Historische Kritik bei Polybios* (Palingenesia 1) (Wiesbaden: Steiner, 1975). *JHS* 97 (1977) 186–87

Review of R. Étienne and D. Knoepfler, *Hyettos de Béotie et la chronologie des archontes fédéraux entre 250 et 171 av. J.-C.* (*BCH* Supplément 3) (Athens: École française d'Athènes, 1976). *JHS* 97 (1977) 209

Review of J. von Ungern-Sternberg, *Capua im zweiten punischen Krieg: Untersuchungen zur römischen Annalistik* (Vestigia, Beiträge zur alten Geschichte 23) (Munich: Beck, 1975). *Gnomon* 49 (1977) 630–32

Review of A. Tovar and J. M. Blázquez, *Historia de la Hispania romana: la peninsula Ibérica desde 218 a.C. hasta el siglo V* (Madrid: Alianza Editorial, 1975). *Bulletin of Hispanic Studies* 54 (1977) 84

Review of Ch. M. Danov, *Altthrakien* (Berlin and New York: de Gruyter, 1976). *LCM* 2 (1977) 215–16

1978

La pavorosa revolución: la decadencia del imperio romano en occidente, trans. Doris Rolfe. Madrid: Alianza Universidad, 1978 (cf. 1969)

1979

A historical commentary on Polybius 3: *Books 19–40*. Oxford: Clarendon Press, 1979

Introduction to *Polybius: the rise of the Roman empire,* trans. Ian Scott-Kilvert (Harmondsworth: Penguin Books, 1979) 9–40

"Egypt in Polybius." In *Glimpses of Ancient Egypt: studies in honour of H. W. Fairman,* ed. J. Ruffle, G. A. Gaballa and K. Kitchen (Warminster: Aris and Phillips, 1979) 180–89

"Storiografia tragica e storiografia pragmatica: la scelta di Polibio." In *La storiografia greca: guida storica e critica,* ed. D. Musti (Bari and Rome: Laterza, 1979) 32–40

"Alexander Hugh MacDonald." *JRS* 69 (1979) 249–50

1980

"The idea of decline in Polybius." In *Niedergang: Studien zu einem geschichtlichen Thema,* ed. R. Koselleck and P. Widmer (Stuttgart: Klett-Cotta, 1980) 81–94

"The surrender of the Egyptian rebels in the Nile delta (Polyb. xxii. 16.1–4)." In Φιλίας χάριν: *miscellanea di studi classici in onore di Eugenio Manni* (6 vols., Rome: Giorgio Bretschneider, 1980) 6.2187–97

Review of P. Brulé, *La piraterie crétoise hellénistique* (Centre de recherches d'histoire ancienne de l'Université de Besançon 27) (Paris: Les Belles Lettres, 1978). *CR* n.s. 30 (1980) 82–83

Review of R. Urban, *Wachstum und Krise des achäischen Bundes: Quellenstudien zur Entwicklung des Bundes von 280 bis 222 v.Chr.* (*Historia* Einzelschriften 35) (Wiesbaden: Steiner, 1979). *JRS* 70 (1980) 199–200

1981

"The Hellenistic kingdoms in the third century." Map 11b (drawn by David Cox) in *Atlas of the Greek and Roman world in antiquity,* ed. N. G. L. Hammond (Park Ridge, N.J.: Noyes Press, 1981)

The Hellenistic world (Fontana history of the ancient world). London: Fontana-Collins (paperback); Brighton: Harvester Press and Atlantic Highlands, New Jersey: Humanities Press (hardback), 1981

Contribution to *Seminario di ricerca: Polib. i.11.1ff.,* ed. S. Calderone (estratto dagli *Quaderni Urbinati di cultura classica* 36 [1981] 7–78) 43–46.

"Il giudizio di Polibio su Roma." *Atti dell' Istituto Veneto di Scienze, Lettere ed Arti: Classe di scienze morali, lettere ed arti* 140 (1981–1982) 1–20

"Prelude to Spartacus: the Romans in southern Thrace, 150–70 B.C." In *Spartacus: Symposium rebus Spartaci gestis dedicatum 2050 a.* (Sofia, 1981) 14–27

"Livy, Macedonia and Alexander." In *Ancient Macedonian Studies in honor of Charles F. Edson,* ed. H. J. Dell (Thessalonica: Institute for Balkan Studies, 1981) 335–56

Review of P. A. Stadter, *Arrian of Nicomedia* (Chapel Hill, N.C.: University of North Carolina Press, 1980). *History* 66 (1981) 112

Review of Olivier Picard, *Chalcis et la confédération eubéenne: étude de numismatique et d'histoire (IVe–Ier siècle)* (Bibliothèque des écoles françaises d'Athènes et de Rome 234) (Athens: École française d'Athènes; Paris: de Boccard, 1979). *JHS* 101 (1981) 202

1982

The Hellenistic world. Cambridge, Mass.: Harvard University Press, 1982 (paperback: corrected edition of 1981)
Articles in German translation in *Polybios*, ed. K. Stiewe and N. Holzberg (Darmstadt: Wissenschaftliche Buchgesellschaft, 1982): "Philippos tragoidoumenos" (cf. 1938) 1–23; "Polybios über die römische Verfassung" (cf. 1943) 79–113; "Der Aufbau des sechsten Buches des Polybios" (cf. 1954: with C. O. Brink) 211–58; "Polemik bei Polybios" (cf. 1962) 377–404; "Drei Anmerkungen zu Polybios Buch xii" (cf. 1963) 415–28
"Sea-power and the Antigonids." In *Philip II, Alexander the Great and the Macedonian heritage*, ed. W. L. Adams and E. N. Borza (Washington, D.C.: University Press of America, 1982) 213–36
Review of N. G. L. Hammond, *Alexander the Great: king, commander and statesman* (London: Chatto and Windus, 1981), and D. W. Engels, *Alexander the Great and the logistics of the Macedonian army* (Berkeley: University of California Press, 1978). *History* 67 (1982) 300–301

1983

Il mondo ellenistico. Bologna: Universale Paperbacks il Mulino, 1983 (cf. 1981)
Die hellenistische Welt. Munich: dtv, 1983 (cf. 1981)
"*Via illa nostra militaris:* some thoughts on the Via Egnatia." In *Althistorische Studien: Hermann Bengtson zum 70. Geburtstag dargebracht von Kollegen und Schülern*, ed. H. Heinen, K. Stroheker and G. Walser (*Historia* Einzelschriften 40) (Wiesbaden: Franz Steiner Verlag, 1983) 131–47
"Polibio nel giudizio di Gaetano De Sanctis." *RFIC* 111 (1983) 465–77
"Polybius and the *aitiai* of the Second Punic War." *LCM* 8 (1983) 62–63
"What made a Hellenistic king?" Résumé in *PCA* 80 (1983) 19–20
"Macedonia from 323 to 168 B.C.: political history, political social and economic institutions, intellectual life." In *Macedonia: 4000 years of Greek history and civilization*, ed. M. B. Sakellariou (Athens: Ekdotike Athenon, 1983) 133–69 (also published in Greek)
Review of G. W. Trompf, *The idea of historical recurrence in western thought: from antiquity to the reformation* (Berkeley: University of California Press, 1979). *CP* 78 (1983) 84–86
Review of G. E. M. de Ste. Croix, *The class struggle in the ancient Greek world from the archaic age to the Arab conquests* (London: Duckworth, 1981). *JHS* 103 (1983) 199–200
Review of Simon Hornblower, *Mausolus* (Oxford: Clarendon Press, 1982). *Antiquaries Journal* 63 (1983) 160–62

Review of Jane Hornblower, *Hieronymus of Cardia* (Oxford Classical and Philosophical
Monographs) (Oxford: University Press, 1981). *Antiquaries Journal* 63 (1983)
162–63

1984

Coeditor with A. E. Astin, M. W. Frederiksen, R. M. Ogilvie, *The Cambridge ancient
history* 7.1^2: *The Hellenistic world*. Cambridge: University Press, 1984. Chapters
on "Sources for the period" (1–22); "Monarchies and monarchic ideas" (62–100);
"Macedonia and Greece" (221–56); "Macedonia and the Greek leagues" (446–81)
"Howard Hayes Scullard, 1903–1983." *Gnomon* 56 (1984) 189–91
"Howard Hayes Scullard, 1903–1983." *Proc. Brit. Ac.* 89 (1983) 111–26 (London:
Oxford University Press for the British Academy, 1984)
Review of E. E. Rice, *The grand procession of Ptolemy Philadelphus* (Oxford Classical
and Philosophical Monographs) (Oxford: University Press, 1983). *LCM* 9 (1984)
52–54
Review of P. Roesch, *Études béotiennes* (Centre de recherches archéologiques, Institut
Fernand-Courby, units recherches archéologiques 15) (Paris: de Boccard, 1982).
JHS 104 (1984) 243–44

1985

Selected Papers: Studies in Greek and Roman history and historiography. Cambridge: Uni-
versity Press, 1985
El mondo helenistico, trans. F. J. Lomas. Madrid: Taurus Ediciones, 1985 (cf. 1981)
"Two misplaced Polybian passages from the Suda (xvi.29.1 and xvi.38)." *Xenia:
scritti in onore di Piero Treves,* ed. F. Broilo (Rome: "L'Erma" di Bretschneider, 1985)
227–34
"The Via Egnatia: its original scope and date." In *Studia in honorem Christo M.
Danov Univ. prof. D.Dr. collegae et discipuli dedicaverunt,* ed. A. Fol, M. Tatcheva, N.
Nedjalkov (Terra Antiqua Balcanica 2) (Sofia, 1985) 458–64
Review of C. W. Fornara, *The nature of history in ancient Greece and Rome* (Berkeley:
University of California Press, 1983). *JHS* 105 (1985) 211
Review of A. N. Sherwin-White, *Roman foreign policy in the East 167 B.C.–A.D. 1* (London:
Duckworth, 1984). *JRS* 75 (1985) 235–37

1986

The Hellenistic world. London: Fontana-Collins, 1986 (revised edition)
"The Via Egnatia: some outstanding problems." In *Ancient Macedonia* 4: Proceed-
ings of the Fourth International Symposium, Thessaloniki, Sept. 21–25, 1983
(Thessalonica: Institute for Balkan Studies, 1986) 673–80
Review of Sir Fred Hoyle, *The small world of Fred Hoyle: an autobiography* (London:
Michael Joseph, 1986). *Cambridge Review* 107 (1986) 188–90
Review of Rainer Bernhardt, *Polis und römische Herrschaft in der späteren Republik, 149–
31 v.Chr.* (Berlin and New York: de Gruyter, 1985). *Gnomon* 58 (1986) 515–18

Review of K. Buraselis, *Das hellenistische Makedonien und die Ägäis: Forschungen zur Politik des Kassandros und der drei ersten Antigoniden im ägäischen Meer und in Westkleinasien* (Münchener Beiträge zur Papyrusforschung und antiken Rechtsgeschichte 73) (Munich: Beck, 1982). *JHS* 106 (1986) 243

1987

"Trade and industry under the later Roman Empire in the West." In *Cambridge economic history of Europe* 2^2, ed. M. M. Postan, E. Miller (Cambridge: University Press, 1987) 71–131, bibliography 878–87 (cf. 1952)

"Könige als Götter: Überlegungen zum Herrscherkult von Alexander bis Augustus." *Chiron* 17 (1987) 365–82

Review of M. Vercruysse, *Het thema van de waarheidsverdraaiing in der Griekse geschieds-schrijving: een onderzoek van Polybius en zijn voorgangers* (Verhandelingen van de Koninklijke Academie voor Wetenschappen, Letteren en Schone Kunsten van België, Klasse de Letteren 46, 115) (Brussels: Paleis der Academiën, 1984). *JHS* 107 (1987) 209

1988

The Hellenistic world (Japanese translation). Tokyo: Kyobunken Inc., 1988

A history of Macedonia 3: *336–168 B.C.* Oxford: Clarendon Press, 1988 (joint with N. G. L. Hammond)

Review of Amélie Kuhrt and Susan Sherwin-White, ed., *Hellenism in the East: the interaction of Greek and non-Greek civilizations from Syria to central Asia after Alexander* (London: Duckworth, 1987). *LCM* 13 (1988) 108–12

"Polybius." In *The Blackwell dictionary of historians*, ed. J. Cannon, R. C. H. Davies, W. Doyle, J. P. Greene (Oxford: Blackwell, 1988) 334–35

1989

"Antigonus Doson's attack on Cytinium (*REG* 101 [1988] 12–53)." *ZPE* 76 (1989) 184–92

Coeditor with A. E. Astin, M. W. Frederiksen, R. M. Ogilvie, *The Cambridge ancient history* 8^2: *Rome and the Mediterranean to 133 B.C.* Cambridge: University Press, 1989

"Polybius, Mr Dryden and the Glorious Revolution." In *Studia Pompeiana et Classica in honor of Wilhelmina F. Jashemski* 2: *Classica*, ed. R. I. Curtis (New Rochelle, N.Y.: Caratzas, 1989) 255–71

Coeditor with A. E. Astin, M. W. Frederiksen, R. M. Ogilvie, A. Drummond, *The Cambridge ancient history* 7.2²: *the rise of Rome to 220 B.C.* Cambridge: University Press, 1989

Review of Ramsay MacMullen, *Corruption and the decline of Rome* (New Haven and London: Yale University Press, 1988). *LCM* 14.7 (1989) 108–12

Review of A. Mehl, *Seleukos Nikator und sein Reich 1. Seleukos' Leben und die Entwicklung seiner Machtposition* (Studia Hellenistica 28) (Leuven, 1986). *JHS* 109 (1989) 254–55

Review of Peter Brown, *Body and society: man, woman and sexual renunciation in early Christianity* (New York: Columbia University, 1988; London: Faber and Faber, 1989). *Cambridge Review* 110 (1989) 177–80

Review of Lionel Pearson, *The Greek historians of the Roman west* (Philological Monographs of the American Philological Association 35) (Atlanta: Scholars' Press, 1987). *JRS* 79 (1989) 183–84

1990

"Polybios' Sicht der Vergangenheit." *Gymnasium* 97 (1990) 17–30

"Profit or amusement: some thoughts on the motives of Hellenistic historians." In *Purposes of History: Studies in Greek historiography from the 4th to the 2nd centuries B.C.* (Studia Hellenistica 30), ed. H. Verdin, G. Schepens, E. De Keyser (Leuven, 1990) 253–66

"Polybius, historian of Rome's rise to power." *Omnibus* 20 (September 1990) 21–23

Review of *Kleines Wörterbuch des Hellenismus,* ed. H. H. Schmitt, E. Vogt (Wiesbaden: Harrasowitz, 1988). *Gnomon* 62 (1990) 128–31

Reviews of A. B. Bosworth, *Conquest and empire: the reign of Alexander the Great* (Cambridge: University Press, 1988) and *From Arrian to Alexander: Studies in historical interpretation* (Oxford: University Press, 1988). *JHS* 110 (1990) 254–56

1991

"Timaeus' views on the past." *SCI* 10 (1989/1990) 41–54

Review of *Polybe: Histoires Tome VIII* (*Livres x et xi*), ed. E. Foulon, R. Weil (Paris: Les Belles Lettres, 1990). *CR* n.s. 41 (1991) 35–37

Review of *Staat und Staatlichkeit in der frühen römischen Republik,* ed. W. Eder (Stuttgart: Franz Steiner Verlag, 1990). *CR* n.s. 41 (1991) 144–45

Review of H. Volkmann, *Die Massenversklavungen der Einwohner eroberter Städte in der hellenistisch-römischen Zeit*[2], ed. G. Horsmann (Stuttgart: Franz Steiner Verlag, 1990). *CR* n.s. 41 (1991) 508–509

Review of Peter Green, *Alexander to Actium: the Hellenistic age* (London: Thames and Hudson, 1990). *The Spectator* (26 January 1991) 37–38

1992

Timaios und die westgriechische Sicht der Vergangenheit (*Xenia*: Konstanzer Althistorische Vorträge und Forschungen 29, ed. W. Schuller). Konstanz: Universitätsverlag, 1992

The Hellenistic world, revised edition. London: Fontana (Harper-Collins), 1992

"The Hellenistic world: new trends and directions." *SCI* 11 (1991/1992) 90–113

Review of Peter Green, *Alexander to Actium: the historic evolution of the Hellenistic age* (Berkeley: University of California Press, 1990). *Ancient History Bulletin* 6.1 (1992) 45–54

Review of *The Cambridge ritualists reconsidered: Proceedings of the first Oldfather conference held at Urbana-Champaign, April 27–30, 1989*, ed. W. M. Calder III (Atlanta: Scholars Press, 1991). *Cambridge Review* 113 (1992) 30–32

Review of K. S. Sacks, *Diodorus Siculus and the first century* (Princeton: University Press, 1990). *JRS* 82 (1992) 250–51

Review of E. Gabba, *Dionysius and the history of archaic Rome* (Berkeley: University of California Press, 1991). *JRS* 82 (1992) 257–58

Review of E. Grzybek, *Du calendrier macédonien au calendrier ptolémaïque* (Basel: Reinhardt, 1990). *CR* n.s. 42 (1992) 371–72

Review of R. Orriga, *Il confine conteso: lettura antropologica di un capitolo sallustiano (Bell. Jug. 79)* (Bari: Edipuglia, 1990). *CR* n.s. 42 (1992) 448

Review of J. Grainger, *Hellenistic Phoenicia* (Oxford: Clarendon Press, 1991). *CR* n.s. 42 (1992) 369–70

Review of J. M. O'Brien, *Alexander the Great: the invisible enemy. A biography* (London: Routledge, 1992). *Review: a literary supplement to "Education"* 2 (November 20, 1992) 7

Review of T. P. Wiseman, *Talking to Virgil: a miscellany* (Exeter: University Press, 1992). *Cambridge Review* 113 (1992) 183–84

1993

Ὁ Ἑλληνιστικὸς Κόσμος. Thessalonica: Ekdoseis Vanias, 1993 (cf. 1992)

"The Hellenistic age." In *The Penguin encyclopaedia of classical civilizations*, ed. A. Cotterell (London: Penguin Books, Viking, 1993) 41–80

Review of Domenica P. Orsi, *L'alleanza acheo-macedone: studio su Polibio* (Monumenti e studi 9) (Bari: Edipuglia, 1991). *CR* n.s. 43 (1993) 197–98

Review of J. M. Alonso-Nuñez, *La historia universal di Pompeyo Trogo: coordinades espaciales y temporales* (Madrid: Ediciones clasicas, 1992). *JRS* 83 (1993) 217

1994

"Albania in antiquity." In J. Pettifer, *Albania: Blue Guide* (London: A. and C. Black, 1994) 15–22

"Polybius and the past." In *Tria Lustra: essays and notes presented to John Pinsent* (Liverpool classical papers 3) (Liverpool: *LCM*, 1993, actually 1994) 15–23

"Supernatural paraphernalia in Polybius' *Histories*." In *Ventures in Greek history* (Hammond Festschrift), ed. I. Worthington (Oxford: Clarendon Press, 1994) 28–42

"Response" to papers by K. Bringmann and L. Koenen on "The Social and religious aspects of Hellenistic kingship." In *Images and ideologies: Self-definition in the Hellenistic world*, ed. A. Bullock, E. S. Gruen, A. A. Long, A. Stewart (Berkeley: University of California Press, 1994) 116–24

"Ἡ ΤΩΝ ὉΛΩΝ ᾽ΕΛΠΙΣ and the Antigonids." *Ancient Macedonia: Fifth International Symposium* (Thessalonica, 1994) 3.1721–30

Die hellenistische Welt, revised edition. Munich: dtv, 1994 (cf. 1992)

Review of S. Sherwin-White and A. Kuhrt, *From Samarkhand to Sardis: a new approach to the Seleucid empire* (London: Duckworth, 1993). *JHS* 114 (1994) 211–12

1995

Ἱστορία τῆς Μακεδονίας 3 (Athens and Thessalonica: Malliaris Paideia, 1995), 221–374 (joint with N. G. L. Hammond) (cf. 1988)

" 'Treason' and Roman domination: two case-studies, Polybius and Josephus." In *Rom und der griechische Osten: Festschrift für Hatto H. Schmitt zum 65. Geburtstag,* ed. Ch. Schubert and K. Brodersen (Stuttgart: Franz Steiner Verlag, 1995) 273–85

"Polybius' perception of the one and the many." In *Leaders and masses in the Roman world: Studies in honor of Zvi Yavetz,* ed. I. Malkin and Z. W. Rubinsohn (Leiden: Brill, 1995) 201–22

1996

Il mondo ellenistico, revised edition with new translation. Bologna: Società editrice il Mulino, 1996 (cf. 1992)

"Ennius" and "Polybius." In *Reference guide to world literature,* ed. L. S. Berger (London: St. James Press, 1996) 396–97, 959–60

"Akarnanien in Polybios' Geschichtswerk." In *Akarnanien: eine Landschaft im antiken Griechenland* (Oberhummer-Gesellschaft-München e.V.), ed. P. Berktold, J. Schmid, C. Wacker (Würzburg: Ergon, 1996) 215–22

"Recent work in Hellenistic history (Review article)." *Dialogos: Hellenic Studies Review* 3 (1996) 111–19

"Two Hellenistic processions: a matter of self-definition." *SCI* 15 (1996) 119–30

"Sir Moses Finley." *Dictionary of national biography 1986–1990,* ed. C. S. Nicholls (Oxford: University Press, 1996) 134–36

Review of *The age of Pyrrhus,* ed. T. Hackens, N. D. Holloway, M. R. Holloway, G. Moucharte (Archaeologica Transatlantica 11; Publications d'histoire de l'art et d'archéologie de l'Université Catholique de Louvain 75) (Providence R.I., Louvain-la-Neuve, 1992). *AJA* 100 (1996) 442

Review of *Greek Historiography,* ed. S. Hornblower (Oxford: Clarendon Press, 1994, paperback 1996). *Histos* 1 (December 1996) 1–11 (electronic publication)

GENERAL BIBLIOGRAPHY

Africa, T. *The Immense Majesty: A History of Rome and the Roman Empire.* New York, 1974.

Alcock, S. E. "Tomb Cult and the Post-classical Polis." *AJA* 95 (1991) 447–67.

———. *Graecia Capta: The Landscapes of Roman Greece.* Cambridge, 1993.

———. "Breaking up the Hellenistic World: Survey and Society." In Morris, ed., 171–90.

———. "Minding the Gap in Hellenistic and Roman Greece." In S. E. Alcock and R. G. Osborne, eds., 247–61.

Alcock, S. E., and R. G. Osborne, eds. *Placing the Gods: Sanctuaries and Sacred Space in Ancient Greece.* Oxford, 1994.

Alexandru, A. "Bemerkungen zu den Mariandynern von Herakleia am Pontos." *Studii Clasice* 22 (1984) 19–28.

Allen, R. E. "Attalos I and Aegina." *BSA* 66 (1971) 1–12.

———. *The Attalid Kingdom.* Oxford, 1983.

Anagnostou-Canas, B. "Rapports de dépendance coloniale dans l'Egypte ptolémaïque I: L'appareil militaire." *BIDR*[3] 31–32 (1989/90) 151–236.

———. "Rapports de dépendance coloniale dans l'Egypte ptolémaïque II: Les rebelles de la chôra." In *Proceedings of the XIXth International Congress of Papyrology* II, 323–72. Cairo, 1992.

———. "La colonisation du sol dans l'Egypte ptolémaïque." In S. Allam, ed., *Grund und Boden in Altägypten (Rechtliche und sozio-ökonomische Verhältnisse). Akten des internationalen Symposions Tübingen 18–20 Juni 1990,* 355–74. Tübingen, 1994.

Andreau, J. "Introduction." In M. Rostovtzeff, *Histoire économique et sociale du monde hellénistique* (French trans. of Rostovtzeff, 1941), i–xxix. Paris, 1989.

Antonaccio, C. *The Archaeology of Early Greek "Hero Cult."* Ph.D. Diss. Princeton, 1987.

———. "The Archaeology of Ancestors." In C. Dougherty and L. Kurke, eds., *Cultural Poetics in Archaic Greece,* 46–70. Cambridge, 1993.

———. "Placing the Past: The Bronze Age in the Cultic Topography of Early Greece." In S. E. Alcock and R. G. Osborne, eds., 79–104.

————. *An Archaeology of Ancestors: Tomb Cult and Hero Cult in Early Greece.* Lanham, Maryland, 1995.

Arnim, H. von. *Stoicorum veterum fragmenta.* 4 vols. Leipzig, 1903–1905, 1924.

Asch, R. G., and A. M. Birke, eds. *Princes, Patronage and the Nobility: The Court at the Beginning of the Modern Age.* Oxford, 1991.

Ashcri, D. "Uber die Frühgeschichte von Herakleia Pontike." *Ergänzungsbände zu den Tituli Asiae Minoris,* nr. 5. Wien, 1972.

Ashton, J. *Understanding the Fourth Gospel.* Oxford and New York, 1991.

Astin, A. E. *Scipio Aemilianus.* Oxford, 1967.

————. *Cato the Censor.* Oxford, 1978.

Atkins, E. M. "The Virtues of Cicero's *De Officiis.*" Ph.D. Diss. Cambridge, 1989.

Austin, M. M. "The Age of Kings from Alexander to the Roman Conquest." In R. Browning, ed., *The Greek World,* 185–200. London and New York, 1985.

————. "Hellenistic Kings, War and the Economy." *CQ* 36 (1986) 450–66.

Badian, E. "The Treaty between Rome and the Achaean League." *JRS* 42 (1952) 76–80.

————. *Foreign Clientelae (264–70 B.C.).* Oxford, 1958.

————. "The Hellenistic World." In H. Lloyd-Jones, ed., *The Greeks,* ch. 10. Harmondsworth, 1965.

————. "Rome, Athens and Mithridates." *AJAH* 1 (1976) 105–28.

————. "Hegemony and Independence: Prolegomena to a Study of the Relations of Rome and the Hellenistic States in the Second Century B.C." *Actes du VIIᵉ Congrès de la F.I.E.C.* I (1983) 397–414.

————. "The Consuls, 179–49 BC." *Chiron* 20 (1990) 371–413.

Bagnall, R. S. *The Administration of the Ptolemaic Possessions Outside Egypt.* Leiden, 1976.

————. "Greeks and Egyptians: Ethnicity, Status, and Culture." In *Cleopatra's Egypt: Age of the Ptolemies* (Exhibition Catalogue, Brooklyn Museum), 21–26. New York, 1988.

————. *Egypt in Late Antiquity.* Princeton, 1993.

————. *Reading Papyri, Writing Ancient History.* London, 1995.

Bagnall, R. S., and B. W. Frier. *The Demography of Roman Egypt.* Cambridge, 1994.

Baldwin, J. G. *Daniel: An Introduction and Commentary.* Downers Grove, 1978.

Bar-Kochva, B. *The Seleucid Army: Organization and Tactics in the Great Campaigns.* Cambridge, 1976.

Bauslaugh, R. A. *The Concept of Neutrality in Classical Greece.* Berkeley, 1991.

Bell, C. *Ritual Theory, Ritual Practice.* New York, 1992.

Beloff, M. *The Age of Absolutism 1660–1815.* London, 1954.

Benton, S. "Excavations in Ithaca, III: The Cave at Pólis, I." *BSA* 35 (1934–1935) 45–73.

————. "A Votive Offering to Odysseus." *Antiquity* 10 (1936) 350.

————. "Excavations in Ithaca, III: The Cave at Pólis, II." *BSA* 39 (1938–1939) 1–51.

Bernal, M. *Black Athena: The Afro-Asiatic Roots of Classical Civilization.* 2 vols. London, 1987–1991.

Bernhardt, R. *Polis und römische Herrschaft in der späteren Republik (149–31 v.Chr.).* Berlin and New York, 1985.

Berve, H. *Das Alexanderreich auf prosopographischer Grundlage*. Munich, 1926 (Arno repr. 1973).

Beye, C. R. *Epic and Romance in the Argonautica of Apollonius*. Carbondale and Edwardsville, 1982.

Bichler, R. *"Hellenismus": Geschichte und Problematik eines Epochenbegriffs*. Darmstadt, 1983.

Bickerman, E. J. *Institutions des Séleucides*. Paris, 1938.

———. "Origines Gentium." *CP* 47 (1952) 65–81.

———. *Studies in Jewish and Christian History* I. Leiden, 1976.

———. *Chronology of the Ancient World*. 2nd ed. London, 1980.

———. *Four Strange Books of the Bible: Jonah, Daniel, Koheleth, Esther*. New York, 1984.

Bilde, P., T. Engberg-Pedersen, L. Hannestad, J. Zahle, and K. Randsborg, eds. *Centre and Periphery in the Hellenistic World*. Aarhus, 1994.

Bingen, J. "Grecs et Égyptiens d'après PSI 502." In *Proceedings of the XIIth International Congress of Papyrology*, 35–40. Toronto, 1970.

Black, M. *An Aramaic Approach to Gospels and Acts*. 3rd ed. Oxford, 1967.

Boardman, J. *Athenian Black Figure Vases*. London, 1974.

———. *Athenian Red Figure Vases: The Archaic Period*. London, 1975.

———. *The Greeks Overseas: Their Early Colonies and Trade*. 3rd ed. London and New York, 1980.

———. *Athenian Red Figure Vases: The Classical Period*. London, 1989.

Boccaccini, G. *Middle Judaism: Jewish Thought, 300 B.C.E. to 200 C.E.* Minneapolis, 1991.

Boethius, C. A. "Excavations at Mycenae, XI: Hellenistic Mycenae." *BSA* 25 (1921–1923) 409–28.

Boren, H. C. *Roman Society*. Chapel Hill, 1977.

Bowie, E. L. "Greeks and their Past in the Second Sophistic." In M. I. Finley, ed., *Studies in Ancient Society*, 166–209. London, 1974.

Bradley, R. *Altering the Earth*. Edinburgh, 1993.

Braswell, B. K. *A Commentary on the Fourth Pythian Ode of Pindar*. Berlin and New York, 1988.

Braudel, F. *Les structures du quotidien: Le possible et l'impossible*. Paris, 1980.

Braund, D. *Georgia in Antiquity: A History of Colchis and Transcaucasian Iberia 550 BC–AD 562*. Oxford, 1994.

Bravo, B. *Philologie, histoire, philosophie de l'histoire: Étude sur J. G. Droysen, historien de l'antiquité*. Wroclaw, Warsaw, and Cracow, 1968.

Brillante, C. "Myth and History: History and the Historical Interpretation of Myth." In L. Edmunds, *Approaches to Greek Myth*, 91–140. Baltimore, 1990.

Bringmann, K. *Geschichte und Psychologie bei Posidonius*. *EntrHardt* 32 (1986) 29–66.

———. "The King as Benefactor." In A. W. Bulloch, E. S. Gruen, A. A. Long, and A. Stewart, eds., 7–24.

Briscoe, J. "Q. Marcius Philippus and Nova Sapientia." *JRS* 54 (1964) 66–77.

———. "Rome and the Class Struggle in the Greek States, 200–146 B.C." *P&P* 36 (1967) 3–20. Repr. in M. I. Finley, ed., *Studies in Ancient Society*, 53–73. London, 1974.

———. *A Commentary on Livy, Books XXXI–XXXIII*. Oxford, 1973.

———. *A Commentary on Livy, Books XXXIV–XXXVII*. Oxford, 1981.

Broughton, T. R. S. *Magistrates of the Roman Republic*. 3 vols. Cleveland, 1968.

Browning, R. *History, Language and Literacy in the Byzantine World*. Northampton, 1989.

Brunt, P.A. "On Historical Fragments and Epitomes." *CQ* 30 (1980) 477–94.

——— . *The Fall of the Roman Republic*. Oxford, 1988.

——— . *Roman Imperial Themes*. Oxford, 1990.

——— . *Studies in Greek History and Thought*. Oxford, 1993.

Buffière, F. *Les mythes d'Homère et la pensée grecque*. Paris, 1956.

——— . *Héraclite: Allégories d'Homère*. Paris, 1962.

Bugh, G.R. "Athenion and Aristion of Athens." *Phoenix* 46 (1992) 108–23.

Bulloch, A.W., E. S. Gruen, A. A. Long, and A. Stewart, eds. *Images and Ideologies: Self-definition in the Hellenistic World*. Berkeley, 1993.

Burkert, W. *Greek Religion*. trans. J. Raffan. Cambridge, Mass., 1985.

——— . "Concordia Discors: The Literary and the Archaeological Evidence on the Sanctuary of Samothrace." In N. Marinatos and R. Hägg, eds., *Greek Sanctuaries: New Approaches*, 178–91. London, 1993.

Burstein, S. M. *Outpost of Hellenism: The Emergence of Heraclea on the Black Sea*. Berkeley, 1976.

——— . "Heraclea Pontica: The City and Subjects." *AncW* 2 (1979) 25–28.

——— . "The Aftermath of the Peace of Apamea, Rome and the Pontic War." *AJAH* 5 (1980) 1–12.

——— . *The Hellenistic Age from the Battle of Ipsos to the Death of Kleopatra VII*. Cambridge, 1985.

Bury, J. B., E. A. Barber, E. Bevan, and W. W. Tarn. *The Hellenistic Age*. Cambridge, 1923.

Buxton, R. *Imaginary Greece: The Contexts of Mythology*. Cambridge, 1994.

Cadell, H. "Problèmes relatifs au sel dans le documentation papyrologique." In *Atti dell' XI congresso internazionale di papirologia*, 272–85. Milan, 1966.

Callaghan, P. F. "The Medusa Rondanini and Antiochus III." *BSA* 76 (1981) 59–70.

——— . "Stylistic Progression in Hellenistic Crete." *BICS* 30 (1983) 33–35.

Campbell, M. "Further Notes on Apollonius Rhodius." *CQ* 21 (1971) 402–23.

Canfora, L. "Posidonio nel VI libro di Ateneo: La schiavitù 'degenerata.'" *Index* 11 (1982) 43–56.

——— . *Ellenismo*. Rome, 1987.

Capelle, W. "Griechische Ethik und römischer Imperialismus." *Klio* 25 (1932) 86–113.

Caragounis, C. C. "History and Supra-history: Daniel and the Four Empires." In A. S. van der Woude, ed. 387–97.

Cardauns, B. "Juden und Spartaner." *Hermes* 95 (1967) 317–24.

Cartledge, P. *Sparta and Lakonia: A Regional History 1300–362 B.C.* London, 1979.

——— . *Agesilaos and the Crisis of Sparta*. London, 1987.

——— . *The Greeks: A Portrait of Self and Others*. Oxford, 1993 (rev. ed. 1997).

Cartledge, P., and A. Spawforth, *Hellenistic and Roman Sparta: A Tale of Two Cities*. London and New York, 1989.

Cary, M. *A History of the Greek World from 323 to 146 BC*. 2nd ed. London, 1951.

Catling, H. W. "Archaeology in Greece, 1975–76." *Archaeological Reports* (1975–1976) 3–33.

———— . "Excavations at the Menelaion, Sparta 1973–76." *Archaeological Reports* (1976–1977) 24–42.

Catling, H. W., and Cavanagh, H. "Two Inscribed Bronzes from the Menelaion, Sparta." *Kadmos* 15 (1976) 145–57.

Chamoux, F. *Cyrène sous la monarchie des Battiades.* Paris, 1953.

———— . "Le lancement du navire Argo." *BullSocNatAntiqFrance* (1983) 45–49.

Charles, R. H. *Apocrypha and Pseudepigrapha of the Old Testament* I. Oxford, 1913.

———— . *A Critical and Exegetical Commentary on the Book of Daniel.* Oxford, 1929.

Charlesworth, J. H. *The Old Testament Pseudepigrapha.* Vol. 2. New York, 1985.

Chiranky, G. "Rome and Cotys, Two Problems II: The Date of Sylloge^3, 656." *Athenaeum* 60 (1982) 470–81.

Clarysse, W. "Greeks and Egyptians in the Ptolemaic Army and Administration." *Aegyptus* 65 (1985) 57–66.

———— . "Some Greeks in Egypt." In Johnson, J.H., ed., 51–56.

———— . "Jews in Trikomia." In *Proceedings of the XXth International Congress of Papyrologists,* 193–203. Copenhagen, 1994.

Clarysse, W., and D. J. Thompson. "The Salt-tax Rate once again." *ChrEg* 70 (1995) 223–29.

———— . *Counting the People* (forthcoming).

Clauss, J. J. *The Best of the Argonauts: The Redefinition of the Epic Hero in Book One of Apollonius' Argonautica.* Berkeley, 1993.

Cohen, S. J. D. "Alexander the Great and Jaddus the High Priest according to Josephus." *AJS Review* 78 (1982–1983) 41–68.

———— . "Religion, Ethnicity and 'Hellenism' in the Emergence of Jewish Identity in Maccabean Palestine." In P. Bilde, T. Engberg-Pedersen, L. Hannestad, and J. Zahle, *Religion and Religious Practice in the Seleucid Kingdom,* 204–23. Aarhus, 1990.

Cohn, B. S. *An Anthropologist among the Historians and Other Essays.* Delhi, Oxford, and New York, 1987.

Coldstream, J. N. "Hero Cults in the Age of Homer." *JHS* 96 (1976) 8–17.

Cole, S. G. *Megaloi Theoi: The Cult of the Great Gods at Samothrace.* Leiden, 1984.

Collins, J. J. *Between Athens and Jerusalem: Jewish Identity in the Hellenistic Diaspora.* New York, 1983.

———— . *Daniel: A Commentary on the Book of Daniel.* Minneapolis, 1993.

Comaroff, J. and J. *Ethnography and the Historical Imagination.* Boulder, 1992.

Connor, W. R. "Historical Writing in the Fourth Century B.C. and in the Hellenistic Period." In P. Easterling and B. Knox, eds., *The Cambridge History of Classical Literature.* Vol. I: *Greek Literature,* 458–71. Cambridge, 1985.

Conze, A. *Untersuchungen auf Samothrake.* Vienna, 1875.

Cook, J. M. "The Cult of Agamemnon at Mycenae." In *Geras Antoniou Keramopoullou,* 112–14. Athens, 1953.

———— . "Mycenae 1939–52: The Agamemnoneion." *BSA* 48 (1953) 30–68.

———— . *The Troad.* Oxford, 1973.

———— . "The Topography of the Plain of Troy." In L. Foxhall and J. K. Davies, eds., *The Trojan War: Its Historicity and Context,* 163–72. Bristol, 1984.

Corradi, G. *Studi ellenistici.* Turin, 1929.

Criscuolo, L., and G. Geraci, eds. *Egitto e storia antica dall'ellenismo all'età araba: Atti del colloquio internazionale, Bologna, 31 agusto–2 settembre 1987*. Bologna, 1989.

Crook, J. A. *Consilium Principis*. Cambridge, 1955.

Culham, P. "Chance, Command, and Chaos in Ancient Military Engagements." *World Futures* 47 (1989) 191–205.

Dack, E. van't. "La date de la lettre d'Aristée." *Studia Hellenistica* 16 (1968) 263–78.

Daly, L.W. *Contributions to a History of Alphabetization in Antiquity and the Middle Ages.* Brussels, 1967.

Daux, G. *Delphes au IIe et au Ier siècle*. Paris, 1936.

Davies, J. K. "Cultural, Social, and Economic Features of the Hellenistic World." In *CAH* VII.1 (2nd ed.), 257–320. Cambridge, 1984.

Deininger, J. *Der politische Widerstand gegen Rom in Griechenland, 217–86 v.Chr.* Berlin and New York, 1971.

Delcor, M. "L'histoire selon le livre de Daniel." In A. S. van der Woude, ed., 365–86.

Della Corte, F. *Catone censore*. 2nd ed. Florence, 1969.

Delling, G. "Die Begegnung zwischen Hellenismus und Judentum." *ANRW* II.20.1 (1987) 3–39.

Dengate, J. A. "Coins from the Mycenae Excavations, 1939–62." *BSA* 69 (1974) 95–102.

Derow, P. S. "Polybius, Rome and the East." *JRS* 69 (1979) 1–15.

Deselaers, P. *Das Buch Tobit*. Freiburg and Göttingen, 1982.

Dickie, M. "Talos Bewitched: Magic, Atomic Theory and Paradoxography in Apollonius' Argonautika 4.1638–1688." In F. Cairns and M. Heath, eds., *Papers of the Leeds International Latin Seminar*. Vol. 6: *Roman Poetry and Drama, Greek Epic, Comedy, Rhetoric*, 267–96. Leeds, 1990.

Diels, H., and W. Kranz, *Die Fragmente der Vorsokratiker*. 12th ed. 3 vols. Dublin and Zürich, 1966.

Dodds, E. R. *The Greeks and the Irrational*. Berkeley, 1951.

Dorandi, T. *Filodemo, Storia dei filosofi: La Stoa da Zenone a Panezio*. Leiden, 1994.

Dowden, K. *The Uses of Greek Mythology*. London and New York, 1992.

Dräger, P. *Argo Pasimelousa: Der Argonautenmythos in der griechischen und römischen Literatur.* Teil 1: *Theos Aitios*. *Palingenesia* XLIII. Stuttgart, 1993.

Ducat, J. *Les Hilotes*. Athens, 1990.

———. *Les Pénestes de Thessalie*. Paris, 1994.

Dumont, J.-C. "Conquête et esclavage chez Cicéron: De Re Publica III 36–7." *Ktema* 8 (1983) 113–28.

———. *Servus: Rome et l'esclavage sous la république*. Rome, 1989.

Eckstein, A. M. "T. Quinctius Flamininus and the Campaign against Philip in 198 B.C." *Phoenix* 30 (1976) 119–42.

———. *Moral Vision in the Histories of Polybius*. Berkeley, 1995.

Eddy, S. K. *The King is Dead: Studies in the Near-Eastern Resistance to Hellenism*. Lincoln, 1961.

Edelstein, L., and I. G. Kidd, eds. *Posidonius*. I: *The Fragments*, II: *The Commentary*. Cambridge, 1972 and 1988.

Eder, W.   Review of William V. Harris, *War and Imperialism in Republican Rome 327–70 B.C. Gnomon* 54 (1982) 549–54.

———, ed.   *Die athenische Demokratie im 4. Jahrhundert v.Chr.* Stuttgart, 1995.

Ehrenberg, V.   *The Greek State.* London, 1969.

———.   "The Hellenistic Age." *Encyclopedia Britannica.* 1974 (= *Man, State and Deity,* 64–106).

———.   *Man, State and Deity: Essays in Ancient History.* London, 1974.

Ehrhardt, II.   *Samothrake: Heiligtümer in ihrer Landschaft und Geschichte als Zeugen antiken Geistlebens.* Stutttgart, 1985.

Eilers, C. P.   "Roman Patrons of Greek Cities." Unpublished thesis, Oxford.

———.   "Cn. Domitius and Samos: A New Extortion Trial." *ZPE* 89 (1991) 167–78.

Eissfeldt, O.   *The Old Testament.* trans. P. R. Ackroyd. Oxford, 1965.

Elias, N.   *Die höfische Gesellschaft.* (1976) trans. E. Jephcott as *The Court Society.* Oxford, 1983.

Elton, G.   *Studies in Tudor and Stuart Politics and Government* III. Cambridge, 1983.

Empson, W.   *Collected Poems.* London, 1955.

Errington, R. M.   "Philip, Aratus and the 'Conspiracy of Apelles.'" *Historia* 16 (1967) 19–36.

———.   *Philopoemen.* Oxford, 1969.

———.   *The Dawn of Empire: Rome's Rise to World Power.* London, 1971.

Erskine, A. W.   *The Hellenistic Stoa: Political Thought and Action.* London, 1990.

———.   "Culture and Power in Ptolemaic Egypt: The Museum and the Library of Alexandria." *G&R* 42 (1995) 38–48.

Farnell, L. R.   *Greek Hero Cults and Ideas of Immortality.* Oxford, 1921.

Feeney, D. C.   *The Gods in Epic: Poets and Critics of the Classical Tradition.* Oxford, 1991.

Feldman, L. H.   *Jew and Gentile in the Ancient World: Attitudes and Interactions from Alexander to Justinian.* Princeton, 1993.

Ferguson, W. S.   "Researches in Athenian and Delian Documents II." *Klio* 8 (1908) 341–45.

———.   *Hellenistic Athens.* London, 1911.

Ferrary, J.-L.   "Le discours de Laelius dans le troisième livre du De Re Publica de Cicéron." *MEFRA* 86 (1974) 747–71.

———.   "Le discours de Philus (Cic. de De Re Publica III,8,31) et la philosophie de Carnéade." *REL* 55 (1977) 128–56.

———.   *Philhellénisme et impérialisme: Aspects idéologiques de la conquête romaine du monde hellénistique.* Rome, 1988.

———.   "Traités et domination romaine dans le monde hellénistique." In L. Canfora, M. Liverani and C. Zaccagini, eds., *I trattati nel mondo antico: Forma, ideologia, funzione,* 217–35. Rome, 1990.

———.   "The Statesman and the Law in the Political Philosophy of Cicero." In A. Laks and M.S. Schofield, eds., 48–73.

Festa, N., ed.   *Mythographici Graeci* III.2: *Palaephatus* περὶ ἀπίστων. Leipzig, 1902.

Finley, M. I.   "Between Slavery and Freedom." *CSSH* 6 (1964) 233–49. Repr. in B. D. Shaw and R. P. Saller, eds., *Economy and Society in Ancient Greece,* 116–32. London, 1981.

————. "Colonies: An Attempt at a Typology." *TransRoyHistSoc* 5 ser. 26 (1976) 167–88.

————. *Politics in the Ancient World*. Cambridge, 1983.

Flower, H. I. *Ancestor Masks and Aristocratic Power in Roman Culture*. Oxford, 1996.

Foertmeyer, V. "The Dating of the Pompe of Ptolemy Philadelphus." *Historia* 37 (1988) 90–104.

Forsdyke, J. *Greece before Homer: Ancient Chronology and Mythology*. London, 1956.

Foxhall, L., and H. A. Forbes, "Σιτομετρεία: The role of grain as a staple food in classical antiquity." *Chiron* 12 (1982) 41–90.

Fränkel, H. *Noten zu den Argonautika des Apollonios*. Munich, 1968.

Fränkel, M. *Die Inschriften von Pergamon* VIII.I. Berlin, 1890–1895.

Franko, G. F. "Sitometreia in the Zenon Archive: Identifying Zenon's personal Documents." *BASP* 25 (1988) 13–98.

Fraser, P. M. Review of Hadas, *Hellenistic Culture: Fusion and Diffusion*. *CR* 11 (1961) 145–48.

————. *Ptolemaic Alexandria*. 3 vols. Oxford, 1972.

————. *Rhodian Funerary Monuments*. Oxford, 1977.

Frazer, J. G. *Pausanias' Description of Greece*. Vol. 5. London, 1898.

————. *Folklore in the Old Testament*. London, 1918.

Freudenthal, J. *Alexander Polyhistor und die von ihm erhaltenen Reste judäischer und samaritanischer Geschichtswerke*. Breslau, 1875.

Friedländer, P. "Kritische Untersuchungen zur Geschichte der Heldensage: I, Argonautensage." *RhM* 69 (1914) 299–317.

Fritz, K. von. *The Theory of the Mixed Constitution in Antiquity: A Critical Analysis of Polybius's Political Ideas*. New York, 1954.

Fuks, A. "Patterns and Types of Social-Economic Revolution in Greece from the Fourth to the Second Centuries B.C." *AncSoc* 5 (1974) 51–81 (= *Social Conflict*, ch. 2).

————. *Social Conflict in Ancient Greece*. Jerusalem and Leiden, 1984.

Fusillo, M. *Il tempo delle Argonautiche: Un' analisi del racconto in Apollonio Rodio*. Filologia & Critica vol. 49. Rome, 1985.

Galinsky, G. K. *Classical and Modern Interactions: Postmodern Architecture, Multiculturalism, Decline, and Other Issues*. Austin, 1992.

Gallis, K. I. "Nea Epigrafika Eurêmata apo tê Larisa." *AAA* 13 (1980) 246–62.

Gallo, I. *Frammenti biografici da papiri*. Vol. 2. Rome, 1990.

Gantz, T. *Early Greek Myth: a Guide to Literary and Artistic Sources*. Baltimore, 1993.

Garlan, Y. *Slavery in Ancient Greece*. Ithaca and London, 1988.

Garnsey, P. *Ideas of Slavery from Aristotle to Augustine*. Cambridge, 1996.

Gauthier, P. "Les villes athéniennes et un décret pour un commerçant (IG, II^2, 903)." *REG* 95 (1982) 275–90.

————. *Les cités grecques et leurs bienfaiteurs*. *BCH* Suppl. 12. Paris, 1985.

————. "Les cités hellénistiques." In Hansen, ed., 11–31.

Geertz, C. "Religion as a Culture System." In M. Banton, ed., *Anthropological Approaches to the Study of Religion*, 1–46. London, 1966.

Georges, P. *Barbarian Asia and the Greek Experience: From the Archaic Period to the Age of Xenophon*. Baltimore and London, 1994.

Gera, D. "On the Credibility of the History of the Tobiads." In A. Kasher, U. Rappaport, and G. Fuks, eds., *Greece and Rome in Eretz Israel.* Jerusalem, 1990.

Giangrande, G. *Zu Sprachgebrauch, Technik, und Text des Apollonios Rhodios.* Amsterdam, 1973.

Giovannini, A. "Philip V, Perseus und die delphische Amphiktyonie." In B. Laourdas and C. Makaronas, eds., *Ancient Macedonia,* 147–54. Thessaloniki: Institute for Balkan Studies, 1970.

——— . "Greek Cities and Greek Commonwealth." In A. W. Bulloch, E. S. Gruen, A. A. Long, and A. Stewart, eds., 265–86.

Golan, D. "Der Besuch Alexanders in Jerusalem." *BerlTheolZeitschr* 8 (1991) 19–30.

Goldhill, S. "The Naive and Knowing Eye: Ecphrasis and the Culture of Viewing in the Hellenistic World." In S. Goldhill and R. G. Osborne, eds., *Art and Text in Ancient Greek Culture,* 197–223. Cambridge, 1994.

Goldstein, J. A. "The Tales of the Tobiads." In J. Neusner, ed., *Christianity, Judaism and other Greco-Roman Cults: Studies for Morton Smith at Sixty,* Part III, 85–123. Leiden, 1975.

——— . "Jewish Acceptance and Rejection of Hellenism." In E. P. Sanders, ed., *Jewish and Christian Self-Definition,* 70–81. Philadelphia, 1981.

Gómez Espelosin, F. J. "Filósofos al poder o algunas consideraciones sobre las tiranías atenienses del 88 a.C." *Polis* 2 (1990) 85–97.

Gould, J. "On Making Sense of Greek Religion." In P. E. Easterling and J. V. Muir, eds., *Greek Religion and Society,* 1–33. Cambridge, 1985.

Grabbe, L. *Judaism from Cyrus to Hadrian.* Minneapolis, 1992.

Green, P. *From Alexander to Actium: The Historic Evolution of the Hellenistic Age.* 2nd corr. printing, 1993. Berkeley, 1990.

——— . "The Metamorphosis of the Barbarian: Athenian Panhellenism in a Changing World." In R. W. Wallace and E. M. Harris, eds., *Transitions to Empire: Essays in Greco-Roman History, 360–146 B.C., in Honor of E. Badian,* 5–36. Norman, Oklahoma, and London,1996.

——— , ed. *Hellenistic History and Culture.* Berkeley, 1993.

Griffin, M. *Seneca: A Philosopher in Politics.* Oxford, 1976.

Griffith, G. T. "The Reign of Philip II." In N. G. L. Hammond and G. T. Griffith, *A History of Macedonia.* II, 203–646. Oxford, 1979.

Grote, G. *A History of Greece.* 10 vols. New York, 1888.

Gruen, E. S. "The Origins of the Achaean War." *JHS* 96 (1976) 47–69.

——— . "Greek πίστις and Roman *fides*." *Athenaeum* 60 (1982) 50–68.

——— . *The Hellenistic World and the Coming of Rome.* 2 vols. Berkeley, 1984.

——— . *Studies in Greek Culture and Roman Policy.* Leiden, 1990.

——— . *Culture and National Identity in Republican Rome.* Ithaca, 1992.

——— . "The Polis in the Hellenistic World." In R. M. Rosen and J. Farrell, eds., *NOMODEIKTES: Festschrift M. Ostwald,* 339–54. Ann Arbor, 1993.

Habicht, C. "Herrschende Gesellschaft in den hellenistischen Monarchien." *Vierteljahresschrift für Sozial- und Wirtschaftsgeschichte* 45 (1958) 1–16.

——— . "Hellenismus und Judentum in der Zeit des Judas Makkabäus." *Jhrb-HeidAkad* (1974) 97–110.

——— . *Studien zur Geschichte Athens in hellenistischer Zeit.* Göttingen, 1982.

——— . *Pausanias' Guide to Ancient Greece.* Berkeley, 1985.

——— . "Zu neuen Inschriften aus Thessalien." *Tyche* 2 (1987) 23–28.

——— . "The Role of Athens in the Reorganization of the Delphic Amphictiony after 189 B.C." *Hesperia* 56 (1987) 59–71.

——— . "Athen und die Seleukiden." *Chiron* 19 (1989) 7–26.

——— . "The Seleucids and their Rivals." *CAH* VIII (2nd ed.), 324–87. Cambridge, 1989.

——— . "Athens and the Attalids in the second century B.C." *Hesperia* 59 (1990) 561–77.

——— . "Zu den Epimeleten von Delos, 167–88." *Hermes* 119 (1991) 194–216.

——— . "Athens and the Ptolemies." *CA* 11 (1992) 68–90.

——— . "Zur Geschichte Athens in der Zeit Mithradates VI: Der eponyme Archon im Jahr der 'Anarchie' (88/7)." *Chiron* 6 (1976) 127–35 (= *Athen in hellenistischer Zeit,* 216–23. Munich, 1994).

——— . *Athen in hellenistischer Zeit.* 2nd ed. Munich, 1994.

Hadas, M. "Aristeas and III Maccabees." *HTR* 42 (1949) 175–84.

——— . *The Third and Fourth Books of Maccabees.* New York, 1953.

——— . *Hellenistic Culture: Fusion and Diffusion.* New York and London, 1959.

Hägg, R. "Gifts to the Heroes in Geometric and Archaic Greece." In T. Linders and G. C. Nordquist, eds., *Gifts to the Gods,* 93–99. Uppsala, 1987.

Hahm, D. E. "Posidonius' Theory of Historical Causation." *ANRW* XXXVI 2 (1989) 1325–63.

——— . "Polybius' Applied Political Theory." In Laks and Schofield, eds., 7–47.

Hall, E. *Inventing the Barbarian: Greek Self-Definition through Tragedy.* Oxford, 1989.

Hammond, N. G. L. "Royal Pages, Personal Pages, and Boys Trained in the Macedonian Manner During the Period of the Temenid Monarchy." *Historia* 39 (1990) 261–90.

Hammond, N. G. L., and G. T. Griffith. *A History of Macedonia* II. Oxford, 1979.

Hammond, N. G. L., and F. W. Walbank. *A History of Macedonia* III. Oxford, 1988.

Hansen, E. V. *The Attalids of Pergamon.* 2nd ed. Ithaca and London, 1971.

Hansen, M. H., ed. *The Ancient Greek City-State.* Acta of the Copenhagen Polis Centre, vol.1. Copenhagen, 1993.

Hanson, A. E. "Ancient Illiteracy." In *Literacy in the Ancient World. JRA* Suppl. Series 3 (1991) 159–98.

Hanson, J. O. de G. "The Secret of Medea's Success." *G&R* 12 (1965) 54–61.

Hanson, V. D. *The Other Greeks: The Family Farm and the Agrarian Roots of Western Civilization.* New York, 1995.

Harl, M., G. Dorival, and O. Munnich. *La Bible grecque des Septante.* Paris, 1988.

Harmond, L. *Un aspect social et politique du monde romain: Le patronat sur les collectivités publiques des origines au Bas-Empire.* Paris, 1957.

Harris, W. V. *War and Imperialism in Republican Rome, 327–70 B.C.* Oxford, 1979 (new ed. 1984).

Hartman, F. L., and A. A. DeLella. *The Book of Daniel.* Anchor Bible XXIII. Garden City, 1978.

Hassall, M., M. Crawford, and J. Reynolds. "Rome and the Eastern Provinces at the End of the Second Century B.C." *JRS* 64 (1974) 195–220.

Heath, M. *The Poetics of Greek Tragedy.* London, 1987.

Hedreen, G. "The Cult of Achilles in the Euxine." *Hesperia* 60 (1991) 313–30.

Helly, B. "Grands dignitaires attalides en Thessalie à l'époque de la 3e guerre de Macédoine." *AAA* (1980) 296–301.

Hengel, M. *Judaism and Hellenism.* London, 1974.

———. *Jews, Greeks and Barbarians: Aspects of the Hellenization of Judaism in the pre-Christian Period.* London, 1980.

———. "Die Septuaginta als 'christliche Schriftensammlung', ihre Vorgeschichte und das Problem ihres Kanons." In M. Hengel and A. M. Schwemer, eds., *Die Septuaginta zwischen Judentum und Christentum*, 182–284. Tübingen, 1993.

Henrichs, A. "Two Doxographical Notes: Democritus and Prodicus on Religion." *HSCP* 79 (1975) 93–123.

———. "The Atheism of Prodicus." *BCPE* 6 (1976) 15–21.

———. "The Sophists and Hellenistic Religion: Prodicus as the Spiritual Father of the Isis Aretalogies." In J. Harmatta, ed., *Actes du VIIᵉ Congrès de la Fédération Internationale d'Études Classiques.* Vol. II, 339–53. Budapest, 1984.

Henry, A. S. "Athenian Financial Officials after 303 B.C." *Chiron* 14 (1984) 49–92.

Herman, G. "The 'Friends' of the Early Hellenistic Rulers: Servants or Officials?" *Talanta* 12/13 (1980–1981) 103–49.

———. *Ritualised Friendship and the Greek City.* Cambridge, 1987.

Hermann, P. "Antiochos der Grosse und Teos." *Anadolu* 9 (1965) 29–160.

———. "Zum Beschluss von Abdera aus Teos Syll. 656." *ZPE* 7 (1971) 72–77.

———. "Cn. Domitius Ahenobarbus, Patronus von Ephesos und Samos." *ZPE* 14 (1974) 257–58.

Himmelmann, N. "Realistic Art in Alexandria." *PBA* 67 (1981) 193–207.

Hind, J. G. F. "Mithridates." In *CAH* IX (2nd ed.), 129–64. Cambridge, 1994.

Hirsch, S. W. *The Friendship of the Barbarians: Xenophon and the Persian Empire.* Hanover, 1985.

Hobsbawm, E. J., and T. O. Ranger, eds. *The Invention of Tradition.* Cambridge, 1983.

Hoffman, W. "Hannibal und Rom." In K. Christ, ed., *Hannibal,* 40–74. Darmstadt, 1974.

Holladay, C. R. *THEIOS ANER in Hellenistic Judaism.* Missoula, 1977.

———. *Fragments from Hellenistic Jewish Authors.* Vol. 1: *Historians.* Chico, Calif., 1983

———. *Fragments from Hellenistic Jewish Authors.* Vol. 3: *Aristobulus.* Atlanta, 1995.

Holleaux, M. *Études d'épigraphie et d'histoire grecques* 2 (1938) 153–78.

Hooker, J. "The Cults of Achilles." *RhM* 131 (1988) 1–7.

Howard, G. "*The Letter of Aristeas* and Diaspora Judaism." *JTS* 22 (1971) 337–48.

Hubbe, R. O. "Decrees from the precinct of Asklepios at Athens." *Hesperia* 28 (1959) 169–201.

Hunter, R. L. *Apollonius of Rhodes: Argonautica Book III.* Cambridge, 1989.

———. *The Argonautica of Apollonius: Literary Studies.* Cambridge, 1993.

Huxley, G. L. *Greek Epic Poetry from Eumelos to Panyassis.* London, 1969.

Ingholt, H. "Aratos and Chrysippos on a lead medallion from a Beirut Collection." *Berytus* 17 (1967/1968) 143–77.

Jacoby, F. *Die Fragmente der Griechischen Historiker.* Vols. II A and C. Berlin, 1926.

Jameson, M. "Perseus, the hero of Mykenai." In R. Hägg and G. C. Nordquist, eds., *Celebrations of Death and Divinity in the Bronze Age Argolid*, 213–22. Stockholm, 1990.

Jameson, M., C. N. Runnels, and T. van Andel. *A Greek Countryside: The Southern Argolid from Prehistory to the Present Day*. Stanford, 1994.

Jellicoe, S. "The occasion and purpose of the letter of Aristeas: A re-examination." *NTS* 12 (1966) 144–50.

Jessen, O. "Argonautai." *RE* II.1: 743–87. Stuttgart, 1895.

Johnson, J. H., ed. *Life in a Multi-Cultural Society: Egypt from Cambyses to Constantine and Beyond*. SAOC 51. Chicago, 1992.

Jones, A. H. M. "The Hellenistic Period." *P&P* 27 (1964) 3–22.

Jones, C. P., and C. Habicht. "A Hellenistic Inscription from Arsinoe in Cilicia." *Phoenix* 43 (1989) 317–46.

Jouguet, P. *L'impérialisme macédonien et l'hellénisation de l'Orient*. Paris, 1937 (repr. 1972).

Katzoff, R. "Jonathan and Late Sparta." *AJP* 106 (1985) 485–89.

Kearns, E. *The Heroes of Attica*. London, 1989.

———. "Between God and Man: Status and Function of Heroes and their Sanctuaries." In A. Schachter and J. Bingen, eds., *Le sanctuaire grec*, 65–99. Vandœuvres-Geneva, 1990.

Kidd, I. G. "Posidonius as Philosopher Historian." In M. Griffin and J. Barnes, eds., *Philosophia togata: Essays on Philosophy and Roman Society*, 39–46. Oxford, 1989.

Kirk, G. S. "Ships on Geometric Vases." *BSA* 44 (1949) 93–153.

Kirk, G. S., J. E. Raven, and M. Schofield. *The Presocratic Philosophers: A Critical History with a Selection of Texts*. 2nd. ed. Cambridge, 1983.

Kreissig, H. *Wirtschaft und Gesellschaft im Seleukidenreich: Die Eigentums und die Abhängigkeitsverhältnisse*. Berlin, 1978.

———. *Geschichte des Hellenismus*. Berlin, 1984.

———. "Weiteres zum Hellenismus." *Klio* 67 (1985) 603–607.

Kromayer, J., and G. Veith. *Heerwesen und Kriegführung der Griechen und Römer*. Munich, 1928.

Kuhrt, A. *The Ancient Near East c. 3000–330 B.C.*, 2 vols. London and New York, 1995.

Kuhrt, A., and S. M. Sherwin-White, eds. *Hellenism in the East: The Interaction of Greek and Non-Greek Civilizations from Syria to Central Asia after Alexander*. London, 1987.

Laks, A., and M. S. Schofield, eds. *Justice and Generosity: Studies in Hellenistic Social and Political Philosophy*. Cambridge, 1995.

Lamberton, R., and J. J. Keaney, eds. *Homer's Ancient Readers*. Princeton, 1992.

Lang, A. *Custom and Myth*. London, 1885.

Launey, M. *Recherches sur les armées hellénistiques*. 2 vols. Paris, 1949–1950 (repr. with add. 1987).

Leaf, W. *Troy: A Study in Homeric Geography*. London, 1912.

Lesky, A. "Medeia." *RE* XV.1: 29–65. Stuttgart, 1931.

Lewis, N. *Greeks in Ptolemaic Egypt: Case Studies in the Social History of the Hellenistic World*. Oxford, 1986.

Lind, L. R. "Concept, Action and Character: The Reasons for Rome's Greatness." *TAPA* 103 (1972) 235–83.

Lindsay, J. *The Clashing Rocks*. London, 1965.

Livrea, E. *Apollonii Rhodii Argonautikon Liber IV*. Florence, 1973.

Lloyd, A. B. *Herodotus Book II: Commentary*. Leiden and New York, 1988.

Long, A. A. "Stoic Readings of Homer." In Lamberton and Keaney, eds., 41–66.

Long, A. A., and D. N. Sedley. *The Hellenistic Philosophers*. 2 vols. Cambridge, 1987.

Lonis, R. *L'étranger dans le monde grec: Actes du colloque organisé par l'Institut d'Études Anciennes*. Nancy, 1987.

Lotze, D. *Metaxy Eleutheron kai Doulon. Studien zur Rechtsstellung unfreier Landbevölkerung bis zum 4. Jahrhundert v.Chr.* Berlin, 1959.

MacDonald, G. *Catalogue of Greek Coins in the Hunterian Collection* III. Glasgow, 1905.

Malitz, J. *Die Historien des Posidonius*. Munich, 1983.

Mann, M. "The Autonomous Power of the State: Its Origins, Mechanisms and Results." *Archives européennes de sociologie* 25 (1984) 185–213.

Martinez Lacy, J. R. *Dos aproximaciones a la historiografía de la antigüedad clasica*. Mexico City, 1994.

———. *Rebeliones populares en la Grecia helénistica*. Mexico City, 1995.

Mason, S. "Josephus, Daniel and the Flavian House." In F. Parente and J. Sievers, eds., *Josephus and the History of the Greco-Roman Period*, 161–91. Leiden and New York, 1994.

Mattingly, H. B. "Notes on some Roman Republican Moneyers." *NC* 9 (1969) 95–109.

———. "Some Problems in second century Attic Prosopography." *Historia* 20 (1971) 26–46.

———. "Some Third Magistrates in the Athenian New Style Coinage." *JHS* 91 (1971) 85–93.

McCredie, J. R. "A Samothracian Enigma." *Hesperia* 43 (1974) 454–59.

———. "Recent Investigations in Samothrace, 1965–74." In U. Jantzen, ed., *Neue Forschungen in griechischen Heiligtümern*, 91–102. Tübingen, 1976.

McNamee, K. "Aristarchus and 'Everyman's' Homer." *GRBS* 22 (1981) 247–55.

Meritt, B. "Greek Inscriptions." *Hesperia* 4 (1935) 525–85.

———. "Greek Inscriptions." *Hesperia* 15 (1946) 169–263.

———. "Greek Inscriptions." *Hesperia* 23 (1954) 233–83.

———. "Greek Inscriptions III: Decrees and Other Texts." *Hesperia* 26 (1957) 51–95.

———. "Greek Inscriptions." *Hesperia* 33 (1964) 168–227.

———. "Greek Inscriptions." *Hesperia* 36 (1967) 57–101.

Meuli, K. *Odyssee und Argonautika: Untersuchungen zur griechischen Sagengeschichte und zum Epos*. Berlin, 1921.

Milani, P. A. *La schiavitù nel pensiero politico: Dai Greci al basso medio evo*. Milan, 1972.

Mill, J. S. *Principles of Political Economy* III. Toronto, 1965 (first ed. 1845).

Millar, F. "The Background to the Maccabean Revolution: Reflections on Martin Hengel's *Judaism and Hellenism*." *JournJewStud* 29 (1978) 1–21.

———. "The Greek City in the Roman Period." In M. H. Hansen, ed., 232–60.

Miller, S. G. *Nemea: A Guide to the Site and the Museum*. Berkeley, 1990.

Minns, E. H. *Scythians and Greeks*. Cambridge, 1913.

Momigliano, A. D. "Genesi storica e funzione attuale del concetto di ellenismo." In *Contributo alla storia degli studi classici*, 165–93. Rome, 1955.

————. "J. G. Droysen between Greeks and Jews." *H&T* 9 (1970) 139–53. (= *Studies on Modern Scholarship*, 147–61).

————. *Alien Wisdom: The Limits of Hellenization*. Cambridge, 1975.

————. "Ebrei e Greci." *RivStorItal* 88 (1976) 425–43 (= *Essays on Ancient and Modern Judaism*, 10–28. Chicago, 1994).

————. "Flavius Josephus and Alexander's Visit to Jerusalem." *Athenaeum* 57 (1979) 442–48 (= *Settimo contributo alla storia degli studi classici e del mondo antico.* Rome, 1984).

————. "Greek Culture and the Jews." In M. I. Finley, ed., *The Legacy of Greece: A new Appraisal*, 325–46. Oxford, 1981.

————. "The Origins of Universal History." *AnnScNormSupPisa* ser. 3, 12.2 (1982) 533–60 (= *On Pagans, Jews and Christians*, ch. 3)

————. *On Pagans, Jews and Christians*. Middletown, 1987.

————. *Pagine Ebraiche: English Essays on Ancient and Modern Judaism*. Chicago, 1994.

————. *Studies on Modern Scholarship*. Berkeley, 1994.

Mommsen, Th. *Römische Geschichte* II.2. Berlin, 1889.

Mooren, L. *La hiérarchie de cour ptolémaïque*. Louvain, 1977.

Moreau, J. "Le troisième livre des Maccabées." *ChrEg* 31 (1941) 111–22.

Moretti, L. *Iscrizioni storiche ellenistiche* I. Firenze, 1967.

————. "Un decreto di Arsinoe in Cirenaica." *RFIC* 104 (1976) 385–98.

Morgan, C., and T. Whitelaw. "Pots and Politics: Ceramic Evidence for the Rise of the Argive state." *AJA* 95 (1991) 88–90.

Morgan, M. G. "Politics, Religion and the Games in Rome, 200–150 B.C." *Philologus* 134 (1990) 14–36.

Morris, I. M. "The Use and Abuse of Homer." *CA* 5 (1986) 81–138.

————. "Tomb Cult and the 'Greek Renaissance': the Past in the Present in the 8th Century B.C." *Antiquity* 62 (1988) 750–61.

————, ed. *Classical Greece: Ancient Histories and Modern Archaeologies*. Cambridge, 1994.

Morris, I., and B. Powell, eds. *A New Companion to Homer*. Leiden, New York, and Köln, 1997.

Morrison, J. S., and R. T. Williams. *Greek Oared Ships 900–322 B.C.* Cambridge, 1968.

Morrow, G. R. *Plato's Law of Slavery*. Urbana, 1939.

Mossé, C. "La crise de la 'polis' et la fin de la civilisation grecque." In E. Will, C. Mossé, and P. Goukowsky, eds., 187–244.

Murray, G. *Greek Studies*. Oxford, 1947.

Murray, O. "Aristeas and Ptolemaic Kingship," *JTS* 18 (1967) 337–71.

————. Review of Schneider, *Kulturgeschichte*. *CR* 19 (1969) 69–72.

————. "Forms of Sociality." In J.-P. Vernant, ed., *The Greeks*, 218–53. Chicago, 1995.

Mussies, G. "The Interpretatio Judaica of Thot-Hermes." In H. M. van Voss, D. J. Hoens, G. Mussies, D. van der Plas, H. Te Velde, eds., *Studies in Egyptian Religion*, 89–120. Leiden, 1982.

Nadel, B. I. "The Euxine Pontos as seen by the Greeks." *Epigraphica* 53 (1991) 268–75.

Nagle, D. B., and S. M. Burstein, eds. *The Ancient World: Readings in Social and Cultural History.* Englewood Cliffs, 1995.

Nestle, W. *Vom Mythos zum Logos: Die Selbstentfaltung des griechischen Denkens von Homer bis auf die Sophistik und Sokrates.* 2nd ed. Stuttgart, 1942 (repr. Aalen, 1966).

Nickelsburg, G. W. E. *Resurrection, Immortality and Eternal Life in Intertestamental Judaism.* Cambridge, 1972.

Nicolet, C. "Mithradate et les ambassadeurs de Carthage (et Posidonius fr. 41)." In Raymond Chevallier, ed., *Mélanges d'archéologie et d'histoire offerts à André Piganiol* II, 807–14. Paris, 1966.

——— . *L'ordre équestre à l'époque républicaine,* II: *Prosopographie des chevaliers romains.* *BEFAR,* 207. Paris, 1974.

——— . "Polybe et les institutions romaines." *EntrHardt* 20 (1974) 209–65.

Nicols, J. "Zur Verleihung öffentlicher Ehrungen in der römischen Welt." *Chiron* 9 (1979) 243–60.

——— . "Pliny and the Patronage of Communities." *Hermes* 108 (1980) 365–85.

——— . "Tabulae patronatus: A Study of the Agreement Between Patron and Client-community." *ANRW* II.13 (1980) 535–61.

——— . "Patrons of Greek Cities in the Early Principate." *ZPE* 80 (1990) 81–100.

——— . "Patrons of Provinces in the Early Principate: The Case of Bithynia." *ZPE* 80 (1990) 100–108.

Niese, B. "Die letzten Tyrannen Athens." *RhM* 42 (1887) 574–81.

Nilsson, M. "Die Griechengötter und die Gerechtigkeit." In *Opuscula Selecta* III, 303–21. Lund, 1951–1960.

——— . *The Mycenean Origin of Greek Mythology.* Berkeley, 1932. Repr. with intro. and bib. by E. Vermeule, 1972.

Nissen, H. *Kritische Untersuchungen über die Quellen der vierten und fünften Dekade des Livius.* Berlin, 1862.

Nussbaum, M. C. *The Therapy of Desire: Theory and Practice in Hellenistic Ethics.* Princeton, 1994.

Oates, J. F., R. S. Bagnall, W. H. Willis, and K. A. Worp. *Checklist of Editions of Greek and Latin Papyri, Ostraca and Tablets.* 4th ed. *BASP* Supp. 7. Atlanta, 1992.

Orlandos, A. K. "Ergasiai en tôi tholôtôi taphôi Orchomenou." *AD* 1 (1915) 51–53.

Orrieux, C. *Les papyrus de Zénon: L'horizon d'un grec en Égypte au IIIe siècle avant J.C.* Paris, 1983.

——— . *Zénon de Caunos, parépidêmos, et le destin grec.* Paris, 1985.

Osborne, M. J. *Naturalization in Athens* I. Brussels, 1981.

Parente, F. "The Third book of Maccabees as ideological document and historical source." *Henoch* 10 (1988) 143–82.

Paul, A. "Le troisième livre des Machabées." *ANRW* II.20.1 (1987) 298–336.

Pédech, P. "Polybe et l'éloge de Philopoemen." *REG* 64 (1951) 82–103.

Peremans, W., and E. van't Dack. *Prosopographica Ptolemaica.* Louvain, 1950.

Pfeiffer, R. *A History of Classical Scholarship from the Beginnings to the End of the Hellenistic Age.* Oxford, 1968.

Phillipson, R. "Philonides." *RE* XX.1: 61–73. Stuttgart, 1941.

Piérart, M. "Le héraut du conseil et du peuple à Athènes." *BCH* 100 (1976) 443–47.

Pohlenz, M. *Die Stoa: Geschichte einer geistigen Bewegung.* 2nd ed. Göttingen, 1959.

Polignac, F. de. *La naissance de la cité grecque.* Paris, 1984 (rev. Eng. trans. Chicago, 1995).

——— . "Mediation, competition and sovereignty: the evolution of rural sanctuaries in Geometric Greece." In S. E. Alcock and R. G. Osborne, eds., 3–18.

Pollitt, J. J. *Art in the Hellenistic Age.* Cambridge, 1986.

Pomeroy, S. B. *Women in Hellenistic Egypt from Alexander to Cleopatra.* New York, 1984.

——— . "Family History in Ptolemaic Egypt." In *Proceedings of the XXth International Congress of Papyrologists,* 593–97. Copenhagen, 1994.

Pounder, K. L. "Honors for Antioch of the Chrysaoreans." *Hesperia* 47 (1978) 49–57.

Préaux, C. *L'économie royale des Lagides.* Brussels, 1939.

——— . "Réflexions sur l'entité hellénistique." *ChrEg* 40 (1965) 129–39.

——— . *Le monde hellénistique: La Grèce et l'Orient (323–146 av. J.-C.).* 2 vols. Paris, 1978.

Price, S. R. F. *Rituals and Power: The Roman Imperial Cult in Asia Minor.* Cambridge, 1984.

Price, T. H. "Hero Cult in the 'Age of Homer' and earlier." In G. W. Bowersock, W. Burkert, and M. C. J. Putnam, eds., *Arktouros: Hellenic Studies Presented to Bernard M. W. Knox on the Occasion of his 65th Birthday,* 221–22. Berlin, 1979.

Pritchett, W. K. *The Greek State at War.* Vol. 2. Berkeley, 1974.

Pucci Ben Zeev, M. "Greek and Roman Documents from Republican times in the *Antiquities*: What was Josephus' Source?" *SCI* 13 (1994) 46–59.

Radermacher, L. *Mythos und Saga bei den Griechen.* 2nd ed. Munich and Vienna, 1943 (repr. Darmstadt, 1968).

Rajak, T. "The Jews under Hasmonean rule." *CAH* IX (2nd ed.), 274–309. Cambridge, 1994.

——— . "The Jewish Reception of the LXX in the First and Second Centuries AD: Some Thoughts on Josephus and LXX Daniel." Forthcoming.

Rathbone, D. W. "The Ancient Economy in Greco-Roman Egypt." In L. Criscuolo and G. Geraci, eds., 159–76.

——— . "Egypt, Augustus and Roman Taxation." *Revue d'histoire ancienne* 4 (1993) 81–111.

Rawson, E. "The Eastern Clientelae of Clodius and the Claudii." *Historia* 22 (1973) 219–39.

——— . "More on the Clientelae of the Patrician Claudii." *Historia* 26 (1977) 340–57 (= *Roman Culture and Society,* 102–124, 227–44. Oxford, 1991).

——— . "The Expansion of Rome." In J. Boardman, J. Griffin, and O. Murray, eds., *The Oxford History of the Classical World,* 417–37. Oxford, 1986.

Reden, S. von. "Money and Coinage in Ptolemaic Egypt." In *Proceedings of the XXIst International Congress of Papyrologists* (Berlin, August 1995). Forthcoming.

Reger, G. *Regionalism and Change in the Economy of Independent Delos, 314–167 B.C.* Berkeley, 1994.

Reinhardt, K. "Poseidonios." *RE* XXII:1, 558–826.

Reynolds, J. M. "A Civic Decree from Tocra in Cyrenaica." *ArchClass* 25/6 (1973/1974) 623–30.

——— . *Aphrodisias and Rome.* *JRS* monograph 1. London, 1982.

Rice, E. E. *The Grand Procession of Ptolemy Philadelphus.* Oxford, 1983.

Robert, C. *Die griechische Heldensage*. 4th rev. ed. Berlin, 1921 (= L. Preller, *Griechische Mythologie* II.3.1).

Robert, J. and L. Review of Harmond. *Bull Epigr* 66 (1959) 169–70.

———. Review of H. Ingholt. *Bull Epigr* 184 (1969) 448–49.

———. *Claros I: Décrets hellénistiques*. Paris, 1989.

Robert, L. *La Carie*. Vol. II. Paris, 1954.

———. "Décret d'Athènes pour un officier d'Antiochos Epiphane." *Hellenica* 11/12 (1960) 92–115.

———. "Théophane de Mytilène à Constantinople." *CRAI* (1969) 42–64 (= *Opera Minora Selecta* 5, 561–83. Amsterdam, 1989).

———. *Études anatoliennes: Recherches sur les inscriptions grecques de l'Asie Mineure*. Amsterdam, 1970.

———. "Bulletin Epigraphique." *REG* 90 (1977) 314–448.

———. "Bulletin Epigraphique." *REG* 91 (1978) 385–510.

———. "Une épigramme satirique d'Automédon et Athènes au début de l'empire." *REG* 94 (1981) 338–61.

Robertson, C. M. *A History of Greek Art*. Cambridge, 1975.

———. "The Death of Talos." *JHS* 97 (1977) 158–60.

———. "What is 'Hellenistic' about Hellenistic art?" In Green, ed., 67–103.

Rogers, G. *The Sacred Identity of Ephesos: Foundation Myths of a Roman City*. London, 1991.

Romm, J. S. *The Edges of the Earth in Ancient Thought: Geography, Exploration, and Fiction*. Princeton, 1992.

Rosenstein, N. "Competition and Crisis in Mid-republican Rome." *Phoenix* 47 (1993) 313–39.

Rostovtzeff, M. *A Large Estate in Egypt in the Third Century BC.* Madison, 1922 (Arno repr. 1979).

———. *The Social and Economic History of the Hellenistic World*. 3 vols. Oxford, 1941 (corr. ed., 1953).

Rostropowicz, J. "The Argonautica by Apollonius of Rhodes as a Nautical Epos: Remarks on the Realities of Navigation." *Eos* 88 (1990) 107–17.

———. "Das Heraklesbild in den Argonautika des Apollonios Rhodios." *ActaClassUnivScientDebreceniensis* 26 (1990) 31–34.

Roussel, P. *Délos colonie athénienne*. Paris, 1916.

Roux, M. "Recherches sur les aspects militaires de la conquête du monde gréco-hellénistique par Rome au IIe siècle avant Jésus-Christ." *REA* 95 (1993) 443–57.

Rowland, C. *The Open Heaven: A Study of Apocalyptic in Judaism and Early Christianity*. New York, 1982.

Runciman, W. G. "Origins of States: The Case of Archaic Greece." *CSSH* 24 (1982) 351–77.

Ruschenbusch, E. "Der Endpunkt der Historien des Poseidonios." *Hermes* 121 (1993) 70–76.

Rusten, J. S. *Dionysius Scytobrachion: Papyrologia Coloniensia* X. Opladen, 1982.

Said, E. W. *Culture and Imperialism*. New York, 1993.

———. *Orientalism*. 2nd ed. Harmondsworth, 1995.

Sallares, R. *The Ecology of the Ancient Greek World*. London, 1991.

Saller, R. P. *Personal Patronage under the Early Empire.* Cambridge, 1982.

Samuel, A. E. "Ptolemaic Chronology." *Münchener Beiträge zur Papyrusforschung und antiken Rechtsgeschichte* 43. Munich, 1962.

————. "Year 27 = 30 and 88 B.C." *ChrEg* 40 (1965) 376–400.

————. *From Athens to Alexandria: Hellenism and Social Goals in Ptolemaic Egypt.* Studia Hellenistica 26. Leuven, 1983.

————. *The Shifting Sands of History: Interpretations of Ptolemaic Egypt.* Lanham and London, 1989.

Sandbach, F. H. *Aristotle and the Stoics.* Cambridge, 1985.

Sanders, E. P. *Judaism: Practice and Belief 63 BCE–66 CE.* London and Philadelphia, 1992.

Scala, R. von. *Die Studien des Polybios* I. Stuttgart, 1890.

Schachermeyr, F. "Minyas." *RE* XV.2: 2014–18. Stuttgart, 1932.

Schachter, A. *Cults of Boeotia,* I: *Acheloos to Hera.* London, 1981.

Schefold, K. *Die Sagen von den Argonauten, von Theben und Troia in der klassischen und hellenistischen Kunst.* Munich, 1989.

————. *Götter- und Heldensagen der Griechen in der früh- und hocharchäischen Kunst.* Munich, 1993.

Schliemann, H. "Exploration of the Boeotian Orchomenos." *JHS* 2 (1881) 122–63.

Schmitt, H. H. *Rom und Rhodos.* Munich, 1957.

Schmitt, H. H., and E. Vogt, eds. *Kleines Lexikon des Hellenismus.* 2nd ed. Wiesbaden, 1993.

Schmitt Pantel, P. *La fête, pratique et discours.* Paris, 1981.

————. *La cité au banquet: Histoire des repas publics dans les cités grecques.* Paris and Rome, 1992.

Schneider, C. *Kulturgeschichte des Hellenismus.* 2 vols. Munich, 1967–1969.

Schoene, A., H. Peterman, and E. Roediger. *Eusebii Chronicorum Quae Supersunt.* Berlin, 1866 (repr. Dublin and Zürich, 1967).

Schofield, M. S. "Ideology and Philosophy in Aristotle's Theory of Slavery." In G. Patzig, ed., *Aristoteles' "Politik,"* 1–27. Göttingen, 1990.

————. *The Stoic Idea of the City.* Cambridge, 1991.

Schürer, E. *The History of the Jewish People in the Age of Jesus Christ* II. Rev. ed. by G. Vermes, F. Millar, and M. Black. Edinburgh, 1979.

————. *The History of the Jewish People in the Age of Jesus Christ.* III.1–2. Rev. ed. by G. Vermes, F. Millar, and M. Goodman. Edinburgh, 1986–87.

Schwartz, S. "Israel and the Nations Roundabout: 1 Maccabees and the Hasmonean Expansion." *JournJewStud* 42 (1991) 16–38.

Scott, D. "Innatism and the Stoa." *PCPS* n.s. 34 (1988) 123–53.

Scott, J. C. *Weapons of the Weak: Everyday Forms of Peasant Resistance.* New Haven, 1985.

Sedley, D. N. "Colloquium 4: Commentary on Mansfield." In J. J. Cleary, ed., *Proc. Boston Area Coll. in Anc. Phil.* 7 (1991) 146–53.

Segal, C. *Pindar's Mythmaking: The Fourth Pythian Ode.* Princeton, 1986.

Seyrig, H. "Sur l'antiquité des remparts de Samothrace." *BCH* 51 (1927) 353–68.

————. *Trésors du Levant anciens et nouveaux.* Paris, 1972.

Sharples, R. W., and D. W. Winter. "Theophrastus on fungi: Inaccurate citations in Athenaeus." *JHS* 103 (1983) 154–56.

Sherk, R. K. *Roman Documents of the Greek East.* Baltimore, 1969.

Sherwin-White, S. M. "The Hellenistic world." *History Today* 33 (December 1983) 45–48.

Sherwin-White, S. M., and A. Kuhrt, eds. *From Samarkhand to Sardis: A New Approach to the Seleucid Empire.* London and Berkeley, 1993.

Shipley, G. "Distance, Development, Decline? World-systems Analysis and the 'Hellenistic' World." In P. Bilde, T. Engberg-Pedersen, L. Hannestad, J. Zahle, and K. Randsborg, eds., 271–84.

Six, J. "Ein Porträt des Ptolemaios VI. Philometor." *AM* 12 (1887) 212–22.

Smith, N. D. "Aristotle's Theory of Natural Slavery." *Phoenix* 37 (1983) 109–22. (Repr. in D. Keyt and F. D. Miller, eds., *A Companion to Aristotle's Politics*, 142–55. Oxford, 1991).

Smith, R. R. R. *Hellenistic Sculpture.* London and New York, 1991.

Snell, B. *Die Entdeckung des Geistes: Studien zur Entstehung des europäischen Denkens bei den Griechen.* 4th rev. ed. Göttingen, 1975.

Snowden, F. M. *Before Color Prejudice.* Cambridge, Mass., 1983.

Stamires, G. A. "Greek Inscriptions II: Attic Decrees." *Hesperia* 26 (1957) 29–51.

Stanford, W. B. *The Ulysses Theme.* Oxford, 1954.

Ste. Croix, G. E. M. de. *The Class Struggle in the Ancient Greek World: From the Archaic Age to the Arab Conquests.* London and Ithaca, 1981.

Sterling, G. E. *Historiography and Self-Definition: Josephos, Luke-Acts, and Apologetic Historiography.* Leiden, 1992.

Stern, M. *Greek and Latin Authors on Jews and Judaism* II. Jerusalem, 1980.

Stewart, A. F. *Faces of Power: Alexander's Image and Hellenistic Politics.* Berkeley, 1993.

Strasburger, H. "Poseidonios on Problems of the Roman Empire." *JRS* 36 (1946) 40–53.

Strauss, B. S. "From Ethnicity to Status: Polyethnic Armies and the Making of the Hellenistic Kingdoms" (forthcoming).

Symeonoglou, S. *Topography of Thebes from the Bronze Age to Modern Times.* Princeton, 1985.

Tarn, W. W. "The Social Question in the Third Century." In J. B. Bury, E. A. Barber, E. Bevan, and W. W. Tarn, *The Hellenistic Age*, 108–40.

Tarn, W. W., and G. T. Griffith. *Hellenistic Civilization.* 3rd ed. London, 1952.

Tcherikover, V. "*Syntaxis* and *laographia.*" *JJP* 4 (1950) 179–207.

———. "The Ideology of the Letter of Aristeas." *HTR* 51 (1958) 59–85.

———. *Hellenistic Civilisation and the Jews.* Philadelphia, 1959.

Theiler, W. *Poseidonios. Die Fragmente* I: *Texte.* Berlin and New York, 1982.

Thomas, R. *Oral Tradition and Written Record in Classical Athens.* Cambridge, 1989.

Thompson, D. J. *Memphis under the Ptolemies.* Princeton, 1988.

———. "Literacy and the Administration in Early Ptolemaic Egypt." In J. H. Johnson, ed., 323–26.

———. "Literacy and Power in Ptolemaic Egypt." In A. K. Bowman and G. Woolf, eds., *Literacy and Power in the Ancient World*, 67–83. Cambridge, 1994.

————. "Policing the Ptolemaic Countryside." In *Proceedings of the XXIst International Papyrological Congress* (Berlin, August 1995). Forthcoming.

Thompson, H. A. "Activities in the Athenian Agora: 1956." *Hesperia* 26 (1957) 99–107.

————. "The Tomb of Clytemnestra Revisited." In K. DeVries, ed., *From Athens to Gordion: The Papers of a Memorial Symposium for Rodney S. Young*, 3–9. Philadelphia, 1980.

Tiede, D. L. *The Charismatic Figure as Miracle Worker*. Missoula, 1972.

Toer, A. *This Earth of Mankind*. [1975] Trans. M. Lane. New York, 1990.

————. *Child of All Nations*. [1980] Trans. M. Lane. New York, 1991.

————. *Footsteps*. [1985] Trans. M. Lane. New York, 1994.

————. *House of Glass*. [1988] Trans. M. Lane. New York, 1996.

Touloumakos, J. "Zu Poseidonios fr. 36 (Jac.)." *Philologus* 110 (1966) 138–42.

————. *Der Einfluss Roms auf die Staatsform der griechischen Stadtstaaten des Festlandes und der Inseln im ersten und zweiten Jhdt. v. Chr.* Diss. Göttingen, 1967.

————. "Zum römischen Gemeindepatronat im griechischen Osten." *Hermes* 116 (1988) 304–24.

Tracy, S. V. "Greek Inscriptions from the Athenian Agora: Third to First Centuries B.C." *Hesperia* 51 (1982) 57–64.

————. "Maccabees and Pseudo-Aristeas: A Study." *YCS* 1 (1982) 241–52.

————. "The Date of the Athenian Archon Achaios." *AJAH* 9 (1985) 43–47.

————. "The Date of the Athenian Archon Achaios." *GRBS* 29 (1988) 383–88.

————. *Attic Letter Cutters of 229–86 B.C.* Berkeley, 1990.

————. "The Date of IG XI 1056 and Pharnakes I of Pontos." *AM* 107 (1992) 307–313.

Tracy, S. V., and C. Habicht. "New and Old Panathenaic Victor Lists." *Hesperia* 60 (1991) 189–236.

Travlos, J. *Pictorial Dictionary of Ancient Athens*. London, 1971.

Trevor-Roper, H. R. "Jacob Burckhardt." *PBA* 70 (1984) 359–78.

Troiani, L. "Il libro di Aristea ed il giudaismo ellenistico." In B. Virgilio, ed., *Studi Ellenistici* II, 31–61. Pisa, 1987.

Tronson, A. "Satyrus the Peripatetic and the Marriages of Philip II." *JHS* 104 (1984) 116–26.

Ulrich, E. "Daniel Manuscripts from Qumran, I." *BASOR* 268 (1987) 17–37.

————. "Daniel Manuscripts from Qumran, II." *BASOR* 274 (1989) 3–26.

Valbelle, D. "Les recensements dans l'Egypte pharaonique des troisième et deuxième millénaires." *CRIPEL* 9 (1987) 33–49.

Vallauri, G. *Euemero di Messene*. Turin, 1956.

van Groningen, B. A. *In the Grip of the Past: Essay on an Aspect of Greek Thought*. Philosophia Antiqua 6. Leiden, 1953.

Vermes, G. *Jesus the Jew*. London, 1973.

————. "Josephus' Treatment of the Book of Daniel." *JournJewStud* 42 (1991) 149–66.

————. "Qumran Forum Miscellanea I." *JournJewStud* 43 (1992) 299–305.

————. *The Dead Sea Scrolls in English*. 4th ed. Baltimore, 1995.

Vermeule, C. C., III. "Neon Ilion and Ilium Novum: Kings, Soldiers, Citizens and Tourists at Classical Troy." In J. B. Carter and S. P. Morris, eds., *The Ages of Homer*, 467–82. Austin, 1995.

Veyne, P. *Did the Greeks Believe in Their Myths? An Essay on the Constitutive Imagination.* trans. P. Wissing. Chicago, 1988.

Vian, F., and E. Delage, eds. and trans. *Apollonios de Rhodes: Argonautiques.* Vol. 1. Paris, 1974. Vol 2. 1980. Vol. 3. 1981.

Vidal-Naquet, P. "Réflexions sur l'historiographic grecque de l'esclavage." In *Actes du Colloque 1971 sur l'esclavage*, 25–44. Ann. litt. de Univ. de Besançon 140, 1972. (Repr. in *Le Chasseur noir* [new ed.], 223–48. Paris, 1983.)

Virgilio, B. *Studi Ellenistici.* 3 vols. Pisa, 1984–1990.

Vlastos, G. *Platonic Studies.* Princeton, 1973.

Vojatzi, M. *Frühe Argonautenbilder. Beitr. zur Archäol.* XIV. Würzburg, 1982.

Wace, A. J. B., M. S. F. Hood, and J. M. Cook. "Mycenae 1939–52: The Epano Phournos Tholos Tomb." *BSA* 48 (1953) 69–83.

Wace, A. J. B., M. S. Thompson, and J. P. Droop, eds. "Laconia I. Excavations at Sparta, 1909: The Menelaion." *BSA* 15 (1908–1909) 108–157.

———. "Excavations at Mycenae, IX: The Tholos Tombs." *BSA* 25 (1921–1923) 292–376.

Walbank, F. W. "Φίλιππος Τραγῳδούμενος: A Polybian Experiment." *JHS* 58 (1938) 55–68. (= *Selected Papers*, 210–23.)

———. "The Causes of Greek Decline." *JHS* 64 (1944) 10–20.

———. *A Historical Commentary on Polybius.* 3 vols. Oxford, 1957–1979.

———. "History and Tragedy." *Historia* 9 (1960) 216–34 (= *Selected Papers*, 224–41).

———. "Political Morality and the Friends of Scipio." *JRS* 55 (1965) 1–16. (= *Selected Papers*, 157–80).

———. *Polybius.* Berkeley, 1972.

———. "Polybius between Greece and Rome." *EntrHardt* 20 (1974) 1–31 (= *Selected Papers*, 280–97).

———. "Were There Greek Federal States?" *SCI* 3 (1976/1977) 27–51 (= *Selected Papers*, 20–37).

———. "Monarchies and Monarchic Ideas." In *CAH* VII.1 (2nd ed.), 62–100. Cambridge, 1984.

———. Review of Rice, *The Grand Procession of Ptolemy Philadelphus. LCM* 9 (1984) 52–54.

———. *Selected Papers: Studies in Greek and Roman History and Historiography.* Cambridge, 1985.

———. "Könige als Götter: Überlegungen zum Herrscherkult von Alexander bis Augustus." *Chiron* 17 (1987) 365–82.

———. "The Hellenistic World: New Trends and Directions." *SCI* 11 (1991/1992) 90–113.

———. *The Hellenistic World.* Rev. ed. London, 1992.

———. "Supernatural Paraphernalia in Polybius' *Histories*." In I. Worthington, ed., *Ventures into Greek History*, 28–42. Oxford, 1994.

————. "Polybius' Perception of the One and the Many." In I. Malkin and Z. W. Rubinsohn, eds., *Leaders and Masses in the Roman World: Studies in Honor of Zvi Yavetz*, 201–22. Leiden, 1995.

————. "Two Hellenistic Processions: A Matter of Self-Definition." *SCI* 15 (1996) 119–30.

Walcot, P. *Hesiod and the Near East*. Cardiff, 1966.

Wallace, P. W. "The Tomb of Hesiod and the Treasury of Minyas at Orkhomenos." In J. M. Fossey and H. Giroux, *Proceedings of the Third International Conference on Boeotian Antiquities*, 165–71. Amsterdam, 1985.

Wallace, S. L. "Census and Poll-tax in Ptolemaic Egypt." *AJP* 59 (1938) 418–42.

Walter, N. *Der Thoraausleger Aristobulus*. Berlin, 1964.

————. *Jüdische Schriften aus hellenistisch-römischer Zeit* I.2. Gütersloh, 1973.

Weaver, P. R. C. *Familia Caesaris*. Cambridge, 1972.

Welles, C. B. *Royal Correspondence in the Hellenistic Period*. London, 1934.

————. "Michael I. Rostovtzeff." In *Architects and Craftsmen in History: Festschrift für A. P. Usher*, 55–74. Tübingen, 1956.

Wes, M. A. *Michael Rostovtzeff, Historian in Exile: Russian Roots in an American Context*. Stuttgart, 1990.

West, M. L. *Hesiod: Theogony*. Oxford, 1966.

————. *Hesiod: Works and Days*. Oxford, 1978.

Whitley, J. "Early States and Hero Cults: A Re-appraisal." *JHS* 108 (1988) 173–82.

————. "Tomb Cult and Hero Cult: The Uses of the Past in Archaic Greece." In N. Spencer, ed., *Time, Tradition and Society in Greek Archaeology: Bridging the "Great Divide,"* 43–63. London, 1996.

Wickersham, J. M. "Myth and Identity in the Archaic Polis." In D. C. Pozzi and J. M. Wickersham, eds., *Myth and the Polis*, 16–31. Ithaca and London, 1991.

Wilamowitz-Moellendorf, U. von. "Athenion und Aristion." *SBPreuss* (1923) 39–50 (= *Kleine Schriften* 5.1, 208–29. Amsterdam, 1971).

Wilcken, U. "Alexandros I. Balas." *RE* I.1: 1437–38. Stuttgart, 1893.

Wilhelm, A. "Ψήφισμα Ἀθηναίων." *Eph. Arch.* (1901) 49–158.

————. "Proxenie und Euergesie." In *Attische Urkunden V*, 11–86. *SBWien* 220.5. Vienna, 1942.

Wilken, R. L. *John Chrysostom and the Jews*. Berkeley, 1983.

Will, E. "Le monde hellénistique." In E. Will, C. Mossé, and P. Goukowsky, *Le monde grec et l'Orient*, II, 337–645.

————. *Histoire politique du monde hellénistique*. 2 vols. 2nd ed. Nancy, 1979–1982.

————. "Pour une 'anthropologie coloniale' du monde hellénistique." In J. W. Eadie and J. Ober, eds., *The Craft of the Ancient Historian: Essays in honor of C. G. Starr*, 273–301. Lanham, 1985.

————. "Poleis hellénistiques: Deux notes." *EMC/CV* n.s. 7 (1988) 329–52.

Will, E., C. Mossé, and P. Goukowsky. *Le monde grec et l'Orient*, II: *Le IVe siècle et l'époque hellénistique*. Paris, 1975.

Will, E., and C. Orrieux. *Ioudaismos–Hellenismos*. Nancy, 1986.

Williamson, H. G. M. *The New Century Bible Commentary: 1 and 2 Chronicles*. Grand Rapids and London, 1982.

————. *World Biblical Commentary 16: Ezra, Nehemiah*. Waco, Texas, 1985.

Winiarczyk, M., ed. *Euhemeri Messenii Reliquiae*. Stuttgart and Leipzig, 1991.

Wörrle, M., and P. Zanker, eds. *Stadtbild und Bürgerbild im Hellenismus*. Munich, 1995.

Woude, A. S. van der, ed. *The Book of Daniel in the Light of New Findings*. Leuven, 1993.

Wunderer, C. *Polybios: Lebens- und Weltanschauung aus dem zweiten vorchristlichen Jahrhundert*. Leipzig, 1927.

Wyss, B., ed. *Antimachi Colophonii Reliquiae*. Berlin, 1936.

Zanker, P. "Brüche im Bürgerbild? Zu bürgerlichen Selbstdarstellungen in den hellenistischen Städten." In Wörrle and Zanker, eds., 251–63.

Ziegler, J., ed. *Susanna, Daniel: Bel et Draco*. Göttingen Septuagint. Vol. 16.2. Göttingen, 1954.

Ziehen, L. "Thebai (Boiotien)." *RE* VA.2: 1514–15. Stuttgart, 1934.

INDEX

Abdera, 106–7
Abraham, 74–76, 76–77, 87
Acarnanians, 178
Achaeus (Seleucid general), 209–10, 220–21
Achaia and Achaian League 10; and Athens, 141, 142, 144; and Delian exiles, 141; demise, 118, 142; and Macedon, 116, 133, 218, 220; patronage, 106; Polybius on unsoldierliness, 178; Ptolemy III supports, 133; and Rome, 106, 116, 117–18, 126, 142, 144, 193; and Seleucids, 116, 124, 126
Achilles, tomb of, Troad, 26–27, 30
Acilius Balbus, L. (praetor 197), 108
Acilius Glabrio, M'. (cos. 191), 115
Aemilia Tertia, 193–94
Aemilii Paulli, 193–94
Aemilius Lepidus, M. (cos. 187), 108
Aemilius Lepidus, Q. (procos. 15–10), 111n27
Aemilius Paullus, L. (cos. I 219), 189n44
Aemilius Paullus Macedonicus, L. (cos. I 182), 192, 193
Aemilius Regillus, L., 108
Aemilius Zosimus, A., 112
Aeschylus, spurious fragments assigned to, 87
aetiology, Alexandrian, 63, 71
Aetolia. *See* Aitolia
Africa, 76, 77

Agamemnon, cult of, 23–25, 29, 30
Agamemnoneion, Mycenae, 23–25, 29, 30
Aglaos of Kos, 132
Agrius Publianus Bassus, L., 112
Aiaia, 47, 53–54
Aigina, 130, 133
Aischylos son of Zopyros, 139
Aitolia and Aitolian League 10, 123; and Macedon, 120–21, 133, 218, 220; Polybius on unsoldierliness, 177, 178
Alabanda (Antiocheia), 122–23
Alexander (captain of bodyguard), 215, 216
Alexander III, the Great, of Macedon, 26, 62, 90–91, 217–18; Jews and, 78–79, 81, 90–91, 101, 103
Alexander Balas, king of Syria, 127, 129, 133, 214
Alexander Polyhistor, 76, 77, 84n36
Alexandria: aetiology, 63, 71; alphabetization, 254; Antiochus IV abandons siege, 89, 90, 126; Apollonius Rhodius in, 16; deracination, 62–63; expulsion of intellectuals, 133; festivals, 242, 247, 257; Jews, 82, 85; Library, 81–83, 247; Museum, 132, 247; palace, 204; papyri lost, 253; rationalism and traditionalism, 68
Alexandros (Egyptian courtier), 131
allegorization of myth, 44, 46, 57, 58–59;

Theopompus, *Histories*, 165
Thera, 54, 130
Therapne, Lakonia, 26
Thermum, 219
Theseus myth, 47
Thessaly, 121, 165, 167n14, 171n23
tholos tombs: Bronze Age, 22, 24, 28,
    31–32; Hellenistic imitations, 20, 21,
    22, 29, 34
Thraseas son of Aetos from Aspendos,
    129–30
Thucydides, 18, 43n25, 45
Tiberius, emperor, 36
Timaeus, 18
Timarchos, of Cypriot Salamis, 125n23,
    131
time, creative and mythic, 66–67
Tithonos and Eos, 48
Tobiads, tales of, 83–84
Tobit, book of, 92–93
tomb cult, post-classical, 20–34
trade, 13, 41, 140; Egyptian tax, 245,
    251
Trasimene, battle of Lake, 180
Troad; tomb of Achilles, 26–27, 30
Tullius Cicero, M.: *De officiis*, 161–62;
    De Re Publica III, 162–63; *Paradoxa*

Stoicorum V, 174; on patronage, 111–12,
    113–14; on slavery, 161, 162, 174

Valerius Flaccus, L. (procos. 62), 111n27
Varro. *See* Terentius Varro
visual representations of myth, 48–52, 56
votive offerings, 25

Walbank, Frank, vii, 4, 6, 36, 120; pub-
    lications, 259–79
Wandering Rocks, 47, 67
wealth: courtiers', 217–18; differences
    in, 10, 12; from farming, 196. *See also*
    display
women, revaluation of status, 10

xenia, 208–10, 223n46
Xenoetas (Seleucid general), 177, 180,
    217
Xenophanes, 58, 68
Xenophon; *Anabasis*, 204

Zeno of Citium, 160–61, 171
Zenon archive, 7, 225–26, 237–38, 240
zero, Greek lack of symbol for, 254
Zeus, 44, 69
Zoilos (Egyptian courtier), 131

Indexer:	Barbara Hird
Compositor:	Humanist Typesetting & Graphics, Inc.
Text:	10.5/12.5 Monotype Baskerville
Display:	Monotype Baskerville
Greek:	Ibycus, designed by Silvio Levy
	modified by Pierre A. MacKay
Printer and binder:	Edwards Brothers, Inc.